ADULT BIPOLAR DISORDERS

DISORDERS

Understanding Your Diagnosis
& Getting Help

Mitzi Waltz

O'REILLY®

Beijing • Cambridge • Farnham • Köln • Paris • Sebastopol • Taipei • Tokyo

Adult Bipolar Disorders: Understanding Your Diagnosis & Getting Help
by Mitzi Waltz

Published by O'Reilly & Associates, Inc., 1005 Gravenstein Hwy, Sebastopol, CA 95472.

Editor: Nancy Keene

Production Editor: Tom Dorsaneo

Cover Designer: Kristen Throop

Printing History: February 2002, First Edition

Many of the designations used by manufacturers and sellers to distinguish their products are claimed as trademarks. Where those designations appear in this book, and O'Reilly & Associates, Inc. was aware of a trademark claim, the designations have been printed in caps or initial caps.

This book is meant to educate and should not be used as an alternative for professional medical care. Although we have exerted every effort to ensure that the information presented is accurate at the time of publication, there is no guarantee that this information will remain current over time. Appropriate medical professionals should be consulted before adopting any procedures or treatments discussed in this book.

Library of Congress Cataloging-in-Publication Data:

Waltz, Mitzi.
    Adult bipolar disorders : understanding your diagnosis and getting help / Mitzi Waltz.—1st ed.
        p. cm.—(Patient-centered guides)
    Includes bibliographical references and index.
    ISBN 0-596-50010-6 (pbk.)
    1. Manic-depressive illness. 2. Depression, Mental. 3. Affective disorders. I. Title. II. Series.

    RC516 W25 2002
    616.89'5--dc21   2001051001

This book is printed on acid-free paper with 85% recycled content, 15% post-consumer waste. O'Reilly & Associates, Inc., is committed to using paper with the highest recycled content available consistent with high quality.

[M]

Table of Contents

Preface

WHEN YOU OR SOMEONE YOU CARE ABOUT is diagnosed with a medical problem, no matter what it is, it turns your world upside down. There are so many questions you want to ask, and so few minutes available to talk openly with your doctor about your concerns and fears.

If your health issue is mental illness, the concern can be even greater. Everyone in our society has been exposed to frightening, and incorrect, images of mental illness through the media. There's still a lot of stigma attached to having a mental illness, and fear of what people may think can cut you off from your usual sources of help and solace.

The reality is that coping with a bipolar disorder is difficult, but not impossible. There are reliable treatments available. Recovery, not just handling symptoms, is more possible than ever.

This book is intended to bring together all the basic information needed by people diagnosed with a bipolar disorder. Family members and friends can learn from the material presented, and helping professionals should find it useful as well.

The first three chapters provide a broad overview of the entire family of bipolar disorders, explaining what causes uncontrollable mood swings and how these conditions are diagnosed. Subsequent chapters cover treatment options, dealing with insurance problems and the healthcare system, and strategies for coping with the ways that having a bipolar disorder can affect your relationships, education, career, and lifestyle.

Appendix A, *Resources,* lists books, web sites, organizations, special diagnostic and treatment centers, and more. Two more appendices provide the latest information on the genetics of bipolar disorders in table form, and list and explain psychological tests that may be used during the diagnostic process.

Bipolar disorders occur in both men and women, so I've tried to alternate between pronouns when talking about patients, as well as healthcare practitioners.

I've done my best to provide accurate information about resources in the English-speaking world, including North America, the UK, the Republic of Ireland, Australia, and New Zealand. Bipolar disorders are a universal phenomenon, however, and occur in people of all races and nationalities. Readers in other parts of the world may be able to find local resources and current information in languages other than English on the Internet: some of the web sites and email discussion groups listed in Appendix A can point you toward resources in your part of the world. Simply because I am writing in the US and UK, some information will be skewed toward American or British readers. Most, however, will be useful to all.

Throughout the text I present findings from the latest medical research. This information is not intended as medical advice. Please consult your physician before starting, stopping, or changing any medical treatment. Some of the health information provided comes from small studies or is experimental or controversial in nature.

Readers should carefully examine any claims made by healthcare facilities, pharmaceutical firms, therapists, supplement manufacturers, and others before implementing new treatments.

You will find the words of other people who are coping with bipolar disorders throughout the book. These quotes are offset from the rest of the text and presented in italics. In many cases, names and other identifying details have been changed at the person's request.

Acknowledgments

About 30 people with bipolar disorders took the time to answer questions about their personal experiences, including Eileen Blackwood, Pamela Cabine, Staci R. Dougherty, Leslie Ann Ellis, Shannon C. Flynn, Heidi Hermanson, Norman Keegel, Benjamin J.P. Lee, Monique Lewis, F. Anthony Nordstrom, Randy Norman, Jane McPherson, Sharon Roseme, Shoshana Anne Simon, and Raymond W. Wolters. They deserve much of the credit for this book, because their advice, ideas, and stories guided its structure and contents.

Portions of a draft of this book were reviewed by Dr. Hagop Akiskal, Professor of Psychiatry and Director of the International Mood Center at the University of California at San Diego; Dr. Mark S. Bauer, Associate Professor of Psychiatry at Brown University; and Dr. Max Dine; among others. Their comments and criticisms were invaluable, and much appreciated.

The National Alliance for the Mentally Ill has also been a primary, and extraordinarily valuable, resource. The Depression and Related Affective Disorders Association and the National Depression and Manic Depression Association have also provided much-appreciated assistance. These organizations give voice to the concerns of people affected by mental illness and their family members. They work in the nation's legislatures, in the media, online, and person-to-person to provide information, help, and hope.

Contacts made through two online mailing lists, Pendulum and Bipolar Planet, have also been essential to this project. I thank everyone who shared their experiences and concerns with me, particularly the many individuals who patiently told me their stories, answered my latest questions, and encouraged me to make the book as comprehensive as possible.

Linda Lamb, Nancy Keene, Shawnde Paull, and all of the extraordinarily professional editorial and production staff at O'Reilly & Associates have my utmost respect and admiration. This was a long and difficult project, and it couldn't have happened without their support and hard work.

Despite the inspiration and contributions of so many, any errors, omissions, misstatements, or flaws are entirely my own.

— Mitzi Waltz
University of Sunderland
UK
February 2002

If you would like to comment on this book or offer suggestions for future editions, please send e-mail to *guides@oreilly.com* or write to O'Reilly & Associates, Inc., at 1005 Gravenstein Hwy, Sebastopol, CA 95472.

CHAPTER 1

What Are Bipolar Disorders?

EVERYONE EXPERIENCES the occasional unexplained mood swing. Maybe it's the weather, or PMS, or just a bad day that throws you into the blue zone. Maybe it's sunny skies, hearing your favorite song first thing in the morning, or looking forward to a special event that kicks off one of those "good vibrations" days when nothing can go wrong. The important thing is that the blues go away before too long, and the enjoyable sense of euphoria doesn't turn into an unstoppable high that gets you into trouble.

People with bipolar disorders, however, experience mood swings that go far beyond the norm. Their moods swing low and keep dropping until life doesn't feel worth living anymore. They swing so high that they lose touch with reality, making rash decisions and behaving wildly. Moods may cycle so rapidly that they literally can't function.

This chapter discusses the states of mind and behaviors that characterize bipolar disorders. It explains the diagnostic system used by most psychiatrists and tells what is currently known about genetics, nervous system differences, and other factors that may cause bipolar disorders to begin or become worse. It also looks at gender, culture, and other factors that can relate to diagnosis.

Bipolar disorders: a definition

Bipolar disorders are changes in the brain and nervous system that cause severe mood swings, from the deepest suicidal depression to overwhelming elation. Some of the most famous artists, musicians, politicians, and writers of our time have been bipolar. Sadly, so have been a disproportionate number of people in our psychiatric hospitals and prisons.

Left untreated, bipolar disorders can plunge a person into absolute hell. Education and work opportunities, self esteem, friends, and family support may be lost. Dependence on public assistance, legal difficulties, expensive hospitalizations, substance abuse, and suicide can occur. With state-of-the-art treatment, however, people with bipolar disorders can be creative, productive, and independent.

Over two million adults in the US are diagnosed with a bipolar disorder. Usually bipolar disorders are first recognized and diagnosed during adulthood. However, a groundbreaking survey of bipolar adults who are members of the of National Depressive and Manic Depressive Association, a support and advocacy group in the US, found that 60 percent of the respondents reported onset of the disorder's symptoms before the age of nineteen.[1] It often takes between five and eight years from first symptoms to diagnosis, so that is not too surprising.

Today researchers know that bipolar disorders are medical problems, not the result of faulty thinking, lack of willpower, or childhood trauma. Although no cure has been found, these conditions are treatable—medications and other interventions are available that can help most people with bipolar disorders gain more control over their mood swings and improve their quality of life.

Types of bipolar disorders

There are several kinds of bipolar disorders, although all of them include the basic symptom of drastic and debilitating mood swings. In the US, diagnosis is confirmed when a person's inner feelings and outward behavior fit the criteria for one of the bipolar disorders listed in the fourth edition of the *Diagnostic and Statistical Manual of Mental Disorders (DSM-IV)*. This book, which is used by psychiatrists and other physicians to define brain-based medical problems, assigns a number to each defined disorder and its subtypes.

In Europe and most other parts of the world, a diagnosis of bipolar disorder is made if a person fits the criteria for one of the similar classifications in the World Health Organization's *ICD-10 Classification of Mental and Behavioural Disorders*. The *ICD-10* also assigns numbers to each psychiatric condition that it lists.

The unusual moods associated with bipolar disorders—depression, hypomania, mania, and mixed states—are defined later in this chapter (see "States of mind in bipolar disorders"). Depending on which of these moods you experience and how often they occur, a diagnosis will be chosen from one of the following major types.

Bipolar I disorder

"Manic depression" is the old name for bipolar I disorder (BPI). People with BPI swing into depression and have had at least one manic episode. Some have also had hypomanic or mixed episodes.

BPI is considered the most serious form of bipolar disorder, but paradoxically, it can be easier to treat than others. People with this form of the condition tend to have fewer mood swings, and their episodes are longer-lasting and further apart. This tends to lead to a more predictable response to medication. The diagnosis should be followed by one of the following modifiers:

- Most Recent Episode Depressed (*DSM-IV* 296.5)
- Most Recent Episode Hypomanic (*DSM-IV* 296.40)
- Most Recent Episode Manic (*DSM-IV* 296.4x)
- Most Recent Episode Mixed (*DSM-IV* 296.6x)
- Most Recent Episode Unspecified (*DSM-IV* 296.7)
- Single Manic Episode (*DSM-IV* 296.0x)

Sharon, age 47, has experienced the life-changing effects of bipolar I disorder:

> *My symptoms have changed my life completely. I was, and am, a high-powered, high-functioning, corporate attorney. Now I cannot handle stress, as it triggers mania no matter how medicated I am, so I am semi-retired and choosing clients and tasks very carefully. Even so, I'm still subject to long manic episodes. I'm reluctant to take the most powerful drugs because side effects (slurred words, slowed mental function, physical tremors, short-term memory loss) all interfere with my ability to function in my life.*
>
> *It's a constant balancing act.*

Bipolar II disorder

Bipolar II disorder (BPII, *DSM-IV* 296.89) is defined as recurrent depression with hypomania, but not mania or mixed states. People with BPII also tend to be more emotionally labile (moody) in between actual mood swings.

Although BPII is sometimes described as milder than bipolar I, it can actually be harder to treat and cope with because you may have fewer periods of normal mood in between depressed and hypomanic periods.

Shannon, now 33, had the very common experience of being treated first for depression, and only later diagnosed with BPII:

> I had already been hospitalized three or four years before with psychotic depression, and was on antidepressants with occasional antipsychotics, but no mood stabilizers. The tricyclic antidepressants started causing rapid cycling between depression and hypomania. During the depressions, I would exhibit psychomotor retardation, hypersomnolence, hopelessness, lack of ability to function, thoughts of suicide, self-mutilation, and sometimes delusions. During the hypomanias, I became irritable and anxious (with occasional euphoria), and experienced racing thoughts, loss of sleep, pacing, increased energy, and preoccupation with projects I'd suddenly take up and then drop.
>
> I was in college at the time, and my ability to concentrate and complete schoolwork was suffering. My parents took me to get a "second opinion"; we were all feeling that my illness had changed in form. The psychiatrist diagnosed me with "bipolar II, rapid cycling" and seemed to feel that all along I had actually been suffering from bipolar II, not depression, as had been originally thought. I agree with this, because I remember other periods of what I now call hypomania, including one immediately preceding my first severe psychotic depression.

Cyclothymic disorder

Cyclothymic disorder (cyclothymia, *DSM-IV* 301.13) is described as a chronic mood disturbance for at least a year. Both depressed and hypomanic moods are present, but there are no major depressive, manic, or mixed episodes. To get diagnosed with cyclothymic disorder, your history must include more than two months without normal mood during the previous year. The cycles and moods are not normally as severe as those seen in bipolar type II.

Cyclothymia appears to come from a milder version of the same chemical imbalance that causes BPI and BPII, generally with shorter cycles and less severity. A cyclothymic temperament can also coexist with bipolar II.[2] That doesn't make it much easier to handle for the person affected and may make accessing treatment resources more difficult.

Some researchers feel that the severest form of pre-menstrual syndrome (PMS), called premenstrual dysphoric disorder (PMDD), is a type of cyclothymic disorder caused by uncontrolled hormonal fluctuations.[3] The same medications used to treat bipolar disorders are sometimes successfully used to treat PMDD.

Mood disorder NOS

If you have some characteristics of bipolar I, bipolar II, or cyclothymic disorder but do not fit all the requirements, your doctor might use the diagnosis "mood disorder NOS" (Not Otherwise Specified), which is *DSM-IV* 296.80. Sometimes this kind of non-committal diagnosis is a stopgap measure, meant to ensure that you receive needed services until your actual diagnosis is made. But sometimes a person really is a "diagnosis of one": he has a mood disorder, but it just refuses to obey the *DSM-IV* rules.

Other mood disorders

Experienced clinicians know that individuals are just that—individuals—not entries in the *DSM-IV.* They tend to believe there is a wider range of bipolar disorders than those mentioned above, a spectrum of temperamental and behavioral differences that could include up to 5 percent of the population. You may, for example, hear about "bipolar III" disorder. This isn't an official *DSM-IV* diagnosis yet, but Dr. Hagop Akiskal has proposed it as a separate category. Dr. Akiskal, a well-known researcher, is director of the International Mood Center at the University of California in San Diego.

Dr. Akiskal defines bipolar III as moods that swing from major or slight depression to periods of normal mood. Many people who fit this profile come from families in which other members have bipolar disorders. Like others with bipolar disorders, these individuals may be at risk of becoming dangerously hypomanic or even manic if they take certain medications or illegal drugs. See Chapter 3, *Differential Diagnosis,* and Chapter 4, *Medical Care,* for more information about this phenomenon.

Dr. Akiskal has also defined another unofficial category, "bipolar IV." These patients have major depressions but no clear-cut episodes of hypomania despite having a driven, voluble temperament.[4]

People who fit the "bipolar III" or "bipolar IV" profiles may not need special medical care, but would benefit from understanding their mood swings and temperament and from avoiding drugs and medications that can push them into mania. Dr. Akiskal and others believe that other similar, definable patterns exist within a larger bipolar spectrum.[5,6]

Seasonal affective disorder (SAD) is a mood disorder that follows the seasons of the year. People with SAD tend to get depressed in the dark months of winter, and some also experience hypomania or mania in the sunnier times of year. Others may have a different pattern. As many as 85 percent of people with seasonal mood swings may actually warrant a bipolar II diagnosis.[7]

Indeed, most people with bipolar disorders are slightly more sensitive than the average person to changes in the amount of light, the weather, even their latitude on the planet. Psychiatrists have been known to joke about "the manic month of May," but it's not funny to those whose moods swing way too far up with the spring sunshine. Identifying predictable cycles of any sort can help you design a good treatment plan.

The Axis system

The American Psychiatric Association uses a special diagnostic system to assess people in five areas of function, each called an "Axis": a center line about which something (in this case, psychiatric and behavioral symptoms) revolves. Each Axis is considered individually and then graphed as a separate part of the diagnosis.

- Axis I: Major psychiatric disorders, such as bipolar disorder or schizophrenia
- Axis II: Personality disorders (ingrained personality traits that cause the person difficulty in life), mental retardation, or developmental delay
- Axis III: Physical disorders that can affect thought or behavior, such as epilepsy
- Axis IV: Stresses in the person's life, such as being the victim of domestic abuse
- Axis V: Level of function described on a scale of 0 (minimal function) to 100 (perfect function)

Disorders listed on Axis I are taken from the *DSM-IV*. Those listed on Axis II and III may affect both the body and the mind. Items listed on Axis IV come from interviews with you or from people who help to take care of you, such as family members or hospital staff.

The score listed on Axis V is based on everything the doctor has learned. It is a subjective measure of how well you are able to handle everyday life at home and in the community and of how you respond to stressful situations.

If your doctor isn't sure that you have a bipolar disorder, he may put the Axis I code for a single episode of depression, mania, or hypomania on the chart and continue to observe for future mood swings before making a diagnosis. If this is the case, the *DSM-IV* code for the episode in question may be followed by one of these modifiers:

- .x1-Mild
- .x2-Moderate
- .x3-Severe Without Psychotic Features
- .x4-Severe With Psychotic Features
    - Mood-Congruent Psychotic Features
    - Mood-Incongruent Psychotic Features
- .x5-In Partial Remission
- .x6-In Full Remission
- .x0-Unspecified

States of mind in bipolar disorders

As the earlier definitions suggest, the type of bipolar disorder a person is diagnosed with is based on which states of mind she has been in—depressive, hypomanic, manic, or mixed—and how often. All four of these are extremes of mood. When they are anything other than transitory states of mind, they can cause dangerous lapses in judgment, which can put your life in danger.

The *DSM-IV* defines these states of mind fairly precisely. Real life is not always so clear-cut. Some people experience mixed moods or cycle so rapidly between states that it's hard to pin down the most pressing problem. Many people experience depression as extreme irritability and anger rather than sadness. This can be confusing for the doctor and maddening for the person experiencing these rollercoaster emotions.

George, age 61, tells how he has experienced the states of mind associated with bipolar disorders:

> *Severe depression is just horrible—I can't think, concentrate, or read. I have to check everything or have someone check it for me. When I'm depressed, I'm afraid to drive, and I can't make decisions. My wife has to function as an agent to negotiate everything for me.*
>
> *Mania is great, just a wonderful feeling. I feel omnipotent! I don't need much sleep, I don't really need to eat. The problem is that I get in trouble with it, because I don't make good decisions.*

*Hypomania is not that bad. The problem is that you can't judge if
you're getting worse or not when you're hypomanic. You may be getting
higher and higher without knowing it, until you're full-blown manic.*

Depression

Most people have experienced a depressed mood due to a sad event, such as the
death of a relative or friend. Clinical depression is characterized by a depressed mood
that does not go away after two weeks or so, or after a normal period of grieving
(usually about two months, although this depends on the situation and the mourner's
cultural background). Symptoms of clinical depression can include the following:

- Sadness that does not go away

- Crying for no reason or for very small reasons

- Change in appetite (lack of appetite, gorging on food)

- Change in sleep pattern (insomnia, oversleeping, sleeping at unusual times)

- Irritability and agitation

- Anger

- Worrying and anxiety

- Pessimism or a "who cares?" attitude

- Lack of energy for normal activities

- Feelings of guilt and worthlessness

- Inability to concentrate or make decisions

- Loss of pleasure in usual interests

- Withdrawal from friendships and other relationships

- Aches and pains, seemingly without medical cause

- Recurring thoughts of death, suicide, or other frightening possibilities

Of all the behaviors listed above, irritability, overeating, and oversleeping are particularly common in people with bipolar disorders who are depressed.

To meet the *DSM-IV* criteria for an episode of clinical depression, at least five or six
conditions from the list above must be present. The depressed mood must last for at
least two weeks, and it cannot meet the criteria for a mixed state, as described later
in this chapter. The symptoms must not be due to a medical condition, drug use or

abuse, or normal bereavement. The symptoms must also cause significant emotional distress or affect how well you can carry out daily life activities. Some people who are depressed have delusions that fit their mood—for example, you may have delusional feelings of guilt or worthlessness or have auditory hallucinations that include voices saying you deserve to die or delivering other negative messages. Delusions that don't fit with the depressed mood (such as thinking you have been sent by God to save the world) indicate that something else is going on, as do most kinds of visual hallucinations.

Mania

Clinical mania occurs when manic thoughts and behavior continue over a period of time and impair how the person functions socially, at work, or in school. A person who is manic can't complete normal daily activities and needs immediate treatment. Symptoms of a manic episode follow:

- A abnormally euphoric, optimistic mood that is not a transitory state
- Exaggerated sense of self-confidence
- Decreased need for sleep
- Compulsively cleaning or doing other tasks, often into the wee hours
- Grandiosity: a delusional sense of self-importance and superiority over others
- Excessive irritability
- Aggression
- Increased level of mental and physical activity (hyperactivity)
- Pressured speech: speaking at a rapid pace, often loudly, and almost constantly (motormouth)
- Flight of ideas: Thoughts race through the mind, jumping from topic to topic
- Missing steps in logical thinking
- Extreme impulsiveness and distractibility
- Poor judgment
- Reckless, out-of-character behavior, which may include compulsive sexual behavior, gambling, substance abuse, and other risky pursuits
- Changes in style of dress, in the direction of the wild and unusual
- In some cases, hallucinations (auditory or visual) that fit with the mood

You'll note that irritability is a characteristic symptom of both depression and mania. Aggression, too, can be seen in either state. Irritability and aggression may take the form of rages, which can seemingly be triggered by the smallest request or mistake. Apart from suicidal behavior, aggression and rages are probably the most difficult aspects of bipolar disorders. Dealing with this frightening symptom is tough, and coping strategies are discussed in greater detail in Chapter 8, *Living with Bipolar Disorders*.

Hypomania

When the average person thinks of a manic mood, he thinks of a day when he was in a frenzy of purposeful but exhilarating activity, such as frantically furnishing a nursery the night before a new baby's anticipated arrival. Most people have the ability to gear up for an occasional day like this. They enjoy the extra energy that these natural highs bring and are also ready for the crash effect that usually follows. This perfectly normal and useful frame of mind is very much like the mood called hypomania in people with bipolar disorders. It's a sense of heightened awareness and activity that, unfortunately, has a tendency to occur too often and for too long, or to spin out of control to become full-blown mania.

This ability to sustain a hypomanic state is the main reason that bipolar disorders are often associated with creative, driven personalities. A hypomanic artist can focus intently on a painting or musical composition, working through the night to create a masterpiece. A hypomanic businesswoman can come up with a long list of ideas for new products. A hypomanic construction worker can pour on the juice to finish a project in record time. The burst of activity may be followed by 24 hours in bed, but as long as the finished product is appreciated, the hypomanic state is often seen as a gift, not a curse.

Jane, age 46, explains what hypomania has been like for her:

> When you are hypomanic, it is a great feeling—you are invincible. You can't see what others are worried about. I have an inability to understand why people can't see what I can see when I am hypomanic. Your mind is brilliant, and you can con people into doing things or joining projects. I have done this on numerous occasions in the past, setting up massive community projects involving many people, making lots of money. People admire you, and then bang! You crash, and everything is left mid-project or there is no follow-up. You end up looking like an incompetent fool.

When it's controllable, hypomania may be useful to those with a willingness to keep their activities strictly within bounds. The problem is that it's very hard to control your behavior in a hypomanic state, and the activity that takes place may become increasingly reckless and extreme. Without an appropriate outlet for this excess energy, hypomania is often translated into fast driving, hard drinking, drug-taking, sexual promiscuity, profligate spending, and a host of other risky behaviors.

To meet the *DSM-IV* criteria for a hypomanic episode, the state must be uncharacteristic of your normal behavior, last for at least four days, and be obvious to outside observers, such as friends and coworkers. It must not be due to another medical condition, drug use or abuse, or some form of antidepressant treatment. It must not be so severe that you cannot manage most normal functions or require hospitalization, nor can psychotic features be present. At least three of the following symptoms must be seen:

- Inflated self-esteem or grandiosity
- Decreased need for sleep
- Pressured speech
- Flight of ideas
- Difficulty paying attention
- Agitation, hyperactivity, feeling driven to pursue activities
- Involvement in reckless activities

Mixed state (mixed mania/depression)

A mixed state has features of both mania and depression. These symptoms may occur at the same time, or you may cycle back and forth between depression, hypomania, and mania over a period of days. The latter is called rapid cycling.

To meet the *DSM-IV* criteria for a mixed episode, you must meet the criteria for a manic episode and the criteria for a depressed episode, for almost every day of a one-week period. This disturbed mood must be serious enough that it prevents you from carrying out normal activities or causes you to require hospitalization, or it must have psychotic features. The symptoms should not be caused by drug or alcohol use, medication, or another medical condition.

Eileen, age 47, says recurring mixed episodes are by far the most difficult reminders of her bipolar disorder.

The "mixed state" is the worst. All of my life, I did the swing, every three years. High, then low, then normal for a couple of years. The last episode was at age 39, when I went high, but never came down. It was hell.

Ever since I became a "medicated bipolar" I don't swing "normally" anymore. I stabilize, until some outside stressor makes me crazy, and it leads to a mixed state that I can't get out of without a change in meds, or more meds, and/or therapy.

The official criteria for a mixed state may be overly stringent, according to some clinicians. Often a mixed state will not quite meet the full requirements for a diagnosis for depression or mania, but has enough qualities of each to be intensely uncomfortable for the person experiencing it.

Rapid cycling

People who are rapid cyclers have had four or more episodes of depression, hypomania, mania, or mixed states in a twelve-month period. Children and women are more likely to be rapid cyclers.[8] Ultra-rapid cyclers swing between moods so quickly that they may seem to be in a near-constant mixed state.

Rapid cyclers are the most difficult bipolar patients to treat. They tend to be more sensitive to some medications and to get no benefit from others. Because their behavior and thought patterns are very unpredictable, they sometimes have difficulties in therapy sessions.

Psychosis

The possibility of having a psychotic episode—or the experience of actually having one—is one of the scariest aspects of bipolar disorders. When most people think of being insane, it is psychosis that they think of.

Most people who have never experienced psychosis get their ideas about it from movies, television, or books, but these dramatic recreations tend to be inaccurate.

A person in a psychotic state is out of touch with objective reality in some way. She may be cataleptic (unresponsive)—a person in this state will tend to retain whatever posture they are in. Alternatively, she could be catatonic, responding to the environment with unusual physical activity, which could range from the waxy flexibility of catalepsy to negative and agitated reactions. She may experience auditory hallucinations, visual hallucinations, or sensory hallucinations: hearing, seeing, feeling, even smelling or tasting things that are not there. She may be completely swept away from reality by delusions, such as believing that she is a supernatural being or that she is under attack by unseen forces.

Psychotic symptoms differ in intensity and power. Auditory symptoms can range from hearing unidentifiable and indistinct sounds, to hearing a blur of voices, to hearing direct commands from an internal or external voice. A full spectrum of visual phenomena has been reported, from seeing vague auras around other people to seeing frightening monsters. Psychotic symptoms can include perceptual errors that you might find merely odd, such as "seeing" musical tones as colors. The intensity of sensory hallucinations can range from a prickly sensation to feeling as though you're being battered by an invisible force.

If this sounds like someone's description of an acid trip, you're right: hallucinogenic drugs like LSD affect the very same brain chemicals that produce psychotic symptoms in people with mental illness. Drugs can do this to people who are otherwise normal in every way. In other words, everyone in the world has the capacity to become psychotic in response to certain triggers, either ingested drugs or something occurring within the brain itself. Drug experiences end after a few hours. Untreated psychosis, however, can literally last for years.

Psychosis is a medical condition, as biological as heart failure or diabetic shock and in many ways just as serious. When a person has psychotic symptoms, some kind of chemical or electrical process in the brain has gone terribly wrong. The problem cannot be fixed by psychotherapy, although therapy is often a useful part of a total treatment plan. Therapists can help patients identify the beginning of a psychotic thought pattern or behavior, so that they can develop coping skills and know when to seek help. The therapist can also provide reassurance: as you can imagine, psychosis can be intensely frightening to the person who experiences it.

Shoshana, age 56, tells about one of these experiences:

> Once I was walking down the middle of the highway, intending to go to
> the Yucatan to find a curandero to cure me, and a nice policeman took me
> home. People who are psychotic can be very literal, and I thought the
> "middle of the road" was a safe place to be.

It's important to note that a person can appear to be functioning normally while having psychotic symptoms. In fact, some people who have experienced psychotic states report that they can sometimes make their symptoms go away for a little while by throwing themselves into a frenzy of cleaning or exercising or by deliberately thinking other thoughts. These stop-gap measures eventually fail, but it's important to identify activities that may help shut out these scary symptoms temporarily, giving you time to get to a safe place and seek medical attention.

Some people with an undiagnosed bipolar disorder have lived with mild, untreated psychotic symptoms for years, somehow getting through life despite these phenomena. This takes incredible courage and stamina, but you don't have to fight these symptoms alone. Medications are available that can usually treat psychosis successfully. These are discussed at length in Chapter 4. Helpful interpersonal therapies are discussed further in Chapter 5, *Talk Therapy*.

Sometimes people with a bipolar disorder have strongly delusional thought patterns without actually being psychotic. For example, in a manic state you might come to believe you are a brilliantly talented rock musician and lay elaborate plans for your imminent rise to stardom. Right after reading a magazine article about a cool record label, you might catch a plane to Los Angeles and seek out this company, thinking it will surely sign you to a record deal on the spot. You may have actual talent, but an outsider could easily see that the rest of your assumptions make no sense. This is delusional thinking, not psychosis—but if no one intervenes before you act on your delusions, you may well slide into psychosis.

What causes bipolar disorders?

The human nervous system is an amazing organic machine, creating and reacting to a complex stew of chemical, electrical, and magnetic impulses. It's constantly humming away, taking in information from all of our senses and reacting to that data in ways that control every bodily activity, from basic breathing and circulation on up. A single misstep in one of these processes can set in motion a chain of events that lead to a neurological event, such as a memory lapse, a seizure, or a manic episode. If such missteps occur constantly, the person has a neurological or psychiatric disorder. Bipolar disorders are caused by differences in how a person's central nervous system regulates basic feelings and behaviors.

Circadian rhythms

The nervous system of a person with a bipolar disorder frequently makes specific types of regulatory errors. Many of them involve the body's internal clock, which controls the phenomena known as circadian rhythms. These are regular rhythmic changes in waking and sleeping, waxing and waning activity levels, even sensations of hunger or thirst and their satisfaction.

The chemical "clock" that governs these rhythms is located in the hypothalamus, a tiny gland deep within the brain. One part of the hypothalamus, the suprachiasmatic nucleus, regulates the secretion of the hormone melatonin by the nearby pineal gland, among other functions. You've probably heard about melatonin supplements, which are sold as a treatment for insomnia. This hormone is the body's own shut-down mechanism, and it is normally produced automatically as dusk begins. The suprachiasmatic nucleus sets itself based on the past several days' pattern of light and dark, slowly adjusting melatonin production and other actions in pace with the seasons. For this process to work properly, exposure to at least some strong, direct light (sunlight or artificial) around mid-day seems important, as is a slow and natural change in the overall patterns of dark and light as each 24 hour period passes.

People with bipolar disorders appear to have difficulty with regulating this system naturally. It's a chicken-and-egg situation: the rhythms are disordered, so sleep, waking, and other patterns are disturbed. As insomnia, hypersomnia (oversleeping), changes in eating habits, and higher or lower activity levels set in, the "clock" gets harder to reset, and the person becomes more and more ill.[9]

Production of the neurotransmitter serotonin is also affected by a reduced amount of light in the environment. Neurotransmitters are chemicals that send signals to all parts of the nervous system. Serotonin affects mood, appetite, and much more. In people with bipolar disorders, serotonin and other neurotransmitters may be created in the wrong amounts, absorbed by the wrong parts of the brain or other sites in the body that rely on them, or refused admittance at specific sites that should accept them.[10]

With each regulatory error, your symptoms become more noticeable and more serious. It's like a snowball rolling downhill: eventually the circadian rhythms and other regu-latory systems are completely off track, resulting in extreme mood swings and bring-ing on depression, mania, or other abnormal states of mind. You may start to have noticeable errors in thinking. You may even hear sounds or voices that aren't there or feel that you're being watched.

The nervous system's disordered condition will eventually show up outwardly as well. Movements may become rapid or very slow, jerky or super-precise. The tone and pace of your speech may change. For example, speedy, disjointed speech is asso-ciated with mania.

What is it about the bodies and minds of people with bipolar disorders that permits this devastating chain reaction to occur? As of this writing, no one can point to a specific gene or brain difference with absolute certainty, but bipolar disorders are probably caused by a complicated mix of inherited genetic differences, differences in brain structure and chemistry, unusual electrical or magnetic activity in the brain, and environmental factors.

Genetic differences

There is currently no doubt that a susceptibility to bipolar disorders runs in families. Several studies have made the genetic links clear, even though the exact mechanism isn't understood.[11,12] As with other psychiatric disorders known to have genetic underpinnings, the inheritance pattern of bipolar disorders probably involves a complex interaction of several different genes.

Ben, age 45, was well aware of his mother's mental illness, but not that it might be inherited:

> My mother had eighteen shock treatments. I was my mother's caretaker since I was in grade school.
>
> I had a long history of interaction with my illness, without knowing that I had a neurobiological brain disorder. My whole life has been "fight or flight"—artist, hippy, chef, high-tech jobs, anger, jail for injunction violation, divorce, disability. I thought I had a drinking problem I couldn't beat. I was three times in rehab before an enlightened psychiatrist told me about bipolar disorder. It was good news. I could then start to rebuild my life.

Clues about the genetics of bipolar disorders are slowly emerging. One of the most interesting is the link between bipolar disorder and velo-cardio-facial syndrome (VCFS), as reported by a team headed by psychiatric researcher Dr. Demitri Papolos. VCFS includes a set of physical abnormalities such as a characteristically long face with a large nose, small ears with a folded portion, narrow squinty eyes, and a relatively expressionless mouth. People with VCFS have a very nasal vocal tone, may be born with a cleft palate, experience heart problems, and have learning disabilities. VCFS is known to be associated with a deletion on chromosome 22.[13]

VCFS is relatively rare, and the majority of people with bipolar disorders do not have this syndrome. However, most people with VCFS have bipolar disorder. By studying the genetic differences seen in VCFS, researchers believe they may be able to identify some of the genes that are also responsible for bipolar disorders in general.

Researchers have also proposed possible genetic differences on chromosomes 5, 12, 18, 21, and the X chromosome, based on genetic studies of people with bipolar disorders. Appendix B, *Genetics,* includes a chart showing some of the genes that researchers think may be connected to bipolar disorders.

Although genetic testing can show whether a person has VCFS, there is no diagnostic genetic test for bipolar disorders at this time.

Brain differences

Genetic differences may lead to structural differences in the developing brain. The eyes are a sense organ tightly bound to the brain, and differences in how they absorb light may also be a factor. Recent research into cryptochromes—special light-sensitive proteins found in retina of the human eye—indicates that they play a role in establishing and maintaining circadian rhythms.[14]

The brain is the most complicated and least understood organ in the body. The brain and spinal cord are called the central nervous system, or CNS. The CNS receives, processes, and sends billions of signals every day by way of chemicals and electrical impulses. Scientists are only starting to identify how these chemicals and power surges work, and what they know right now is woefully inadequate for reliably getting these processes back on track.

The brain is made up of several complex parts, all of which work together to control body functions, produce thought and emotion, and store and retrieve memories. (See Figure 1-1, "Parts of the human brain.") Researchers are not absolutely sure which parts of the CNS are affected by bipolar disorders, although a clearer picture is

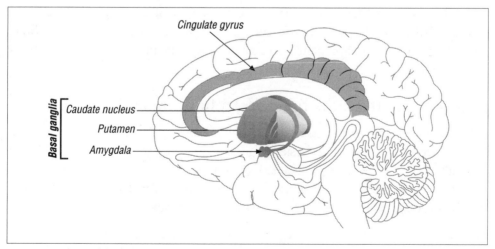

Figure 1-1. Parts of the human brain.

emerging every year thanks to brain-imaging technologies. These include computer tomography (CAT), magnetic resonance imagery (MRI), and single photon emission computed tomography (SPECT or NeuroSPECT) scans.

Although they aren't used to diagnose bipolar disorders just yet, brain scans can show where abnormal activity is occurring or whether the brain is structured differently than usual. The Bipolar Disorders Clinic at Stanford University has been at the forefront of brain imaging research, and its preliminary findings implicate differences in the prefrontal and anterior paralimbic areas of the brain, including the almond-shaped portion called the amygdala.[15] These differences are subtle, not major.

The amygdala is one of several small structures called the basal ganglia. Located deep within the brain, these structures are involved with governing automatic movements and behaviors. They are connected to the hypothalamus gland by nerve fibers. The basal ganglia are part of the brain's inhibitory system, and when they're not working properly, compulsive movements (tics), compulsive or obsessive thoughts and behaviors, and the loss of normal inhibitions can occur. There is a higher prevalence of bipolar disorder among people diagnosed with Tourette's syndrome, a neurological disorder known to involve differences in the basal ganglia that result in tics.[16] It could be that the basal ganglia play a role in mood regulation as well as in regulating movements.

The brain's limbic system has also long been known to affect mood and behavior.

More bipolar-specific findings from brain scans include an enlarged caudate nucleus (part of the basal ganglia) and white matter hyperintensities (white spots of unknown origin that appear on the scans).[17] These are not seen in all imaging studies, and the total number of studies done is still fairly small. No one is sure what these brain differences might mean, nor are they yet leading medicine in new diagnostic or treatment directions.

Neurotransmitters: the brain's telephone system

Although differences in brain structure may play a role in bipolar disorders, researchers are currently much more interested in what's happening at the cellular level within the brain. There are definitely differences in how the cells that make up the nervous system communicate with each other in persons with bipolar disorders. There might even be some differences in cellular structure or in the number of certain types of cells.

Two kinds of cells make up most of the brain: neurons and glial cells. Neurons are the brain's internal communication centers, but they don't trade messages directly.

Neurons have a central cell body with long arms called axons and smaller tentacle-like structures called dendrites. (See Figure 1-2, "The structure of a neuron.") Inside a neuron, all the messages are sent via electrical impulses. Where two neurons meet to swap information, however, there's a small space between them called the synaptic cleft. Electrical impulses are translated into chemical signals in the form of neurotransmitters, the chemicals mentioned earlier in this chapter, which cross the synaptic

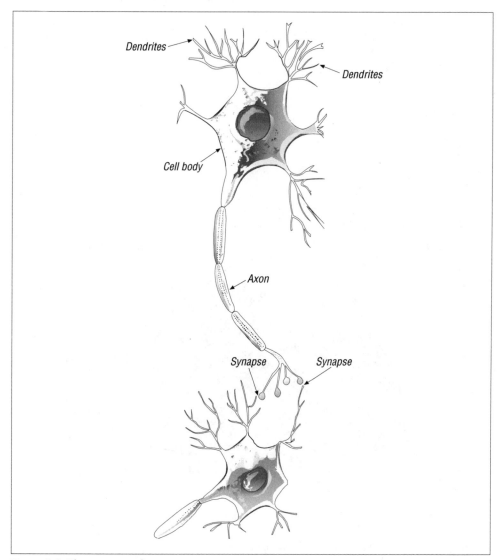

Figure 1-2. The structure of a neuron

cleft and are then re-translated into electrical signals on the other side. (See Figure 1-3, "Neurotransmitters crossing the synaptic cleft.")

Glial cells have the less glamorous jobs of making sure the neurons have enough nutrients and other chemicals, repairing the brain if it is injured, and confronting bacteria that try to attack the brain. These cells combine to form a vastly intricate architecture.

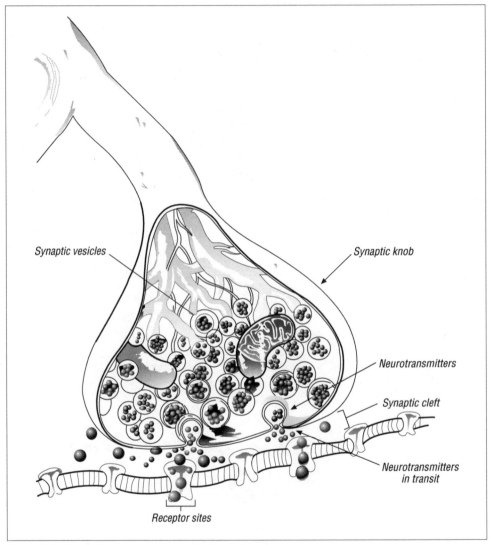

Figure 1-3. Neurotransmitters crossing the synaptic cleft

There are many different neurotransmitters and related hormones at work in the human brain and throughout the body. They're all site-specific chemicals that are absorbed only by certain cells and only at certain spots, called binding sites. When this process works normally, it ensures that only the right kinds of messages get through. Neurotransmitters are also used and absorbed differently in various areas of the body and sometimes turned into other kinds of chemicals.

Along with the hormone melatonin, several neurotransmitters appear to be involved in bipolar disorders, including:

- **Serotonin**. Serotonin, also called 5-hydroxytryptamine or 5-HT, is part of the system that controls sleep, mood, some types of sensory perception, body-temperature regulation, and appetite. It affects the rate at which hormones are released and plays a role in inflammation.

- **Dopamine**. Dopamine, sometimes abbreviated as DA, helps control body movements and thought patterns and also regulates how hormones are released.

- **Norepinephrine**. Norepinephrine is used by both the central nervous system and the peripheral sympathetic nervous system (the nerves that communicate with the rest of the body). It governs arousal, the fight or flight response, anxiety, and memory.

Medications can increase or decrease the production of certain neurotransmitters or alter how these chemicals are absorbed in the brain. In turn, these actions can produce changes in symptoms—that's one of the clues that has let researchers know which chemicals have something to do with various brain-based health conditions.

For people with bipolar disorders, current medicines don't cure the underlying problem or problems, but they can create major improvements in behavior and emotional stability by directly affecting neurotransmitter function and/or use. It's a bit like taking the hormone insulin for diabetes: you're still a diabetic and you still must watch your diet, but insulin injections can help you control the illness and prevent its most debilitating effects. See Chapter 4 for more information about medications used to treat bipolar disorders and how they work.

Exercise, diet, vitamins, and herbal supplements can also affect neurotransmitter production or activity. That's one of the reasons you need to be as careful about choosing alternative treatments as you would be about taking prescription drugs. For more information about nonpharmaceutical treatments for bipolar disorders, see Chapter 6, *Complementary Therapies*.

There is even some evidence that positive or negative life experiences, including talk therapy and behavior modification, can help create actual neurological change over a period of time.[18] Therapy is definitely very helpful for learning to handle the negative aspects of bipolar disorders, from embarrassing public behavior to difficulties in personal relationships. Also, a good relationship with a therapist is often the key to ensuring that you keep taking helpful medication, stop taking medication that isn't helping, and maintain a healthy lifestyle. For more about talk therapy and related concepts, see Chapter 5.

Electrical miswiring

The brain's electrical system is intimately intertwined with its chemical messaging system. Problems can occur during the electrical side of the communication process when uncontrolled surges of electricity, called seizures, take place inside the brain. Many people with bipolar disorders have unusual electrical activity that will show up on an electroencephalogram (EEG) test. Usually the activity observed is not the type associated with seizure disorders (epilepsy). However, seizure disorders are somewhat more common in people with bipolar disorder, and many of the same medications can work for both conditions. These are all clues that abnormal electrical activity may sometimes be involved in causing mood swings or may happen as a result of mood swings.

Some types of seizures are hard to recognize, even with sophisticated equipment. For example, some doctors believe that the inexplicable temper tantrums and rages occasionally experienced by people with bipolar disorders may be related to seizures occurring deep within the brain.[19] Others suspect that an increase in a theoretical phenomenon called kindling—sort of an electrical blip in brain activity that can be caused by environmental triggers—may be at fault.[20] In people with epilepsy, a kindling process might lead to a seizure; in those with migraine, a different kind of kindling process may precede a migraine headache or other symptom. Perhaps in some people with bipolar disorders, the result of an as yet undefined kindling process is behavioral or psychiatric disturbances. No one really knows just yet.

Chapter 3 presents more information about the connection between bipolar disorders and epilepsy, and explains how seizure disorders are diagnosed and treated.

Immune system impairment

It's not a totally mainstream idea, but some scientists think that bipolar disorders may include an immune system problem.[21] There's a certain amount of good sense to this theory, because the immune system is tightly bound to the endocrine (hormonal) system, which in turn affects neurotransmitter production. In addition, people with known immune disorders, such as lupus, often experience mood swings.

One intriguing clue has come from research into toxoplasmosis, a common parasitical disease caused by an organism carried in the feces of some birds and cats and also found in raw meat, raw vegetables, and the soil. Toxoplasmosis has an interesting ability: it can hide within the body for years, seemingly in a dormant state. Most people have been exposed to this parasite at some time in their lives with no ill effects, but when a person develops immune system problems it can reemerge from hiding and cause both physical illness and mood swings.[22]

Researchers are currently exploring the possible role of toxoplasmosis in some cases of bipolar disorders.[23] Others have proposed that one of the human herpes viruses could play a part in some cases. Members of this large family of viruses are responsible for a number of physical ailments, ranging from genital herpes to chickenpox.[24] Like toxoplasmosis, herpes viruses can hibernate in the body for years, reemerging during times of poor immune function to cause trouble.

Interestingly, lithium, the most popular medication for bipolar disorders, also seems to have some anti-viral effects.[25]

There hasn't been enough research done on this angle yet, but for at least some people immune system problems could be a cause, or perhaps a side effect, of manic-depressive illness. Chapters 3 and 4 include the latest information on diagnosing and treating infections and immune system problems when they are related to bipolar disorders or when they make your symptoms worse.

Dual and multiple diagnoses

When psychiatrists say the words "dual diagnosis," they are almost always referring to a person who has a mental illness and a substance abuse problem. Drug and alcohol abuse are far more common among people with bipolar disorders than in the general population or in those with any other Axis I psychiatric disorder. The lifetime prevalence of drug and alcohol abuse is an astonishing 50 to 60 percent—or more— among those who have bipolar disorders.[26] Drug and alcohol abuse usually starts during the teenage years, sometimes even earlier, so early onset of a bipolar disorder seems to make this problem even more likely.

Choice of drug may even be a diagnostic clue: up to 30 percent of cocaine addicts fit the criteria for bipolar disorder, as do a sizable portion of alcoholics and amphetamine users.[27] It's not yet known whether these individuals abuse drugs as a result of their bipolar illness or have bipolar-like symptoms as a result of their drug use. There is some pretty compelling evidence that the former, rather than the latter, is usually the case.[28]

Substance abuse can complicate diagnosis and treatment of bipolar disorder. In the past, the conventional wisdom was that the alcoholic or drug addict had to be "clean and sober" before psychiatric treatment could succeed, but current clinical experience indicates that it's essential to treat the underlying bipolar disorder along with the substance abuse problem. In fact, mood stabilization may be a very necessary part of substance abuse treatment for this population. Medication and therapy can greatly reduce the relapse rate.[29]

For Steven, age forty-five, substance abuse and bipolar disorder have been a double whammy:

> *I suffered for countless years. I abused alcohol, and smoked a little weed too. I was finally told that my problems stemmed from being bipolar—I was using alcohol to control the cycling of my moods. I used alcohol to relieve my high moods, and in return got sicker than a dog for days on end. I would not get out of bed or bathe myself for more than four days.*
>
> *I have lost a lot with the combination of the two: houses, cars, jobs, marriages, the whole gamut. I need to rebuild all I have torn down, and move on.*

Many people with bipolar disorder have other psychiatric or medical problems to contend with, a fact that can complicate their treatment. Several neurological and physical problems appear to occur more often in people with bipolar disorder than in the general population. The list includes migraines, fibromyalgia, seizure disorders, attention deficit hyperactivity disorder (ADHD), developmental delays, obsessive-compulsive disorder (OCD), Tourette's syndrome, anxiety disorders, autism and other pervasive developmental disorders, autoimmune disorders, and gastrointestinal problems. Many of these conditions have symptoms like those of bipolar disorder (see Chapter 3 for more information), which often causes the coexisting bipolar disorder to go untreated.

Other factors in bipolar disorders

Gender can influence medical diagnosis more than one might expect. Women are diagnosed more often with depressive disorders in general. There is some evidence that childhood bipolar disorder is diagnosed more commonly among males.[30]

Other studies have found more diagnoses of adolescent bipolar disorder among females.[31]

It seems likely that women are sometimes misdiagnosed as bipolar due to problems that are actually caused by hormonal cycles—although men, too, can have hormonal disorders that cause mood swings. Culture has an impact, too. The stress experienced by women and girls in a sexist culture can produce emotional problems, and normal behavior for a particular girl or woman can be pathologized when seen through certain cultural lenses. A female with a tempestuous, artistic, assertive, even aggressive temperament might be called mentally ill in a culture that does not value these attributes in females. Women may also seek medical help more often than males who have similar symptoms.

Bipolar women do seem to be more prone to rapid cycling than male patients and to have more depressed and mixed moods. Hormonal activity definitely plays a role in how and when bipolar illness expresses itself, particularly right after pregnancy.[32]

Males can also be affected by gender bias. A man with undiagnosed bipolar disorder may come to the attention of the criminal justice system before he sees a mental health professional. He may find himself with a police record rather than a treatment plan, simply because moody, unpredictable, aggressive behavior in males is generally seen as a personal problem, not a medical one. Males with bipolar disorder are more likely to get involved in potentially criminal, aggressive, assaultive, or risky behavior than females—and therefore are more likely to end up in the criminal justice system rather than in treatment.[33] There may also be more cultural acceptance of aggressive, risky, and even assaultive behavior among males, leading to missed diagnosis and missed opportunities for intervention. Males are also more likely to kill themselves, even though females are more likely to attempt suicide.[34]

Other cultural issues, including race, religion, economic status, and nationality, can have an impact on diagnosis as well. Psychiatric professionals, families, and affected individuals all carry some cultural baggage, ranging from assumptions about what is proper behavior to stereotypes about the behavior of other cultural or racial groups. These ideas can play a role in who gets diagnosed, how they are treated, and what resources are made available.

Although bipolar disorders run in families, there is no evidence that any ethnic group is immune, nor is there evidence that any particular group has a far higher prevalence. Characteristics that often accompany these disorders, such as the ability to hyperfocus, enhanced creativity, and (within bounds) aggressiveness, are so valuable that, despite the disorder's down side, individuals with bipolar disorders have always been desirable as mates—and so are found in every community.

It's important to keep those good characteristics in mind. It's not right to think of everything about bipolar disorders as being bad, nor should anyone say that people with bipolar disorders are abnormal. Many people with bipolar disorders feel that they have received special gifts along with challenges, and these gifts can actually help them overcome their difficulties.

Whether it's a creative streak, an ability to produce massive amounts of work in short bursts, or simply the gift of conversational wit that characterizes many people with bipolar disorder, there is much that's special and wonderful about these individuals. If you are a person with bipolar disorder, your goal should be not only achieving good mental health, but reaching your full creative potential as an individual. If you are someone who cares for a person with bipolar disorder, keeping both of these goals in mind will help you provide an optimal level of support.

As Shannon puts it:

> The message I would like to give to all of us who struggle with bipolar disorder, is never to give up. Bipolar people are smart, talented, intense, creative people with much to offer the rest of the world. And I believe that, with new and better meds and other treatments being created all the time, the hope of recovery has never been stronger. Let your light shine!

CHAPTER 2

Getting a Diagnosis

DIAGNOSING BIPOLAR DISORDERS is not an exact science. These conditions can be obscured by or mistaken for other disorders of the mind or body. There's no blood test, brain imaging machine, or written exam that can provide certainty. Careful observation of your mood, demeanor (affect), and behavior is the key to accurate diagnosis.

In this chapter, we talk about finding an expert in bipolar disorders and about how a diagnosis is made. Medical conditions that can mimic the symptoms of bipolar disorders are covered in Chapter 3, *Differential Diagnosis*.

Where to begin

Most people begin their search for help by seeing a general practitioner. That's a good place to start, but while most family physicians are experts in sore knees, stomachaches, and other common medical problems, they are not usually experts in neurology or psychiatry.

Diagnosing bipolar disorders can be especially difficult. People with mood swings tend to see their doctor for the first time while they are in a depressed state. Because a primary care physician is less likely than a psychiatrist to take a complete personal and family history, misdiagnosing the problem as unipolar depression is common.

Jane, age 46, was not diagnosed until three years ago. It wasn't for want of trying:

> I saw social workers, psychologists, doctors, women's health
> professionals, naturopaths, alternative health services, etc., etc.,
> always searching for an answer for not feeling right. At age 24, I was
> taking an infant welfare course. My lecturer pulled me aside, told me
> that she felt that I needed help, and advised me to seek professional
> services. I must have been manic.

> *I went to my general practitioner, who was a family friend, and told him what the teacher had said to me. I think he did me the biggest disservice ever, saying "Don't be silly, Jane, there is nothing wrong with you." I was happy, and went on with life in my manic way. I know my drinking was way out of control—I was drunk every night of the course, and don't know how I passed the exams.*
>
> *When my kids were babies, it seemed like I was at the doctor's every five minutes with worries and fears about their health. In the end, a young doctor told me to go home and not come back. Missed again.*

As Jane's story illustrates, a psychiatrist who specializes in bipolar disorders is the best choice for diagnostic help. To find a doctor who is knowledgeable about the latest research, look for a board-certified psychiatrist who has a working relationship with a good hospital, preferably one affiliated with a university medical school. "Board-certified" means that the doctor has completed a very rigorous training program, has already practiced psychiatry as a supervised resident for three to four years, and meets the most rigorous qualifications in the field as set by an official board of his peers.

You can reach the American Board of Psychiatry and Neurology at (847) 945-7900. You can also check a doctor's certification status with the American Board of Medical Specialties at (800) 776-CERT or on the Web at *http://www.certifieddoctor.org*.

Some board-certified psychologists or neurologists also have expertise in diagnosing bipolar disorders. However, psychologists will not be able to prescribe medication, and neurologists rarely provide ongoing care for persons with bipolar disorders unless they have additional conditions, such as seizures, that impact treatment.

One source for referrals is the psychiatry or neurology department of a nearby medical school. Many medical schools have excellent clinics staffed by both experienced doctors and residents who are learning the ropes. Some of the foremost experts in bipolar disorders are affiliated with university programs. These doctors are often (but not always!) aware of the latest research findings and treatments. Several university-affiliated programs with special expertise in bipolar disorders are listed Appendix A, *Resources*.

You might also begin your search for an expert by calling a support or advocacy group, like the National Alliance for the Mentally Ill (NAMI) or the Depression and Related Affective Disorders Association (DRADA), and asking for suggestions. Several helpful organizations are listed in Appendix A.

Internet discussion groups are sometimes a good source of tips and advice about doctors in your area. There's more about the value of support groups, both traditional and online, in Chapter 8, *Living with Bipolar Disorders,* but the best time to make first contact with these is when you are still in search of a diagnosis and help. You can avoid dead ends, unqualified doctors, and much heartache by tapping into these resources right away. Even if it turns out that your problems are due to another condition, you'll be glad to have found out so quickly.

Of course, the best doctors are also the busiest and the hardest to get an appointment with. Make sure you have a second choice in the wings, just in case. Once you have identified your experts, make sure they are currently taking new patients. You may also want to ask if they have worked with your health plan or HMO before. Insurance regulations, or the rules of your national health plan, usually govern just how you go about accessing a specialist. Chapter 7, *Healthcare and Insurance,* covers problems that frequently occur and provides ideas for dealing with them.

Consultation appointment

Now that you know who you should eventually see, you have to go back to square one—unless you will be paying the psychologist or psychiatrist directly rather than going through your insurance or national health plan. Usually you must put the diagnostic process in motion by requesting a consultation appointment with your primary care physician (PCP) or general practitioner (GP), the doctor who provides your regular medical care. This kind of appointment is a little different from the typical visit. In fact, it may take place in a meeting room or office rather than in an examination room. It should also be longer in length: a half-hour at least, preferably an hour.

Your doctor will want to know a lot of details about your family's health history, including mental health. If you're not sure, ask relatives what they know. Often people with bipolar disorder were never officially diagnosed, but will be described by those who remember them as moody, depressed, hyper, wild, bad-tempered, alcoholic, married and divorced multiple times, or "difficult." You may get some surprises at this stage of the game, such as tales of a grandparent's secret trips to the hospital or sanitarium.

You may need to check family medical records or talk with doctors who knew older family members well. Physicians are duty-bound not to give you personal information about living persons, but they are generally more forthcoming about patients who are deceased. Once you have this family history in hand, you might want to put it in very simple "family tree" form for your physician.

Keeping a daily diary is also an excellent way to prepare for the consultation appointment. Many people have learned a great deal about themselves during this process. Use your diary to record activities, diet, mood, and other symptoms each day for a period of two weeks or more, with the time and duration of items noted. Not only can this diary provide a very complete picture of your symptoms to a professional, it can also help to identify patterns.

If you can, use a calendar, personal diaries, medical notes, and your own recollections to create a rough chart of your major mood swings over the past year or so. That can help a doctor find out if there is a seasonal pattern to your mood swings or if there are other identifiable triggers, such as holidays, times of particular stress, or use of medication for another condition.

For Norman, his wife's observations turned out to be helpful during diagnosis and have also assisted him in maintaining stability during treatment:

> *I've known for quite awhile that I have depression, but I was able to keep working through all the episodes of depression without medication until recently. Seven or eight years ago my wife and I went overseas, and she had a chance to observe my younger brother. He has been diagnosed bipolar, and his behavior at both ends is more extreme than mine, but she saw similarities. I had never thought about bipolar disorder much until then.*
>
> *My wife said that when I'm hypomanic or manic, my behaviors had more impact on her than anyone else. She said I tend to have less time for her because I'm involved in so many other things. Typically when I'm depressed I don't go out in the evenings, but when I'm "up" I'm out seven nights a week. I'm less available emotionally as well—and when I'm there, she describes my behavior as being rude. I'm more likely to argue with her about something than just go along with something she says. I also have a tendency to spend a lot of money when I'm hypomanic or manic. Before I met her, I got something like $50,000 as a payout from work, and that went in about a year. It's not that any one thing was a big expense, but looking at the totality of it you have to wonder about the possibility of mania, especially since normally I sort of border on stingy.*
>
> *Anyway, the first time I went in on my own to a psychiatrist, my wife gave me a one-page written list some of the things she had noticed about my behavior in the past twelve months, and that helped.*

Now I take my wife along for appointments. The doctor would always ask me what happened, and sometimes I couldn't remember. My wife was reluctant to do that—I think she was thinking it was like being my mother—but she ended up having a good relationship with my psychiatrist.

It definitely helps if you, or someone close to you, can summarize your concerns in writing. The records already mentioned can help you gather your thoughts. You don't have to be an eloquent writer to express what worries you. You can jot down a simple numbered list rather than writing whole paragraphs if you prefer. Be sure to include specific information about episodes of suspected depression, hypomania, mania, and mixed moods, including the symptoms you have experienced and the timing and length of these episodes. Also list any behaviors, such as suicide threats or attempts, aggressive behaviors, self-mutilation, sudden onset of phobias, anxiety or panic attacks, and substance abuse that you want to make sure the doctor knows about. Some people send their summary of concerns to the doctor in advance; others prefer to use it as an agenda for discussion during the consultation.

If you have seen other doctors, you must sign releases to have your medical records transferred to your current physician before the consultation appointment, and to your expert later on. Transfers always seem to take longer than you would expect, so get releases taken care of early and make sure the records were actually sent and received. Alternatively, if you have your own copies of these records, you may photocopy and deliver them yourself.

You might also want to talk to a nurse or physician's assistant who works most closely with your doctor. In large medical practices and HMOs, nurses and assistants are an especially important part of the organization. They can be allies for people who need referrals to specialists or even just a listening ear. If you are lucky enough to find a knowledgeable and sympathetic nurse, his or her input can help greatly.

If possible, your information and your complete medical file should be available to the doctor at least a week before the consultation appointment. These should be accompanied by a request that she read the material in advance and review your file before the meeting. You want ensure that your case is fresh in the doctor's mind at the consultation appointment.

When you arrive for the consultation, bring any additional records you have gathered, copies of your earlier letter (just in case it never reached the doctor), your summary of concerns, and any questions that you want to ask. A small notebook or tape recorder can help you keep a record of the discussion.

If the consultation seems to be getting off to an awkward start, start with your summary of concerns or list of questions. Always keep your goal in mind: referral to one of the experts you have already identified. You're there to make a case for this referral, and your information is the evidence you'll need to convince your primary care physician. Think of yourself as a salesperson trying to convince a customer. You want to be the one in charge of this meeting, and keeping that image in your mind can help.

It's likely that your doctor will simply discuss the situation with you and make the referral. Sometimes, however, medical practitioners need help in making decisions. They may use tools like the *DSM-IV* or *ICD-10* criteria (see Chapter 1, *What Are Bipolar Disorders?*); structured interviews where you answer a list of questions; less structured discussions; direct observation in a medical setting; direct observation in a more natural setting, such as at home; and standardized questionnaires for you or your family to fill out. Sometimes your doctor will first order certain medical tests to rule out health conditions that affect mood.

It's important to tell your doctor about any symptoms you have that appear to be purely physical, such as unexplained aches and pains or menstrual problems. These may indicate a different cause for your mood swings. However, some people tend to express mental pain with physical symptoms, such as headaches or insomnia, a process known as "somatization."

For Shoshana, age 56, unexplained physical issues could have provided an early clue to her deteriorating mental state:

> *For about a year before I went completely nuts, I had increasing pain in my neck and shoulders and, as a result of the pain (or so I thought), I started to have bouts of insomnia. My concentration became impaired, and eventually my judgment. I was verbally skilled, so none of the physicians I saw suspected psychiatric problems for over a year. I coped with the inability to read my notes at work by having my secretary brief me on what was happening; no one guessed I couldn't concentrate enough.*
>
> *Finally my husband took me to a nearby university hospital outside our medical plan. I was diagnosed within a couple of weeks, and hospitalized.*

Referral roadblocks

It isn't always easy to get a referral to a specialist. Sometimes the main problem is communication between you and your doctor. Sometimes reluctance stems from corporate considerations, including capitation arrangements in HMOs.

If your doctor is reluctant to make a referral, there are several possible responses.

- Go back over your evidence, explaining how your behaviors and mood swings are affecting you at home, at work, and in the community. If you believe that your life or the safety of others is in danger, make this fact very clear.

- Let the doctor know what interventions you've already tried, such as treatment for other disorders or counseling.

- Emphasize any special factors that you feel support the possibility that you could have a bipolar disorder. These include knowledge that other people in your family have been diagnosed as bipolar; presence in your family of other disorders with strong links to bipolar disorder, such as migraine, ADHD, or epilepsy; and suggestions by a previous doctor or other professional that you should be evaluated for a bipolar disorder.

- Ask the doctor to put his refusal to refer in writing. This may not be something he'd like to commit to paper, so you might end up getting the referral after all.

- If the doctor does put his refusal in writing, you can choose to call your diagnostic facility of choice and set up an appointment directly. Be prepared to pay for this visit out-of-pocket. However, if the specialist confirms your suspicions, you should be able to bill your insurance company for reimbursement due to refusal of an appropriate referral.

- If your doctor won't refer but won't put his refusal in writing either, you can still self-refer, but it will be harder to get reimbursed. You should send a letter to the doctor explaining why you have made this choice over his objections. Send a copy to your insurance company as well. This creates a paper record, allowing you to pursue a claim for improper refusal later on, if warranted.

- Go up the chain of command if your doctor is in a managed care organization or HMO. In these medical groups there is a board that considers patient complaints. You can petition the board to approve your referral even if your doctor refuses. Usually this is done in writing, not in person. You can have a patient advocate help you with these procedures.

In the US, most doctors share the risks and expenses of caring for patients, including those who need specialized care, with business partners or an HMO group. Doctors who make too many referrals can face financial penalties, even if the extra services were absolutely necessary. Physicians may also feel constrained by directives from insurance companies, which want to minimize expenses.

Low-income Americans who are uninsured face the biggest barrier of all: lack of access to health care. Your county health or mental health department should be your first stop. Chapter 7 provides many ideas for getting diagnostic help and ongoing care if you are not covered by private insurance.

In Canada and Europe, where the single-payer system of nationalized healthcare predominates, doctors have a different set of constraints on their ability make referrals. Resources are focused on providing basic healthcare to everyone, so specialists are more rare and harder to access than in the US. If you want prompt care, you may be forced to pay out-of-pocket to doctors who practice outside the national healthcare scheme. The expenses can be considerable. Some people gain more timely access with help from a sympathetic social worker or health visitor or call on advocacy groups for assistance.

In countries where neither private insurance nor the single-payer model predominates, you should seek out—and pay for—a specialist directly, without going through a preliminary consultation appointment. Reduced-fee or free help may be available through state-run hospitals and clinics, medical facilities owned by religious orders or charities, or individual physicians who are willing to take a case at a lower cost than usual.

Seeing a specialist

Technically, psychologists, neuropsychologists (psychologists with special training in neurological disorders), and psychiatrists are the appropriate professionals for diagnosing bipolar disorders. You may end up seeing a neurologist instead, especially if the diagnosis is complicated by another neurological problem, such as epilepsy.

In areas with limited medical resources, you may only be able to see a therapist, social worker, or counselor. These professionals are not legally qualified to diagnose bipolar disorders, but some have ample experience in this area and can at least help you get started. They may be able to consult with a medical doctor at a distance or arrange for a visit to the closest qualified physician for the final diagnosis.

In some health plans, a therapist or counselor acts as a gatekeeper: you must see this person before you are allowed to see a psychiatrist. Therapists, counselors, and social workers can administer many of the standardized tests used in the diagnostic process, they can observe and interview you, and they can talk to you about your family, medical, social, and educational history. A good therapist, counselor, or social worker can be a very important part of the diagnostic team by handling the paperwork and finding out what needs you and your family have.

Although therapists, counselors, and social workers can offer suggestions to the psychiatrist, psychologist, or neurologist, they should not give you a diagnosis themselves. They also cannot prescribe medication—and neither can a psychologist. In practice, however, these professionals often know quite a lot about medication and can work productively with a psychiatrist, neurologist, or other medical doctor. After the diagnosis has been made, they can provide more information, offer therapy sessions, help you locate resources in the community, and provide a listening ear when needed.

When you finally see a psychiatrist, psychologist, or neurologist, your visit is unlikely to resemble the stereotypical trip to the shrink as seen in a Woody Allen film. Psychiatrists and psychologists usually have an office with a desk, comfortable chairs and perhaps a sofa. They may administer standardized tests, or you may simply chat together about your concerns. Neurologists usually work in a medical office, complete with examining table. They will give you a physical examination and perform tests of neurological function as well as discussing your symptoms.

Pay attention to your feelings in this meeting. Sometimes a particular doctor is not a good fit. Just as some people respond best to a fatherly Marcus Welby-style doctor, others prefer a no-nonsense clinical manner, and still others do best in a collaborative relationship with their physician.

Rachel, mother of 19-year-old Lillian, says:

> *My daughter saw three doctors and two therapists before she finally found someone who clicked with her, and with us. Dr. B listened to all of us, and made it clear to our daughter that her health, safety, and happiness were the primarily concerns. That made her feel much more comfortable. Some of the other people she had seen seemed bent on turning her into a perfect, conformist teenager, and focused on minor things like her hair or clothes when she was worried about far greater problems.*

*Dr. B was willing to hear her out about some health worries she
had, and as it turned out, dealing with these was very important
in her recovery. Because this doctor gained her trust, our daughter
was willing to tell her about symptoms she had not revealed to the
others. She was also more willing to listen to the doctor about
taking medication, and to call her right away when she needed
help.*

Regardless of her personal style, a psychiatrist, psychologist, or neurologist should always be a good listener. Your questions should be answered with information that helps you understand what's going on and take charge of your medical care. Sometimes it's comforting when a professional takes control of the situation right away, but in reality you must have the ability to communicate freely and without fear of having your queries brushed aside. The psychiatrist, psychologist, or neurologist may see you only once, on a monthly basis for medication management, or even for weekly or more frequent therapy sessions. You, however, must live with your symptoms every day of the year. A smart doctor knows that your observations and input are essential at every stage of your treatment.

It may take awhile for the doctor to make a diagnosis. This can be frustrating, but it's much better than having a doctor who jumps to conclusions! However, it's possible to treat dangerous symptoms, such as suicidal or assaultive behavior, without knowing for certain what the psychiatric diagnosis is. Day treatment and hospitalization are other options that can keep everyone safe if you are in crisis during the diagnostic process.

Tests for bipolar disorders

As noted earlier in this chapter, the most important tools for diagnosing bipolar disorders are direct observation, personal interviews, and your personal and family history. Many evaluators will also use some standardized questionnaires to find out about and assess symptoms. You may hear these referred to as "tests" for bipolar disorders, but they're really just questionnaires. You can't accurately diagnose someone with a mental illness because of answers on a piece of paper. These standard questionnaires are helpful for screening new patients, and sometimes the questions asked will unearth new information about symptoms you haven't talked about before, but they're not a sure thing.

Some tests are just screening instruments: simple lists of questions for you or a care-giver that can identify "red flags" for mental or neurological disorders in general. Others are targeted more precisely, such as the Attention Deficit Disorders Evaluation Scale, which is used to diagnose or rule out ADHD. The information gained from targeted tests, if properly administered, is valuable when designing treatment and recovery programs.

Some tools for gauging emotional disturbance ask people to draw pictures or interpret the pictures or words of others. These projective tests are highly subjective. Nonetheless, some practitioners administer tests like the well-known Rorschach Blot interpretation test, the House-Tree-Person test, and many variations on the same theme. Projective tests might give an evaluator a better feel for your state of mind than your direct answers to questions, but using them well requires training and experience that not all possess. In other words, you are far more likely to get useful, reliable information from interviews, direct observation, and objective diagnostic tools.

Standardized diagnostic tools that you may encounter are listed and explained in Appendix C, *Diagnostic Tests*.

One tool that many doctors find useful is a "mood diary." If you already keep a journal, you could create a retrospective mood diary based on past entries. Otherwise, it's a great idea to work on one in the weeks leading up to your first appointment. Chapter 8 includes a daily mood and behavior worksheet that you can copy and use. Keep track of things like sleep problems, eating problems, and feeling sick, as well as mood changes.

Leslie, age 44, said bringing her journals along for a consultation appointment with an expert was very helpful:

> *I took journals with me, years of descriptions of cyclic moods and repeated behavioral patterns—you know, the symptoms of hypomania—and the doctor thought bipolar was a good possibility.*
>
> *I also underwent a week of testing to rule out some other illnesses that can cause mood swings. So many other illnesses cause mood swings. Treating the symptoms while missing the diagnosis of, say, lupus can be dangerous. The tests literally took several days and included a glucose tolerance test, a dexamethasone suppression test, a 24-hour urine cortisol level, and thyroid, kidney, and liver function test.*

As Leslie notes, it's important for doctors to look at your physical health as well, especially in light of emerging information about infection, hormonal problems, and other factors that can cause or worsen mood swings. In the next few years, it's likely that doctors will begin using more physical tests during the diagnostic process. Some employ these now, although they are used mostly to rule out other conditions. See Chapter 3 for more information about this process.

The diagnostic report

Once the psychiatrist, psychologist, or neurologist has completed his observations, interviews, and testing, he'll be ready to make a diagnosis. This will probably be done in a report that describes your symptoms; summarizes the events, observations, and tests that led up to the diagnosis; and presents the doctor's diagnosis. Most practitioners also include suggestions for therapy, medications, or rehabilitative help based on what they have learned.

Sometimes you'll see notes in the report about specific manic, hypomanic, mixed, or depressive episodes. Often these describe the most recent episode (usually the one that brought you in for treatment). Sometimes there are notes on several episodes.

Some people interviewed for this book mentioned that they were never given a copy of the diagnostic report. Instead, they may have been informed of the diagnosis verbally—even over the phone—without getting much information or a chance to ask questions. This is not an acceptable practice.

Bipolar disorders are chronic medical conditions that can be hard to treat. A good diagnostician knows that a label alone isn't much help. It must be accompanied by information about what should happen next and what you can expect in the future. If your diagnosing professional isn't forthcoming with this level of information, tell him that you keep detailed records and would appreciate more information. If you still do not get thorough answers to your questions, you may need to move on to someone else who is more committed to working closely with you. Ask for copies of any reports, including scores on standardized tests.

Other people interviewed said the diagnostic report was hard to read. Usually the doctor writes out the diagnosis in full, either on an Axis chart or elsewhere on the report. If numbers were used instead, ask her to give you the full definition for them. If the doctor is too busy to explain the report to you, seek out someone who can. This is another area where a therapist or social worker can come in handy. They have a background in psychiatric jargon and testing terminology, but they're also accustomed to using real-world language with their clients.

One thing to ask for in the evaluation report is a prognosis. Doctors are often reluctant to give this information—after all, they aren't mind readers, and they don't want to raise false hopes. Simply explain that you want to know what might be possible with the interventions they recommend.

Also ask how progress in areas of deficit might best be measured. For example, if you are re-evaluated after completing a period of treatment, your Axis V score should inch upward if the treatment has been successful. It's possible for a person diagnosed with a major mental disorder to end up with a perfectly adequate Axis V score, meaning that he is coping well with life despite it.

To measure progress, your practitioner may want to use the same checklists and observations again after a certain period of time.

Alternatively, you may want to address specific, individual symptoms rather than measuring overall function.

The meaning of a diagnosis

When all is said and done, a diagnosis is just a label. It's what is done with that label that really counts. The best model for effective mental health treatment is one that has recovery, not just effective medication, as its goal. Recovery doesn't mean that the underlying condition is cured or even in complete remission—sadly, that is currently beyond the ability of today's medicine—but that you have persevered and succeeded despite it.

There was a time when the label of bipolar disorder usually indicated a steadily worsening condition with a poor prognosis. This need not be the case anymore. Effective treatments are available, as are personal support and professional help for weathering the storms to come. Recovery is an achievable goal for most persons with bipolar disorders.

Steven, age 45, was just diagnosed last year. With recovery from both bipolar disorder and substance abuse as his goal, he is relishing this chance to start over:

> *I have now come to realize, after so many years, that I am mentally*
> *ill and will be for the rest of my life. I need to know how to live with that.*
> *I will have to take medications to control my symptoms, and balance my*

life too. God has given me a decent brain—a little short-circuited, but it is a good one, and I want to use it to all of its abilities.

You know the old saying, "I burnt my bridges"? Well, I have found a few still worthy to be crossed, and I am doing so now.

CHAPTER 3

Differential Diagnosis

A NUMBER OF EMOTIONAL DISTURBANCES, neurological problems, and medical illnesses can look like bipolar disorders—or can occur along with bipolar disorders, masking symptoms and making treatment more complicated. There's also the tricky issue of deciding whether someone has simple depression or manic depression. For these reasons, making a diagnosis is often a process of elimination.

Doctors call this process "differential diagnosis," which means finding the right medical diagnosis by eliminating others that don't fit. This chapter describes these conditions and should help you understand how doctors tell the difference.

Investigating possibilities

There's no need for people with mood swings to be checked out for every possible cause. Experienced doctors take a thorough medical history as well as a mental health history. They can use this information to rule out any likely possibilities. If you have physical symptoms that point toward a medical disorder that can cause mood swings, such as diabetes or thyroid dysfunction, your doctor may order blood tests or other medical tests specifically for that condition.

A complete neurological checkup can give your doctor clues about your condition as well. Minor differences in neurological function (so-called "soft signs," such as lack of hand preference) are slightly more common in persons with bipolar disorders, but are also common enough in the general population not to be a cause for worry. A neurological exam can pinpoint any major problems, however, and give you peace of mind about the overall condition of your brain.

Differentiating partial seizures from mood swings is a particularly tough area of differential diagnosis. The most common physical test now used to diagnose seizures is an electroencephalogram, or EEG. There are actually several different types of EEGs, but all of them have a common purpose—looking for electrical activity in the brain that indicates seizures. Minor brainwave pattern differences are fairly common in people with bipolar disorders, but they are different from the abnormal patterns associated with seizures and are not consistent enough from person to person for EEG results alone to be a true diagnostic tool for bipolar disorders. Unfortunately, EEG testing cannot always detect seizures, either, unless a seizure actually occurs during the test. Special forms of EEG testing or the use of additional brain imaging technologies may be recommended if an EEG is not conclusive in ruling out seizures as a cause for mood swings.

For persons who have mood swings and also report feeling sick frequently, doctors may order immune-system testing. Depending on your personal history and other factors, this may include a blood chemistry screen, white blood-cell count, or tests for specific viruses, such as HIV, hepatitis, or Epstein-Barr.

Joe, age 33, had a diagnostic experience that followed a very typical pattern:

> *For a while it wasn't clear whether I had regular (unipolar) depression or bipolar disorder. At 15 I had a depressive episode with hypomanic features. I remember going on a whale-watching cruise with my parents, and I was so withdrawn into my own thoughts that the whales hardly made any impression on me at all. At other times, I was agitated, and had "ideas of reference" on a couple of occasions—suspecting that newspaper articles were about me, for instance. My parents took me to a psychiatrist, who may have suspected I was bipolar, although to me he only said he thought I was depressed. I eventually recovered, thanks to medications, time, and changes in circumstance.*
>
> *At 19 I had another episode, and by then it was clear that I was bipolar. First I was diagnosed as bipolar type II, then with my first real mania and hospitalization, as bipolar type I.*

Horses, zebras, and hybrids

Every medical professional has her own frame of reference. A psychiatrist uses the *DSM-IV*, along with his training and experience, to make a diagnosis. A neurologist tests for seizures and brain damage. It's not feasible to consider every single possibility, but doctors do need to rule out (or rule in) certain common causes for symptoms.

First-year medical students are always taught the old saw, "If you hear hoofbeats, think horses, not zebras." That means they should first consider common problems when trouble emerges, rather than investigating rare and unusual diseases. It's good basic advice, but some people really do have stripes! If you do not respond to the usual treatment options, it is usually worthwhile to consider other causes for your difficulties, especially if particular symptoms or family history indicate that you should.

It's also important to base diagnostic and treatment decisions on a broad view of a person's total health and functioning. Sometimes those hoofbeats aren't coming from either a horse or a zebra, but from a complex hybrid that doesn't follow the expected pattern. Each person with a bipolar disorder has a unique set of personal circumstances and symptoms. A person with ADHD and bipolar disorder type II will respond best to a particular set of interventions; someone with rapid cycling bipolar type I and thyroid problems will need different forms of treatment. Due to medical specialization, it can be hard to find one professional who understands how all of your health, mental health, and lifestyle issues affect each other. That's why a team approach to diagnosis and care is so much better, especially for those whose needs are unique or complex.

The following sections cover a wide variety of health conditions that may mimic or complicate bipolar disorders.

ADHD

Bipolar disorder in children is frequently misdiagnosed as Attention Deficit Hyperactivity Disorder (ADHD). An investigation by Dr. Jane Wozniak at Harvard Medical School found that, although 20 percent of the children in her study who had been diagnosed with ADHD also met the criteria for mania, a full 98 percent of the children who had been diagnosed with manic features fit the criteria for ADHD.[1] To fit the *DSM-IV* criteria for ADHD, some hyperactive, inattentive, or impulsive symptoms must appear before the age of 7; symptoms must be present in two or more settings (such as at school and at home); and the symptoms must cause real difficulty.

Today, many people feel that ADHD has become a fad diagnosis, and that too many children are diagnosed who do not have a neurological problem. However, when today's adults with bipolar disorders were children, ADHD was not recognized as often, and childhood-onset bipolar disorders were usually missed altogether. Many adults who never had an ADHD label as a child are now being diagnosed in adulthood.

Getting a diagnosis of ADHD as an adult is not an easy process, because the official ADHD criteria are written with children in mind. The criteria also state that symptoms must not be due to another mental disorder, including bipolar disorder. This either/or position is controversial with some clinicians, who see ADHD and bipolar disorder as overlapping, but separate, conditions—particularly in children, but also in some adults who present with both mood swings and attention difficulties. These two disorders are usually treated with different types of medication and other interventions. In fact, the stimulants used to treat ADHD sometimes cause mania to emerge.

Joe experienced his first manic episode after taking a prescribed stimulant:

> *When I was a child, a psychiatrist gave me Ritalin, thinking I might have Attention Deficit Disorder (hyperactivity). I became manic. I have heard that this is a common reaction of people with bipolar mood disorder. It was short-lived, once I stopped taking the medication.*

To meet the criteria for ADHD, you must have six or more of the following symptoms, persisting for at least six months, occurring frequently, and occurring to a degree inconsistent with your developmental level. These criteria have been adapted slightly from the *DSM-IV* list to make them apply to adults rather than to children:

* Failure to pay attention to details, making careless mistakes in work or other activities
* Difficulty sustaining attention in work, chores, or community activities
* Difficulty listening and maintaining consistent attention when spoken to directly
* Failure to follow instructions, or failure to finish work or chores (not due to deliberate oppositional behavior or failure to understand instructions)
* Difficulty organizing tasks and activities
* Avoidance, dislike, or reluctance to try tasks that require sustained mental effort
* Loss of things needed for tasks or activities
* Distractibility when faced with noise or other external stimuli
* Forgetfulness in daily activities

OR

Six or more of the following symptoms of hyperactivity/impulsivity, persisting for at least six months, and to a degree that is inconsistent with your developmental level:

* Hyperactivity
  - Fidgeting with hands or feet, squirming in seat
  - Inability to remain seated in places where it is expected
  - Inner feelings of restlessness

- – Difficulty remaining quiet
- – Physically very active—acting as if "driven by a motor"
- – Excessive talking
- Impulsivity
  - – Blurting out answers before questions have been completed or out of turn
  - – Inability to wait for one's turn
  - – Interrupting or intruding on others by butting into conversations, invading others' personal space, etc.

Based on these criteria, the *DSM-IV* separates ADHD into four categories:

- ADHD, Predominantly Inattentive Type (314.00): person meets the criteria in section 1, but not in section 2.

- ADHD, Predominantly Hyperactive-Impulsive Type (314.01): person meets the criteria in section 2, but not in section 1.

- ADHD, Combined Type (314.01): person meets the criteria in both section 1 and section 2.

- ADHD NOS (314.9): person has prominent symptoms of hyperactivity/impulsivity and/or attention deficit, but doesn't meet all of the required criteria for any of the other three types (NOS stands for "not otherwise specified"). This diagnosis is sometimes used when the person has another primary condition, such as a bipolar disorder, but also has additional symptoms of ADHD.

As you can see, there's a great deal of overlap between the features of ADHD and bipolar disorder. Diagnosticians trying to tell one from the other look for features like psychosis, depression, rapid mood swings, waxing and waning of symptoms, inappropriate affect, and disregard for the feelings of others. These are more characteristic of bipolar disorders than of ADHD.

Other telltale factors can include angry destructiveness, which is sometimes seen in bipolar disorders, as opposed to careless destructiveness in ADHD; rages that can last for hours in bipolar disorders, as opposed to thirty to forty minutes in childhood ADHD and rarely if ever in adult ADHD; and the incredibly high level of energy expended during manic episodes or bipolar rages, which goes far beyond even that of the most hyperactive person. Persons with a bipolar disorder may move, talk, and think differently than usual during and after a rage, while the behavior and affect of a person with ADHD is relatively consistent. Some bipolar people will not even remember a rage or destructive event, giving it a seizure-like quality.

Another difference is seen mostly in the morning. People with ADHD tend to bounce out of bed, ready to take on the world with an overabundant supply of energy. People with bipolar disorders are more likely to be hard to wake up, slow to get going, and irritable.

There are also differences in daily function, including work. Although some people with ADHD can focus intently on a topic of interest and complete projects (at least on that topic, if not in general), this ability to hyperfocus is somewhat more characteristic of people with bipolar disorders. That means you're more likely to see an uneven pattern of attention in persons with bipolar disorders, with periods of intense focus and periods of complete distractibility.

People with bipolar disorder are also less likely to have been diagnosed with specific learning disabilities than people with ADHD. Many are early talkers and readers and use language with special skill. They may be quite brilliant conversationalists, able to tell jokes effectively, use puns and plays on words, and employ expressive body language to full effect. There is often an evident flair for the dramatic.

A troubling symptom that may be noticed even in young children with bipolar disorder is sexual precociousness. Children with bipolar disorder seem to become aware of gender differences early, and some may have difficult-to-manage crushes or even touch other children inappropriately. Parents of bipolar girls in particular often note that their daughters were unusually giggly, flirtatious, and ultra-feminine, even as toddlers. In adulthood, these individuals may be very impulsive about their sexual expression, having multiple partners and difficult relationships. This symptom is not seen in all persons with bipolar disorders, but it is common enough to bear mentioning. It may have to do with hormonal differences, which are often seen in bipolar adults.

Other personality traits seen in bipolar disorders but not normally in ADHD include a rebellious streak that seems to bring the person into deliberate conflict with authority figures and reckless behavior based on grandiose thinking.

Some clinicians working with bipolar children and adolescents have reported that their patients are traumatized by unusually violent, gory nightmares.[2] Although it isn't yet known whether this symptom extends to bipolar adults, nightmares may explain the pattern of frequent waking throughout the night, morning tiredness, and literal fear of going to sleep seen in many. Vivid dreams may result in part from interruptions in circadian rhythms caused by sleep disturbances or from neurotransmitter differences. It has long been known that certain medications have the side effect of causing more vivid dreams, and natural variations in brain chemistry could do the same.

Anxiety

Anxiety disorders are common enough that almost everyone knows someone who has one. They include panic disorders and extreme phobias of all sorts, from claustrophobia (fear of being in small, enclosed places) to arachnophobia (fear of spiders). Basically put, they all involve an extreme reaction to certain situations or stimuli, as the body puts its fight or flight system in motion for no good reason.

Some people with anxiety disorders have panic attacks so severe that they could almost be mistaken for mania. They may make rapid movements, have an increased heartbeat, and talk a lot to calm themselves down. Panic attacks and phobias are embarrassing and can limit your activities, so it's only natural that people with severe anxiety disorders may have low self-esteem or feel depressed.

Anxiety disorders are more common in people with bipolar disorders than in the general population.[3] Often it's the anxiety disorder, with its totally debilitating panic attacks or phobias, that will bring a bipolar person into treatment for the first time.

Leslie, age 44, says that professionals she saw before her diagnosis mistook her mood swings for episodes of anxiety or unipolar depression:

> I was misdiagnosed with "depression and anxiety" several times. They invariably pronounced me "cured" when the depression lifted. Then I'd run out and ruin my life, and be back in therapy again.
>
> After yet another bad experience with a psychologist, I read a book called The Good News About Depression by Dr. Mark Gold. He described clinical depression and also the milder forms of bipolar disorder. Since Dr. Gold's practice was only an hour away, I made an appointment with one of his associates.
>
> Finally, in August 1988 I started on Prozac, which was then a very new drug. Within a week everything had changed. All my life people had told me I had a negative attitude, but I had no frame of reference—suddenly I knew what it meant. And optimism, I'd never had that before. My energy came back, my sex drive increased, and I started drinking again as I ramped up into one of the highest hypomanias of my life.
>
> When I went back in two weeks, the doctor indicated that this hypomania was a sure sign that I had bipolar disorder and not just depression, and he put me on lithium.

That evened me out in a couple of weeks. Slowly emotions became differentiated and not these indistinguishable, overwhelming tides. I was less ruled by impulse, my concentration was better, and I could handle the everyday stress more gracefully.

Conduct disorder

Conduct disorder (CD) is the *DSM-IV's* diagnosis for the classic antisocial personality: the person who deliberately hurts others, destroys property, willfully clashes with authority at every turn, and seems to get great satisfaction out of his behavior. People diagnosed with CD tend to be vindictive, seeking revenge for real or perceived wrongs. They blame others for all their problems—and often for their own actions as well. They are likely to be involved in criminal activity; indeed, many people diagnosed with CD receive this label from a prison psychologist.

The difference between conduct disorder and bipolar disorders is that the person with CD usually has at least a perceived reason for his anger, aggression, and assaultive behavior, while the person with bipolar disorder may feel angry and agitated for no particular reason. Like an episode of depression or euphoria, an angry mood may seem to come out of nowhere, for no reason.

The bad behavior of people with CD may also be strongly influenced by their peers. This is less frequently the case in bipolar disorders, even when the behavior (shoplifting, substance abuse, fighting) looks the same on the surface.

Bipolar persons tend to have an elevated or irritable mood along with their antisocial outbursts; the person with conduct disorder is mostly angry or just plain mean. Psychotic symptoms are also not a part of conduct disorder.

Tony explains how mania can be expressed in disinhibited words and actions:

> *When I was manic, things that seemed obvious to me I would just say—and people don't know how to deal with that. For example, I put up a big hand-painted sign on the roof rack of my car telling people to get out of the passing lane: "Slow? Go Right."*
>
> *Having been manic, I realize how much of a self-imposed prison my mind is in right now. Of course, that's very reasonable, because if people went out and said or did whatever they thought and felt, they would tend to get shunned.*

Many clinicians—and people given the CD label—feel that this term is applied far too frequently. That's a problem, because treatment programs often reject adults labeled as CD. On later review, a great many people initially diagnosed with a conduct disorder prove to be bipolar.[4] The problem first perceived was the behavior, but the real problem was the mood disturbance underlying the behavior.

Cushing's disease

Cushing's disease can result from a tumor on the pituitary gland, a structure located deep in the brain. The tumor will actually secrete a hormone, ACTH, which in turn overstimulates the adrenal glands. This can cause mood swings, as well as physical symptoms like raised blood glucose levels, high blood pressure, excess growth of facial and body hair, weight gain, and reddening of the face and neck.

A related condition, Cushing's disorder, can be caused by a tumor of the adrenal gland, lung, or elsewhere—or by overuse of corticosteroid medications or illegal steroids. The symptoms are much like those of Cushing's disease, although treatment may differ.

Depression

Unipolar, or simple, depression is just that: depressed mood that lasts longer than two weeks and is not due to another medical condition, the side effects of medication, or normal reaction to a major life event (such as grieving after a loved one's death). It is the most common form of depression. Most people with unipolar depression have periods of feeling normal, including feeling happy. These shouldn't be confused with hypomania, but occasionally they are.

Many people with bipolar disorders first seek help during or because of a depressive episode. Doctors then prescribe one of the antidepressant drugs commonly used to treat unipolar depression: Selective Serotonin Reuptake Inhibitors (SSRIs) such as Paxil, Prozac, and Zoloft; or tricyclic antidepressants, such as Anafranil or Tofranil. If the patient is actually bipolar, the result may be a manic episode. Often this is the first clue to the correct diagnosis.

Unfortunately, this clue is all too often overlooked. Many people have endured mania-producing trials on several antidepressants in succession before finally getting a correct diagnosis. Because the behavior that occurs during manic episodes can be so dangerous to you and to others, anyone taking an antidepressant for the first time or switching to a new antidepressant should be carefully monitored for the signs of hypomania or mania.

SSRIs, and sometimes tricyclic antidepressants, can have a place in the treatment of bipolar disorders. Normally mood swings need to be controlled by a mood stabilizer like lithium or Depakote before these drugs can be safely given, however. This combination of medications is discussed in Chapter 4, *Medical Care*.

Diabetes mellitus

Diabetes is a metabolic disorder with autoimmune and genetic components. The body is unable to use carbohydrates and sugars to produce energy due to lack of the pancreatic hormone insulin. The body tries to use fats as an energy source instead, but the by-products of metabolizing fats build up in the bloodstream. This can cause convulsions or even diabetic coma.

Diabetics can have problems with high blood sugar (hyperglycemia) or with hypoglycemia (see "Hypoglycemia," later in this chapter) unless they follow a careful diet. Diabetes can usually be controlled with diet, exercise, and medication. Symptoms of uncontrolled diabetes can include mood swings.

Fibromyalgia

Fibromyalgia is a painful physical problem, also known as myofascial pain syndrome or fibrositis disease. It is characterized by unexplained tenderness and pain in many points around the body, fatigue, and stiffness. Symptoms are sporadic, getting worse or better for no obvious reason and sometimes disappearing entirely for long periods of time. For many years, doctors told people with fibromyalgia symptoms that the problem was all in their head as a way of dismissing them. Many ended up seeing psychiatrists as a result, and the changing nature of their physical complaints and energy levels sometimes led to a mistaken diagnosis of bipolar disorder.

However, it now appears that fibromyalgia is a very real medical disorder, and the American College of Rheumatology has developed a diagnostic system. The cause is still unknown. Viral infection was long the suspected culprit, but the currently prevailing view is that compression of or injury to the brain stem is at fault.

There does appear to be a somewhat higher rate of fibromyalgia among people with bipolar disorder, although no full-scale studies have been done. Researchers looking at both conditions suspect that the connection, if any, may lie in sleep disturbance—people with fibromyalgia frequently experience serious insomnia problems and/or sleep apnea, which can interfere with the operation of the body's natural internal clock, which can in turn lead to mood swings.

Some people with fibromyalgia do find partial relief by taking drugs that affect the serotonin system, including antidepressants. Chiropractic treatment and massage may also be helpful.

Shoshana, age 56, has fibromyalgia. She says a tendency to express her mood swings with physical symptoms made it more difficult to get an accurate diagnosis of bipolar disorder:

> I was diagnosed with fibromyalgia about 25 years ago, long before I found out I was bipolar. Denial is a strong part if the disease is bipolar disorder, and I had great coping strategies, so I was able to get past a lot of doctors for a long time—for me, my symptoms might emerge as something like a stiff neck or a lot of pain in the head.
>
> Finally a doctor said, "Would you mind taking a neuropsychiatric evaluation?" I did, and the diagnosis was bipolar disorder.

Hormonal disorders

Some people have more than the usual behavior number of problems in puberty. Their moods don't ebb and flow, they surge wildly and stop suddenly. These individuals may have very noticeable and debilitating mood swings, including depression, lethargy, irritability, and even aggression. If these symptoms are linked to disorders of the sex hormones or related chemicals—and they aren't always—they can continue into adulthood in some men, although it's rare. Women with hormonal imbalances, however, tend to have long-lasting problems, including serious menstrual irregularities. Unless the underlying hormonal problem is identified and treated, their mood swings may be mistaken for a bipolar disorder.

Hormonal disorders can be identified through medical tests and treated with hormone supplements. Some women find improvement by taking birth control pills, getting injections of Depo-Provera, or getting Norplant implants. All of these are conveniently available ways to change the hormonal imbalance, but all can also cause side effects (including mood swings) that must be carefully balanced against possible benefits. It's important to reiterate that disorders of the sex hormones do not seem to play a major role for most women diagnosed with bipolar disorder, and they are probably a factor for even fewer men.

Thyroid and pituitary disorders are other hormonal problems that can be involved in mood swings. As with the involvement of sex hormones, the effect isn't always direct. The neurotransmitters that are believed to be working improperly or being produced in the wrong amounts in bipolar disorders are substances related to hormones and are also affected by hormone production. In other words, if there's a problem with hormones, such as estrogen, progesterone, androgen, testosterone, or thyroid or pituitary hormones, that problem may also affect the production, transmission, or use of neurotransmitters like serotonin and dopamine. This may be one of the reasons that bipolar symptoms sometimes seem to emerge, worsen, or improve just before or during periods of special hormonal activity, such as puberty, menstruation, pregnancy, the period just after giving birth, and menopause.

For some people, hormonal disorders may mimic the symptoms of bipolar disorders. In others, the two may be intimately intertwined. Getting treatment for an underlying hormonal disorder has contributed greatly to the stability of many people with bipolar disorders.

Rachel, mother of 19-year-old Lillian, says:

> Lillian's bipolar symptoms began with puberty, which came at a very early age. It has always been obvious that her mood swings are closely tied to her menstrual cycle, which is itself disordered in the extreme. One of her most stable periods coincided with being placed on estrogen supplements for several months in an attempt to bring her menstrual cycle into balance. Unfortunately, her doctor was not comfortable with continuing that treatment on a long-term basis due to her young age.
>
> She has since tried Depo-Provera and several types of birth control pills. Each of these choices has an obvious effect on mood, for better or worse, as well as on her hormonal difficulties.
>
> She also responded well to lithium, although the side effects ended up being intolerable. We have often wondered if her symptoms could be fully controlled with just the right hormonal treatment. I wish she could find a doctor who really understands how her fluctuating hormones and moods are connected, and who could design a safe, effective treatment plan for her that addresses both problems.

Hypoglycemia

Hypoglycemia is a deficiency of glucose in the bloodstream: low blood sugar. It can cause confusion, weakness, fainting, sudden loss of energy, or fatigue, all symptoms that can mimic depression. It is treated by ingesting or injecting glucose—and since the results of suddenly ingesting lots of sugar can mimic hyperactivity, the yo-yo behavior and mood swings of a hypoglycemic person could be mistaken for a bipolar pattern. Hypoglycemia is a common side effect of diabetes, but can occur without it.

Lupus

Systemic lupus erythematosus (SLE) is an autoimmune disorder that causes chronic inflammation of the connective tissue, including the skin, internal organs, and sometimes the nervous system and brain. Symptoms can include a scaly, red, butterfly-shaped rash on the face; joint pain; fatigue; and mood swings.

Lupus appears to have at least some genetic component, so if it has appeared in your family before, it's especially important to rule it out. Lupus is more common in women than in men, and it may be more common in people of African or Mediterranean descent.

Lupus can be diagnosed by a blood test. Some medications used to treat lupus, especially the corticosteroids, can also cause mood swings.

Medication side effects

Both prescription and over-the-counter (OTC) medications can cause severe behavioral side effects in some people. Be sure to mention all medications, including herbal medicines and vitamin supplements, to your psychiatrist when a diagnosis of bipolar disorder is under consideration. Even long-term medication users can suddenly have new side effects.

You might be surprised to know how many legal substances can affect mood and behavior. For example, large doses of B vitamins cause increased hyperactivity in some people. OTC stimulants like Vivarin and NoDoz, antihistamines containing ephedrine and similar stimulants, corticosteroids such as Prednisone, and stimulant-based diet pills can seriously disturb moods and the sleep cycle.

The discovery that medication side effects play a role in the problems a person is experiencing does not rule out bipolar disorder. In fact, some undiagnosed bipolar adults self-medicate with OTC stimulants, herbal remedies, and other legal substances. Unfortunately, these substances can also kick off or worsen the course of their mood swings.

Multiple sclerosis

Multiple sclerosis (MS) is a progressive disease of the nervous system characterized by damage to the myelin sheath, the tissue that surrounds and protects the spinal cord and nerves. Early symptoms can include fatigue, irritability, shaky movements, sudden muscle weakness, sleep disturbances, and mood swings.

MS normally affects young and middle-aged adults. The cause of MS is currently unknown. It may be caused by viral or bacterial infection of the nervous system, or it may be caused by an abnormal autoimmune response.

The medication Interferon is sometimes used to treat MS, and can cause mood and sleep disturbances.

Personality disorders

There are two major ways of looking at personality disorders (PDs). The official view is that they are ways of seeing the world, reacting to events, and relating to people that cause problems for the individuals who have them. Most psychologists have been trained to believe that personality disorders arise from childhood difficulties and conflicts.

A second view is that personality disorders are shadows of major mental or neurological disorders—milder, but still debilitating, collections of symptoms.

The *DSM-IV* identifies eleven major personality disorders, which it divides into three groups, Clusters A, B, and C (or I, II, and III). It is believed that some personality disorders—particularly Borderline Personality Disorder—can arise from untreated bipolar disorders. Studies indicate that that the PDs listed under Cluster B are more common in people with bipolar disorders.[5] This may be because people with bipolar disorders sometimes miss out on healthy personality development due to their illness, or perhaps the same genes that cause bipolar disorders determine some personality characteristics. Very briefly defined, the personality disorders are:

- Cluster A
  - Paranoid: Distrustful, suspicious of others and their motives.

- Schizoid: Very limited social and emotional range.
- Schizotypal: Limited social and emotional range coupled with unusual thought and behavior patterns.

- Cluster B
  - Antisocial: Unconcerned about rules, laws, or the rights of others; often violent, aggressive, destructive. Also called sociopathic or psychopathic personality, and very similar to conduct disorder.
  - Borderline: Unstable relationships, values, self-image, and emotions; reckless and impulsive; episodes of aggressive or highly emotional behavior.
  - Histrionic: Attention-seeking, highly emotional.
  - Narcissistic: Self-absorbed, self-important, demanding, limited understanding of other peoples' perspectives.

- Cluster C
  - Avoidant: Feels inadequate, overly sensitive to criticism, avoids social interaction.
  - Dependent: Overly dependent on others for approval or care, clinging and submissive.
  - Obsessive-Compulsive: Overly controlled (and controlling), orderly, and perfectionistic.

Borderline personality disorder can be an especially difficult diagnosis to live with. The symptoms of rapidly fluctuating moods, emotions, and behavior frequently cause unemployment, loss of friends and family support, and other social problems. Unfortunately, it's also true that their unpredictability makes borderline patients notoriously hard for therapists and doctors to treat. Rather than looking for new and better ways to accommodate the needs of these patients, some professionals tend to either exclude them from their caseload or give up on them easily.

Shoshana was mislabeled with this diagnosis as a young woman:

> I was diagnosed with borderline personality disorder in my twenties. This was in 1969 or 1970. I described my symptoms, and the psychiatrist said, "How do you know it's not lupus?" I said, "I don't have the rash and other symptoms." He was surprised that I actually knew what lupus was, and he was upset.
>
> A lot of male doctors in that era didn't like to be challenged, but I had challenged the psychiatrist, and I felt this label was his way to get

> *revenge. I was not aware of the stigma attached to that label, but I felt*
> *that they were blowing me off, that they had no real interest in treating*
> *me. I think a lot of bipolar people are diagnosed with borderline*
> *personality disorder that later "disappears."*

You may hear about other personality disorders that are not currently listed in the *DSM-IV.* One of these is depressive personality disorder, which can be defined as having a chronically gloomy outlook on life without being clinically depressed. Another is passive-aggressive personality disorder, which involves using passive resistance to express anger (for example, playing the long-suffering martyr rather than telling your husband off). To ensure that any other personality problems have a clinical label, some psychiatrists may employ the term "personality disorder, not otherwise specified."

Psychosis

Psychotic symptoms, including visual hallucinations, aural hallucinations (hearing voices or other sounds that are not there), and other major perceptual distortions, are associated with some types of bipolar episodes. They are also seen in other neuropsychiatric disorders, particularly schizophrenia. As discussed in Chapter 1, *What Are Bipolar Disorders?,* psychosis is caused by physical processes, ranging from psychoactive drugs to chemical imbalance in the brain.

However, sometimes other phenomena are mistaken for hallucinations. People with migraines or seizure disorders often report a hallucination-like phenomenon called an aura. Many different types of migraine and seizure auras have been described. If the aura is visual, it often includes seeing geometric designs or patterns of moving light. Auditory auras tend to be buzzing, ringing, or even musical sounds rather than "voices." Some people report experiencing certain smells or tastes before a migraine attack or a seizure. Others may have physical auras, such as feeling a spreading warmth, a sudden stomachache, or a prickly sensation on the scalp. If the underlying migraine or seizure disorder is not diagnosed, people who report these experiences may be diagnosed as having psychosis instead.

Doctors also need to take cultural differences into account when looking at symptoms resembling psychosis. Some religious belief systems include rituals in which people may experience trance states and other psychosis-like phenomena, such as hearing voices, speaking in tongues, or believing that they are communicating with otherworldly beings. Not to discount the spiritual dimension of these experiences, but certain religious practices (dervish dancing and prolonged chanting, to give just two examples) can result in temporary biochemical changes and altered states of consciousness. Otherwise valid religious beliefs can also be distorted by mental illness, turning religious practices into obsessions and compulsions, or gateways to psychotic episodes. Professionals who are sensitive to their patients' spiritual traditions can help them see where a spiritual experience ends and psychosis begins. Sometimes a particular religious practice may not be healthy for a person with a mental illness. Other practices may be very helpful indeed.

When spiritual beliefs are intensely important to a person with a bipolar disorder, a pastor, priest, rabbi, shaman, or other spiritual counselor can become part of the evaluation and treatment team. It's sometimes difficult for psychiatric professionals to work closely with people whose view of their illness or of the world in general is colored by strong religious beliefs, but the team approach should increase their understanding. Sometimes there are also institutional barriers to cooperation with religious leaders. Conversely, medical professionals who have spiritual beliefs of their own must be careful not to push them on people and families who have different opinions.

People should be aware that spiritual counseling alone cannot cure mental illness, although it can provide support, comfort, and strength to believers. Taken together, good medical and spiritual practices help the whole person.

Rheumatoid arthritis

Rheumatoid arthritis is an autoimmune disorder that causes inflammation and degeneration of the joints. When it occurs in young adults, it may not be suspected as the cause for lethargy, unexplained aches and pains, and mood swings. These symptoms may come and go, making diagnosis difficult. Rheumatoid arthritis can range from very mild to completely disabling.

Substance abuse

The use of illegal drugs and alcohol has strong effects on brain chemistry. It can produce personality changes, unusual behavior, mood swings, and even psychotic symptoms. Be forthright with your doctor about any substances you use or abuse and about any past history of substance abuse. It can make a major difference in your medical care, including what medications you should be prescribed and the type of therapy most likely to help.

Tony, age 31, has had some difficulties in this area—but luckily recognized the problem before it got out of hand.

The idea of "self-medication" is interesting... When I think about it, when I was manic, I didn't do anything really hard but I was going out drinking a lot and smoking up a lot of dope. I had never really done that before, but in that state I didn't really see. I did all sorts of things that I normally wouldn't do—laws weren't part of my operational guidebook anymore.

I'm not really sure that when I did that I was trying to get better or get normal, I feel that I was just playing with these things. In the same way, I explored other aspects of my life.

What would have been really dangerous would be to self-medicate with alcohol when I was depressed. I remember thinking about suicide during that period very seriously. Alcohol tends to loosen the gates of decision-making a little further, and I think that if I had been drinking I might not have been able to stop myself.

Drugs that carry a particular risk for causing manic or manic-like states include amphetamines ("speed"), cocaine, and steroids, including those taken for other medical conditions as well as illegal steroids taken by some athletes and body-builders. Steroids can cause major mood swings, including states that mimic depression and sudden angry, aggressive, manic-like behavior (colloquially known as "'roid rage.") Amphetamines and cocaine can cause manic-like episodes in otherwise normal people and can also worsen the course of a pre-existing bipolar disorder.

One area where differential diagnosis is particularly crucial is psychotic symptoms. Illicit drug use can cause a person to temporarily lose touch with reality. Hallucinogens are the most frequent offenders, although some people have had strange experiences with other drugs, including marijuana. Speed and cocaine can both induce psychotic symptoms. Amphetamine abusers are particularly likely to have sensory hallucinations ("speed psychosis"), such as feeling like something is crawling under their skin, and may become both delusional and aggressive. Cocaine psychosis is a well-known phenomenon in detox clinics. Long-term alcohol abuse can also result in hallucinations (the infamous delirium tremens, or "DTs").

A few people have delayed reactions to drugs and may experience unpleasant flashbacks or ongoing distortions of reality due to previous drug use. These may be caused by damage to neural circuits. Therapy can help affected individuals recognize and cope with these episodes. In some cases, medication or biofeedback exercises can help.

Substance abuse can also be a symptom of bipolar disorders, however, because people often feel that drinking or drugging masks their problems for a little while. For that reason, the discovery that a person has been abusing drugs or alcohol does not rule out a bipolar diagnosis. In fact, it may buttress the diagnosis, simply because substance abuse is so common in people with these conditions.

For years, 45-year-old Steven believed his mood swings and other problems were due to alcoholism. Finally an addiction specialist recognized his symptoms, and eventually he was diagnosed as bipolar type I with schizoaffective disorder:

> *There was misdiagnosis all over the place. One episode that seriously sticks in my mind was at my hometown hospital. I called for help, they sent the police, and I ended up in a detox ward for three days, never receiving any mental health help. Prior to that I was hospitalized twice for 21 and 24 days each.*
>
> *If there is even the suspicion of mood swings, you should get diagnosed and get help. I found help in an intensive treatment program.*

Schizophrenia

Psychotic features, such as hallucinations, grandiose thinking, or delusions, are more often experienced by bipolar children than bipolar adults (this is probably because children have a less fully developed sense of reality and fantasy: even normal children occasionally confuse the two). These symptoms sometimes cause persons with bipolar disorder, regardless of age, to be misdiagnosed as having schizophrenia or schizoaffective disorder (see "Schizoaffective disorder," below).

Schizophrenia is a major mental illness characterized by psychotic symptoms, often including complete loss of connection with reality. One difference between schizophrenia and bipolar disorders involves affect, which can be defined as how one's emotions are projected outward to others and how one reacts to experiences. People with schizophrenia usually have what's called a blunt affect. They don't react much to outside stimuli, and they don't have much personality. It can be hard to tell this from the demeanor of a person who's in a depressed state, which can bring on an apathetic attitude and delayed response to stimuli. Generally speaking, though, people with bipolar disorders tend to be over-reactive to outside stimuli and to have lots of personality when normal, with even greater extremes during hypomanic or manic episodes.

Another difference between schizophrenia and bipolar disorders is that bipolar mood swings can be sudden, but schizophrenia almost always has a slow, gradually worsening onset. It also does not normally wax and wane like bipolar disorders, except for periods of remission due to successful treatment. People with schizophrenia rarely have the characteristic signs of true mania, namely hyperactivity and pressured speech (speaking rapidly and flitting from idea to idea).

A third difference is that people with schizophrenia are more likely to suffer from a thought disorder. While people in either group may hallucinate or be delusional, a person with bipolar disorder is more likely to realize, at least intermittently, that the phenomena she is experiencing are not normal. For example, she may hear voices and fully realize some of the time that the voices are not real, and that they are a psychiatric symptom. A person with schizophrenia, however, is usually not connected enough with objective reality to tell the voices in his head from voices on the radio.

Persons with schizophrenia are also more likely to have truly bizarre delusions, including psychotic symptoms that don't jibe with their outward mood. For example, they may seem quite cheerful while informing you that the walls are dripping with blood.

Sometimes differential diagnosis is made via medication, either accidentally or on purpose. Schizophrenia does not respond to lithium, and bipolar mood swings are not well-controlled by the neuroleptic drugs most useful for schizophrenia. Some people with bipolar disorder do benefit from neuroleptics, however, usually in addition to a mood stabilizer.

In the US, some recent studies indicate that African-Americans with bipolar disorders run a higher than average risk of being misdiagnosed with schizophrenia.[6] No one is quite sure why, although clinician bias and poor communication between patient and doctor are likely factors.

Monique, age 30, was alarmed when a doctor misdiagnosed her as having schizophrenia:

> I had just moved to a new state when I had my first manic episode, and no one really knew what was wrong with me. At first, they thought I was depressed and hospitalized me. When I went back to my home state, I saw a psychiatrist and she said I was schizophrenic.
>
> Often people don't know much about mental illness, and I can say that from what I've heard, from what I had seen in the media, I was not comfortable with that label. I kept going to different doctors until I found

one who could tell me what was really going on. I didn't really receive a correct diagnosis until almost four years later—I was having episodes that whole time, and I have no idea how I was getting through them.

Finally I had another episode and I explained it to my doctor— I was having all kinds of grandiose thoughts. She finally said, "I know what you have, and I know a medication that will help you." I didn't feel that content about being manic-depressive either—"What do you mean there's something wrong with my brain?," was what I thought—but it was also a relief.

Schizoaffective disorder

The terms schizoaffective disorder or schizoaffective depression indicate that a person has some characteristics of a mood disorder, such as a bipolar disorder or unipolar depression, and some characteristics of schizophrenia. When this diagnosis is correctly made, it indicates that treatment will need to cover both conditions.

However, this diagnosis is probably applied too often to people with a bipolar disorder. As noted previously, psychotic symptoms are not necessarily signs of schizophrenia.

Thyroid disorders

The thyroid is a small butterfly-shaped gland located in front of the trachea in the neck. It enlarges and becomes more active during puberty, pregnancy, and times of great stress. It also alters its size and shape during women's menstrual cycles.

The thyroid glad secretes three hormones: thyroxin (T_4), triiodothyronine (T_3), and calcitonin. T_3 and T_4, which contain iodine, have far-reaching effects on almost all tissues in the body. They are intimately involved in physical and mental development during childhood and adolescence and affect metabolism throughout life. Calcitonin helps regulate the amount of calcium in the body. If T_3 and T_4 levels are low or nonexistent, growth hormone secretion is decreased and what is released is not effective.

Hyperthyroidism is overactivity of the thyroid gland; hypothyroidism is underactivity of the thyroid gland. According to the Thyroid Society, about 10 percent of people with diagnosed depression have thyroid dysfunction.[7] Some people have a fluctuating level of thyroid function and may present with bipolar-like symptoms.

It's hard to tell whether thyroid dysfunction causes mood disorders or simply coexists with them, but treating the thyroid condition often helps depressive symptoms.

A simple blood test can be used to detect thyroid problems, and they can be treated with hormone supplementation. Chapter 4 includes more information on treating thyroid disorders that may occur with bipolar disorders.

Infectious illness and mood swings

Several forms of serious infectious illness can also cause mood swings. That's because certain kinds of viruses and bacteria can cross the blood-brain barrier and wreak havoc within the brain, especially when your immune-system defenses are down.

Some doctors believe that infection may play a much larger role in mood disorders than is currently thought, either directly or as a result of the complex interactions between neurotransmitters, hormones, and the immune system. Research is ongoing into possible viral and bacterial effects on mood, thought, and behavior.

AIDS

Sexually active persons and those who inject illicit drugs are at risk for Acquired Immune Deficiency Syndrome (AIDS), and over the past twenty years many people have been born carrying the HIV virus that causes this severe immune-system disorder. HIV erodes the immune system's effectiveness by killing off protective T4 cells, leaving the body and brain open to various types of infections. The Epstein-Barr virus (see "Mononucleosis," later in this chapter), other human herpes viruses, and some other types of infections can cause mood swings and even psychotic episodes.

People with AIDS are also more susceptible to overgrowth of yeasts and fungi in the body, including Candida albicans (a yeast normally found in the digestive tract in small amounts) and cryptosporidium, which can cause unusual behaviors and physical symptoms if left untreated.

Actual psychosis is not usually seen in AIDS until the very late stages of the disease. However, disturbances in mood, sleep, and energy levels can be among the early warning signs of this illness.

A diagnosis of AIDS or a related immune-deficiency condition does not rule out the possibility of a bipolar disorder. In fact, it's safe to assume that people with untreated bipolar disorders are at greater risk for contracting AIDS, because compulsive sexual activity and substance abuse are more common in this population. It is currently believed that people with mental illness are one of the largest populations of HIV-infected persons.

Chronic fatigue syndrome

Chronic fatigue syndrome, also known as chronic fatigue immune deficiency syndrome (CFIDS) and myalgic encephalopathy (ME), is a debilitating disorder of unknown origin, although some sort of virus or other infection of the nervous system is the suspected cause.

People with chronic fatigue syndrome have some symptoms that mimic those of depression, including irritability, extreme fatigue, unexplained aches and pains, and changes in sleep and mood. During brief periods of remission, they may become virtual whirlwinds of activity, trying to make up for everything they've missed while ill. This swing from seeming depression to seeming hypomania could be mistaken for cyclothymia, seasonal affective disorder (SAD), or bipolar type II. And, of course, depression can also be mistaken for CFIDS.

Hepatitis

Hepatitis is an inflammation of the liver. It is usually caused by infection with one of several Hepatitis viruses (Hepatitis A, B, C, D, E, and G, and perhaps others that have not been identified), although hepatitis can be a side effect of other diseases, including mononucleosis and lupus. It can also be caused by poisons, drugs, or alcohol.

Hepatitis A and E can be spread through food or drink contaminated with fecal matter from an infected person. These two viruses rarely cause long-term liver damage, although they may cause a flu-like illness and other symptoms.

Hepatitis B and C are carried in the bloodstream. Both are spread by sexual activity, IV drug use, accidental contact with bodily fluids, or infected blood products. Untreated hepatitis B or C can result in cirrhosis or cancer of the liver, along with a flu-like illness, fatigue, and other symptoms. Hepatitis B also may permit later infection with hepatitis D, which never occurs alone.

Vaccines are available for prevention of hepatitis A and B.

Because the liver is the body's center for eliminating toxic substances, varied symptoms occur when it isn't working properly. The most common include fever, nausea, weakness, persistent headache, jaundice (a yellow discoloration of the skin and sometimes of the whites of the eyes), and dark urine. People with untreated hepatitis or with one of the forms of infectious hepatitis that cannot currently be easily treated may also experience mood swings. These are generally in the direction of depression, although some patients also experience grandiose thinking, aggression, and other symptoms that could look like hypomania or mania.

Medications used to treat resistant forms of hepatitis, such as Interferon, can also cause mood and sleep disturbances.

Infectious mononucleosis

Mononucleosis ("mono," also known as glandular fever) is an infection of the lymphatic system caused by the Epstein-Barr virus, a common virus in the herpes family that usually does not cause illness. Symptoms can mimic those of depression, including fatigue, loss of energy, unexplained aches and pains, and changes in sleep and mood. It is characterized by high levels of white blood cells in the blood stream and can be diagnosed with a blood test.

Mono tends to strike children and teenagers more frequently than adults, and it has an affinity for people with compromised immune systems. It can be extraordinarily difficult to recover from, with episodes of illusory wellness during which you may try to make up for lost time. This swing from seeming depression to seeming hypomania could be mistaken for cyclothymia, SAD, or even bipolar type II.

Untreated mono may lead to hepatitis, which can also cause severe mood swings.

Seizure disorders

Seizures can be compared to an electrical storm in the brain. Epilepsy is defined as repeated episodes of seizure activity. About 1 percent of all people have epilepsy, but many more will have a single seizure at some time in their life. Around 40 different types of seizures or seizure disorders have been identified.

When a seizure begins in a single area of the brain, it's called a partial seizure. When seizure activity seems to begin simultaneously in many different areas of the brain, it's called a generalized seizure. Partial seizure disorders are more common.

Partial seizures are further divided into simple partial and complex partial seizures. Although simple and complex partial seizures usually do not include convulsions or loss of consciousness, they can have serious consequences. The physical and emotional effects of partial seizures—dissociation, loss of coordination, memory loss, fatigue, mood swings, and physical pain, among others—can make them very difficult to live with.

Some people who suffer from severe mood swings do have epilepsy, either instead of or in addition to a bipolar disorder. Be sure to tell your doctor if you have any symptoms that are associated with seizures. These include episodes of repetitive body movements, such as a shaking leg or fluttering eye, that you cannot control; brief episodes of impaired consciousness or blackouts; or aura phenomena.

A seizure aura is actually a type of partial seizure. It can occur on its own, or it may occur before a more serious type of seizure.

Auras are highly individualized. Some people see flashing lights, others smell a strange odor, some simply have an odd mental sensation, such as a floating feeling. It all depends on where the seizure focus is in your brain and where the process catches hold. Auras reported by people with seizure disorders may include symptoms like the following.

- A sense of déja vu: the feeling of having been somewhere before, when one has not

- A sense of jamais vu: the feeling that a familiar place is suddenly strange and unfamiliar

- Ringing or buzzing in the ears

- Hearing other sounds that are not there, ranging from bells to a clamor of human voices

- Smelling odors that are not there, including such pungent smells as gasoline, burning rubber, feces, peanuts, bananas, or even the scent of a specific perfume

- Feeling disoriented

- Feeling larger or smaller than normal, like Alice in Wonderland in her "drink me" phase

- Experiencing other distortions of perception, like feeling that the room is tilting or revolving

- Experiencing sudden dilation of pupils

- Feeling lightheaded

- Feeling dizzy

- Suffering from numbness in a part of the body

- Experiencing tremors in hands, feet, arms, or legs

- Feeling a spreading warmth or chilliness

- Feeling as though the stomach is rising, heaving, or being pulled upwards in the abdomen

- Feeling prickly sensations ("pins and needles"), especially on the feet and hands

- Feeling sudden emotions, such as dread, fear, anger, rage, happiness, or euphoria, that come out of the blue and are not related to the situation

- Seeing patterns or colors

- Suffering from sudden headaches, stomachaches, or other sorts of unpleasant or unusual physical sensations

Obviously, these symptoms could have many other causes. Your doctor will probably order an EEG or other medical tests if seizures are suspected.

Seizure disorders can be successfully treated with medication and lifestyle changes. Interestingly, most of the medications used as mood stabilizers for bipolar disorders were originally developed to treat seizure disorders.

The relationship between low-level seizure activity and bipolar disorders is still largely unexplored, and the linkage is controversial. However, there is no controversy about the fact that mood and personality changes can be a side effect of untreated seizure activity. Many clinicians recommend that all persons reporting severe mood swings should have a thorough neurological evaluation, including an EEG, to rule out seizures as a cause or an additional diagnosis. Given the overlap in symptoms, this seems like wise advice.

The future

For now, diagnosing bipolar disorders is based primarily on observation and records. However, medical tests, such as special brain scans or even blood tests, may eventually be used to rule out or uncover specific causes for mood swings. When that day comes, test results will help doctors definitively diagnose these conditions and pinpoint the best medical treatment for each individual.

Very little is currently known about bipolar disorders and their relationship to hormonal imbalances, thyroid function, the long-term effects of substance abuse, seizures, and other complicating or contributing factors. That's one reason that people with bipolar disorders need to keep abreast of the latest medical research— new discoveries are being made every day, and it's likely that they will give rise to new treatment options in the very near future.

CHAPTER 4

Medical Care

MEDICATIONS ARE THE MAINSTAY of any treatment plan for bipolar disorders. Until other reliable treatments are developed, most people with a bipolar disorder will need to take one or more medications for life, although the type and amount of medication may change with age. It is extremely rare for someone to experience a complete and permanent remission from bipolar symptoms, except through the use of medication.

Several different medications are used to treat bipolar disorders, and they work with varying degrees of effectiveness. This chapter covers all of the current options and reveals what's known about new drugs that are under development. It includes a look at some of the problems involved in treating people who have epilepsy, substance abuse problems, or other conditions in addition to bipolar disorders. This chapter lists and discusses all of the medications you may hear about, starting with lithium. Finally, it includes a look at evaluating and working with outpatient and inpatient mental health treatment programs.

Although talk therapy is not a medical treatment, it's a very important part of an overall treatment plan for people with bipolar disorders. See Chapter 5, *Talk Therapy*, for more information about this topic.

Taking charge of medication choices

The idea of taking medication for the rest of your life is scary. Many people with bipolar disorders are used to thinking of their condition as something outside themselves, something they have or are affected by, but not something they are. It might feel easier to fight your symptoms when they are perceived this way, but it can make recovery harder. Addressing the way that a bipolar disorder adversely affects your life requires first accepting that you have a chronic illness whose impact you truly want to diminish.

The chemical processes that cause your mood swings are an intrinsic part of you, just as the chemical processes that lead to diabetes or high blood pressure are part of the people who have those conditions. Like these chronic illnesses, bipolar disorders can be successfully treated, and recovery is possible—but it almost always comes from a combination of judiciously used medication and lifestyle changes, not just one or the other.

You have the power to make gaining and maintaining mental and physical health your top priority. Only you can take medication. Only you can follow that decision with others that enhance the beneficial effects of medication, such as building a solid relationship with a trustworthy therapist, rebuilding relationships with your family and friends, and making daily choices that improve your life.

There will be stops and starts along the way. Today's medication choices are far from perfect and may cause unwanted or even intolerable side effects. You may have difficulty finding professional helpers, such as psychiatrists and therapists, whom you feel comfortable with. Sometimes you may feel that recovery is an unattainable goal.

Don't give up—new medications, new medical discoveries, and forms of therapy better suited for persons with bipolar disorders are being developed every year. If the choices you are able to make now lead to less than perfect control of your bipolar symptoms, you can definitely look forward to improved treatments in the future.

Why medication doesn't always work

Some people with a bipolar disorder have tried almost everything. Leslie, age 44, jumped at the chance to share her long, "been there, done that" list of personal medication reviews:

> *Prozac: I've tried adding other SSRIs for depression, but none work for me so I always come back to Prozac.*
>
> *Paxil: Didn't work, was like not being on a med.*
>
> *BuSpar: That was a long time ago… I can't remember why now, but I didn't take it long.*
>
> *Wellbutrin: Made me suicidal.*
>
> *Ativan: I've been taking this for anxiety since before I was diagnosed with bipolar disorder type II.*

Klonopin: This is to help me sleep if I need it. The first time I took it (this is embarrassing) it made me wet the bed. Years later I tried it again, and now I can take it without that side effect.

Lithium: Best med in the book, but it makes me feel like my brain is wrapped in cotton, and I can't handle hot weather or salty foods due to edema (water retention and swelling).

Depakote: This anticonvulsant worked well, but caused edema and hair loss.

Tegretol: This anticonvulsant was good for intrusive thoughts or OCD symptoms, but it gives me hangovers.

Neurontin: This anticonvulsant made me sleepy and gave me hangovers. Now I add it at night as an extra weapon against impending hypomania.

Mellaril: It's an antipsychotic—makes you feel like you're wearing plexi-glass armor. The next day is emotionally flat, and feels very safe.

Risperdal: This antipsychotic was too sedating, gave me hangovers, and made me horribly depressed the next day.

Zyprexa: This antipsychotic was too sedating and sometimes made me depressed.

Lamictal: Another anticonvulsant, it works well for me. My mood is a little higher on Lamictal than on, say, just lithium. I have to watch for hypomanias and add Neurontin when I notice one sneaking up on me.

Elavil: This stuff made me too stoned to function. Plus I would literally pass out when I stood up too fast.

Chloral hydrate: I took this to help me sleep. Yeah, right—hypomania wins every time.

Of course, that's just Leslie's list. If you talk to anyone who has been around the block a few times when it comes to taking psychiatric meds, you'll find that reactions to different drugs are highly personal. One person may experience relief from their most hated symptoms with a drug that causes someone else to have intolerable side effects. But according to many doctors, the biggest problem that people with bipolar disorders have with medication is refusing to take it. Doctors employ the term "noncompliant" to describe patients who refuse to take their medication.

Dictionary definitions of compliant use words like yielding, obedient, and submissive. These may be qualities that make people easy to manage, but they are not necessarily qualities that help you gain control over your health. Even the best doctors are not omnipotent and omniscient. Enlightened physicians want you to think of them as a primary part of your support system and of medication as a key tool in your recovery process. What they really need from you is active engagement in your own healing process, not blind compliance.

Noncompliance generally isn't a conscious, deliberate flouting of medical advice. For most people, it's a decision based on past experiences with the effects and side effects of psychiatric medications. It's perfectly natural to want to avoid difficult side effects— especially if those side effects are unexplained and unexpected, and especially if benefits did not seem to outweigh the negative effects in the past. Each time you have a bad experience with a psychiatric medication or hear a scary story about a particular drug, it gives you one more reason to be "noncompliant" in the future.

Joe, age 33, says he always fights an internal battle over taking lithium, despite its benefits for him:

> Some psychiatrists have suggested that patients who have reservations about lithium really want to experience the mania again, because in some ways it feels good. I don't believe this, partly because my mania really doesn't feel good to me. The side effects of lithium are what has made me reluctant to take the normal dose.
>
> I think of it with this analogy: many people are drawn to buy natural supplements to gain an edge in some way, to be more relaxed or smarter, to live longer, to have bigger muscles or shinier hair. These supplements may carry some risks. I think of my lower dose of lithium as wanting to gain a slight edge, while minimizing risk. Certainly most people would be eager to take a pill that would improve their memory, help them lose weight, increase their creativity, give them a more colorful experience of life, clear up their skin, make their hair thicker, and strengthen their kidneys and thyroid. I feel I get all these benefits from reducing the amount of lithium I take. The risk is another episode, but I went three and a half years between my first and second episodes without any medication, and it is still possible to have "breakthrough" episodes even while on medication.

As Joe notes, medication isn't an either/or decision. If you are fully informed about both risks and benefits, you can make wise decisions about which medications to take, how much you can safely and comfortably take, and what side effects are and are not worth the trade-offs involved. There's certainly no magic pill on the market. Indeed, every medication that has shown benefit also has its drawbacks. It helps to occasionally look at the situation from your doctor's point of view as well as from your own. It takes a lot of experience (and sometimes a healthy helping of intuition, too) to treat bipolar disorders effectively and safely. Doctors must research medications very carefully, including checking for interactions with other medicines you might be taking. They must introduce new drugs cautiously, explaining about possible side effects and how to prevent or address them.

Even when doctors prepare well and do their best, differences in individual chemistry may result in unexpected problems. Some people with bipolar disorders are exquisitely sensitive to medications, especially to antidepressants that might be tried after manic symptoms are controlled but depression remains. It's not always possible for even a highly experienced doctor to predict how you will respond to various types of medications.

The physical changes responsible for causing mood swings are poorly understood. There is also still much to learn about the effect of other physical factors, such as the hormonal system, on brain chemistry. Current medications can lessen symptoms and improve functioning, but they do not address the root biological causes of bipolar disorders. This is frustrating for doctors, but it's much more difficult for people who must rely on medication to stay on an even keel. Someday it may be possible to not just control, but actually reverse the biological causes of bipolar disorders.

Ask your doctor to make time for discussing your past experiences with medication. These experiences may provide important clues as to what results she may expect from trying different drugs. Be open about fears you have about medication, and about which side effects are and aren't acceptable to you.

As Joe mentioned earlier in this chapter, a few doctors say the real reason some people with bipolar disorders refuse medication is that they are addicted to the highs. This is only partially correct. People do miss the highs of hypomania and even mania, of course—when you've become used to wildly fluctuating, intense emotions, anything else can feel like emotional deadening. Many people with bipolar disorders crave extreme sensations. It's simply part of their nature. Smart doctors work with this personality trait, not against it.

The trick is helping people find safer, healthier, life-affirming outlets for this need, whether it's pursuing artistic expression, strengthening interpersonal relationships, or even pursuing extreme sports. Like drugs and alcohol, unchecked mania provides only temporary, illusory, and unsafe highs. Lifestyle changes can create happiness and excitement that's lasting and real. Peer support groups and sometimes therapists can help you recapture the intensity and drive that you may feel is missing when you're medicated.

Emotional deadening is not something that you will just have to live with forever—it's how people accustomed to living with internal intensity perceive a downshifting of that intensity. When treatment is truly successful, you will experience the full range of human emotions and still enjoy personal stability and safety. Getting to that place can take time, but arriving will be worth it.

Eileen, age 47, is still on that journey:

> *Bipolar disorder is a life sentence. I didn't know that when I was first diagnosed. I thought then that if I took my lithium, like a diabetic takes insulin, I was protected forever. That is not true... I am learning that I must take care of my bipolar disorder forever.*
>
> *The hardest part of being medicated is the dumbing-down effect. We are used to thinking and acting so fast that when the medication kicks in, we feel robbed of our minds. It takes longer, and more clues, to tease the information out of my brain. The information is there, it is just harder to access.*
>
> *Still, I've been one of the rare ones who has never yet quit taking the meds. I am too afraid to do that, probably because I was older when the illness began, and what I lost due to it was greater.*

A skilled therapist can help you work through your feelings about the emotional changes that medication can put you through and about the difficult life experiences you may have had as a result of your upbringing or your illness.

Another common reason people stop taking their medication is continued substance abuse. If you tend to rely on drugs or alcohol, it's extremely important to pursue substance abuse treatment at the same time as treatment for your bipolar disorder. Your use of mood-altering substances not only reduces the effectiveness and safety of the medication you take, it can sabotage your treatment and cloud your judgment.

You don't have to be an addict or alcoholic to benefit from substance abuse treatment or self-help/support groups like Alcoholics Anonymous or Narcotics Anonymous. If drinking or drug use causes you even occasional problems, counseling and peer support can help you minimize its impact and give you strategies for maintaining abstinence.

Dosage details

Each person's body chemistry is different, and some people have unusual responses to certain medications. Selecting the correct dose is more of an art than a science. Often you will notice side effects long before you notice benefits. Minor side effects, such as dry mouth or sleepiness, occur as your body struggles to get used to the new medication. These usually pass within a few days or weeks.

Doctors who are unfamiliar with a medication may start with the manufacturer's guidelines, which set typical dosages based on weight and/or age. Differences in individual metabolism, as well as the use of other medications, vitamins, or herbal supplements at the same time, can make a lot of difference in what the optimal dose should really be.

There is one dosage rule that should almost always be followed: start low and go slow. If you are given too high a starting dose or if medications are increased to the full therapeutic dose over just a few days, difficult side effects are far more likely to occur. Gradual titration (increase in dosage) over a period of weeks can make all the difference, even though you are less likely to see dramatic effects right away.

Increasing medications slowly is a problem if you are experiencing acute depression or mania or if you are actively suicidal or aggressive. When things are really bad, it's human nature to want to fix the problem as quickly as possible. You may find it easier to handle major medication changes while in a hospital or day-treatment program, or you may simply need extra personal support from your doctor, friends, and family members.

If possible, start, add, or increase the dose of only one medication at a time. You shouldn't make major dietary changes or start taking an herbal remedy, vitamin, or supplement at the same time as starting a new medication. Otherwise, it's hard to tell what the culprit is should a side effect occur.

Here are some more points to keep in mind when starting a new medication:

- Do not start or stop taking any prescription medication on your own. This includes taking medication prescribed for someone else.

- Know both the trade and generic names of all your medications—this can come in handy when you need to make sure you've been given the right drug. Ask your doctor if there is a less expensive generic version of your medication and if it is as effective as the brand-name product. Some generics are fine, while others are far less effective than their branded counterparts.

- Be sure you understand how much of the medication to take daily and when it should be taken. If it is prescribed for use on an "as needed" basis, discuss what that means with your doctor.

- Follow dose size, dosage time, and other instructions (take with food, etc.) to the letter.

- Ask your doctor what you should do if you forget a dose.

- Ask your doctor or pharmacist about both common and rare side effects. Ask specifically about effects on vision, dental health, energy level, and sexual function. Make sure you know what to do if side effects occur.

- Ask your physician or pharmacist about any side effects specifically related to contraceptive effectiveness, pregnancy, and breastfeeding if you are pregnant, are breastfeeding, or could become pregnant.

- Ask about the risks of male reproductive side effects if you are actively trying to father a child.

- Tell both your physician and pharmacist about all other prescription medications you take.

- Inform your physician and pharmacist about over-the-counter (OTC) drugs you take. Aspirin, ibuprofen, decongestants, non-prescription asthma inhalers, Alka-Seltzer and similar medications, and cough syrup are just some of the common substances that sometimes cause dangerous side effects when mixed with prescription drugs.

- Tell your doctor about any supplements, herbs, vitamins other than a regular daily multivitamin, and special diets that you are trying. If your doctor is unsure about how a medication might interact with an herbal remedy or supplement, you may need to help him find more information. Most doctors are not well-informed about the chemical action of nutritional supplements, herbal medicines, and dietary changes, but many are willing to work with you on these matters.

- Inform your doctor about your use of alcohol, tobacco, and any illegal drugs. Ask her how this may affect your health when combined with your medication. If your current level of use is likely to cause harm, or if you know you have a substance abuse problem, get help right away.

- Call your pharmacist right away if you suspect that you have been given the wrong medication or the wrong dosage. Errors do occur, and the pharmacist should be able to either reassure you or fix the problem.

No matter what psychiatric medications you take, make sure they are listed on your chart if you enter the hospital for surgery. Neuroleptics affect what kind of anesthesia should be chosen, and you may have to discontinue other psychiatric medications a few hours before your surgery because of their effect on blood pressure. Psychiatric medications can also interact with a wide variety of drugs commonly given to treat other illnesses. The descriptions of medications given in this chapter list some well-known or highly dangerous interactions, but you should always ask your pharmacist to check for others when a new drug is added to your regimen.

Special drug formulas for sensitive people

Side effects aren't the only reason to lower a medication dose. Sometimes when a medication doesn't seem to be working, lower is the way to go, not higher. Many people with a bipolar disorder have found this to be the case with antidepressants, such as Prozac, which is sometimes prescribed if you still have problems with depression after your mood swings have been stabilized with lithium, Depakote, or similar medications. In some cases, a low dose of an antidepressant (sometimes very low) helps, but a higher dose (such as might be prescribed to someone with unipolar depression) causes mania despite the use of a mood stabilizer.

Unfortunately, drugs tend to come in just a few dose sizes. Even the least powerful pill may be too much for some people to start with and may be too high altogether for others. Options that can help include the following.

- A number of psychiatric medications, including lithium, Prozac, Haldol, and Risperdal, are available in liquid form. Liquids can be measured out in tiny doses and increased very gradually. You may even be able to mix liquid medications with food or drinks (check with your pharmacist first).

- You can break some medications into fractions. Pill splitters are available at most pharmacies for just this purpose. Make sure that it's okay to split a medication before you go this route, however. Time-release medications and some pills with special coatings will not work properly when broken. Generally speaking, if the pill is scored down the middle, you can split it. If it isn't, ask your pharmacist or call the manufacturer's customer hotline.

- Some pills that are too small or oddly shaped to split can be crushed and divided into equal parts. Again, ask your pharmacist before doing this, because it's difficult to get precise doses with crushed pills. Tiny mortar and pestle sets can be found at health-food or cooking shops. You can buy empty gel caps to put the powder in, or you may be able to mix it into food or drink.

- If you are taking an antidepressant that lasts a long time, such as Prozac (which takes three or more weeks to completely clear your system), talk to your doctor about taking it every other or every third day. It sounds odd, but it has worked for some.

Compounding pharmacies make medications to order in their own lab. For example, they can make a liquid version of a prescription normally available in tablet form only. These pharmacies are especially helpful to individuals with allergy problems. Many pills and syrups contain common allergens, including eggs, soy, corn, and dyes. If a hypoallergenic version isn't available from the manufacturer, seek out a compounding pharmacy. If there isn't one where you live, several allow patients with valid prescriptions to order over the Internet. The International Association of Compounding Pharmacies (IACP), a trade association, can provide referrals. You can search by zip code at the IACP web site (*http://www.iacprx.org/*), or call the IACP at (281) 933-8400 or (800) 927-4227. As always, check the references of the pharmacy you choose before you pay for goods or services.

Follow any instructions about eating or drinking before, with, or after your medication. Also, avoid taking medications with grapefruit juice—it may sound strange, but grapefruit juice can prevent the breakdown of certain drugs for up to twelve hours. In particular, it increases blood levels of the drugs Ambien, Anafranil, BuSpar, Elavil, Halcion, Luvox, Tegretol, Valium, and Zoloft. Pay attention to interactions with other medications and over-the-counter drugs, too. Many times drugs that didn't work were actually being counteracted by something as simple as the Alka-Seltzer tablets or calcium supplements you were taking at the time.

Keep an eye out for unusual symptoms and let your physician know about your concerns right away. Most people remember to do this when they first start taking a drug, but forget about it after they've had the same prescription for a long time. Your body may build up a tolerance to a drug, or changes in your lifestyle, weight, or diet may affect its potency.

Kristi, age 52, says:

> *Three years ago I started menopause and my mood swings got worse. I upped my dose of lithium, which had always worked before, but it didn't this time. In fact, lithium seemed to almost stop working altogether!*
>
> *My doctor ended up switching me to Neurontin after about six months of things being really bad. It is not as effective for me as lithium used to be, but at least I have some control over my mood again.*

Vigilance is especially important when using newer medications. The FDA and similar government bodies in Canada and Europe require studies showing that new medications are effective and safe in the short term. Long-term studies are not required, and they are rarely done.

Of course, not every unusual symptom you experience will be a drug side effect. For example, if you're having flu-like symptoms and everyone else at the office is too, it's much more likely that you're getting the flu than having a medication problem.

Discontinuing medication

One of the most important tools a person with a bipolar disorder can use is a mood diary (see Chapter 8, *Living with Bipolar Disorders,* for a mood diary template and more information). Making a daily habit of charting your symptoms gives you and your doctor a realistic picture of your medication's effectiveness and any patterns of symptoms. It also can provide an early warning system by helping you recognize signs that tend to precede depressive, hypomanic, and manic episodes.

Your mood diary also gives you a way to figure out whether a medication is effective or not. It is much more reliable than simply answering a question in your doctor's office with a yes or no. By looking at your mood diary together, you and your doctor can see if your symptoms are improving steadily, if they are improving but you are still experiencing breakthrough symptoms, if they are not improving, or if your symptoms are actually worsening. If you see worsening or no improvement, your doctor will probably want to either add a second medication, switch mood stabilizers, or discontinue one or more of your medications.

Sometimes a doctor will ask that all medication be withdrawn for a while to give him a baseline look at which symptoms are being caused by the disorder and which are due to over-, under-, or mis-medication. This process can be exceptionally trying if it is not managed well. There are very few medications that can be stopped cold without causing distress—stopping a mood stabilizer too soon can actually worsen your stability, and with some medications, stopping suddenly is life-threatening.

George, age 61, made the mistake of stopping a drug cold and suffered the consequences:

> *My lithium stopped working in the late '80s, after about fifteen years of effectiveness. I started to get depressed even with a normal lithium level, and got fired from my job. I went to see a new psychiatrist. She did a CAT*

scan of my brain to make sure there wasn't something physical going on. After that, she kept me on lithium but also put me on Tegretol.

A few years later, however, I had a stomach problem with H. pylori, a bacteria that can cause stomach ulcers, and some of the drugs they wanted to put me on interacted with Tegretol. I spoke to a psychopharmacologist, who said I needed to cut the dose of Tegretol down—but I just stopped taking it instead. Within 48 hours I was manic. I lasted a couple weeks, but then I had to go in for help. I should have listened to the psychopharmacologist and just cut back—but because I'm a doctor myself, sometimes I make the mistake of thinking I know best.

Stopping one of the SSRI antidepressants or Effexor suddenly can be especially uncomfortable. You may experience symptoms that resemble the flu, with an achy, tired, sick feeling for a couple of weeks.

Ask your doctor if there are any symptoms you might expect during the withdrawal period. He might recommend over-the-counter or dietary remedies for likely problems, such as diarrhea or nausea. Decide in advance on non-medication strategies for dealing with problem behaviors and bipolar symptoms that may occur as drugs are tapered off.

Gradually tapering off to a lower dose and then to none is almost always the best approach, if possible. You should be carefully monitored for signs of trouble. In some cases (such as for discontinuing benzodiazepine tranquilizer use after several years), medication withdrawal may need to take place in a hospital setting or under extra-careful home supervision.

Blood tests and EKGs

Blood levels are a regular routine for some people who take medications for bipolar disorders. For example, liver or heart function tests are sometimes needed before a particular drug is tried and perhaps at regular intervals during its use. Liver function is assessed with a blood test that checks the level of certain enzymes.

The insert that comes with your medication will include recommendations about how often you need blood tests, if at all. Experienced doctors have found that repeated blood tests are rarely needed on otherwise healthy patients whose medication is effective. If you have a health problem that places you at special risk, such as a heart or liver condition, blood tests become more important. Talk to your doctor about what kind of tests he recommends when using your medication, how often you need the tests, and why they are necessary.

Good phlebotomists (blood-draw specialists) do not usually cause bruising or more than a twinge of pain when they do their job, unless you bruise very easily or have a low pain threshold. If this is the case, let the phlebotomist know—she may have a better way to obtain the sample. Numbing ointments like EMLA cream can help, as can using tiny butterfly needles.

People who do not have regular access to quality lab facilities, such as those living in remote areas, may have a difficult time keeping up with a frequent testing schedule. Talk to your health care provider about alternative ways to handle monthly testing, such as having a visiting home-health nurse do the blood draw in your home and then mailing the vial to a lab for testing.

Lithium levels and other blood levels

Other blood tests measure how much of a medication is found in the bloodstream. These are especially important for people who take lithium, which works best at a dose just below the level at which it could cause harm.[1] Your doctor can compare your blood level to a chart of therapeutic blood levels: amounts of the medication that have been found to be effective in people of various sizes and ages.

Doctors usually aim for a "trough" level, meaning taking blood toward the end of a dose's presumed effectiveness (twelve hours or less after you took your medication). For example, if you normally take your medication at 8 A.M., evening would be your best choice for having blood drawn to obtain a trough level. Don't have your lithium level taken on a Friday, because the results will probably not arrive until Monday. If your level is toxic (too high,) you could be in real danger.

Often some other tests of body function can be run at the same time as the lithium level, such as thyroid or liver function tests.

Always ask where your therapeutic blood level and current blood level are when you are tested, rather than assuming that your doctor will call if there's a problem. Observant people can catch potentially dangerous mistakes. Typical problems include blood assessed with the wrong blood test, misinterpreted levels, and getting someone else's paperwork. A physician's assistant or nurse can help you understand what your test results mean.

Troy, age thirty, has learned to keep a close eye on his lithium level:

> *In order to be really successful at living with both the illness and the lithium, I've had to become aware of my internal body. I always know roughly how much lithium is in me at any given time. I used to play a game and predict my level before getting a blood draw. I was almost always right, and knew when I was at .5, .7, or .9.*

Once a therapeutic level has been reached (usually between .5 and 1.5, with .7 to .9 considered optimal), your main job is to keep that level steady. Usually this means taking the same dose, although occasionally it requires raising the dose of medication over time. For a few people, it's as if the body gets used to the drug and requires more to get the same effect. This isn't the same as becoming addicted. Except for the benzodiazepine tranquilizers, the drugs commonly prescribed to people with manic-depressive symptoms are not addictive when used as directed.

Also, your metabolism tends to increase when you are manic, and a temporarily higher dose may be needed during these periods.

Understanding blood test results

Unless you're a doctor, it's hard to interpret blood test results. Here's some basic information about three of the most common tests requested for people taking medications to treat bipolar disorders:

- **Liver function tests.** The liver is the body's organ for eliminating toxins. Blood tests can check the levels of liver (hepatic) enzymes found in the bloodstream. These enzymes result from the death of liver cells. Because the liver is constantly regenerating itself, some of these enzymes are always present. When you take a medication that's metabolized by the liver, they will be a bit higher than usual. What your doctor looks for is an enzyme level that's much too high, indicating dangerously increased stress on the liver or liver disease. The three liver enzymes most commonly checked are:

  - **AST (aspartate amino transferase).** AST is also known as SGOT (serum glutamic-oxaloacetic transaminase) or aspartate transaminase.

  - **ALT (alanine amino transferase).** ALT is also known as SGPT (serum glutamate pyruvate transaminase) or alanine transaminase.

  - **GGT (gamma glutamyl transpeptidase).** For people in good health, the levels of all three liver enzymes are usually below 25. Simply taking certain medications can double the level of liver enzymes. If the level goes over 70, that's generally considered cause for concern. If you have known or suspected liver problems, levels between 35 and 70 might also concern your doctor. High liver enzyme levels may also indicate heart problems, because poor heart function puts increased stress on the liver as well.

- **WBC count.** A healthy number of white blood cells (lymphocytes) in your blood indicates a properly functioning immune system. A very elevated number usually indicates the presence of infection; a very low number can indicate either a suppressed immune system or an infection that has overwhelmed your body's defenses. The WBC count is included in a CBC count (see below). A slightly higher than normal WBC count is normal in people taking lithium.

- **CBC count.** A complete blood cell (CBC) count measures the numbers of various types of cells present in your blood. It measures the numbers of red and white blood cells, blood platelets, and subgroups of these cells. Normal values returned from a CBC count are listed in the following table.

CBC test component	Expected result
WBC (white blood cells)	5,000 to 10,000 WBCs per cubic millimeter of blood; often higher when taking lithium
HGB (hemoglobin)	12 to 15 grams per 100 cubic centimeters of blood
Hct (hematocrit)	36 to 43 percent of whole blood
RBC (red blood cells)	4 to 5.2 million RBCs per cubic millimeter of blood
Platelets	130,000 to 500,000 platelets per cubic millimeter of blood
MCV (mean corpuscular volume)	74 to 85, an expression of the average size of red blood cells

Normal blood values depend on your age, size, state of general health, and what medications you use regularly. If one of the results on your CBC or any other blood test is outside the normal range, ask your doctor whether it should be a concern or not. Individual variations do occur and may not indicate a problem.

Electrocardiogram (EKG)

In addition to blood tests, your heart function may need to be monitored with regular blood-pressure tests, physical exams, and sometimes an electrocardiogram (EKG). The EKG can be done in the doctor's office. It uses wires applied to the chest with an adhesive patch or gooey substance, and it doesn't hurt at all. The wires are attached to a mechanical device or to a computer, much like an EEG machine, resulting in a graph of your heart's activity. Your doctor can read this graph to discern problems with or changes in heart function.

Medication side effects

The same dose of a medication can cause terrible side effects in one person and none at all in another. The difference isn't the drug itself, but differences in each person's body chemistry.

Some of these are probably genetically based, but there are tests only for the very few differences that have been identified. For example, one study found that between 5 and 8 percent of Caucasians produce abnormally low levels of an enzyme needed to metabolize common antidepressant and blood pressure medications.[2] These people either can't take these drugs safely or can take only tiny doses. On the other hand, fully one-third of persons of Somali descent were found to have a genetic difference that prevents them from benefiting from all but the highest doses of these same drugs.[3]

The emerging science of figuring out who can and can't take certain medications is known as pharmacogenomics, and it's still in its infancy. Until reliable tests have been developed—and until some of the issues surrounding confidentiality of genetic information have been addressed—most people will continue to find out about their susceptibility to drug side effects through trial and error.

Certain side effects are associated with psychiatric drugs, including those used to treat bipolar disorders. You may experience none, one or two minor problems, or even one or more serious side effects. The best way to avoid side effects is to work with a physician who believes in careful, gradual increases of medications and who watches out for interactions with other drugs.

Minor side effects

Although some people call the following side effects minor because they usually don't endanger health, you may consider them quite major. If these or other side effects really bother you, talk to your doctor to find a solution:

- **Unwanted behavior changes.** Sometimes called behavioral side effects (BSEs), these can include increased hyperactivity and abnormally elevated mood, provocative and uninhibited behavior, and in a few cases aggression: in other words, symptoms consistent with hypomania. These changes are usually mild and may fade in time or respond to lowering the dose slightly. For people with bipolar disorders, they are most likely to occur when taking antidepressants. If behavior changes are more severe or long-lasting, you may need to stop taking the medication, or your doctor may need to adjust your mood-stabilizing medication.

- **Dry mouth.** Dry mouth is the result of decreased saliva production. It's caused by the secondary action of certain drugs on the neurotransmitter acetylcholine. Usually dry mouth is a minor annoyance, but it can contribute to tooth decay, especially if you wear braces or partial plates, and it can also exacerbate tooth-grinding. Drink plenty of water to relieve the dryness, and brush your teeth frequently. Using a fluoride mouthwash should also help. Sugarless mints or gum sometimes improve comfort by increasing saliva production. In extreme cases, you may want to use a nighttime mouth guard to prevent tooth damage from grinding, or a dentist may recommend or prescribe a special moistening spray, mouthwash, or medication. One medication often prescribed for dry mouth is Urecholine (bethanichol).

- **Nausea.** This side effect results mostly from the action of medications on serotonin receptors concentrated in the gastrointestinal tract. It usually goes away after a few weeks. In the meantime, changes in diet and eating small, frequent meals can relieve symptoms. Check with your doctor before using any over-the-counter stomach remedy.

- **Weight gain or loss.** Serotonin is the target of many psychiatric drugs. This neurotransmitter controls the inner feeling of having eaten enough food. People taking drugs that affect serotonin may report increased or decreased appetite and ensuing weight gain or loss. Weight gain is a frequent problem for people who take neuroleptics, which affect both serotonin and the histamine system. It can also occur with SSRIs. These symptoms are best addressed by dietary changes and, for weight gain, regular exercise. Some clinicians think these drugs may reset the metabolism, because sometimes people on controlled diets still gain weight. In these cases, adjustments to dose or adding another medication to treat this side effect may be tried. Stimulants are the most commonly used medications to offset weight gain, although some clinicians report success from using low doses (25 to 50 micrograms per day) of the thyroid hormone Cytomel. A recent study showed that nizatidine, normally used to treat stomach ulcers, helped limit weight gain in people taking the neuroleptic Zyprexa.[4] People with eating disorders need to be especially careful about medications that cause appetite changes. New versions of current atypical neuroleptics are now being formulated to address this issue. One, Geodon, has already been released but is not appropriate for everyone.

- **Sexual side effects.** Many psychiatric medications tend to dampen sexual impulses and lower responsiveness to sexual stimulation. They may affect your ability to achieve erection or orgasm. Strategies including lowering the medication dose; adding a second medication, such as Effexor, Wellbutrin, BuSpar, or Edronax, that may increase sexual responsiveness; using Viagra; trying herbal remedies that may affect sexual response; or working on sensitization techniques with a professional sex therapist. Ritalin, Dexedrine, and presumably other stimulants may actually increase sexual response for some people. People frequently cite sexual side effects as their reason for discontinuing psychiatric medications, so this issue is actually more important than clinicians may think. The important thing to know is that there are ways to continue taking useful medications without destroying your libido.

Major side effects

If you ever experience a seizure—or more frequent seizures if you have epilepsy— call your doctor right away. Other reasons to call are heart palpitations or blood in your urine or stools. If your doctor is not available on short notice, go to an emergency room. These problems signify either a health condition that needs immediate attention or a serious adverse reaction to medication. Either way, you need immediate care.

The side effects listed below are also signs of major trouble and always warrant immediate medical help:

- **Agranulocytosis.** This is a severe, potentially fatal loss of white blood cells. A regular WBC or CBC count (see "Blood tests and EKGs," earlier in this chapter) should ensure early detection. Other symptoms include sore throat, sudden onset of fever, severe fatigue, and the eruption of bleeding sores on or near the mouth or genitals.

- **Akathisia.** This is an intense, continual, internal sensation of physical restlessness, itchiness, and jumpiness—a need to move constantly. A person with akathisia will look and feel uncomfortable if she tries to be still.

- **Bradyphrenia.** This term denotes slowed thought processes.

- **Dystonia.** Muscle rigidity and uncontrollable muscle spasms are called dystonia. They are associated primarily with the neuroleptics.

- **Encephalopathic syndrome.** The symptoms of encephalopathic syndrome are similar to those of neuroleptic malignant syndrome (see below), of which it may be a variant. It is usually associated with toxic levels of lithium.

- **Extrapyramidal side effects (EPS).** EPS is a blanket term for a whole spectrum of severe side effects, including tremor, slurred speech, akathisia, dystonia, anxiety, distress, paranoia, and bradyphrenia (cognitive slowing). These may occur alone or in combination. All forms of EPS are related to lowered dopamine activity, so they are seldom caused by drugs other than the neuroleptics. Many of these symptoms mimic the neurological disorder Parkinson's disease, such as muscle and joint stiffness, tremor, and unusually stiff and unstable gait, and so these are sometimes called Parkinsonian symptoms. EPS can be remedied by reducing your neuroleptic dose or changing your medication. Parkinsonian symptoms can also be addressed with Cogentin or similar medications normally used to treat Parkinson's disease (see "Other medications," later in this chapter).

- **Hyperkinesia.** This term means excessive motor activity, the physical expression of akathisia. Unlike common hyperactivity, the movements may seem both driven and purposeless.

- **Neuroleptic malignant syndrome (NMS).** This potentially fatal condition is characterized by rigid muscle movements, fever, irregular pulse and heartbeat, rapid heartbeat, irregular blood pressure, heavy sweating, and strange states of mind. Discontinue the medication immediately and call your doctor if these symptoms occur. In extreme cases, you may need emergency care at a hospital. Physicians should report episodes of NMS to the Neuroleptic Malignant Syndrome Information Service (*http://www.nmsis.org/*), which has set up a registry to help researchers reduce the incidence of this problem. NMS is associated primarily with neuroleptics, although it can also occur with tricyclic antidepressants or other medications.

- **Oculogyric crisis.** A person in the throes of oculogyric crisis has a frozen upward gaze, often a very strange-looking facial expression and eye movements, and has contorted facial and neck muscles. This may be caused by some neuroleptic medications, such as Stelazine.

- **Orthostatic hypotension.** This is dangerously low blood pressure and is associated primarily with tricyclic antidepressants, monamineoxidase inhibitors (MAOIs), and neuroleptics, especially the older ones. Some people who take SSRIs experience dizziness when they stand up suddenly, which is also caused by a drop in blood pressure but is not considered harmful. If you experience dizziness, get up slowly.

- **Seizures.** Some medications can lower your susceptibility to seizures. This is rarely a problem, but it is something to be aware of, especially if there is a family history of seizure disorders. Other than convulsions, which are easy to recognize, mild seizures can mimic fainting spells, dizziness, short-term memory loss, strange sensations (such as feeling as if your mind is detached from your body or feelings of déjà vu), and hearing or seeing things that aren't there.

- **Serotonin syndrome.** When the brain is bombarded with too much serotonin (for example, from combining two antidepressants), a person may experience shivers, headaches, diarrhea, profuse sweating, confusion, and akathisia. If this happens, stop taking the medication and see your doctor without delay. In extreme cases, serotonin syndrome can be fatal. That's why patients taking prescription antidepressants should not also take natural antidepressants, such as St. John's Wort.

- **Tardive dyskinesia (TD).** TD is a drug-induced movement disorder characterized by twisting motions of the hands and feet and smacking or chewing movements of the mouth. Rippling movements of the tongue muscles are considered an early warning sign. Discontinue the medication immediately and call your doctor if these symptoms occur. Between 10 and 20 percent of long-term users of the older neuroleptic drugs, such as Haldol and Thorazine, eventually develop this disorder.[5] The newer atypical neuroleptics seem far less likely to cause TD, and those patients who do get TD have usually taken very large doses over many years. A very few cases of TD have been associated with tricyclic antidepressants and some mood stabilizers. If TD is caught early, it may reverse itself once the medication is stopped.

    - Some physicians recommend that people who take drugs that carry a risk for tardive dyskinesia also take Vitamin E supplements, which may prevent the disorder in some people, although research has been inconclusive.

    - Some people experience TD-like symptoms while discontinuing a neuroleptic drug. This "withdrawal dyskinesia" should pass in time.

    - For those who are already affected by TD, only one medication is currently known to help: tetrabenazine (Regulin or Nitoman), which will be discussed later in this section.

These are difficult and painful side effects, the kind that understandably make people worry about taking their medicine. Careful medication choices and dosage adjustment should reduce them, and complementary relaxation techniques and adjustments to diet, vitamins, and supplements may also help you cope.

Sometimes physicians add another medication specifically to address side effects. The following three drugs are occasionally used for this purpose.

Cogentin

Generic name: Benztropine mesylate.

Use: Parkinson's disease, Parkinsonian symptoms caused by psychiatric drugs.

Action, if known: Cogentin counteracts the effects of acetylcholine, the neurotransmitter responsible for a number of unwanted side effects associated with some psychiatric medications.

Side effects: Cogentin can interfere with perspiration, which may cause overheating or even heatstroke. It may also cause dry mouth, constipation, painful or infrequent urination, increased light sensitivity, or blurred vision.

Known interaction hazards: This medication's action is strengthened by other anticholinergic drugs, including antihistamines and some antidepressants. It should not be taken with benzodiazepine tranquilizers or with other CNS depressants.

Tips: Cogentin is not recommended for people with narrow-angle glaucoma, heart disease, myasthenia gravis, or GI tract obstruction.

Habitrol, Nicoderm, Nicotrol, ProStep

Generic name: Nicotine.

Use: Aid to stopping smoking; may be prescribed to strengthen the action of neuroleptics or atypical neuroleptics without increasing the actual dose.

Action, if known: Nicotine definitely affects many CNS functions, but not all of its actions are known. It may reduce tics and anxiety in some people.

Side effects: You may experience diarrhea, insomnia, or nervousness while taking this drug. Nicotine is addictive.

Known interaction hazards: Caffeine interferes with the absorption of this drug.

Tips: People with insulin-dependent diabetes, heart problems, liver or kidney disease, high blood pressure, or pheochromocytoma should be carefully monitored when using nicotine in any form (including cigarettes).

Regulin, Nitoman

Generic name: Tetrabenazine (TBZ).

Use: Tetrabenazine is the only drug currently known to ease the effects of tardive dyskinesia.

Action, if known: Tetrabenazine depletes dopamine in nerve endings.

Side effects: This drug can cause depression.

Known interaction hazards: Tetrabenazine may interact with other drugs that affect dopamine production or use.

Tips: Tetrabenazine is not FDA-approved for sale in the US, but is widely available elsewhere. US patients may obtain it through compassionate use programs or through mail-order arrangements.

Mood stabilizers

Many people with bipolar disorders find relief from a single medication—usually lithium. Many others need two or more medications, carefully balanced to address their individual symptoms without causing undesirable side effects.

Treatment should almost always start with a mood stabilizer, either lithium or one of the antiseizure drugs that has been found to be effective for this purpose. Of these, lithium is the only one known to both stabilize mood in general and also lift depression. Once your mood swings are under control, your doctor may want to add other medications to treat additional problems, such as continued depression or ADHD.

For Norman, combining a mood stabilizer and an antidepressant has turned out to be the best choice:

> I was not interested in getting therapy, so my psychiatrist just talked about medication and got me a referral to someone who was a psychopharmacologist. He was very good at explaining the effects of the medications that were available. After looking at the choices, I chose a combination.
>
> I didn't want to take a mood stabilizer all the time at first. The doctor went along with that, because he felt my wife would blow the whistle, even if I didn't notice.

We had arguments each time she said "Norman, I think you're depressed." Eventually the psychiatrist said that if I could do without the highs, we could do something else. He felt my highs were inevitably followed by depression. He convinced me to try taking a mood stabilizer all year round, and an antidepressant when I'm depressed, and I've been doing that. I think this is oversimplified, but the way he explained it was that if you're hypomanic or manic you're using up your neurotransmitters, and when you use them all up you hit a depression for a few months, That's the idea I based my decision on—what made me decide to try it for twelve months was that the cost of being depressed was worse than what the highs were worth, even though I enjoyed them.

Most of the drugs listed in this section are available in the US and Canada. They are listed under their primary US brand name. Some are available in less-expensive generic forms, while others are not (although all have a generic chemical name). Brand names and formulations may vary in other countries, and some drugs may not be available elsewhere.

Many of the medications routinely prescribed to treat the symptoms of bipolar disorders do not have formal approval for this use. This is called "off-label" use. It is both common and legal, although you should always ask your doctor why an off-label medication is a better choice for you than one that has undergone more testing and been approved.

Of course, new medications are always under development. In fact, as this book went to press several drug companies were hard at work on new antidepressants and mood stabilizers.

Medications approved for use in Asia or Europe are not always available in North America, and vice versa. If you're curious about an unfamiliar medication, look it up by its generic name to find the names of brand-name equivalents, or ask your doctor whether something similar is available where you live.

Sometimes medications that have not been formally approved by government regulators are available under compassionate use laws, including drugs that normally would only be available overseas. It is sometimes possible—if not absolutely legal— for a physician in one country to prescribe a medication available only overseas, and for patients to then have the prescription filled at an overseas pharmacy. Sometimes new drugs are made available to participants in human research trials. If you don't have success with any of the usual treatments for bipolar disorders, this may be an avenue to pursue. The US National Institutes of Mental Health (NIMH) runs many clinical trials each year and usually knows of others at major research centers or pharmaceutical companies. Your nearest medical school or large research hospital may also have studies you could take part in.

The National Alliance for the Mentally Ill is one of the best resources for information on new drugs for neurological disorders. Its Web site (*http://www.nami.org/*) often has "reviews" of new drugs and previews of medications that are undergoing clinical trials.

Not all of the medications listed in this chapter are highly recommended by patients or physicians—some, such as the old-line neuroleptics and the MAO inhibitors, are very much out of favor. That said, it's important to know as much as possible about drugs you may be prescribed or may hear about from others.

This book lists only commonly reported side effects and certain rare, but especially dangerous, side effects. Less common and rare side effects may be associated with any medication, and you may experience side effects that no one else has ever had. If you experience unusual symptoms after taking medicine or after combining more than one medication, call your doctor right away. You may also want to consult the drug reference sheet packaged with your medication by the pharmacy or a detailed medication reference book, such as those listed in Appendix A, *Resources,* to make you aware of all possible side effects and interactions

The information in this chapter was taken from the *Physician's Desk Reference,* the *British National Formulary,* pharmaceutical company literature, mental health consumer publications, and other reputable sources. It is accurate as of this writing, but new information may emerge.

Lithium

Lithium carbonate is still tops for treating bipolar disorders, and for many, many people it is indeed a miracle pill. It is usually the first medication that a doctor prescribes for a newly diagnosed person.

There are many good things that can be said about lithium. It's an inexpensive, naturally occurring mineral salt that is mined out of the ground, not concocted in a lab. It has been in use for thousands—that's right, thousands—of years. Native Americans were well aware of the beneficial effect of drinking water from lithium springs, and many tribes sent their mentally ill family members to take the cure at these bodies of water. Several place names on the US map, such as Lithia Springs in Oregon, indicate that European settlers also quickly grasped the health-promoting value of this water. Lithium was the secret ingredient in many patent medicines and health drinks, including "Bib-Label Lithiated Lemon-Lime Soda," a turn-of-the-century concoction better known today as 7-Up (of course, 7-Up no longer contains lithium).[6] But despite this long history of casual use as a remedy for emotional distress, lithium was not discovered by modern medicine until 1949. An Australian doctor was the first to figure out its usefulness for patients with manic depression. The US Food and Drug Administration approved it as a treatment for depression twenty years later.

Now lithium is available in tablets and capsules that deliver carefully measured doses of pure lithium carbonate at various strengths. A time-release version is also available. Unlike drinking or soaking in lithium-rich water, this method of dosing is more reliable and much more convenient.

Because lithium has been in medical use for more than forty years, there's plenty of information available about side effects you might expect. Most of these are minor. For a few patients, however, lithium can have dangerous effects on the body. This is the case for almost every medication used to treat the symptoms of bipolar disorders. The section that follows highlights some essential information about lithium.

Important facts about lithium

Since lithium has been in use for so long, much has been learned about ways to prevent side effects and ensure that it works well. Here are some hints gathered from medical researchers, doctors, and people who have successfully taken lithium for many years:

- It takes awhile for lithium (and most other mood stabilizers) to start working. While some people respond to lithium in two weeks, it may be several months before you see positive results.

- Stopping lithium suddenly can sometimes bring on a manic episode, and there is about one chance in five that lithium may not work again when you restart it after stopping. Always taper off or stop your dose under a doctor's supervision.

- Lithium is usually most effective for people who have fewer than four manic or depressive episodes per year.

- Lithium may have some antiviral effects, including the ability to suppress the herpes simplex virus (and possibly other herpatiform viruses).[7]

- Some medications, including ACE inhibitors, tetracycline antibiotics, thiazide diuretics, and non-steroidal anti-inflammatories (NSAIDs) like ibuprofin (Advil, Motrin, Midol-IB, etc.), may increase your lithium level.

- Calcium channel blockers, frequently used to treat heart conditions, can lower your lithium level. So can caffeine, theophylline, and carbonic anhydrase inhibitors.

- Sodium bicarbonate (baking soda) counteracts lithium. People taking lithium don't need to worry about the minuscule amount of baking soda found in typical baked goods. You do need to watch out for common antacids that are based on sodium bicarbonate, however, including Alka-Seltzer and Bromo Seltzer.

- Mannitol, a sweet alcohol found mainly in olives, beets, and celery, also counteracts lithium. The amount found naturally in unprocessed foods probably won't cause problems. Larger amounts of mannitol, which is manufactured commercially from corn sugar and hydrogen, are used to sweeten many sugarless foods, including many gums, candies, powdered drink mixes, and diet foods. It may also be found in other powdered food products, chewable medicines and vitamins, and cereals. Mannitol is the main active ingredient of a few powdered laxatives. (These laxatives are also commonly used by illicit drug dealers to cut their product.)

- Some people find that they must avoid eating sweets (including fruit) until a couple of hours after taking lithium. For these individuals, sugar seems to make the medication metabolize too quickly.

- Inositol, a sugar present in organ meats, whole grains, vegetables, nuts, and beans, is available in supplement form and in the health-food staple lecithin. Inositol is also produced within the human body. People with bipolar disorders appear to better regulate this internal inositol level when taking lithium, which indicates that there is an interaction between the two. Accordingly, taking inositol supplements might not be such a good idea when taking lithium—even though small clinical studies have shown that inositol supplements taken alone can help stabilize some people with affective disorders, including bipolar disorders.[8]

- Urea counteracts lithium. Urea is a normal product of the body's ongoing internal detoxification efforts—this is an essential process, and there's no need to worry about the effect of this urea on lithium. Some very few people may be especially sensitive to urea from other sources, including animal milk and blood, urea-based fertilizers, and the release of chemical gasses from products containing formaldehyde or other substances mixed with urea.

- There is a major interaction between lithium and salt in the body. The amount of lithium excreted by the kidneys is determined, to a large extent, by the amount of salt you eat. Reducing your salt intake will cause your lithium level to increase, and increasing your salt intake will cause your lithium level to fall. It is important to maintain a relatively stable salt intake while you take lithium.

- Adequate water intake is very important when you are on lithium. Drink several glasses of water daily and be aware that dehydration can increase your lithium level. This is especially important information for anyone who does strenuous physical work or heavy exercise, such as long-distance running or bicycling. These activities are actually very beneficial for many people with bipolar disorders, but you must take extra care to replenish liquids and electrolytes for safety. If you exercise heavily, you may want to try drinking an electrolyte solution regularly, such as Gatorade.

Troy has taken lithium successfully for almost thirteen years. Here are his tips for success:

> When I was an adolescent, the main side effect that upset me was acne. I was taking a generic brand of lithium. I was eventually informed that the difference in capsule brands has to do with the filler (not lithium carbonate) that they put in them. Since more than 80 percent of the capsule is filler, this is important. I switched to Eskalith ("the Ferrari of lithium"), and most of my acne disappeared, along with my stomachaches. This wasn't a tough decision, since Eskalith cost me about four cents per capsule, rather than two.
>
> You should trust your body to know what the right dosage of lithium is for you. During the first few months I was taking lithium, my psychiatrist felt it was best to increase my dosage to 1200 milligrams a day. On the second day of doing this I felt spaced out, so I went back to the 900-milligram dose and soon felt "normal" again. I called up my psychiatrist and told him the situation, and we agreed that I was not going to take that extra 300 milligrams.
>
> Once you discover the right dosage for you, if you take the lithium on a regular basis and drink the right amount of water, it isn't too difficult to stay in a good range. I take 900 mgs a day and drink about a gallon of bottled water a day. I drink most of the water in the afternoons and evenings after taking the lithium.
>
> Without fail, if my lithium level gets too high I get toxic and then I get diarrhea. This happened to me often when I was first taking lithium, but it rarely happens now. It would most commonly occur when I wasn't drinking enough water. I've become aware of my thirst enough to know now when that is happening so I can head it off by drinking more water to flush the lithium out of my body. I am most at risk for this when I go on a trip. There are times when traveling where I don't have access to enough water, or I don't want to

drink a lot of water since a bathroom may not be available. I usually head this off by decreasing my lithium dosage during the trip. If you have a stable lithium level, small dosage changes over a couple of days won't really change anything.

When you take lithium for a long time, it becomes so habitual that you can actually take a capsule without remembering that you did so. A trick that's worked for me is to have my three capsules in a little container that I refill every day. Then, when I'm not sure if I've taken it I just check the container.

One side effect lithium has given me is psoriasis of the scalp. I've been able to treat this with shampoo, so for me this is a very small price to pay for the mood balance I've been able to maintain.

When I first started taking lithium I had to have a blood draw every month to check my lithium level. For the past ten years, however, I've only had to see a psychiatrist twice a year for half an hour, and have a blood draw once a year to check my lithium level, and check on my kidneys and thyroid gland.

Lithium (Carbolith, Duralith, Eskalith, Lithane, Lithizine, Lithobid, Lithonate, Lithotabs)

Generic name: Lithium, lithium carbonate, lithium citrate (syrup).

Use: Bipolar disorders, mood regulation, manic psychosis, PMS, eating disorders, thyroid problems, aggression.

Action, if known: Lithium appears to regulate the activity of circuits within the brain, possibly by acting on the enzyme inositol monophosphatase. This enzyme is involved with sending phosphoinositide signals, which are believed to help control the body's circadian rhythms. Lithium also seems to affect the amino acid glycine, which affects metabolism and neurotransmitter production; and protein kinace C (PKC), a substance that inhibits neurotransmitter production and neuronal firing. It may have other, as yet unknown, effects.

Side effects: You may experience hand tremor, excessive thirst and urination, nausea, diarrhea, or blurred vision when taking lithium. These effects are usually temporary. If any occur over a long period of time, it could be a sign of toxicity. Call your doctor if they persist.

Known interaction hazards: Lithium makes neuroleptics more powerful and carries a danger of encephalopathic syndrome. It is counteracted by acetazolamide (Diamox) and by theophylline drugs, such as those used for allergy or asthma. (See "Important facts about lithium," earlier in this chapter, for more information about lithium interactions.) Be especially careful about taking any other drug that puts a heavy load on your kidneys, such as metronidazole or verpamil.

Tips: Before starting lithium, you should have kidney function, thyroid function, blood salts level, and blood cell counts checked. Lithium users must have their creatinine level (a measure of kidney function), thyroid function (TSH), and lithium blood therapeutic level monitored regularly—for most people, that means testing every three to six months once stabilized. Ideal therapeutic lithium levels are usually between 0.7 and 0.8 mEq/ml. Some people may also need regular heart monitoring.

Lithium can be toxic in doses that are not much higher than the therapeutic dose. If you are allergic to tartrazine dyes, ask your pharmacist if these are used in your lithium product. If side effects are a problem, the slow-release Lithobid version may be more tolerable, or you may be able to use several small doses of lithium in tablet or liquid form taken more frequently, rather than a single large dose. People who have diabetes or a family history of diabetes should be very careful with lithium, which may affect the sugar metabolism. Lithium may increase your risk of having a child with birth defects, although it appears to be safer than some other mood stabilizers for use during pregnancy. Talk to your doctor if you could become pregnant.

Other mood stabilizers

All of these medications were originally developed to treat epilepsy, but have since been used as mood stabilizers. If you already take a medication for epilepsy but need to add a second one for mood stabilization, or if you take lithium but it is not fully effective, your doctor will need to adjust your dosage of both drugs carefully.

These drugs tend to have more side effects than lithium, but they work better for some people. Unlike lithium, these drugs stabilize mood but may not prevent depression.

Depakene

Generic name: Valproic acid.

Use: Seizure disorders, bipolar disorders, migraine, panic disorder, rages/aggression.

Action, if known: Depakene increases the levels of gamma-aminobutyric acid (GABA) in the brain and increases its absorption. It also stabilizes brain membranes. It stabilizes mood and works well against mania.

Side effects: Nausea, sedation, depression, psychosis, aggression, hyperactivity, and diarrhea are sometimes associated with this medication. Changes in blood platelet function may also occur and can cause easy bruising. Weight gain and hair loss may also occur.

Known interaction hazards: Do not take Depakene with milk, and do not use charcoal tablets when taking this drug. Be careful with alcohol and with any medication that has a tranquilizing or depressant effect. Side effects may increase if you use anticoagulants, including aspirin, non-steroidal anti-inflammatory drugs, erythromycin, chlorpromazine, cimetidine, or felbamate.

Tips: You will need regular blood tests while taking this drug (every three months once stabilized): therapeutic blood level (VPA: usually 50-125 ug/ml), CBC with platelet count, and SGPT to check your liver. Watch out for increased bruising or bleeding, an indicator of blood platelet problems. Do not crush or chew tablets. Starting with a very small dose and increasing it slowly can often help you avoid even the common side effects. Depakene has recently been linked to polycystic ovary syndrome in women. The symptoms of this endocrine disorder include irregular or missed periods, unexplained weight gain, growth of abnormal body hair, and an inability to get pregnant. Valproate drugs can increase the risk of neural tube birth defects in babies born to mothers who take them before conception and during the early weeks of pregnancy, so be sure to talk to your doctor if you could become pregnant.

Depakote (Epilim, Valpro)

Generic name: Divalproex sodium (valproic acid plus sodium valproate).

Use: Seizure disorders, bipolar disorders, migraine, panic disorder, rages/aggression.

Action, if known: Depakote increases the levels of gamma-aminobutyric acid (GABA) in the brain and increases its absorption. It also stabilizes brain membranes. It stabilizes mood and works well against mania.

Side effects: This drug may cause nausea, sedation (this usually passes after a few days), depression, psychosis, aggression, hyperactivity, changes in blood platelet function, weight gain, or hair loss.

Known interaction hazards: Do not take this drug with milk, and do not use charcoal tablets when taking Depakote. Be careful with alcohol and with any medication that has a tranquilizing or depressant effect. Side effects may increase if you use anticoagulants, including aspirin, non-steroidal anti-inflammatory drugs, erythromycin, chlorpromazine, cimetidine, or felbamate.

Tips: You will need regular blood tests while taking this drug (every three months once stabilized): therapeutic blood level (VPA: usually 50-125 ug/ml), CBC with platelet count, and SGPT to check your liver. Watch out for increased bruising or bleeding, an indicator of blood platelet problems. Therapeutic level tests can be misleading with Depakote: actual therapeutic levels for individuals may be higher or lower than published charts indicate. Do not crush or chew tablets (Depakote is available in a sprinkle form that can be mixed with soft food). Starting with a very small dose and titrating it up slowly can often help you avoid even the common side effects. Hair loss can be avoided by taking 50 mg of zinc daily; some people also take .025 mg of selenium to boost zinc's effect. Depakote has recently been linked to polycystic ovary syndrome in women. The symptoms of this endocrine disorder include irregular or missed periods, unexplained weight gain, growth of abnormal body hair, and an inability to get pregnant. Valproate drugs can increase the risk of neural tube birth defects in babies born to mothers who take them before conception and during the early weeks of pregnancy, so be sure to talk to your doctor if you could become pregnant. A time-release version of Depakote is available and may be less likely to cause side effects.

Gabitril

Generic name: Tiagibine HCL.

Use: Seizure disorders, bipolar disorders.

Action, if known: Gabitril enhances the activity of gamma-aminobutyric acid (GABA), a chemical substance that inhibits electrical activity in the brain.

Side effects: Gabitril is sometimes associated with stomach problems, severe rash, or weakness, and it can lower your white blood cell and blood platelet count. It can bind to parts of the eye—research has not been done into whether this is harmful or not, but you should report any eye-related symptoms to your doctor when taking Gabitril.

Known interaction hazards: Antacids can counteract Gabitril. It may interact with other antiepilepsy drugs and mood stabilizers, causing changes in their availability or strength, so your doctor should monitor all medication doses carefully.

Tips: Watch dosage increases closely to avoid toxic reactions.

Lamictal

Generic name: Lamotrigine.

Use: Seizure disorders. Lamictal has not yet been FDA-approved as a treatment for bipolar disorder, but it has been prescribed by some doctors, with reports of positive results. It is currently undergoing clinical trials for FDA approval.

Action, if known: Lamictal binds to the hormone melatonin. It stabilizes electrical currents within the brain and blocks the release of at least two seizure-stimulating neurotransmitters: aspartate and glutamate. These same neurotransmitters may be involved in causing mood swings. Lamotrigine seems to have some antidepressant activity as well as acting as a mood stabilizer.

Side effects: Lamictal is sometimes associated with headaches, dizziness, nausea, a general flu-like feeling, or increased light sensitivity. If you develop a rash, call your doctor immediately. Although most rashes that develop in patients taking Lamictal are not serious, some rashes may be a warning of a serious, even life-threatening, side effect called Stevens-Johnson Syndrome. Rarely, Lamictal may increase the risk of seizures for some people.

Known interaction hazards: Lamictal interacts with Depakote and Depakene, carbamazepine, and phenytoin. Anti-folate drugs like methotrexate strengthen Lamictal. Phenobarbital and primidone may lessen its effects.

Tips: If you have heart, kidney, or liver disease, use only under careful supervision. Lamictal may act as an antidepressant when added to another mood stabilizer. Like other antidepressants, it may occasionally cause mania. It also appears less likely to cause weight gain than some similar drugs. Slow, gradual introduction of this medication is essential.

Neurontin

Generic name: Gabapentin.

Use: Seizure disorders, especially those that do not respond to other drugs; rage/aggression; anxiety; panic. Neurontin has not yet been FDA-approved as a treatment for bipolar disorder, but some doctors have reported positive results, especially when used in addition to another mood stabilizer.

Action, if known: This medication appears to act by binding a specific protein found only on neurons in the central nervous system. It may increase the GABA content of some brain regions.

Side effects: Neurontin can cause blurred vision, dizziness, clumsiness, drowsiness, swaying, or eye-rolling.

Known interaction hazards: Avoid alcohol and all other CNS depressants, including tranquilizers, over-the-counter (OTC) medications for colds and allergies, OTC sleep aids, anesthetics, and narcotics, when taking this medication. Antacids may counteract the effects of Neurontin.

Tips: Increase doses very slowly to avoid side effects. People with kidney disease should be carefully monitored while taking Neurontin. Corn is used as a filler in the usual formulation of this drug, causing allergic reactions in some. Recent reports indicate that Neurontin can cause mania in some patients, especially younger patients. This can be offset by adding another medication or by changing the dose of Neurontin or other medications used with it. Others report that Neurontin made their psoriasis worse. Neurontin does seem to help with anxiety and insomnia. A new drug under development called Pregabalin is based on Neurontin, but with fewer side effects—however, clinical trials of this drug were restricted in February 2001, when it was flagged as a possible cancer risk. It is not known at the time of this writing when or if Pregabalin will come to market.

Tegretol

Generic name: Carbamazepine.

Use: Seizure disorders, bipolar disorders, rage/aggression, nerve pain, aid to drug withdrawal, restless leg syndrome, Sydenham's Chorea, and similar movement/behavior disorders in children.

Action, if known: This drug appears to work by reducing the activity level within some brain circuits. It appears to work well against mania, in addition to any mood stabilizing properties it may have.

Side effects: Sleepiness, dizziness, nausea, unusual moods or behavior, headache, and water retention can be side effects of Tegretol. It may cause a low white blood cell count. Call your doctor if you have flu-like symptoms or other unusual reactions while taking this drug.

Known interaction hazards: Never take this medication with an MAOI (monoamine-oxidase inhibitor). Tegretol is often used in combination with other mood stabilizers, including lithium, but the dose of Tegretol and drugs used with it must be very carefully adjusted. The action of Tegretol is strengthened by numerous prescription and over-the-counter medications, including many antibiotics, antidepressants, calcium channel blockers, and cimetadine. It also counteracts or changes the effect of many drugs, including Haldol, oral contraceptives, theophylline, and acetaminophen. Because these interactions can be very serious, discuss all medications you take—including all OTC remedies, vitamins, and herbs—with your doctor before beginning to use Tegretol.

Tips: You should have a white blood cell count done before taking Tegretol. You will need regular blood tests while taking this medication (about every three months once stabilized): therapeutic blood level (usually 4-12 ug/ml), CBC, reticulocyte count, and SGPT. Avoid this medication if you have a history of bone marrow depression. Tegretol can be fatal at fairly low doses, so all people taking it should be carefully monitored, particularly since it interacts with so many other medications. This medication can increase the risk of neural tube birth defects in babies born to mothers who take it before conception and during the early weeks of pregnancy, so be sure to talk to your doctor if you could become pregnant. It also passes through breast milk in dangerously high concentrations.

Topamax

Generic name: Topiramate.

Use: Seizure disorders. Topamax has not yet been FDA-approved as a treatment for bipolar disorders, but it has been prescribed for this purpose with reports of good results. Anecdotal reports from physicians also indicate that it may be useful for anxiety and eating disorders.

Action, if known: Topamax enhances the activity of GABA, which inhibits electrical activity in the brain; acts as a calcium-channel blocker; and blocks the excitatory neurotransmitter glutamate.

Side effects: This drug may cause sleepiness, dizziness, loss of coordination, and slowed thinking or speech. Topamax has been reported to cause nearsightedness and glaucoma in a few people who take it. Any changes in vision should be reported to the prescribing physician.

Known interaction hazards: Topamax dosages must be adjusted carefully when it is used with other mood stabilizers or any substance that acts as a depressant, including alcohol.

Tips: Topamax is available in a sprinkle formulation that can be combined with soft food, such as applesauce or ice cream. Topamax may increase your risk of developing kidney stones, especially if you take calcium supplements. To reduce this risk, drink lots of water and take vitamin C. Because of the side effects that can happen with this drug, it is recommended that you start very low and increase the dose very slowly. This drug may increase the risk of birth defects. Talk to your doctor if you could become pregnant.

Trileptal

Generic name: Oxcarbamazepine.

Use: Seizure disorders, bipolar disorders, rage/aggression, nerve pain, aid to drug withdrawal, restless leg syndrome, Sydenham's Chorea, and similar movement/behavior disorders in children. Trileptal has not been FDA-approved as a treatment for bipolar disorders, but its similarity to Tegretol indicates it may be effective.

Action, if known: This drug appears to work by reducing activity in some brain circuits.

Side effects: Trilpetal can cause sleepiness, dizziness, nausea, unusual moods or behavior, headache, retention of water. It may cause low white blood cell count. Call your doctor right away if you have flu-like symptoms or other unusual reactions while taking this drug.

Known interaction hazards: Never take this medication with an MAOI. Trileptal may be used in combination with other mood stabilizers, including lithium, but the doses must be very carefully adjusted. Trileptal is very similar to Tegretol, but its molecular structure has been changed to reduce toxicity. It may interact with other drugs, including oral contraceptives, hormone supplements, calcium channel blockers, and many psychiatric drugs. As with Tegretol, discuss all prescription and OTC medications you take with your doctor before starting this drug.

Tips: You should have a white blood cell count done before taking Trileptal. You may need regular blood tests for serum sodium levels while taking this medication. This medication increases the risk of neural tube birth defects. Talk to your doctor if you could become pregnant.

Antidepressants

The use of antidepressants alone to treat bipolar disorders is rarely a good idea, although there are a few patients who do well. Most experienced clinicians use antidepressants only in addition to a mood stabilizer. That's because antidepressants can trigger a rapid swing into mania.

Marcia, age 26, has been down that road before:

> I have tried Prozac, and it was not good! Originally I was misdiagnosed as having depression. I was placed on Prozac, which caused a manic/hypomanic cycle. I was immediately taken off Prozac and rediagnosed as bipolar II. I was then placed on lithium, and I have been stable ever since.
>
> In addition to the lithium, I also take a small dose of Zoloft. This was done mainly because of the severity of my depressions.

Today's antidepressants are much more advanced than those used just a decade ago, but they're still not as precise as those who take them would like. There are several different types, and related medications may function quite differently. That's why you shouldn't write off a whole family of drugs just because one was a disaster. A slightly different medication may turn out to be infinitely preferable.

All antidepressants should be used with care. Check package inserts and pharmacy information sheets to avoid interactions with other medications. Be sure to tell your doctor about any over-the-counter drugs you use, even aspirin, herbal medicines, or supplements.

SSRI antidepressants

The brain is chock-full of serotonin receptors, tiny sites that bind with serotonin molecules to move chemical impulses through the brain. One type of antidepressants, the Selective Serotonin Reuptake Inhibitors (SSRIs), block certain receptors from absorbing serotonin. Researchers believe this results in lowered or raised levels of serotonin in specific areas of the brain. Over time, SSRIs may cause changes in brain chemistry, hopefully in a positive direction. SSRIs may also cause actual changes in brain structure with prolonged use. There are also receptor sites elsewhere in the central and peripheral nervous systems, so SSRIs can have an impact on saliva production, appetite, digestion, skin sensitivity, and many other functions.

The SSRIs are not identical in either their chemical composition or their effects on the brain. Prozac and Zoloft tend to have an energizing and focusing effect as well as reducing depression, for example, while Paxil may calm anxious or agitated people who are also depressed.

Starting with a very small dose is especially important when adding an antidepressant to the medication regimen of someone with bipolar disorder. Doctors may want to consider creative dosing ideas too, such as pulse (intermittent) dosing or cyclic dosing for women whose mood swings are closely related to their menstrual cycle.

The five drugs currently considered part of the SSRI family follow:

Celexa, Cipramil

Generic name: Citalopram.

Use: Depression.

Action, if known: Celexa increases the amount of active serotonin in the brain and tends to have a calming effect.

Side effects: Dry mouth, insomnia or restless sleep, increased sweating, nausea, or sexual dysfunction may be associated with Celexa. It lowers the seizure threshold. This drug can cause mood swings in people with bipolar disorders.

Known interaction hazards: Avoid alcohol when taking Celexa. Never take it with an MAOI or soon after stopping a MAOI. Use this drug with caution if you take any medication that affects the liver, such as ketoconazole or the macrolide antibiotics.

Tips: People with liver or kidney disease should be monitored regularly while taking Celexa.

Luvox, Faverin

Generic name: Fluvoxamine.

Use: Depression, obsessive-compulsive disorder.

Action, if known: Luvox increases the amount of active serotonin in the brain.

Side effects: Luvox may cause headaches, insomnia, sleepiness, nervousness, nausea, dry mouth, diarrhea or constipation, or sexual dysfunction. It lowers the seizure threshold. Luvox can cause mood swings in people with bipolar disorders.

Known interaction hazards: Never take this drug with an MAOI or soon after stopping an MAOI. Its action is strengthened by tricyclic antidepressants and lithium. It strengthens the action of many medications, including clozapine, diltiazem and perhaps other calcium-channel blockers, methadone, some beta-blockers and antihistamines, and Haldol and other neuroleptics.

Tips: Avoid taking this drug if you have liver disease. Cigarette smoking may make Luvox less effective. Luvox does not bind to protein in the body, unlike the other SSRIs, and may have a very different effect in some people.

Paxil, Seroxat

Generic name: Paroxetine.

Use: Depression.

Action, if known: Paxil increases the amount of active serotonin in the brain and tends to have a calming effect.

Side effects: Headache, insomnia or restless sleep, dizziness, tremor, nausea, weakness, dizziness, sexual dysfunction, or dry mouth may be associated with Paxil. It lowers the seizure threshold. Paxil can cause mood swings in people with bipolar disorders.

Known interaction hazards: Avoid alcohol when taking Paxil. Never take it with an MAOI or soon after stopping a MAOI. Paxil strengthens the action of warfarin, theophylline, paroxetine, and procyclidine. It changes how digoxin and phenytoin act in the body.

Tips: People with liver or kidney disease should be monitored regularly while taking Paxil. Some people who take Paxil for a long period and then stop suddenly experience unpleasant effects, occasionally including the onset of depression. To avoid these difficulties, always reduce your dose gradually under medical supervision.

Prozac

Generic name: Fluoxetine.

Use: Depression, obsessive-compulsive disorder, eating disorders, ADHD, narcolepsy, migraine/chronic headache, Tourette's syndrome, social phobia.

Action, if known: Prozac increases the amount of active serotonin in the brain and tends to have an energizing effect.

Side effects: Prozac may cause headaches, insomnia or restless sleep, dizziness, tremor, nausea, weakness, dizziness, sexual dysfunction, dry mouth, itchy skin, or a rash. It may cause changes in appetite and weight. It lowers the seizure threshold. Prozac can cause mood swings in people with bipolar disorders.

Known interaction hazards: Avoid alcohol when taking Prozac. Never take it with an MAOI or within six weeks of stopping an MAOI. Do not take over-the-counter or prescription cold or allergy remedies containing cyproheptadine or dextromethorphan with this drug. Prozac's action is strengthened by tricyclic antidepressants. It strengthens the action of lithium, phenytoin, neuroleptic drugs, carbamazepine, and cyclosporine. It reduces the effectiveness of BuSpar.

Tips: Prozac has a long life in your body and is metabolized slowly. People with liver or kidney disease should be monitored while taking Prozac.

Zoloft, Lustral

Generic name: Sertraline.

Use: Depression, obsessive-compulsive disorder.

Action, if known: Zoloft increases the amount of active serotonin in the brain and tends to have an energizing quality.

Side effects: Dry mouth, headache, tremor, diarrhea, nausea, and sexual dysfunction are sometimes associated with Zoloft. This medication may precipitate a manic episode in people with bipolar disorders and it can lower the seizure threshold.

Known interaction hazards: Avoid alcohol and all other substances that act as depressants when taking Zoloft. Never take it with an MAOI or soon after stopping an MAOI. Zoloft strengthens the action of benzodiazepine drugs and warfarin. Its action is strengthened by cimetidine.

Tips: People with epilepsy, bipolar disorders, liver disease, or kidney disease should be carefully monitored if they take Zoloft. It may affect the therapeutic level of lithium.

Tricyclic antidepressants

Before Prozac and its cousins became famous, the tricyclic antidepressants were the wonder drugs for depression and obsessive-compulsive disorder (OCD). They are still the best choice for some patients.

Although doctors will usually try an SSRI or two first, these drugs can be added to a mood stabilizer when treating people with bipolar disorders, if they are still depressed despite successful mood stabilization.

The tricyclic antidepressants work by inhibiting the reuptake of various neurotransmitters at nerve terminals.

People taking these drugs require regular monitoring for heart problems and other potentially serious side effects. All of the tricyclics can lower the seizure threshold. They also carry a greater risk of sending people with bipolar disorders into a manic phase than the SSRIs do, and they pose increased overdose risks. Some people also complain of excessive weight gain when taking tricyclics.

There are several tricyclic antidepressants, many of which combine more than one active drug. The most frequently used ones follow:

Anafranil

Generic name: Clomipramine.

Use: Depression, OCD, panic disorder, chronic pain, eating disorders, severe PMS.

Action, if known: Anafranil blocks norepinephrine and serotonin use and works against the neurotransmitter acetylcholine. It also has weak antihistamine properties.

Side effects: Sedation, tremor, seizures, dry mouth, light sensitivity, and weight gain are among the risks associated with this drug. It lowers the seizure threshold and can cause mood swings in people with bipolar disorders.

Known interaction hazards: Alcohol, MAOIs, blood pressure medications (including clonidine and guanfacine), and thyroid medication can interact with Anafranil. Its action may be strengthened by estrogen, bicarbonate of soda (as in Alka-Seltzer and other OTC remedies), acetazolamide, procainamide, the calcium-channel blockers diltiazem and verapramil, and quinidine. Cimetidine, methylphenidate, Thorazine and similar drugs, oral contraceptives, nicotine (including cigarettes), and charcoal tablets may interfere with Anafranil's action in the body.

Tips: Take with food if stomach upset occurs. Take bulk of dose at bedtime to reduce daytime sedation, if so directed by your doctor.

Asendin, Asendis

Generic name: Amoxapine.

Use: Depression, panic disorder, chronic pain, eating disorders, severe PMS.

Action, if known: Asendin blocks norepinephrine and serotonin use and works against the neurotransmitter acetylcholine.

Side effects: You may experience sedation, tremor, seizures, dry mouth, or light sensitivity while taking Asendin. It can cause mood swings in people with bipolar disorders.

Known interaction hazards: Alcohol, MAOIs, blood pressure medications (including clonidine and guanfacine), and thyroid medication may interact with Asendin. Its action may be strengthened by estrogen, bicarbonate of soda (as in Alka-Seltzer and other OTC remedies), acetazolamide, procainamide, the calcium-channel blockers diltiazem and verapramil, and quinidine. Cimetidine, methylphenidate, Thorazine and similar drugs, oral contraceptives, nicotine (including cigarettes), and charcoal tablets may interfere with Asendin's action in the body.

Tips: Take Asendin with food if stomach upset occurs. Asendin tends to be less sedating than other tricyclics. If daytime sedation is a problem nevertheless, take the bulk of your dose at bedtime if so directed.

Aventyl, Allegron, Motipress, Motival, Pamelor

Generic name: Nortriptyline.

Use: Depression, panic disorder, chronic pain, eating disorders, severe PMS.

Action, if known: Aventyl blocks norepinephrine and serotonin use and works against the neurotransmitter acetylcholine.

Side effects: Sedation, tremor, seizures, dry mouth, or light sensitivity can occur while taking this drug. It can cause mood swings in people with bipolar disorders.

Known interaction hazards: Alcohol, MAOIs, blood pressure medications (including clonidine and guanfacine), and thyroid medication may interact with this drug. Its action may be strengthened by estrogen, bicarbonate of soda (as in Alka-Seltzer and other OTC remedies), acetazolamide, procainamide, the calcium-channel blockers diltiazem and verapramil, and quinidine. Cimetidine, methylphenidate, Thorazine and similar drugs, oral contraceptives, nicotine (including cigarettes), and charcoal tablets may also interfere with Aventyl's action in the body.

Tips: Take Aventyil with food if stomach upset occurs. This drug tends to be less sedating than other tricyclics.

Elavil, Lentizol, Tryptizol

Generic name: Amitriptyline.

Use: Depression, panic disorder, chronic pain, eating disorders, severe PMS.

Action, if known: Elavil blocks norepinephrine and serotonin use and works against the neurotransmitter acetylcholine.

Side effects: You may experience sedation, tremor, seizures, dry mouth, or light sensitivity while taking this drug. Elavil can cause mood swings in people with bipolar disorders.

Known interaction hazards: Alcohol, MAOIs, blood pressure medications (including clonidine and guanfacine), and thyroid medication can interact with Elavil. Its action may be strengthened by estrogen, bicarbonate of soda (as in Alka-Seltzer and other OTC remedies), acetazolamide, procainamide, the calcium-channel blockers diltiazem and verapramil, and quinidine. Cimetidine, methylphenidate, Thorazine and similar drugs, oral contraceptives, nicotine (including cigarettes), and charcoal tablets may interfere with Elavil's action in the body.

Tips: Take Elavil with food if stomach upset occurs. Take bulk of dose at bedtime to reduce daytime sedation, if so directed by your doctor.

Etrafon, Trilafon, Triavil

Generic name: Amitriptyline/perphenazine (Trilafon includes only perphenazine).

Use: Depression, panic disorder, chronic pain, eating disorders, severe PMS.

Action, if known: These tricyclic antidepressants also have some of the qualities associated with neuroleptics (see "Neuroleptics," later in this chapter). They block norepinephrine and serotonin use and work against the neurotransmitter acetylcholine.

Side effects: Sedation, tremor, seizures, dry mouth, or increased light sensitivity may occur when taking these drugs. They also carry a risk of tardive dyskinesia, extra-pyramidal side effects, or neuroleptic malignant syndrome. These medications can cause mood swings in people with bipolar disorders.

Known interaction hazards: Alcohol, MAOIs, blood pressure medications (including clonidine and guanfacine), and thyroid medication can interact with these drugs. Their action may be strengthened by estrogen, bicarbonate of soda (as in Alka-Seltzer and other OTC remedies), acetazolamide, procainamide, the calcium-channel blockers diltiazem and verapramil, and quinidine. Cimetidine, methylphenidate, Thorazine and similar drugs, oral contraceptives, nicotine (including cigarettes), charcoal tablets, and estrogen may interfere with their action in the body.

Tips: Avoid extreme heat when taking these drugs. These medications are not recommended for use by people with severe depression, lung disease, severe asthma, or liver disease. Take with food if stomach upset occurs. Take bulk of dose at bedtime to reduce daytime sedation, if so directed by your doctor.

Limbitrol

Generic name: Amitriptyline/chlordiazepoxide.

Use: Depression, panic disorder, chronic pain, eating disorders, severe PMS.

Action, if known: Limbitrol blocks norepinephrine and serotonin use and works against the neurotransmitter acetylcholine.

Side effects: You may experience sedation, tremor, seizures, dry mouth, light sensitivity, or weight gain while taking this drug. Limbitrol can cause mood swings in people with bipolar disorders, and it lowers the seizure threshold.

Known interaction hazards: Alcohol, MAOIs, blood pressure medications (including clonidine and guanfacine), and thyroid medication may interact with Limbitrol. Its action may be strengthened by estrogen, bicarbonate of soda (as in Alka-Seltzer and other OTC remedies), the calcium-channel blockers diltiazem and verapramil, acetazolamide, procainamide, and quinidine. Cimetidine, methylphenidate, Thorazine and similar drugs, oral contraceptives, nicotine (including cigarettes), and charcoal tablets may interfere with Limbitrol's action in the body.

Tips: Take this medication with food if stomach upset occurs. Take bulk of dose at bedtime to reduce daytime sedation, if so directed by your doctor.

Norpramin

Generic name: Desipramine.

Use: Depression, panic disorder, chronic pain, eating disorders, severe PMS.

Action, if known: Norpramin blocks norepinephrine and serotonin use and works against the neurotransmitter acetylcholine.

Side effects: You may experience sedation, tremor, seizures, dry mouth, light sensitivity, or weight gain while taking this drug. Norpramin can cause mood swings in people with bipolar disorders, and it lowers the seizure threshold.

Known interaction hazards: Alcohol, MAOIs, blood pressure medications (including clonidine and guanfacine), and thyroid medication interact with this drug. Its action is strengthened by estrogen, bicarbonate of soda (as in Alka-Seltzer and other OTC remedies), acetazolamide, procainamide, and quinidine. Cimetidine, methylphenidate, Thorazine and similar drugs, oral contraceptives, nicotine (including cigarettes), and charcoal tablets may interfere with Norpramin's action in the body.

Tips: Take this medication with food if stomach upset occurs.

Sinequan

Generic name: Doxepin.

Use: Depression, panic disorder, chronic pain, eating disorders, severe PMS.

Action, if known: Sinequan blocks norepinephrine and serotonin use and works against the neurotransmitter acetylcholine.

Side effects: You may experience sedation, tremor, seizures, dry mouth, light sensitivity, or weight gain while taking this drug. Sinequan can cause mood swings in people with bipolar disorders, and it lowers the seizure threshold.

Known interaction hazards: Alcohol, MAOIs, blood pressure medications (including clonidine and guanfacine), and thyroid medication interact with Sinequan. Its action is strengthened by estrogen, bicarbonate of soda (as in Alka-Seltzer and other OTC remedies), acetazolamide, procainamide, and quinidine. Cimetidine, methylphenidate, Thorazine and similar drugs, oral contraceptives, nicotine (including cigarettes), and charcoal tablets may interfere with Sinequan's action in the body.

Tips: Take Sinequan with food if stomach upset occurs. Take bulk of dose at bedtime to reduce daytime sedation, if so directed by your doctor.

Surmontil

Generic name: Trimipramine.

Use: Depression, panic disorder, chronic pain, eating disorders, severe PMS.

Action, if known: Surmontil blocks norepinephrine and serotonin use and works against the neurotransmitter acetylcholine.

Side effects: You may experience sedation, tremor, seizures, dry mouth, light sensitivity, or weight gain while taking this drug. Surmontil can cause mood swings in people with bipolar disorders, and it lowers the seizure threshold.

Known interaction hazards: Alcohol, MAOIs, blood pressure medications (including clonidine and guanfacine), and thyroid medication can interact with this drug. Its action is strengthened by estrogen, bicarbonate of soda (as in Alka-Seltzer and other OTC remedies), acetazolamide, procainamide, and quinidine. Cimetidine, methylphenidate, Thorazine and similar drugs, oral contraceptives, nicotine (including cigarettes), and charcoal tablets may interfere with Surmontil's action in the body.

Tips: Take this medication with food if stomach upset occurs. Take bulk of dose at bedtime to reduce daytime sedation, if so directed by your doctor.

Tofranil, Janimine

Generic name: Imipramine.

Use: Depression, panic disorder, chronic pain, eating disorders, severe PMS.

Action, if known: Tofranil blocks norepinephrine and serotonin use and works against the neurotransmitter acetylcholine.

Side effects: You may experience sedation, tremor, seizures, dry mouth, light sensitivity, or weight gain while taking this drug. Tofranil can cause mood swings in people with bipolar disorders, and it lowers the seizure threshold.

Known interaction hazards: Alcohol, MAOIs, blood pressure medications (including clonidine and guanfacine), and thyroid medication can interact with Tofranil. Its action is strengthened by estrogen, bicarbonate of soda (as in Alka-Seltzer and other OTC remedies), acetazolamide, procainamide, and quinidine. Cimetidine, methylphenidate, Thorazine and similar drugs, oral contraceptives, nicotine (including cigarettes), and charcoal tablets may interfere with Tofranil's action in the body.

Tips: Take this medication with food if stomach upset occurs. Although Tofranil tends to be less sedating than other tricyclics, take bulk of dose at bedtime if daytime sedation is an issue for you and if so directed by your doctor.

Vivactil

Generic name: Protriptyline.

Use: Depression, panic disorder, chronic pain, eating disorders, severe PMS.

Action, if known: Vivactil blocks norepinephrine and serotonin use and works against the neurotransmitter acetylcholine. It tends to be more energizing than other tricyclics.

Side effects: You may experience sedation, tremor, seizures, dry mouth, light sensitivity, or weight gain while taking this drug. Vivactil can cause mood swings in people with bipolar disorders, and it lowers the seizure threshold.

Known interaction hazards: Alcohol, MAOIs, blood pressure medications (including clonidine and guanfacine), and thyroid medication can interact with this drug. Its action is strengthened by estrogen, bicarbonate of soda (as in Alka-Seltzer and other OTC remedies), acetazolamide, procainamide, and quinidine. Cimetidine, methylphenidate, Thorazine and similar drugs, oral contraceptives, nicotine (including cigarettes), and charcoal tablets may interfere with Vivactil's action in the body.

Tips: Take this medication with food if stomach upset occurs. Vivactil tends to have a stimulating effect, unlike other tricyclics.

MAOI antidepressants

A third class of antidepressants, the monoamineoxidase inhibitors (MAOIs), are also available—but they are rarely used. These medications are effective against depression by inhibiting the metabolization of the neurotransmitters serotonin, norepinephrine, and dopamine. They do so indirectly, by interfering with the enzyme monoamineoxidase (MAO).

The MAOIs have unpleasant and even life-threatening interactions with many other drugs, including common over-the-counter medications. If you take an MAOI, wear a Medicalert bracelet or keep a card in your wallet to ensure that emergency personnel know, just in case you ever have an accident.

People taking MAOIs must also follow a special diet, because these medications interact with many foods. The list of foods to avoid includes chocolate, aged cheeses, beer, and many more. If you must take a MAOI, check for warning labels on everything and familiarize yourself thoroughly with the dietary restrictions.

MAOIs can also produce hallucinations and have been abused by some drug users to get this effect.

The most frequently prescribed drugs in this class are Aurorix (moclobemide), Nardil (phenelzine), and Parnate (tranylcypromine sulfate). If your doctor prescribes an MAOI inhibitor, read the package insert carefully and learn more about its possible side effects from a medication reference book or your physician.

Other antidepressants

Several antidepressants are now available that don't fit one of the three major categories. These include Desyrel (trazodone, Molipaxin), Effexor (venlafacine), Reboxetine (edronax), Remeron (mirtazapine), Serzone (nefaxodone), and Wellbutrin (buproprion). All of these antidepressants can cause mood swings in people with bipolar disorders, particularly manic episodes, and should be used in combination with mood stabilizers. If your doctor prescribes one of these drugs, find out as much as you can about its side effects and interaction profile from your physician or a medication reference book.

Of these, Wellbutrin—also sold under the brand name Zyban as an aid to stopping smoking—is most frequently prescribed to persons with bipolar disorders. Some clinicians report that Wellbutrin is less likely to cause mood swings than other antidepressants. However, it does lower the seizure threshold substantially and can increase the incidence of migraines.

George has found that Effexor works better for him than other antidepressants, because it is less likely to cause mood swings:

> The only time I get manic is from tricyclic antidepressants like Elavil—
> but I've had maybe 25 major depressions and just five manic episodes.
> I would go through stages of being mildly depressed, then severely
> depressed, and then hit rock bottom. I don't think there was ever a time
> I could get out of it without help. I've received antidepressants when I've
> been working, and needed for the doctor to get me out of it fast so I could

keep my job. I didn't realize for almost twenty years that antidepressants were a trigger for mania.

It's a very fine line between when you're depressed and then you feel better, and hypomania. It's difficult to separate out what's a level above just feeling better. Most of the time my mania is diagnosed because I get into trouble, such as getting fired from my job or spending a lot of money.

I'm on Effexor now, and I haven't gotten manic with that. I'm told that Wellbutrin doesn't cause mania as easily either.

Neuroleptics

The neuroleptics are also known as antipsychotics. These medications are used to treat a wide variety of serious mental illnesses, but they are certainly not limited to the treatment of outright psychosis. Most of these medications affect dopamine production or absorption; some also work on serotonin or other neurotransmitters.

The very first neuroleptics were discovered in the 1950s and 1960s and represented the first major breakthrough in medical treatment for mental illness. However, the excitement was short-lived when the results of long-term use and overdose were discovered. Although for some patients they may be the only viable choice, most physicians no longer use the older neuroleptics first. These drugs include the following:

Brand name	Generic name	Brand name	Generic name
Haldol	haloperidol	Navane	thiothixene
Largactil	chlorpromazine	Orap	diphenylbutylpiperdine
Loxipac	loxapine	Pimozide	diphenylbutylpiperdine
Loxipax	loxapine	Prolixin	fluphenazine
Loxitane	loxapine	Serenace	haloperidol
Mellaril	thioridazine hydrochloride	Serentil	mesoridazine
Moban	molindone	Stelazine	trifluoperazine
Motipress	loxapine plus nortriptyline (an anti-anxiety drug)	Thorazine	chlorpromazine
		Vesprin	trifluoperazine
Motival	loxapine plus nortriptyline		

Etrafon (amitriptyline/perphenazine, also sold as Triavil) and Trilafon (perphenazine) resemble neuroleptics, but are normally classed as tricyclic antidepressants. They are described earlier in this chapter.

People involved in the care of institutionalized patients have noted that the older neuroleptics are used more often in these settings than one might think, possibly as an inexpensive way to control patients in understaffed or poorly run facilities. Psychiatric nurses derisively refer to this approach as "using a chemical straightjacket." The potential for misuse or overuse of neuroleptics is something you should be on the lookout for.

Side effects to watch out for with all neuroleptic drugs include agranulocytosis (a dramatic drop in white blood cell count), NMS, tardive dyskinesia, and extrapyramidal side effects (see "Major side effects," earlier in this chapter). Some people also have withdrawal dyskinesias: temporary episodes that occur when the medication is stopped and that have symptoms similar to tardive dyskinesia. Excessive weight gain is also a common problem.

The atypical neuroleptics are more recent discoveries. They blend functionality against psychosis, self-injurious behavior, painful movement disorders, and other major mental-health symptoms with far fewer side effects and dangers than their ancestors.

That's not to say that these are safe, gentle drugs: risk is still there, and they do carry side effects that can be a problem (especially rapid weight gain). However, people taking older neuroleptics should definitely ask their physician about making a switch.

The atypical neuroleptic family includes the following medications:

Clozaril

Generic name: Clozapine.

Use: Schizophrenia, psychosis.

Action, if known: This drug works against the neurotransmitters acetylcholine and dopamine.

Side effects: Sedation, fever (this usually passes), changes in blood pressure or heartbeat, overproduction of saliva, and tremor are among the side effects connected with Clozaril. Major dangers include agranulocytosis (a serious blood condition), seizures, NMS, and tardive dyskinesia.

Known interaction hazards: Alcohol, CNS system depressants, drugs for high blood pressure, tricyclic antidepressants, and similar drugs should be avoided or used with caution. The danger of NMS increases when Clozaril is used with lithium.

Tips: Weekly blood tests are recommended for the first year of use, after which every four weeks will suffice if blood levels are stable. Women, people with low white blood-cell counts, and some people of Ashkenazi Jewish descent have a higher risk of agranulocytosis when taking this drug. People with heart disease, glaucoma, prostate trouble, or liver or kidney disease should be monitored carefully. Smoking cigarettes can affect how quickly your body metabolizes Clozaril.

Risperdal

Generic name: Risperidone.

Use: Psychosis, schizophrenia, rage/aggression.

Action, if known: Risperdal affects serotonin and dopamine and raises the level of the hormone prolactin.

Side effects: You may experience sedation, headache, runny nose, anxiety, or insomnia while taking this drug. Weight gain, especially in children, is a concern. Risperdal carries a risk of NMS and tardive dyskinesia.

Known interaction hazards: Risperdal decreases the action of L-Dopa. It interacts with carbamazepine and clozapine. It may strengthen the action of, or be strengthened by, SSRI antidepressants.

Tips: Doctors recommend having an EKG before starting Risperdal and regular heart monitoring while taking it. In some patients, Risperdal (and possibly other atypical neuroleptics) may increase obsessive-compulsive symptoms.

Seroquel

Generic name: Quetiapine.

Use: Psychosis, rage/aggression.

Action, if known: This medication is believed to increase the availability of serotonin and dopamine at specific receptors in the brain.

Side effects: Drowsiness, dizziness, sedation, agitation, nausea, changes in appetite, weight gain or loss, or sexual dysfunction may occur while taking this drug. Seroquel lowers the seizure threshold. It carries a risk of NMS, extrapyramidal side effects, and tardive dyskinesia.

Known interaction hazards: Avoid alcohol and all CNS depressants, including tranquilizers, sedatives, OTC sleep aids, and narcotics. The action of this drug is strengthened to a high degree by phenytoin. Its action may also be strengthened by other drugs, including ketoconazole, erythromycin, clarithromycin, diltiazam, verapamil, and nefazodone. It may interfere with the effects of drugs for high blood pressure.

Tips: Avoid extreme heat while taking this drug. People with liver or kidney problems, heart disease, thyroid problems, or low blood pressure should be monitored while taking Seroquel.

Zeldox, Geodon

Generic name: Ziprasidone.

Use: Schizophrenia, psychosis, rage/aggression.

Action, if known: Zeldox affects the production and use of dopamine, serotonin, and norepinephrine. It also has some antihistamine effects and is an alpha-adrenergic blocker.

Side effects: You may experience drowsiness, dizziness, agitation, tremor, nausea, reduced appetite, lightheadedness, rash, increased light sensitivity, increased blood pressure, or cold-like symptoms while taking Zeldox. It carries a risk of NMS and tardive dyskinesia. Zeldox can lower the seizure threshold.

Known interaction hazards: Avoid alcohol and all CNS depressants, including tranquilizers, sedatives, OTC sleep aids, and narcotics. Zeldox may strengthen the action of drugs that lower your blood pressure, including clonidine and guanfacine. It may counteract L-Dopa and similar drugs. Its action may be strengthened by carbamazepine and ketoconazole. According to its manufacturer, Pfizer, Zeldox is less likely to interact with other medications than other atypical neuroleptics.

Tips: You should have an EKG before starting Zeldox, as well as regular heart monitoring while taking this drug. It should not be used with other drugs that affect the QT interval (a measure of heart function), including quinidine, dofetilide, pimozide, thioridazine, moxifloxacin, and sparfloxicin. It is not recommended for people with existing heart or liver problems or for people with altered electrolyte balance (such as persons with anorexia). This is a very new drug that just received FDA approval for US use in February 2001. According to research carried out by its manufacturer, it is much less likely to cause rapid weight gain than other atypical antipsychotics and may be safer for people who have diabetes or high cholesterol because it has less effect on insulin and cholesterol. Zeldox capsules contain lactose, so if you are lactose intolerant you may want to use a lactose-free version if available. This drug may increase the risk of birth defects in the children of women who take it. Talk to your doctor if you could become pregnant.

Zyprexa

Generic name: Olanzapine.

Use: Psychosis, rage/aggression, tics; also used in cases of hard-to-treat OCD, depression (usually used in conjunction with an antidepressant), or bipolar disorders (usually used with a mood stabilizer).

Action, if known: Zyprexa blocks uptake of dopamine and serotonin at certain receptors and may have other actions. It appears to work well against mania.

Side effects: You may experience headache, agitation, dry mouth, hostility, disinhibition, insomnia, or slurred speech while taking this drug. Other risks include NMS, tardive dyskinesia, dizziness, and seizures.

Known interaction hazards: Avoid alcohol when taking Zyprexa. This drug's action is strengthened by carbamazepine, which in turn strengthens the action of medications for high blood pressure, such as clonidine and guanfacine.

Tips: Avoid extreme heat. If you smoke, you may need to take Zyprexa more frequently, because nicotine increases the metabolism of this drug.

Stimulants

Ritalin and other stimulant drugs are prescribed for ADD or ADHD and sometimes to counteract the sluggish effects of neuroleptics or other medications. Stimulants affect the level of dopamine available at synapses. They are also believed to increase how much norepinephrine is available to the brain and to increase the flow of blood to all parts of the brain.

All of the stimulants work similarly, but for different lengths of time and with varying danger of the dreaded rebound effect. This phenomenon occurs as the effects of a stimulant wear off. Symptoms range from manic-like euphoria to depression or aggression.

Your doctor can address the rebound effect by careful dosing. Ritalin is the shortest-acting stimulant and, therefore, the one with which the greatest amount of rebound trouble occurs. Doctors often ask that it be given at two-and-a-half to three-hour intervals, with half of a regular dose at bedtime to permit better sleep. A sustained-release version of Ritalin, Ritalin SR, is available, but gets low marks from patients when used without adding a second stimulant. Dexedrine has a longer life (four to six hours), and the time-release Dexedrine Spansule formulation can maintain its beneficial effects for up to eight hours.

Stimulants can and do precipitate mania in some people with bipolar disorders. A list of prescription stimulants follows:

Brand name	Generic name	Brand name	Generic name
Adderall	dextroamphetamine/ amphetamine	Dexedrine	dextroamphetamine sulfate
		Dextrostat	dextroamphetamine sulfate
Cylert	pemoline	Ferndex	dextroamphetamine sulfate
Das	dextroamphetamine sulfate	Oxydess	dextroamphetamine sulfate
Desoxyn	methamphetamine, MTH	Ritalin	methylphenidate hydrochloride
Dexampex	dextroamphetamine sulfate		

Many people with bipolar disorders use and abuse OTC stimulants. These include NoDoz, Vivarin, and similar drugs; herbal stimulants like Ma Huang or Happy Camper; and diet pills. Preparations intended for colds, asthma, and allergies may also contain ephedrine, pseudoephedrine, caffeine, cyproheptadine, dextromethorphan, or other CNS stimulants. These drugs can rapidly knock your circadian clock out of rhythm and put you in the fast lane to mania. Many manic episodes have started off with an all-night cram session made possible by a legal stimulant.

Students with bipolar disorders need to develop study skills that make cramming into the wee hours unnecessary—it's literally a survival skill. If your job requires unpredictable late-night hours, ask for an alternative schedule, look for other employment, or talk to your medical team about developing safe coping strategies. Shift work, especially split-shift or revolving shift schedules that prevent your circadian clock from stabilizing in one pattern, can be truly dangerous for people with bipolar disorder.

Educate yourself by reading the labels on all over-the-counter medications and making sure you recognize the names of common stimulants that may wreak havoc with your mental state.

BuSpar (see "Anti-Anxiety medications," later in this chapter) and clonidine or guanfacine are alternatives for treating ADD and ADHD when stimulants are not well-tolerated or advisable.

Drug and alcohol detox/dependency aids

If you have a dual diagnosis of chemical dependency and a bipolar disorder, you will probably need treatment for both conditions at once. This is often difficult if you are not in a hospital or other residential situation where you do not have easy access to drugs or alcohol. Doctors must exercise caution when mixing medications for bipolar symptoms and those for other purposes.

Drug and alcohol withdrawal is a difficult process. Several neural and hormonal systems are affected by substance abuse, and when it ends they are thrown into confusion. Your blood pressure may soar or become unstable, you may sweat profusely or develop tremors, and you may have seizures or hallucinations. Severe nausea, mental difficulties, and physical discomfort or pain are commonplace.

For years, in-patient detox programs have prescribed benzodiazepine tranquilizers as a way to blunt these difficulties. Unfortunately, these medications are also addictive—and may encourage patients to simply trade one addiction for another. They are still widely used to treat withdrawal from methamphetamine and cocaine, however, simply because there are few other medical options.

Methadone treatment is another option for heroin addicts. It involves swapping an illegal addiction for a legal one, which is controversial. However, methadone treatment has been shown to help keep drug addicts away from criminal behavior and to help them become more productive members of society. When combined with counseling and other strategies, it may be a good first step on the road to actual detox. It certainly can improve the patient's health in many ways, because methadone is administered in a clinic, comes in a reliable dose to eliminate the risk of overdose, and is drunk rather than injected. It is the treatment of choice for pregnant addicts.

Cold turkey detox is always an option—and for some people, it works best despite the temporary discomfort. However, today's addiction specialists do have pharmacological tools at their disposal that can ease the pain and suffering of addicts in detox, and help prevent relapses. Intensive rehabilitation centers for people addicted to heroin and other opiates often use a method that involves completely sedating the patient and administering ReVia or another opiate blocker intravenously. Follow-up care consists of continued use of oral opiate blockers, counseling, and peer support groups. Some programs are also experimenting with implanted ReVia.

Some intensive detox programs claim a 75 to 80 percent success rate, although this cannot be confirmed. The cost of such treatment ranges to well over $7,000.

Currently there are no cocaine or methamphetamine blockers (antagonists) available for those who are addicted to these drugs. Unfortunately, these are the drugs of choice for many people with bipolar disorders, probably because of their paradoxically—and temporarily—calming effects on some individuals. Several potential cocaine antagonists are currently under development, but so far there have been many roadblocks in this research. Cocaine works by preventing certain nerve cells from accumulating the neurotransmitter dopamine, making dopamine widely available to the brain and causing a euphoric high. Blocking dopamine entirely produces many ill effects on the body, however.

Heavy methamphetamine and cocaine abusers often experience the symptoms of psychosis. Neuroleptics (see earlier in this chapter) are used to address these symptoms in some addiction treatment centers.

Supplementing with vitamin C, which can counteract the effects of prescription stimulants, may also help recovering methamphetamine addicts.

The SSRI antidepressants, BuSpar, and tricyclic antidepressants (all of which are listed elsewhere in this chapter) have shown some promise in helping recovering alcoholics stay sober and may also be of use to former drug addicts. People with a bipolar disorder and substance abuse problems may find that recovery from substance abuse is easier if they use an antidepressant in addition to their regular mood stabilizer. Some doctors use clonidine or guanfacine during drug or alcohol withdrawal.

Medications that are sometimes used to treat or prevent substance abuse include the following:

Brand name	Generic name	Brand name	Generic name
Acamprosate	calcium acetylhomotaurinate	NTX	naltrexone hydrochloride
Antabuse	disulfiram	ReVex	nalmefene hydrochloride
Calan	verapamil	ReVia	naltrexone hydrochloride
Isoptin	verapamil	Trexan	naltrexone hydrochloride
Narcan	naloxone hydrochloride		

Years ago, verapamil was also used to treat mania.

Anti-anxiety medications

Most of the drugs prescribed for anxiety are in the benzodiazepine family of tranquilizers. Some of these medications may also help to prevent seizures and ease depression. Doctors try to avoid prescribing these for long-term use. Tranquilizers slow down CNS activity, they often don't mix well with other medications, and they can be addictive.

Shannon, age 33, says anxiety has been a persistent part of her challenges, despite the use of mood stabilizers:

> Anxiety has been the most difficult symptom for me, oddly enough, even more so than depression or mania, or even psychosis. Maybe this is because anxiety underlies all of these types of symptoms. When I get depressed, I worry and ruminate about all the evil things I've done in the past. When I'm hypomanic, I tend to be jazzed up in an irritable, nervous, can't-relax way. When I've been psychotic, my paranoid delusions have caused me much anxiety about the terrible things people are saying about me and terrible thoughts of mine that they're picking up. Also, my anxiety makes it difficult for me to cross busy streets and drive a car.

Despite their drawbacks, benzodiazepine tranquilizers can be very effective. Some people can take these on an as-needed basis, avoiding medication dependency and long-term side effects. The following medications are used to treat anxiety.

Ativan

Generic name: Lorazepam.

Use: Anti-anxiety, panic disorder, PMS, and irritable bowel syndrome. It may also be used in acute mania to bring on sleep and stabilize the patient—some doctors prefer Ativan to antipsychotics, which are commonly used for this purpose.

Action, if known: This benzodiazepine tranquilizer slows CNS activity.

Side effects: Sleepiness (this usually passes after a week), lethargy, confusion, headache, slurred speech, and tremor may occur while taking Ativan.

Known interaction hazards: Avoid alcohol, all tranquilizers (including OTC sleep aids), narcotics, MAOIs, antihistamines (including OTC allergy and cold remedies), and antidepressants while taking this drug. Ativan's action is strengthened by cimetidine,

SSRIs, Depakene and Depakote, disulfiram, isoniazid, ketoconazole, metoprolol, probenecid, propoxyphene, propranalol, rifampin, and oral contraceptives. It strengthens the action of digoxin and phenytoin, but decreases the effectiveness of L-Dopa.

Tips: If you smoke, take theophylline drugs, or use antacids, Ativan may be less effective.

BuSpar

Generic name: Buspirone.

Use: Anxiety, decreasing emotional lability or mood swings, ADHD, PMS.

Action, if known: A non-benzodiazepine tranquilizer, BuSpar enhances serotonin transmission, blocks dopamine receptors, and increases metabolism of norepinephrine in the brain.

Side effects: You may experience dizziness, nausea, headache, fatigue, jitteriness, tremor, sore muscles, heart palpitations, or sweating while taking this medication. Other risks include liver or kidney damage and tardive dyskinesia-like movements or tics.

Known interaction hazards: Do not use this drug with an MAOI antidepressant. It strengthens the action of Haldol and possibly other neuroleptics. BuSpar can cause liver inflammation when used with Desyrel. It may have other side effects when used with antidepressants or similar drugs. This medication prolongs the effectiveness of SSRIs and is sometimes prescribed for this specific purpose.

Tips: Side effects are a frequent problem with BuSpar, especially when taken in combination with other medications, including OTC remedies. The BuSpar patch may be better tolerated and smoother-acting than the pill, especially for treatment of ADHD or mood swings. It has been tested with good results for treatment of ADHD without the same rebound effect as Ritalin and for treating anxiety and irritability. Many physicians like to prescribe BuSpar rather than benzodiazepine tranquilizers, because it is not addictive.

Centrax

Generic name: Prazepam.

Use: Anti-anxiety, muscle spasm, seizures, panic disorder, irritable bowel syndrome.

Action, if known: This benzodiazepine tranquilizer slows CNS activity.

Side effects: Sleepiness (this usually passes after a week), lethargy, confusion, headache, slurred speech, or tremor may occur.

Known interaction hazards: Alcohol, all tranquilizers (including OTC sleep aids), narcotics, MAOIs, antihistamines (including OTC allergy and cold remedies), and antidepressants can interact dangerously with Centrax. Its action is strengthened by cimetidine, disulfiram, SSRIs, Depakene and Depakote, disulfiram, isoniazid, ketoconazole, metoprolol, probenecid, propoxyphene, propranalol, rifampin, and oral contraceptives. It strengthens the action of digoxin and phenytoin, but decreases the effectiveness of L-Dopa.

Tips: Many people should not take Centrax, including people with severe depression, lung disease, liver or kidney disease, sleep apnea, alcoholism, or psychosis. It is intended for short-term use. If you smoke, take theophylline medications, or use antacids, Centrax may be less effective.

Librium

Generic name: Chlordiazepoxide.

Use: Anxiety, panic attacks, irritable bowel syndrome.

Action, if known: A benzodiazepine tranquilizer, Librium depresses CNS activity.

Side effects: You may experience sedation (this should pass), depression, stupor, headache, tremor, dry mouth, or sexual dysfunction while taking Librium.

Known interaction hazards: Avoid other CNS depressants, including alcohol, narcotics, tranquilizers (including OTC sleep aids), MAOIs, antidepressants, and both prescription and OTC antihistamines while taking Librium. Do not take this drug with antacids. It strengthens the action of digoxin and phenytoin, but reduces the potency of L-Dopa.

Tips: Many people should not take Librium, including people with severe depression, lung disease, liver or kidney disease, sleep apnea, alcoholism, or psychosis. It is intended for short-term use. Smoking may reduce the effectiveness of Librium.

Serax

Generic name: Oxazepam.

Use: Anxiety, muscle spasm, seizures, panic disorder, irritable bowel syndrome.

Action, if known: This benzodiazepine tranquilizer slows CNS activity.

Side effects: Sleepiness (this usually passes after a week), lethargy, confusion, headache, slurred speech, or tremor are among the side effects reported.

Known interaction hazards: Alcohol, all tranquilizers (including OTC sleep aids), narcotics, MAOIs, antihistamines (including OTC allergy and cold remedies), and antidepressants can interact dangerously with this drug. Its action is strengthened by cimetidine, disulfiram, SSRIs, Depakene and Depakote, isoniazid, ketoconazole, metoprolol, probenecid, propoxyphene, propranalol, rifampin, and oral contraceptives. It increases the action of digoxin and phenytoin, but decreases the effectiveness of L-Dopa.

Tips: Many people should not take Serax, including people with severe depression, lung disease, liver or kidney disease, sleep apnea, alcoholism, or psychosis. It is intended for short-term use. If you smoke, take theophylline drugs, or use antacids, Serax may be less effective.

Tranxene

Generic name: Clorazepate.

Use: Anxiety, panic disorder, irritable bowel syndrome.

Action, if known: As a benzodiazepine tranquilizer, Tranxene slows CNS activity.

Side effects: Drowsiness (this should pass), confusion, tremor, dizziness, or depression may occur in association with this drug.

Known interaction hazards: Do not take Tranxene with antacids. Alcohol and other CNS depressants, tranquilizers (including OTC sleep aids), narcotics, barbiturates, MAOIs, antihistamines (including cold and allergy medications), and antidepressants all interact negatively with Tranxene. This drug strengthens the action of digoxin and phenytoin. Its action is strengthened by cimetidine, disulfiram, fluoxetine, isoniazid, ketoconazole, metoprolol, probenecid, propoxyphene, propranolol, rifampin, and Depakote or Depakene.

Tips: You should not take Tranxene if you have lung, liver, or kidney disease; psychosis; or depression. It is intended for short-term use. Smoking may interfere with the action of Tranxene.

Valium

Generic name: Diazepam.

Use: Anxiety, muscle spasm, seizures, panic disorder, irritable bowel syndrome.

Action, if known: A benzodiazepine tranquilizer, Valium slows CNS activity.

Side effects: You may experience sleepiness (this usually passes after a week), lethargy, confusion, headache, slurred speech, or tremor while taking this medication.

Known interaction hazards: Alcohol, all other tranquilizers (including OTC sleep aids), narcotics, MAOIs, antihistamines (including OTC allergy and cold remedies), and antidepressants can interact dangerously with this drug. Valium's activity is strengthened by cimetidine, disulfiram, SSRIs, Depakote and Depakene, disulfiram, isoniazid, ketoconazole, metoprolol, probenecid, propoxyphene, propranalol, rifampin, and oral contraceptives. It strengthens the action of digoxin and phenytoin, but decreases the effectiveness of L-Dopa.

Tips: Many people should not take Valium, including people with severe depression, lung disease, liver or kidney disease, sleep apnea, alcoholism, or psychosis. Valium is intended for short-term use. If you smoke, take theophylline medications, or use antacids, Valium may be less effective.

Xanax

Generic name: Alprazolam.

Use: Anxiety, panic disorder, PMS, irritable bowel syndrome.

Action, if known: This benzodiazepine tranquilizer slows CNS activity.

Side effects: Sleepiness (this usually passes after a week), lethargy, confusion, headache, slurred speech, and tremor are among the side effects reported by persons taking Xanax.

Known interaction hazards: Do not use this drug with alcohol, tranquilizers of any kind (including over-the-counter sleep aids), MAOIs, antihistamines (including OTC allergy and cold medicines), or antidepressants, unless under strict medical supervision.

Tips: Many people should not take Xanax, including people with severe depression, sleep apnea, liver or kidney disease, lung disease, alcoholism, or psychosis.

New drugs for bipolar disorders

Most of the drugs likely to gain approval as treatments for bipolar disorders are currently in use as antiseizure drugs. Many of these (Tegretol and Neurontin, for example) are already widely used to treat symptoms associated with bipolar disorders, even though they have not been FDA-approved for this purpose.

Some of the newest antiseizure drugs appear to have particular promise. One of these, Keppra (levetiracetam), is currently undergoing clinical trials as a treatment for bipolar disorders. It has a novel antiseizure action and a much lower risk of side effects than most other drugs in its category. A few doctors are already prescribing this medication to people with bipolar disorders, and early reports are promising.

Another interesting class of drugs is the beta-adrenergic blockers. These medications were originally developed to treat high blood pressure, but have since been found useful on an off-label basis for a number of neuropsychiatric conditions, including ADHD and Tourette's syndrome. They include clonidine (Catapres), guanfacine (Tenex), and propranolol (Inderal). Clonidine is also an alpha-2 agonist, and has been shown to have good anti-manic properties in one clinical trial.[9] Guanfacine, on the other hand, may actually induce manic episodes in some persons. See the section "Other medications" earlier in this chapter for more information about some of these drugs.

Some clinical investigation has been done on calcium channel blockers as a treatment for bipolar disorders. You may have noticed that these medications interact with many established treatments, such as lithium, often strengthening their effect. So far, research indicates that some people do achieve improved mood stabilization with these medications alone.[10] For others, they might be used to deliberately strengthen the therapeutic activity of a mainstream mood stabilizer with a lower risk of side effects. These medications may be especially helpful for people who experience ultra-rapid mood cycles.

A few other medications have been suggested over the years as perhaps having effectiveness for bipolar disorders. These include acetazolamide (Diamox), a carbonic anhydrase inhibitor; anticholinesterase inhibitors such as donepezil (Aricept); and mexiletine (Mexitil).[11]

Some possible treatments have not yet made their way out of the lab. For example, researchers are looking into medications that affect the GABA receptors without causing the addiction risks and side effects of current medications in this class, such as Gabitril and the benzodiazepine tranquilizers. Others are trying to understand how existing treatments, such as lithium, actually work. This type of research may result in new variants of existing drugs that are more effective and safer.

Treatment of depression after mood stabilization is another big issue among people with bipolar disorders. All of the current antidepressants have the potential to cause manic episodes, although they can sometimes be successfully added to a mood stabilizer. A new type of antidepressant called a substance P blocker may eventually be used. It blocks a different brain chemical than today's SSRI, tricyclic, and MAOI antidepressants. Substance P blockers are not yet commercially available, but this area of research bears watching.

Other medications may be prescribed to treat specific symptoms. One group of these, estrogen and related hormones used to treat menstrual irregularities, are discussed in more detail in Chapter 6, *Complementary Therapies.*

Immune system therapies

For decades, people with bipolar disorders have been telling their doctors that they also have other health problems and expressing a feeling that these issues might be related to their mood swings. Serious research on the effect of immune-system dysregulation on mood has finally begun and is already producing interesting results. Specifically, researchers have now found abnormal levels of cytokines, chemicals produced by the immune system that also interact with neurotransmitters, and a higher than normal rate of autoimmune thyroid disorders in persons with bipolar disorders.[12,13] Doctors treating immune disorders, particularly lupus and AIDS, are certainly well aware that mood swings are sometimes a symptom of underlying infection or autoimmune problems.[14,15]

For most bipolar people who experience immune system problems, the issues are minor, nagging, and hard to get a handle on. They get sick a lot and don't get well easily. They experience worse mood swings when ill—or have unexplained remission from psychiatric symptoms while physically ill. For these individuals, lifestyle changes and, perhaps, medications or supplements aimed at gently boosting immune system function may help.

When mood problems are secondary to an infectious illness like AIDS or an autoimmune disorder like lupus, the diagnosis should be "organic mood syndrome." However, it's likely that at least some people are given a psychiatric diagnosis long before the underlying immune system problem is discovered, and it's certainly possible for one person to have both an immune system problem and a bipolar disorder without one causing the other.

This was the case for Randy, age 39, who now works hard to cope with both bipolar disorder and lupus:

> My bipolar disorder diagnosis came many years before I found out that I had systemic lupus erythematosus (SLE), and my bipolar mood swings were brought under control with the classic meds for a year and a half before the SLE started. My SLE hasn't included any clear CNS involvement.
>
> My doctors have been very savvy, and of course view the whole set of presenting symptoms. But perhaps equally important, they and I are confident in my ability to tell the difference between the irrational and horrible depths of the depressive phase of bipolar disorder and the depression that comes with SLE, more as a result of increased pain and fatigue or lack of sleep. Both are aware that the psychiatric symptoms have to be viewed in the context of my SLE activity.
>
> My rheumatologist and psychiatrist have consulted on a number of occasions, and I tell each about what's going on with the other's treatment as well as my status with both illnesses at every visit.
>
> Prednisone and I are not very compatible. At about 35 mgs a day I not only get the feeling of being "wired" and nervous, but I quickly start to space out. So far my SLE has been mild enough that, combined with the usual Plaquenil (hydroxychloroquine) and Ultram (tramadol) for pain, as well as weekly methotrexate (Rheumatrex) injections, I'm able to keep the prednisone dose low.

Unfortunately, treatment for infectious and autoimmune disorders can interfere with treatment of bipolar symptoms. For example, immune-suppression chemotherapy, such as the administration of steroids like prednisone, is common for treating lupus. However, steroids can cause the onset of mania. Mood stabilization becomes extremely important in such cases, along with careful supervision of treatment. Pulse (intermittent) dosing with steroids may be less likely to cause mood swings, although the jury's still out.

When there are issues of viral infection, treatments are occasionally synergistic. For example, recent research indicates that lithium combined with Zidovudine (AZT) may be an effective drug cocktail for AIDS.[16] Normally, HIV infection is treated with a combination of three or more antiretroviral drugs, usually including one of the HIV protease inhibitors. That is still the treatment of choice for most persons with both AIDS and a bipolar disorder—but your doctor can add lithium safely, and even beneficially, to a standard HIV drug combo.

AZT and some other AIDS medications can themselves cause increased anxiety or other psychiatric symptoms, so be sure to talk to your doctor about any new or newly increased mental health problems you may have while taking these drugs.

Unfortunately, persons with bipolar disorder are at heightened risk for AIDS, presumably because of high-risk behaviors such as drug use or impulsive sexual behavior. Recent statistics indicate that between 4 and 23 percent of persons with severe and persistent mental illness (a category that includes many people with bipolar disorders) are also positive for the HIV virus.[17] For the past couple of years, the US National Institutes of Health has been funding new research on helping people with a dual diagnosis of HIV infection and major mental illness. It may be some years before these studies are used to create better prevention, treatment, and support programs, however.

Having an untreated bipolar disorder increases your risk of getting or transmitting the AIDS virus and of contracting dangerous secondary infections, because risky behaviors like unprotected sex and sharing needles are more likely to occur when you are depressed or manic. Mood swings also increase your risk of not taking anti-HIV medications regularly, which can worsen the course of the disorder. If you are living with AIDS, be sure to seek the help of a clinician who is experienced with managing both antiretroviral and mood stabilizing drugs, and ask about support programs in your community.

People with HIV are at special risk of harm from viral infections that can affect the central nervous system, such as some herpes viruses and toxoplasmosis. These viruses can also attack people who do not have AIDS, however, and occasionally may cause bipolar-like symptoms.[18,19,20] For these conditions, antiviral drugs are prescribed. As with antiretroviral drugs, these medications may actually be complemented rather than counteracted by lithium.

Fibromyalgia and chronic fatigue immune dysfunction syndrome (CFIDS) are two illnesses reported more frequently by persons with bipolar disorders than among those without. Indeed, the medical literature on CFIDS specifically states that many people who have been diagnosed with chronic fatigue actually have bipolar disorder instead—but might it sometimes be the other way around, or might the two sometimes be intertwined?

Because these disorders are still poorly defined, treatment options are not set in stone. Stress reduction and lifestyle changes are beneficial to many; others report improvement from a wide variety of drugs. Neurontin and Tegretol have been used, as have antidepressants, antivirals, and pain medication.

Sometimes a single treatment may help with both mood swings and the symptoms of fatigue, pain, and neurological dysfunction associated with fibromyalgia and chronic fatigue syndrome. As in other cases of dual diagnosis, however, you may find your treatments work against each other. For example, pain medications used to treat fibromyalgia can interact with many medications used to treat bipolar disorders and may increase your risk of depression. As mentioned earlier in this section, some antiviral drugs can also affect mood.

As of yet, there isn't much medical literature available on living with immune system disorders and a bipolar disorder. Some web sites covering this situation do exist and may help you find support and information on the latest research (although they are no substitute for medical advice). A list of these sites follows:

Center for Mental Health Research on AIDS
http://www.nimh.nih.gov/oa/mentill.htm

Fibromyalgia and Bipolar Disorder
http://www.pendulum.org/related/FMS/

Lupus and Bipolar Disorder
http://www.geocities.com/HotSprings/Spa/4816/

Thyroid Problems in Bipolar Disorder
http://people.ne.mediaone.net/pmbrig/BP_pharm.html#thyroxine

One area of immune system impairment where clinicians have no doubt about a bipolar disorders link is thyroid dysfunction.[21] People with the rapid cycling variant of bipolar disorder are especially likely to have thyroid problems.[22] In addition, taking lithium can depress thyroid hormone levels. In either case, supplementing with thyroid hormone is a viable option. Information about thyroid hormone replacement follows.

Thyroid hormone replacements (Armour, Cytomel, Euthroid, S-P-T, Thyroid Strong, Thyrar, and more)

Generic name: Levothyroxine (T4), liothyronine (T3).

Use: Thyroid disorders, mood disorders that do not respond to conventional treatment, as an adjunct to antidepressants. T4 is used as an adjuvant (additional) medication for persons with rapid-cycling bipolar disorder, in which case the dose given is somewhat higher than the usual amount suggested for thyroid disorders. T3 is used as an adjuvant treatment for both unipolar and bipolar depression, in doses about the same as those used for thyroid disorders.

Action, if known: These medications replace deficient natural hormones, helping to address the effects of improper thyroid function. Thyroid hormones affect noradrenergic receptor sensitivity, increase the efficiency of noradrenergic neurotransmission, and probably have many other effects.

Side effects: Taking thyroid hormone supplements may negatively affect your body's natural production of thyroid hormone. Overdose symptoms include headache, irritability, nervousness, sweating, and irregular heartbeat—call your doctor if these continue over a period of time.

Known interaction hazards: Do not use these products when taking maprotiline. Thyroid hormones make antidepressants have a stronger effect (and are sometimes used for this specific reason). They also interact with other hormone supplements, including estrogen, birth control pills, and insulin. Aspirin and other salicytates may strengthen the activity of thyroid hormones. Thyroid hormones reduce the effectiveness of some beta-blockers and may strengthen the action of theophylline drugs. Avoid vitamin formulas that contain iron when taking thyroid hormones—iron can block their action.

Tips: Regular blood tests are needed to monitor thyroid hormones. Some people have an allergic skin reaction to thyroid hormone. According to some clinicians, supplementing with T3 or T3 plus T4 is more effective than T4 alone.

Hospitalization

Today, many people with bipolar disorders will never need to see the inside of a mental hospital. Outpatient treatment is readily available and often very effective. However, there are several situations that call for hospitalization, including the following. In most cases, only the first two can be used to start an involuntary hospitalization process:

- Being a danger to yourself, either through suicide threats or attempts or through serious self-injurious behavior

- Being a danger to others because of aggressive, assaultive behavior or serious threats

- Being in an acute manic, depressed, or mixed state that cannot be safely managed at home with the addition of more or different medication and extra support services

- Suffering from severe medication reactions or unusual symptoms that are too difficult medically to handle at home

- Experiencing severe and medication-resistant seizures, for those who have epilepsy in addition to a bipolar disorder

- Having an eating disorder that does not respond to outpatient treatment

- Having a need for intense medical supervision during the substance abuse detox process

Of course, people with bipolar disorders may also fall victim to disease or injury that's not psychiatric in nature. When these problems require hospitalization, confer with the staff to ensure that your diagnosis and current medical treatments are thoroughly understood and that your needs for medication management, therapy, and other services are met in the hospital during your recovery.

Emergency care

If you have been injured due to a suicide attempt, self-injurious behavior, medication or drug overdose, or a reckless bipolar-related accident and need immediate medical care, go directly to the nearest emergency room. Call your psychiatrist to let him know what's going on. It's a good idea if a friend or family member can come with you until a professional who knows you well arrives. Your behaviors and state of mind may be puzzling to workers in the ER. Sometimes patients who come in with self-inflicted injuries are denigrated or forced to wait longer than others by poorly educated medical personnel. The presence of a familiar physician, friend, or relative who can advocate for proper care should help.

When you go to the ER, bring along any medications, supplements, and herbal remedies that you use. If you have recently used any illegal drugs or alcohol, let the emergency room personnel know about it right away. These things affect what medical intervention they can safely use. You may also want to bring a book, a Walkman with tapes of soothing music, and a change of clothes in case you need to be admitted overnight (or longer). If there's no time to collect these items, don't worry—you can have someone else deliver them to you later at the hospital when the situation stabilizes.

You may have to wait a long time to see someone in the ER, especially if it's a busy weekend night or most personnel are attending to car accident victims and other life or death emergencies. Probably the first person you'll see is an intake worker, who will get your identifying and health insurance information.

After intake, you should next see a triage nurse, who's specially trained to assess the severity of your injury or illness. Let this person know what your greatest concerns are, especially if you feel you could be a danger to yourself or others. At this point a decision will be made about whether to admit you to the hospital's emergency room or send you home.

Once you have been formally admitted to the ER, you'll see a doctor and/or nurses. They may take your blood pressure; check your heartbeat; take blood or urine samples to test for drugs, alcohol, lithium toxicity, infection, or other issues; and give emergency medical treatment, including medication. Make sure you understand what drugs are given, especially if you are released immediately after treatment rather than being held for observation.

Keeping a crisis from becoming an emergency

When you need expert help fast, it's very reassuring if you already know what to do, where to go, and whom to see. Because episodes of high—and even sudden—need for medical care are a characteristic of bipolar disorders, it helps to have a plan worked out in advance. When you are affected by a serious episode of mania or depression and want to do something before it becomes an emergency, you'll feel reassured to have a plan in hand.

When you are in crisis, the best place to start is your psychiatrist's office. Call and ask for an emergency evaluation. If it is after hours or your psychiatrist is unavailable, call your primary care provider, general practitioner, or HMO and ask for an immediate appointment or referral. In some cases you should go to the ER for safety's sake until a doctor can arrive to evaluate you.

Tony, age 31, had a psychiatrist who helped him get hospital treatment when he was faced with a suicide crisis:

> After an extended manic episode, I crashed, and I kept going into a depression. I got very desperate and I didn't know if I would end up killing myself. I was seeing a psychiatrist fairly regularly, and one day I just admitted that I didn't know if I could take it anymore. I was checked in as a risk to myself, and was admitted to the hospital.
>
> I was put on suicide watch—this is where the nurse comes in every fifteen minutes to see if you are still alive. It took a few weeks, but I gradually started functioning again.
>
> I was there for six weeks. They used Effexor in the hospital to lift my depression, and discontinued it once that was done. I have been on mood stabilizers ever since.
>
> I missed a few months' work due to my hospital stay, but I am fortunate that the drugs I am taking now seem to be effective. If you reach your psychiatrist or doctor, he should ask you to come in immediately if the situation warrants it. If you think you'll need help getting to his office, say so—he may be able to send a mental health aide or other staff member to assist you. If this kind of help is not available through his office, ask your spouse, other relatives, friends, neighbors, or even the police for help. In some areas your county or provincial mental health department can send someone out to help you get to an urgent care appointment or the hospital.

Some larger cities have a separate crisis triage center for people with mental health issues. In a mental health crisis triage center, trained personnel are on staff 24 hours a day to deal with crisis situations. Psychiatrists, appropriate medications, and security measures are on hand to meet your needs. Whenever possible, the environment is carefully constructed to be as peaceful, quiet, and non-threatening as possible—just the kind of place you would want to be if you were in emotional pain.

At these facilities, a mental health triage specialist will usually meet with you within just a few minutes. As in an ER, the triage nurse will assess your condition and start the process of obtaining emergency treatment. Vital signs checks, blood and urine samples, and interviews are often performed quickly.

Whether you go to your psychiatrist's office, the ER, or a mental health triage center, the criteria for hospital admission is largely the same. If you are stabilized there, you may go home right afterward. Otherwise, the facility can hold you for overnight observation or admit you for short- or long-term treatment.

People with HMOs or managed care plans are sometimes required to jump through some hoops to get urgent care treatment or hospital admission. Many people have reported that it's extremely hard to get admitted even when you are a suicide risk or your family is in danger from violent actions. Others note that some facilities release people far too early, often due less to positive treatment outcomes than to negative news from the insurance company. Your doctor is your most important ally when you need immediate help, hospital admission, or permission for a longer stay.

Psychiatric facilities

There are many different types of hospitals for psychiatric care. Most are a special psychiatric wing at a local hospital. These mental health units are usually locked wards, both to protect the patients themselves and to prevent escape. They are designed mostly for short-term care, giving doctors a safe place to observe people for a few days or weeks.

People in need of long-term hospitalization may be sent to a standalone mental health facility. Choices include private facilities, therapeutic residential care facilities that specialize in treating people with mental illness, and public mental hospitals. Generally speaking, public mental hospitals in the US get only the most difficult-to-treat cases, along with uninsured patients. This is not necessarily the case elsewhere in the world, where publicly funded mental health care may be available to all citizens.

The type of facility matters far less than the appropriateness of its program. All staff members should be knowledgeable about the latest advances in treatment, and the facility should offer therapy options that are appropriate for each person's needs. Programs should have considerable resources for treating drug and alcohol addiction when it occurs along with psychiatric problems. They should be ready and willing to work closely with family members and other outside helpers. Cleanliness and basic safety are important issues too, as are human decency and kindness.

A lot of the time you have to go with your gut instinct. If the staff members you meet appear to be well-trained, competent, and gentle with the people in their care, that's a good sign, as is the presence of a sense of humor and a genuine caring attitude.

If you have time, talk to your local NAMI or NDMDA chapter to get other opinions about facilities you are considering. If you are difficult to treat with the usual medications and therapies, you may want to consider a research-oriented hospital, up to and including the special bipolar disorders unit at the National Institute of Mental Health in Bethesda, MD.

Programs vary greatly, as does their expertise with bipolar disorders. Talk to the head of the program about their typical treatment program for people with your specific diagnosis. Also ask how they will involve your regular psychiatrist, therapist, other outside mental health providers such as a county social worker, and family members.

When you are being cared for in a high-quality hospital or residential care facility, you should feel reasonably comfortable with the situation. The environment should be not unlike any other kind of hospital. It'll probably be less sterile than some, in fact. The food may be a drag, as hospital food usually is. You will probably chafe at some of the rules, too. Many psychiatric units have regulations about appearance, smoking, language, and activities.

When you are first admitted you may not be able to see friends and family members for a period of time, possibly based on your behavior on the ward. If a spouse or relative will be helping to care for you after your release, however, he should be able to meet with the staff during this period and start planning the treatment and after-care program.

If you are in the hospital for a long time or have been admitted before, you will probably adjust to the routine quite well.

You may be disturbed or frightened by the behavior of some other patients. Most psychiatric facilities care for people with a wide variety of conditions, ranging from eating disorders to active psychosis to neurological problems like autism or Tourette's syndrome. Some people will probably be very, very ill. Others will be well on their way to recovery. Talk to your doctor or therapist about anything you see or hear that bothers you. Information about other mental illnesses or neurological disorders should be able to help you better understand what your fellow patients may be experiencing and make the experience of living with them less traumatic.

A good hospital is probably the safest place to be while in a mental or medical health crisis. Medication reactions can be carefully observed, therapy can be delivered on a daily basis, and concerned professionals can design an ongoing treatment and recovery plan.

Hospital problems

For many of us, our image of a mental hospital comes from old movies like *The Snake Pit,* depictions of past years' horrors in films like *Frances* (the story of actress Frances Farmer), or books by people who suffered in horrid institutions. Today, there are many good hospital programs, but there are still some that verge on the criminal. Danger signs include frequent use of physical restraints and isolation rooms to control "dangerous" patients, a reliance on psychoanalysis as the primary cure for major mental illnesses, lack of knowledge about the most current medications, and poor relationships with family members and other outside care providers.

Stephanie, age 32, has unpleasant memories of one such hospital:

> *I would avoid state institutions at any cost. I was watched by a male nurse when I showered. The nurses locked themselves in a glass room, and talked and played cards. The only interaction between them and us was when they handed out meds. I was afraid of being killed by a fellow patient (I almost said inmate!) After almost two days of no sleep due to that fear, a guy I made friends with sat outside my room watching so I could sleep safely. This was not deranged paranoia—this was a very, very scary place.*

Certain treatments used in mental hospitals, or used long ago, have gained notoriety. These include electroconvulsive ("shock") therapy, insulin shock therapy, wet sheet packs, aversives, restraints, and isolation. Any program that relies heavily on these is substandard and should be avoided at all costs.

Electroconvulsive therapy (ECT)

Also called electroshock therapy, this intervention is what many patients fear most when admitted to a hospital for treatment of a mental illness. Scenes from *One Flew Over the Cuckoo's Nest* come to mind, and at the time that book and film were written, those scenes were a grim reality in many mental hospitals. Until the mid-1970s, ECT was used indiscriminately and even punitively in many mental hospitals.

Stephanie tells about her ECT experience:

> *I was hospitalized five or six times in a four-and-a-half year period. I was given everything, none of which worked very well. I also received two series of ECT therapy, in two rounds, for a total of thirty-two treatments.*

ECT is still in use today, still controversial, and probably sometimes misused. However, it remains a treatment option that helps many bipolar patients who have drug-resistant mania or severe, delusional depression. Statistically speaking, ECT is a very effective and safe treatment for depression in adults.

ECT induces a seizure through application of a low-level electric shock to the brain. The patient is given a relaxing medication, so the seizure should not cause pain. Retrograde amnesia almost always prevents memory of the actual ECT and seizure. It occasionally wipes out some other memories, however.

NAMI has been involved for many years in encouraging further study and regulation of ECT. You can learn more about its efforts at *http://www.nami.org/helpline/ect.htm*. Other advocacy groups have sought to limit or ban its use.

Insulin shock

Early in this century physicians discovered that giving schizophrenic or psychotic patients massive doses of the pancreatic hormone insulin—enough to cause convulsions or even coma—seemed to cure some of them. This therapy has not been used in the US or Europe for many years, but was used up into the 1970s and may still be current in other countries. It did appear to work for some patients, at least on a short-term basis, but it could also easily cause death and its use was long ago eclipsed by advances in medical care.

Hydrotherapy

Hydrotherapy, the use of water in some form to ease mental distress, is probably one of the oldest remedies around. The efficacy of lithium springs was probably enhanced by the beneficial effects of a long, relaxing soak. Hydrotherapy is still a mainstay of treatment in many Russian, Eastern European, and Asian mental hospitals, particularly where modern pharmaceuticals are hard to obtain. It is also widely used by naturopathic doctors and other alternative practitioners. Many patients give high marks to warm soaks, some types of wet wraps or compresses, and steam baths as being gentle adjuncts to medications or other treatments.

A particular type of hydrotherapy called wet sheet packs is still used in some US and Canadian facilities to calm manic patients. It involves wrapping the patient tightly in cold, wet sheets. Most people who have actually experienced this practice describe it as uncomfortable and invasive. It is no longer considered proper medical practice.

Aversives

Many mental health facilities use behavior modification techniques to control and improve patient behavior. Linking privileges or rewards with desired behaviors is an example of positive behavior modification. Some facilities do use aversives, however, which can range from removal of privileges on up to mild electric shocks. For obvious reasons, no aversive technique with the capacity to cause physical harm or more than momentary emotional distress should be employed. If this is not the case in a particular facility, most experts would agree that patients are being abused.

Restraints

Restraints are sometimes a necessary part of mental health care when a patient is truly dangerous to himself or others. They are also potentially deadly: every year about fifty mental patients die while restrained in the US, often as a result of suffocation, strangulation, or deliberate self-harm using the restraint mechanism.

If you ever need to be restrained temporarily, you should in no circumstances be left alone and unobserved. Nor should restraints be used as a regular method of "treatment" (they do nothing to treat mental illness), as punishment, or as a substitute for supervision. All too often, restraints are a sign that other forms of care are unavailable or ineffective.

Isolation

Most mental health facilities do have isolation facilities for temporarily containing violent or suicidal people. This should be their sole function, and staff should not leave unobserved patients in isolation. The "rubber room" or padded cell should never be used as a threat, punishment, or routine behavior-control device.

After the hospital

What happens after you leave a hospital or residential care center is almost as important as what happened inside. Without follow-up care, failure is far more likely. The hospital may begin to look preferable to suffering through life on the outside.

Stephanie tells what happened for her when this step was missed:

> I liked the hospital... I would do things to get sent back: cut my wrists, act up in school, etc. I was so miserable inside, but at the hospital, there were people around all the time so I did not feel so lonely. If I could not

sleep, I could play cards or shoot pool with a night nurse. It was my safe haven, and I would act out just enough while I was in there to avoid being discharged.

When you are released, you should have a realistic and complete treatment plan in hand, including full information about any medications you are taking and a schedule of appointments with outside providers. These will include monthly visits with a psychiatrist, psychopharmacologist, or other doctor to manage your new medication, and therapy appointments as needed.

Arrangements for vocational rehabilitation, housing, and other services recommended by the hospital team or necessary for your recovery should also be in place when you leave—and perhaps already started, if practical. Aside from medical intervention and appointments with doctors and therapists, you need to have support that comes from family and peers. If relationships with family members have been stressed by your illness, ask your therapist for help—preferably direct help, such as counseling for all parties. Joining peer support groups or taking advantage of a drop-in center or clubhouse where you can support and be supported by peers who are also in recovery from mental illness can be invaluable. Chapter 5 discusses peer support in more detail.

Most people go directly from the hospital to home, but some have an intermediate stay in a halfway house, supported living community, or other residential center.

Another option is moving from an in-patient unit into a day treatment facility. Day treatment patients live at home, but spend their days in a therapeutic center where they can be carefully monitored and cared for. Some day treatment centers are strongly medical in nature and may be located inside a hospital. Others are stand-alone facilities.

CHAPTER 5

Talk Therapy

MEDICATION ALONE can help reduce the symptoms of bipolar disorder, but it can't cure the illness entirely. Nor can it help you cope with the stress, alienation, and residual symptoms that remain. That's where therapy—the process of exploring feelings, motivations, strategies for change, and personal goals with a trained professional—comes in. Therapy is also not a cure, but when done well, it can contribute greatly to better personal functioning and happiness.

This chapter explains what therapy is, what kinds of professionals work in the field, how to find a therapist, and who can benefit from therapy. It also defines some of the major styles of therapy.

What is therapy?

From time immemorial, people have known about the healing power of a listening ear, a shoulder to cry on, and wise advice. These resources have always been prized, whether they were offered by family members, friends, or religious advisors.

The industrial revolution of the late nineteenth century changed the way people relate to each other, and it also made life more stressful and complex. Many people began looking for professional advisors, and often the person they turned to was a trusted physician. Some physicians did have a high level of expertise at helping people handle everyday emotional problems and did so as a matter of course as they treated their physical troubles. Some, like Austrian neurologist Sigmund Freud, became especially fascinated with the serious life difficulties faced by people with major mental illness.

When Freud and his circle of European colleagues founded the modern practice of psychoanalysis in the late 1800s, not much was known about mental illness, and no effective treatments existed. The Freudians identified many emotional disorders that they believed were based on unresolved sexual conflicts, difficult life experiences, and constitutional weakness. The psychoanalytic process they developed to address these difficulties used conversations between patients and therapists about childhood memories, dreams, and current experiences to uncover the causes of problems and find avenues for healing.

Because many of the thoughts and behaviors associated with major mental illnesses actually came from chemical imbalances, however, efforts at ferreting out their roots in childhood traumas were fruitless. Freud himself believed that bipolar disorders, schizophrenia, and some other major mental illnesses were biological in nature, largely because he found that long-term psychoanalysis didn't seem to help those affected very much. To benefit from psychoanalysis, it seemed to him, the person had to have a great deal of insight into the roots of unusual thoughts or behaviors, not just a desire to change.[1]

That's not to say that no one tried to apply psychoanalysis to major mental illness. Freud treated a few very disturbed patients, with predictably poor results (some of which he did not report accurately, leading later practitioners to think he had succeeded). As psychoanalysis grew as a field, many analysts did start touting it as an effective treatment for major mental illness, despite contrary evidence.

People with bipolar disorders often found the psychoanalytic process enlightening on a personal level, but it rarely afforded any reduction in troublesome symptoms. With the advent of psychiatric medication in the '50s and '60s, and the first glimmerings of other types of psychological therapy around the same time, other options became available.

Modern therapy choices

Today, it's a rare person with bipolar disorder who would look at psychoanalysis as a first-line intervention. Combining medication with highly practical forms of talk therapy appears to get the best possible results. The types of talk therapy often used include the following:

- Cognitive therapy
- Family therapy, including the behavioral family management model
- Interpersonal and social rhythm therapy
- Behavior modification
- Group therapy
- Peer-to-peer support

All of these approaches share one basic characteristic with psychoanalysis: they rely on forging a strong relationship between people to lay the groundwork for change.

Unlike psychoanalysis, however, these methods don't delve into the metaphysical or unconscious aspects of thought patterns and behaviors.

Instead, these disciplines address specific symptoms with targeted intervention techniques. Clients may even have homework assignments that involve applying the lessons learned in therapy to real life. In most cases, intervention is seen as a short-term process, although because of the chronic and fluctuating nature of their illness, many people with manic depression will need ongoing therapeutic help. The section "Therapy styles" later in this chapter provides details about each of these methods.

Some therapists are specialists in a particular method. Jungian therapists use psychoanalysis-like techniques based on the theories of Freud's contemporary, Carl Jung. Gestalt therapists specialize in helping people uncover and meet hidden needs (encounter groups and sensitivity training are two Gestalt-related ideas that were popular in the '60s and '70s) and fall into the general category of humanistic or experiential therapy. Holistic psychologists or therapists suggest diet changes, meditation, and other interventions; they are discussed in Chapter 6, *Complementary Therapies*. There are many other specialized therapy styles. Most of these methods, although interesting, have not been proven useful for treating bipolar disorders.

Many therapists use an eclectic approach: they take the best ideas from each school of thought and employ whatever methods and concepts seem most likely to work with each patient.

Types of therapists

Many different kinds of professionals deliver therapeutic services. Because there are various approaches to therapy, be sure to ask any therapist you are considering about her training and orientation.

The best indicators of a good therapist are personal rapport, experience working with people who have bipolar disorders, and an appropriate level of expertise in handling any additional problems, such as substance abuse. You'll also want to make sure your therapist is properly credentialed and preferably board-certified, both for your own peace of mind and for insurance billing purposes.

The information presented in this chapter applies mostly to professionals practicing in the US. Persons outside the US should contact their national, regional, or provincial government's mental health authority for information about finding a qualified, credentialed practitioner. Those in Canada can also call the Canadian Mental Health Association at (416) 484-7750 for additional information.

Psychiatrists

Psychiatrists are medical doctors (MDs) or, occasionally, osteopaths (DOs) whose special area of expertise is psychiatric disorders. As doctors, they must be licensed by their state medical board and may achieve additional qualifications. Chapter 2, *Getting a Diagnosis,* explains how to check any type of medical doctor's credentials.

Today, psychiatrists are usually busy evaluating patients, diagnosing mental disorders, and prescribing and managing psychiatric drugs. It is rare for a psychiatrist to see people for discussion sessions outside these activities. In small towns and in some special circumstances, however, your psychiatrist might also be your therapist.

Shannon, age 33, sees a single provider for both medication and therapy:

> I am very lucky in that my psychiatrist is also my psychotherapist. I've been working with him for about ten years, and used to see him once a week; now I'm down to once every two or three weeks.
>
> I think his approach is fairly eclectic, although he is decidedly not psychoanalytically inclined, which is just fine with me. He generally uses supportive counseling with some cognitive work from time to time. I keep a journal that I sometimes let him read parts of, and sometimes we discuss my dreams, but not in a Freudian way—he always asks me what I see in them, instead of making stock associations.
>
> I credit my psychiatrist with being the main force behind my being able to quit self-mutilation nine years ago, after a lifetime of hurting myself.

Like Shannon, some people prefer to see a single psychiatrist for their medication and therapy needs. Others note that because therapy can bring up strong emotions, they would rather have medications handled by someone other than their therapist—that way if you decide to quit therapy, you won't also lose your doctor.

Psychiatrists usually (but not always) charge more than other mental health professionals.

Psychiatric nurses

Some clinics and hospitals employ psychiatric mental health nurse practitioners (PMHNPs). A PMHNP is a registered nurse (RN) who has completed several additional years of training and supervised practice in this specialty.

PMHNPs can diagnose patients, and they can prescribe and manage psychiatric drugs. Most do not have specific training in therapy techniques, and they are unlikely to provide therapy services. As with psychiatrists, however, some PMHNPs may play a dual role.

Other psychiatric nurses are simply RNs who work with psychiatric patients. Most will have had at least some specialized training, although due to periodic nurse shortages, it's not rare for this training to be done on the job. That means that, although some psychiatric nurses are experienced and knowledgeable, others may not yet have the breadth of information about mental illness that a good therapist needs.

Psychologists

Psychologists in private practice have a doctorate (PhD), doctorate in psychology (PsyD), or doctorate in education (DEd) degree. They have completed a program of instruction that allows them to diagnose mental illness and to treat it with therapeutic interventions—but not with medication—and they have practiced under supervision as a clinical intern.

Licensed psychologists have passed a national examination to receive credentials from the states where they work. They may go on to become certified in a specialty by the American Board of Professional Psychology [(573) 875-1267, *http://www.abpp.org/*] or the American Board of Clinical Neuropsychology [(734) 936-8269, *http://www.med. umich.edu/abcn/*]. In the latter case, they may use the title clinical neuropsychologist. Those who have achieved the top level of board certification are called Diplomates; if they surpass this level they can add the title Fellow, as in Fellow in the Academy of Clinical Psychology (FAClinP).

Limited licensed psychologists have a master's degree in psychology, have done some doctoral work, and operate under supervision only.

The Certificate of Professional Qualification in Psychology (CPQ) is issued by the Association of State and Provincial Psychology Boards (ASPPB) and is an international credential accepted by many US states and Canadian provinces.

The best psychologists to choose are those who combine expert knowledge of bipolar disorders and a willingness to work closely with your psychiatrist and/or medical doctor. Neuropsychologists tend to do an especially good job of understanding the complexity of bipolar symptoms.

Social workers

Social workers are usually employed by public or private programs that help people in distress. Some social workers have job assignments that are investigative in nature: for example, they might be assigned to check out cases of suspected child abuse. Others help people access community resources. Many do provide interpersonal services that are very much like therapy, or they make therapy a specific part of the services they offer their clients. This is especially true of social workers in private practice. In rural areas, persons in need of therapy services often see a social worker rather than a psychologist or psychiatrist.

Social workers may have a Bachelor of Arts (BA) in social work or a Masters in Social Work (MSW). Certified social workers (CSW or ASCW) have a master's degree, have passed an examination by the National Association of Social Workers (NASW) [(202) 408-8600, *http://www.socialworkers.org/*], and have practiced under supervision for two years. The NASW also offers the school social work specialist (SSWS), qualified clinical social worker (QCSW), and diplomate in clinical social work (DCSW) credentials. Diplomates of the Academy of Certified Social Workers have the highest level of professional certification for social workers.

Licensed clinical social workers (LCSW) have received a license from their state board; some states offer certification rather than licensure. Consult the American Association of State Social Work Boards (*http://www.aasswb.org*) for a list of state boards from all 50 states, several US possessions, and the Canadian province of Alberta.

Therapists and counselors

Depending on where you live, there may or may not be legal restrictions on who can use the professional titles "therapist" and "counselor." In some US states and in many other countries, these terms are not regulated at all—anyone who wishes to can hang out a shingle and start seeing clients.

Ask any therapist or counselor you are considering about his training, and make sure he keeps up with current developments and has all of the other qualities of a good therapist mentioned at the beginning of this section.

Most US states offer a licensed professional counselor (LPC) or certified professional counselor (CPC) credential. Each state's requirements are different, but most include completing an MA or Master's of Education (MEd) degree with a major in counseling, serving a period of supervised practice, and passing an exam. The American Association of State Counseling Boards (*http://pweb.netcom.com/~aascb/aascb.html*) maintains a complete list of credentialing boards for counselors.

Other counselors may practice with a licensed marriage and family counselor (LMFC); licensed marriage and family therapist (LMFT); or marriage, family, and child counseling (MFCC) credential. In most states, these require completing a specific program of college courses in a BA and/or MA program, passing a state exam, and practicing under supervision for several years. Counselors-in-training may use the title marriage, family, and child intern (MFCI) or marriage and family therapy intern (MFTI).

Counselors may go on to become nationally board-certified by meeting requirements set by the National Board for Certified Counselors [(336) 547-0607, *http://www.nbcc.org*]. The NBCC offers the National Certified Counselor (NCC) credential as well as subsequent specialty credentials, including the Certified Clinical Mental Health Counselor (CCMHC) certificate. Another board, the Commission on Rehabilitation Counselor Certification (CRCC), offers the Certified Rehabilitation Counselor (CRC) credential and some specialty credentials as well.

Group therapy is a special technique, and so there is a specific credential for that, too. Ask your group therapist if she is certified by the National Registry of Certified Group Psychotherapists. Its CGP credential requires specific training in group therapy techniques and membership in the American Group Psychotherapy Association.

In the US, some counselors are associated with particular religious denominations and may advertise themselves as Christian counselors or under similar titles. If your religious beliefs are very important to you, finding a qualified therapist who also shares or supports these views can add an extra dimension to the healing process. These pastoral care professionals should have credentials required by your religious denomination (a degree and/or ordination) as well as specialized training in counseling.

Reports indicate that a few Christian counselors reject modern knowledge of mental disorders in favor of ancient demon possession theories and have attempted to treat people with exorcism or prayer only. Others have accused people of causing their own mental illness due to lack of proper religious practice or have made false and painful accusations of Satanic activity or abuse. Obviously, these are not mainstream beliefs among well-educated counselors, Christian or otherwise, and any counselor with these biases should be avoided by people seeking help for bipolar symptoms.

The governing body of your religious denomination should be able to help you locate a qualified mental health practitioner who can also take your spiritual needs into account. Alternatively, your pastor, rabbi, or other spiritual advisor may be able to work with your therapist to create a personal therapeutic plan that incorporates both spirituality and science.

Behavior therapists use behavior modification techniques, which are described later in this chapter. Behavior therapists can come from a number of different educational backgrounds. Some design or oversee behavior modification programs to be carried out by others. Others provide direct services to people at home, or in clinic or hospital situations.

Two other sets of initials you may see after a practitioner's name are QMHA (Qualified Mental Health Associate) and QMHP (Qualified Mental Health Professional). These are basically hiring credentials used by mental health agencies, indicating a basic level of education and experience.

Your state or provincial licensing board can let you know whether a practitioner's credentials are legitimate and may be able to tell you if he has been reprimanded or censured by the board. Your local chapter of NDMDA, NAMI, or another advocacy group should have information about therapists who have worked effectively with bipolar patients.

Finally, always pay attention to your intuition. Because the personal relationship that grows between therapist and client is at the heart of producing results, your therapist must be someone you feel comfortable with.

How to find a therapist

Your primary care physician may be able to recommend a therapist. Your insurance company will also have a list of approved providers. You can get information about local professionals through a county health or mental health department, a crisis line, or a local support and advocacy group, such as NAMI.

Once you have some names to choose from, your criteria for making a decision are up to you. Factors may include the following:

- Credentials of the therapy provider, as described in the preceding section, "Who does therapy?"

- The therapist's approach to working with people who have bipolar disorders, as described in the section "Therapy styles," later in this chapter

- Whether the therapist accepts your insurance plan or charges an affordable rate for out-of-pocket payment

- Location of the therapist's office and the availability of convenient hours

Once you have narrowed down your list to one or two providers, ask for an introductory interview. The purpose of the first meeting is to see if you feel comfortable with the therapist. It's also a chance to learn more about the therapist's treatment philosophy, approach, and personality. Compatibility, trust, and a feeling of genuine caring are essential to a working therapeutic relationship. It is worth the effort to keep looking until you find a good match.

When you are evaluating a therapist, the following are some questions you may want to ask:

- Are you accepting new clients?
- Do you charge for an initial consultation?
- What training and experience do you have working with people who have bipolar disorders?
- What is your preferred methodology? Do you use a brief or long-term approach?
- How and when will treatment goals be set?
- Will my spouse or partner, children, or other family members be involved in treatment?

Tony, age 31, has a few tips to share on choosing and working with a therapist:

> Look for somebody who is fairly open-minded, and who knows how to ask the right questions. I'm not sure about the benefits of one particular technique over another.
>
> If I was a therapist and someone came to me troubled about bipolar symptoms, rather than focusing on the methods, I'd have to wing it. I'd ask, "How does that make you feel?" You'd have to have discussions about reality and how bipolar disorder fits in there.
>
> I have a real problem with therapists who explain everything by saying, "this particular behavior or thinking pattern is 'classically bipolar'." There's an assumption that there's one scientifically proven "normal" state to be in. I would be disappointed if the people who developed the DSM-IV thought it was the source code for the universe.
>
> Therapists have been a good tool for me, but what you need to do is not to burden the therapist with too much of your own self-development. I went into therapy with my wife and while it seemed like I wasn't getting anywhere, they were planting seeds of growth into my brain. What I learned from that experience is, a good teacher helps, but you have to be motivated to go out and do the work in your life.

Therapy goals

You will set your own goals for therapy, in concert with your therapist. Goals are as varied as individuals with bipolar disorders.

Your therapeutic goals might include items like the following:

- Discussing the nature of bipolar disorders and how they can be treated
- Identifying personal mood-swing triggers
- Identifying ways to prevent or shorten mood swings
- Identifying and stopping detrimental thought patterns
- Coping with problem symptoms and medication side-effects
- Improving behavior at home, at work, or in the community
- Gaining support for positive lifestyle changes, such as maintaining sobriety
- Developing personal strengths, resiliency, and self-esteem to counter the detrimental social and personal effects of manic depression

If you don't think a therapeutic relationship is working well or if a therapist tells you something that doesn't seem right, don't be afraid to seek a second opinion.

Therapy styles

This section describes the types of therapy that are frequently useful for people with bipolar disorders and the benefits you might expect from each type. As mentioned previously in this chapter, many good therapists use techniques and concepts from several different disciplines.

Eileen, age 47, recently found a therapist whose style fit her needs:

> I never saw a therapist one-on-one until this year, when I was simply falling apart. I don't know what name her approach had, but, she drew on my spirituality, my ownership of my soul, to guide me into looking at what I needed to do to nurture and care for myself.
>
> The symptoms she concentrated on were the ones that separated me from my reality. This therapy was very helpful.

Cognitive therapy

Cognitive therapy (also called cognitive-behavioral therapy) is an approach that often produces relief from troubling symptoms within a defined, limited period of time. The cognitive therapist begins by helping you identify which negative behavior patterns you would like to work on. Together, you then identify what kinds of thoughts and feelings precipitate these behaviors.

Next, the therapist helps you figure out strategies for replacing thoughts that have negative consequences with new thoughts that have positive consequences. In other words, the cognitive therapist helps you "think yourself well."

For Joe, age 33, this approach wasn't enough on its own—but it has proven effective for many people with bipolar symptoms, usually in connection with medical treatment:

> *In college, at age 19, I went to one of the school psychologists and said that I thought my brain chemicals were going out of whack and that I was going to become depressed. The psychologist, who favored cognitive methods, told me that my problem was my deterministic and reductionistic point of view that depression was something that simply happened to a person as a result of brain chemicals. Well, I think I must have been right, because I did end up depressed in a way that seemed impossible to treat except by medication.*
>
> *Nevertheless, I have been in therapy off and on ever since. I find it most useful to have someone objective to meet with me regularly who can tell if I am about to have an episode. Also, it helps me deal with the stigma and problems with relationships. At the very least, it helps in that I can regularly talk with someone who knows and accepts my illness.*

Cognitive therapy works best for handling specific kinds of problematic thought patterns and behaviors. For example, if you tend to catastrophize when depressed, seeing only the negative side of everything and then becoming further depressed as a result, cognitive therapy can help you find strategies for breaking this negative thought spiral. These strategies might include the use of affirmations, consulting with the therapist or another trusted person to double-check negative thoughts, or learning to recognize the faulty logic that underlies unreasonably negative thoughts.

Does it work? Not always, but more often than one might expect. Cognitive therapy has helped many people identify and combat negative thought patterns. It has even proved useful for stopping thoughts that can lead to the most troubling kinds of behaviors, including self-injurious behaviors. It has a good track record for helping people with compulsive behaviors, those in recovery from substance abuse, and people suffering from anxiety, panic, and other out-of-proportion reactions to daily events. Evidence is mounting that cognitive therapy produces actual physical effects, such as changes in the production and absorption of neurotransmitters.[2]

Cognitive-behavioral therapy has also shown effectiveness for educating people with bipolar disorders about monitoring their mood cycles and symptoms, and for encouraging them to stay the course with medical treatment.[3]

Family therapy

A family is a group formed by individuals for mutual benefit, with each member having his or her own personality, needs, and desires. Whenever one member of the group is ill or in emotional distress, it affects all the other members.

Sharon, age 47, relies on family therapy to help her handle being a single parent with bipolar disorder:

> I use crisis counseling now and then, but I have a long-term family therapist. I see her for life advice on major decisions, or when I feel overwhelmed, or as though I am overwhelming my friends and family. She allows me to exercise my own judgment to a large extent and keeps trying new stuff, so that helps.
>
> It's been very difficult for my 15-year-old daughter, but I do my best to be consistent, firm and stable for her, and to explain and apologize when I'm not. I use the family therapist as a safety valve.

Family therapists work with the entire family together, although they may also see some members individually. They see the family as a system: probably not a perfect one (whose is?), but a system that at least tries to meet everyone's needs. The therapist helps each family member express his or her fears, angers, and wishes, and then helps the group restructure itself in healthier ways.

For adults with bipolar disorders, family therapy usually means treating you, your spouse or partner, and/or your children together. However, sometimes adults use family therapy as a venue for repairing shattered relationships with their own parents and adult siblings.

You don't have to be the classic dysfunctional family to benefit from family therapy. Meeting as a group with a therapist can help a lot, even if only one person's behavior is seriously disordered. In fact, this approach is strongly recommended for families coping with bipolar disorders, even if the affected person is seeing an individual therapist. In family therapy sessions, you'll have a safe place to talk about your frustrations, ask questions, and develop strategies for helping the affected person without neglecting everyone else's needs. Without this opportunity, family members can undergo severe stress.

Tony, age 31, says:

> Family therapy helped greatly. My marriage took a lot of abuse from my mania. I was unmedicated and quite manic for at least four months, during which I hardly spoke to my wife. I did some very strange, risky, rude, bizarre things, and I got myself into a great deal of debt. There were a lot of hurt feelings worked out during our sessions.

The effects of manic depression are very hard for families to handle, and yet a strong support system is essential to the recovery process. Clinical experience has shown that the more family members know about bipolar disorders, the better the prognosis is for the person with a bipolar disorder. That should mean fewer hospitalizations, better medication compliance, and fewer serious legal and educational problems.

A good family therapist is someone who is supportive, and who is also knowledgeable about the biological nature of bipolar disorders and any co-morbid conditions. The last thing you need is a therapist who blames you for your own difficulties or who encourages everyone else to pin the blame on you.

There's no place for the blame game in family therapy. All parties need to acknowledge personal failings, of course, but with the understanding that not everything done wrong is a calculated effort to harm or annoy. The message should be that everyone has shortcomings to work on, everyone makes mistakes, and once they have been dealt with, it's time to move on to a better life together. Even though it's tough to stick with it for the long haul, compliance with medical treatment and ongoing work on personal issues in therapy can make those better lives a reality for all family members.

Family therapy can provide a venue for putting issues on the table, for healing the pain caused by errors and misunderstanding, and, perhaps most importantly, for setting family ground rules that ensure difficult situations are avoided in the future. Family therapy sessions can also focus on the thought styles and symptoms associated with bipolar disorder, helping all family members understand each other better, improve how they relate to each other, and become a more cohesive and supportive unit.

As in any type of interpersonal treatment, there are a few common pitfalls to family therapy. Misplaced assumptions are one. Although piles of self-help books have been written about family relationships, the truth is that every family is a unique blend.

Knowledge of common personal behavior patterns and family structures can certainly be useful, but watch out for any therapist who instantly labels your family as having "typical adult children of alcoholics problems" or uses some other quick pop-psychology explanation. The assumptions that accompany labels can prevent appropriate therapeutic work and may lead the therapist away from concentrating on those needs specifically related to the effects of bipolar symptoms.

Family therapy is not a solution for all problems, although sometimes well-meaning professionals present it that way. Sometimes the goal of family therapy is identifying survival strategies for coping with unmanageable symptoms. In other cases what families really need most is direct services, such as respite care or medical help, not better coping skills.

Troy, age 30, wishes that family therapy was available during the early years of his illness:

> My mother said she almost had a nervous breakdown watching me disintegrate from a student-body president to someone who couldn't finish a single sentence, choose something to eat, or really do much at all except stay in bed and complain a lot. I think I was putting a lot of pressure on her by constantly turning to her for help that she could never give. Our relationship went through the toughest time when I was hospitalized. It took years to heal the wound that occurred from this. It wasn't until years later that I found out the hospital wasn't at all accurate with the information they were giving her.

Behavioral family management (BFM) is a structured approach to family therapy designed specifically for families coping with mental illness. It includes education about the illness itself and its symptoms, directed discussion about the effects of mental illness on the family, and specific instruction on coping and stress-reduction skills.

Many people with bipolar disorders are already estranged from their families by the time they enter treatment. In some cases, one goal of therapy can be reopening the lines of communication; in others, coming to terms with their loss.

Interpersonal and social rhythm therapy (IPSRT)

Interpersonal therapy is a time-limited, very focused approach to helping people cope with the interpersonal problems that can occur in any mental illness. These include issues of family or work disputes, changing roles, grief, and deficits in social skills. Interpersonal therapists usually use a workbook-based approach to assessing how well you are doing, how your symptoms are impacting social functioning, and strategies you can use to improve your relationships. Interpersonal therapy uses many concepts and techniques borrowed from cognitive-behavioral therapy.

For people with bipolar disorders, interpersonal therapy is combined with social rhythm therapy, a technique that tries to help people beat the mood-swing cycle through lifestyle changes. It's based on the idea that people with mood disorders are exquisitely sensitive to changes in social routines, sleep patterns, and daily activities. A therapist who uses this approach would help you develop the most beneficial daily routine and encourage you to maintain it to prevent future relapses.[4]

Behavior modification

Behavior modification, also called behavior therapy or behaviorism, focuses on identifying problem behaviors, finding out what causes them, and eliminating them. That's far less simple than it sounds on paper.

You are most likely to encounter "behavior mod" experts in more restrictive settings, such as day treatment centers, hospitals, and corrections facilities. The quality of their training and expertise varies widely. A behaviorist's role in your treatment might include analyzing your behavior and helping you develop a plan to address problem areas. Some behavior therapists work one-on-one with people, using techniques that are very similar to the related practice of cognitive-behavioral therapy.

In restrictive settings, behaviorists are often involved in helping to motivate people. They may design incentive programs to encourage medication compliance, therapy session attendance, or specific types of behavior improvement. For example, the behaviorist might develop a system that lets you earn privileges, or credits toward getting desired items, if you follow through on desirable actions.

In private practice, a behaviorist may help you build incentives into your plan for improved mental health. She can help you understand what motivates you to follow through with difficult activities and set up a personal system of rewards that will encourage you to meet your goals.

Unfortunately, some behavior therapists are purists who feel that all human activity is based on conditioned responses to outside environmental stimuli. It's important to find a professional in this discipline who understands, accepts, and works with the role of neurochemistry in the origin and treatment of bipolar symptoms.

Group therapy

Group therapy brings together several people who are dealing with the same or similar problems, placing them under the guidance of a professional therapist. Members try to help themselves and each other in the group's meetings.

Like family therapy, group therapy is often a very positive experience. You can form supportive relationships with peers as well as with a therapist, and benefit from the real-life experiences and insight they offer. Group therapy also is usually less expensive than individual therapy sessions.

As long as the therapist in charge is knowledgeable and supportive, group therapy can be very useful for almost anyone coping with a serious mental illness. Most residential centers, day treatment facilities, and hospitals provide some form of group therapy to their patients. It is also available through many outpatient clinics, private practitioners, and community organizations that serve people with mental illness. Groups that are geared toward your specific issues are more likely to be successful than groups that include all patients in a clinic or hospital or that have a different focus.

Joe had some experiences with mandatory group therapy during his hospitalizations, which he did not feel were worthwhile:

> *I have been in two community rehabilitation hospitals. There were frequent activities of little use to a bipolar patient without a dual diagnosis of substance abuse and mental illness. They did have various "goal groups" and groups that were geared more to recovering alcoholics or substance abusers.*
>
> *I remember how these discussion groups emphasized taking responsibility for your actions, which is really impossible when actively manic and swept away by delusions.*

Also, some people never feel comfortable in a group situation. For introverts and people who have a hard time trusting others, individual therapy is probably a better fit. However, your ability to function in a group may be one of the goals of that therapy, leading to group therapy later on.

Peer-to-peer support

Peer support groups are a little like group therapy—but without the therapist in charge. Peer support groups range from ad hoc groups formed by patients to professionally mediated support groups at a mental health clinic or public agency.

Usually peer support groups do not charge participants, although a collection for snacks or meeting-room expenses might be taken up. Clinic-run groups, of course, may carry a fee.

Alcoholics Anonymous, Narcotics Anonymous, and other programs that use the twelve-step model or a similar supported self-help approach are a particularly advanced kind of peer support group. These well-known programs use mutual support methods for effecting personal change, and they work extremely well for many people. In groups that use the 12-step model, more experienced members help newcomers. You are usually assigned a sponsor, who will help you learn the methods used and whom you can call when you need help. If substance abuse is a problem for you, do look into these resources.

Local chapters of support and advocacy organizations, such as NAMI and the National Depressive and Manic-Depressive Association (NDMDA), are often involved in setting up and sponsoring peer support groups for people with bipolar disorders and other forms of mental illness.

For Benjamin, age 45, both the 12-step model and peer-to-peer support groups have been important:

> I dig the 12-step program of AA—I think the 12 steps of AA are a whole lifestyle, and the self-examination and taking stock of one's own actions are essential to recovery. I just input the words "mental illness" where they use the word "alcoholic."
>
> Support groups are helpful. I was able to start a NAMI-Care group with the support of the local NAMI branch. NDMDA's model is also good if it is a well-honed group with an educated facilitator, and able to be faithful to NDMDA's national guidelines.

The information shared and friendships made in a peer support group can be very helpful to people coping with bipolar disorder. The best support groups provide a wonderful healing environment where you can share your experiences with others who have been there.

Always find out as much as you can about a group before joining. There are some AA and NA groups that discourage the use of psychiatric medication, for example, and this can inadvertently sabotage your treatment. In other peer support groups, misinformation can be spread, especially when trained mediators or advisors are not available to step in. Strong personalities may dominate a particular group, making some participants feel uncomfortable and miss out on getting the help they need.

Peer-to-peer support is available online as well as in person. These groups are discussed more in Chapter 8, *Living with Bipolar Disorders*.

Joe says the peer-to-peer aspects of support groups are most valuable for him:

> *Probably the greatest positive contribution of support groups is seeing that others in all walks of life can thrive with these problems. Also, one can feel useful by sharing what one knows of one's experience. When you ask yourself, "what good has it done me that I have this condition?" you can say, "at least I've been able to help others." It has been useful for me to meet other people who also deal with the stigma and the fear of reoccurrence—they are also people from whom I don't have to fear any stigma.*

> *A problem with many such groups is that one meets people with different forms of the disorder who are in different mood stages. Often the manic people dominate the discussion, while those who are depressed remain quietly resentful of that attention. Some people even questioned whether others were really bipolar or had the wrong diagnosis—and some people did indeed show up saying, "I think I may be bipolar, I'm here to see what people with the disorder are like."*

> *My first group was at the university, and was organized by a staff psychologist. There was no over-arching theme to this group. The people I met there were by and large "high functioning." The process was that we would simply meet together in the psychologist's office, usually about five of us, and talk about our lives and problems, with the psychologist as mediator.*

> *My second group was through the NDMDA and was split into different groups. It was a much larger system, and each of the sub-groups had ten to twenty members. The sub-groups usually included one specifically for manic issues, another for depressive issues, one for family support, one for youth issues, and sometimes another group would focus on a special issue. Even in the "manic issues" group, though, there was a split between people whose symptoms were more dramatic at the moment and those who needed to deal with more long-term issues like stigma. This group seemed very professional: they had a ground rule that you don't recommend medication for other members, as that was the job of a doctor. They were very organized in their political advocacy, and I remember a concert benefit they organized.*

I've also been part of an online support group, Pendulum. Pendulum seems dominated by a core group who know each other well, although newcomers are welcome. I mostly "lurk" (listen in) and contribute only rarely.

It's worth mentioning that support groups are different from group therapy. Joining a support group can also carry responsibilities. For example, I met a member of my first group on campus once, and thought she was having a manic episode. I tried to contact her therapist, who was out of town; a substitute therapist was contacted, and the group member was eventually hospitalized. I had to wonder how much responsibility I bore for what happened, and how much my influence was positive.

Benefits of therapy

Generally speaking, therapy cannot produce much change until your most troubling symptoms are intermittent or starting to recede. A person who is actively psychotic, extremely manic, or depressed to the point of needing hospitalization may greatly appreciate a therapist's support while weathering these storms. Once medication is starting to help or the state is receding on its own, there is a window of opportunity for therapeutic work.[5]

Over a period of time, you should expect therapy sessions to help you develop better strategies for handling mood swings and other symptoms. As these strategies begin to work, you will become even more able to benefit from therapy. You can think of it as a building process: first you must make the necessary tools, and then the greater work can be done.

Non-talk therapies

Chapter 6 discusses a variety of approaches to manic-depressive symptoms that are therapeutic, but that do not rely on talk as the primary principle. These include body-work, light therapy, and other interventions that you may hear about. Most of these are considered alternative medicine by psychiatrists and psychologists—although many professionals support or even recommend trying them.

Chapter 8 covers self-help strategies for organizing your life, dealing with stress, and handling issues that may emerge at work or in your family. These skills will help you build on what you learn in therapy, turning your improved self-understanding into practical action.

CHAPTER 6

Complementary Therapies

BECAUSE BIPOLAR DISORDERS ARE ILLNESSES of the nervous system, they have varied physical roots and may cause many repercussions. This chapter describes ways to address some bipolar symptoms in addition to talk therapy and psychiatric drugs.

First, it defines the major types of complementary therapies, explains who practices each method, and talks about what they do. Specific sections then cover light therapy, non-pharmaceutical approaches to sleep problems, essential fatty acids, special diets and combating medication-related weight gain, allergy treatments, hormonal treatments, and anti-viral and immune system treatments. It also discusses the role of vitamins, minerals, herbal remedies, and dietary supplements for some people with bipolar disorders. Finally, it provides information about auditory integration therapy and stress reduction techniques.

Experts agree that no one should rely entirely on herbal remedies or other non-medical therapies when confronting a chronic, serious illness like manic depression—but these options may have an important place in your total treatment plan. They can complement psychiatric medication and therapy, promote your sense of well-being and general health, help you prevent or diminish medication side effects, and give you increased personal control over your health.

Careful choices

Many non-pharmaceutical interventions are widely accepted, such as taking saw palmetto extract for prostate problems or avoiding wheat products to ease the pain of celiac disease. In fact, medical studies are proving that quite a few of the vitamins, supplements, tonics, exercises, and diets long touted for various illnesses can be quite effective and often do not carry the same risks and side effects as prescription drugs. When these interventions are used to complement mainstream medical practices, this combination approach is called complementary or adjunctive treatment: using the best of what medical science has to offer and complementing it with less invasive techniques. If they are used instead of mainstream treatments, they become alternative therapies—an approach that's definitely not recommended for coping with bipolar disorders.

It is very unwise to rely solely on non-pharmaceutical measures to treat bipolar disorders, with the possible exception of mild cyclothymia or seasonal affective disorder. The risks of going without medical treatment include death by suicide or misadventure and the terrible personal consequences of self-injurious behavior, manic spending sprees, hypersexuality, and all the rest.

There is also much misinformation about complementary healthcare measures, some of it deliberate. Botanical formulas can differ wildly in their potency, both from manufacturer to manufacturer and from vial to vial. There is a potentially dangerous lack of scientific and regulatory oversight in this field and, sometimes, a blatantly anti-science attitude. Some practitioners are well-trained and highly competent; others are charlatans.

Accordingly, you must be wary of claims you read in advertisements, in magazine and newspaper articles, and on the Internet. Check the credentials of practitioners before you heed their advice, especially if it involves expensive tests or remedies. And be doubly doubtful if a practitioner encourages you to forgo prescription medications. None of the herbal remedies or other complementary treatments available today can cure bipolar disorders: in fact, if you see or hear such claims made, that should make you highly suspicious right away.

Despite the ease with which some people demand the latest prescription pill for everything from premature balding to weight loss, many still take a very negative view of psychiatric medications. Well-meaning friends and relatives may approach you with information about natural cures and get angry if you say you're not interested. Often these people either don't know your actual diagnosis or have no idea what a serious illness it is. Just as you have a right to consider other treatments, you also have a right to stick with your doctor's regimen—especially if it's working.

The role of complementary treatments

A holistic approach to health takes all aspects of physical, emotional, and spiritual well-being into account. That's important when treating bipolar disorders, because of their far-reaching impact on personal functioning. You may be able to enhance pharmaceuticals with complementary treatments, often reducing medication doses and thereby eliminating some dangers and side effects.

Eileen, age 47, relies on a complementary approach:

> I take lithium and Depakote. It took about six to eight weeks to get used to it—the gastrointestinal effects were something else! Now, I am fine, except my liver functions are slowly degrading, according to my blood work. I know this is probably partly due to the fact that I take Depakote, and also because I drink beer and smoke. I do take milk thistle twice daily, and that helps. I feel less well when I forget it for a few days.
>
> I take a "senior" vitamin—I had to hunt for a multivitamin that did not have iron. Iron interferes with thyroid medication, which I depend upon now that I have had my thyroid destroyed because of Graves's disease. The senior vitamin also has gingko, ginseng, and grapeseed extract in it. I literally "know" when I've been taking my vitamins. They help a lot.
>
> I also take 400 units of vitamin E, and I take a soy supplement for the perimenopausal hot flashes and night sweats. It too, is helping.
>
> I drink water instead of coffee all day long. That helps. I do know that no matter what meds I have taken, when I eat a completely balanced diet and drink plenty of water, things always work so much better.

Complementary treatments rarely produce dramatic changes. When they work, they usually assist your body's own self-righting mechanisms, promoting better sleep, fewer and less severe mood swings, improved general health, and a better frame of mind.

Many of these treatments have a preventative focus, rather than merely treating symptoms of illness after they emerge. Practitioners also stress empowering people to be more responsible for their own self-care. Even if all that does is make you feel more in charge of your treatment program, the effects can be powerful.

There are other reasons to consider complementary therapies. For example, occasionally a person has very valid health reasons for giving up pharmaceutical treatments that are actually working. Almost all of the medications used to treat bipolar disorders can increase the risk of birth defects, so pregnant women who are bipolar can find themselves faced with a terrible choice. Temporary reliance on complementary methods under careful supervision, with a return to the use of effective medication as soon as possible, can protect both the developing fetus and the mother's health.

Should you develop another serious health condition, such as cancer, conflicting medications might have to be temporarily discontinued during chemotherapy, preparation for surgery, or certain types of medical treatment. So even if non-pharmaceutical treatments are not right for you now, they might be useful someday.

Evaluating complementary therapies

To assess claims made about complementary therapies, rely on reputable reference books for your basic information, rather than on advertisements or the popular press. You can check with the National Center for Complementary and Alternative Medicine (listed in Appendix A, *Resources*) to see if any scientific evidence backs up the treatment that interests you.

Check the credentials of non-medical care providers, just as you would with any other specialist. The section "Complementary treatment systems," later in this chapter, includes information on how to check these credentials. Beware of any practitioner who will see you only if you stop using conventional treatments.

Talk with other people who have gone through the treatment. Be sure to find out how much the therapy costs, because your insurance company may not pay for complementary treatments.

Take all the information you have gathered to your doctor to discuss any positive or negative impact that it may have on current medical treatment.

Monique, age 30, says she would be very careful about trying alternative approaches that could interfere with medication:

> Before I try anything new, even prescribed medication, I do some research on it. Right now my research method is mostly going on the Internet. I do a search on that medication or whatever to see what information is available about it, what it's used for, what the side effects and complications are, what kind of research has been done on it, and what it's approved for, if anything.
>
> With alternative stuff, I would be a little wary and would not necessarily trust what I read. I would like to hear from the person who actually took it, and see what their results were. I also like to talk to a doctor that I trust about it. But in my experience, most psychiatrists don't seem to be in touch with alternative medicine, much less suggesting it.

Evaluating supplements

Once upon a time, only the health enthusiasts crowed about the virtues of herbs from the Peruvian rain forest or purchased multivitamin bars. Now soft drinks are spiked with St. John's Wort and gingko biloba, and One-a-Day vitamins share a shelf with a One-a-Day herbal mood supporter.

Although the glossy veneer of today's supplements makes them look very attractive, being a smart consumer is just as important in this area as it is with traditional medicine. Being well-informed is sometimes more difficult, however. Medications with approval from the FDA or similar government bodies undergo rigorous testing. Study results and detailed information about these compounds are available in numerous books, online, or directly from the manufacturers.

With supplements, that's not always the case. It seems like every week another paperback book appears making wild claims for a new antioxidant compound or herbal medication. These books—not to mention magazine articles, web sites, and semi-informed friends—sometimes wrap conjecture up in a thin veneer of science. They may reference studies that are misinterpreted, that appeared in disreputable journals, or that were so poorly designed or biased that no journal would publish them.

Supplement salespeople, and particularly those who take part in multi-level marketing schemes, seem to have taken lessons from their predecessors in the days of the traveling medicine show. They have little to lose by making outrageous claims for their products, and much to gain financially. Here are just a few of the unsupported claims found in a single five-minute sweep of supplement-sales sites on the Internet:

- "Glutathione slows the aging clock, prevents disease and increases life."
- "Pycogenol dramatically relieves ADD/ADHD, improves skin smoothness and elasticity, reduces prostate inflammation and other inflammatory conditions, reduces diabetic retinopathy and neuropathy, improves circulation and enhances cell vitality." (And, according to this site, cures almost anything else that ails you!)
- "Sage and Bee Pollen nourish the brain."
- "Soybean lecithin has been found to clean out veins and arteries—dissolve the gooey sludge cholesterol—and thus increase circulation, relieve heart, vein and artery problems. It has cured many diabetics—cured brain clots, strokes, paralyzed legs, hands and arms!"

Take the time to browse your local store's shelves, and you'll probably spot a number of dubious products. Some companies try to deceive you with sound-alike names, packaging that mimics other products, or suggestive names that hint at cures.

Other colorful bottles of pills contain substances that the body can't absorb in oral form—for example, DNA (deoxyribonucleic acid, the building block of human genetic material) graces the shelves of some shops. One site for a manufacturer of this useless supplement claims, "it is the key element in the reprogramming and stimulation of lazy cells to avoid, improve, or correct problems in the respiratory, digestive, nervous, or glandular systems." Some brands of DNA are apparently nothing but capsules of brewer's yeast. Brewer's yeast is high in nucleic acids, the compounds the body uses to build DNA, but there's no evidence that your body can use nucleic acids taken orally to build better DNA. Brewer's yeast is a good, inexpensive source of vitamin B and the mineral chromium, but these pills cost 40 times as much as an equivalent amount of brewer's yeast.

Some other supplements provide end products of internal metabolism, such as glutathione, instead of the precursors needed for the body to make a sufficient supply on its own, such as Vitamin E. This approach may not work. Consult with your doctor, pharmacist, or a competent nutritionist before taking supplements.

Watch out for any product whose salespeople claim it will cure anything. Supplements and vitamins may enhance health and promote wellness, but they rarely effect cures. Be wary of universal usefulness claims. The worst offenders in supplement advertising tout their wares as cure-alls for a multitude of unrelated conditions.

Be especially cautious when sales pitches are written in pseudoscientific language that doesn't hold up under close examination with a dictionary. This is a popular ploy. For example, one supplement sold by multi-level marketers claims to "support cellular communication through a dietary supplement of monosaccharides needed for glyco-conjugate synthesis." Translated into plain English, that means it's a sugar pill.

Even when you have examined the science behind a vitamin or supplement treatment, there's still the problem of quality and purity. It's almost impossible for consumers to know for sure that a tablet or powder contains the substances advertised at the strength and purity promised. Whenever possible, do business with reputable manufacturers, companies that back up their products with potency guarantees or standards. In most European countries, potency is governed by government standards; in the US, it's a matter of corporate choice.

Leslie, age 44, says:

> I own The Herbal PDR, *and look things up before I take them.*
> *Herbs are drugs too, and can have interactions with each other and*
> *with allopathic meds. Alternative medicine is adjunctive, not primary,*
> *therapy.*

Natural does not mean harmless. Whenever a vitamin or supplement is powerful enough to heal, it also has the power to harm if misused. Be sure to work closely with your physician, pharmacist, or nutritionist if you will be taking anything more complex than a daily multivitamin.

One thing at a time

Desperate to find something that works to reduce difficult symptoms, people tend to pile on the interventions. That makes it hard to tell when something really is working—or if it would work without interference from some other remedy. To get the clearest picture possible of any complementary treatment, you must introduce it independent of others and independent of pharmaceuticals or therapeutic interventions. Obviously, this is often impractical. You wouldn't stop taking lithium just to see if B vitamins might be useful, for example. However, you could add one complementary therapy to your regimen after checking with your doctor and assess any improvement after several weeks.

Keep careful, daily records of supplements and dietary changes you introduce, when they are given and in what amounts, what brands you used, and any visible effects that you observe. If after four to six weeks you have not seen improvements with a supplement, benefits are unlikely. Dietary changes, bodywork, and other interventions may take much longer to show beneficial effects.

Complementary treatment systems

Although there is no secret natural cure for bipolar disorders, the holistic approach to patient care used by good complementary medicine practitioners often helps people maintain optimal general health. Complementary treatments may be suggested by your family doctor or psychiatrist or by a specialist in a particular type of treatment. Common complementary practices include the following:

Acupuncture

Developed in China, acupuncture is based on the concept of ch'i, an energy force that is believed to course through the human body. Acupuncture theory states that if your ch'i is blocked, illness results. Acupuncturists use tiny needles inserted into the skin at specific points to undo these blockages.

Modern acupuncturists use disposable needles to ensure sterility. Some also employ heat (moxibustion), noninvasive lasers, magnetic devices, essential oils, or electrical stimulation. Many have expertise in other Chinese or Western complementary therapies, such as herbal medicine.

If you do try acupuncture, you may encounter terms and practices that are unfamiliar to you. Acupuncture, and Chinese medicine in general, works from a different set of core beliefs than Western medicine. Ask your practitioner about anything you don't understand.

Studies funded by the National Institutes of Health have found that acupuncture does help some conditions, including chronic pain, and works well as an adjunct to other methods in the treatment of drug addiction. Some researchers think that the needles influence the body's production of natural opioid chemicals and neurotransmitters.[1]

Reputable research indicates that properly applied acupuncture treatments may help regulate gastrointestinal functions, which could be good news for people with GI distress due to medication.[2] Other studies have indicated (but not proven) that acupuncture may heal nerve damage, which may in turn reduce anxiety and mood swings.[3]

The National Certification Commission for Acupuncture and Oriental Medicine (NCCAOM) is the main US accreditation group for acupuncture. It can be reached at (703) 548-9004 or on the web at *http://www.nccaom.org.*

There have been anecdotal reports about acupuncture as an effective treatment for manic episodes—for instance, actress Margot Kidder, who has bipolar disorder type I, claimed to have been successfully treated with acupuncture and other complementary practices after a much-publicized manic/psychotic episode a few years ago.[4] If you can find a good acupuncturist, it might be a worthwhile adjunct to traditional medical care.

Acupressure and reflexology are other complementary treatments that borrow much from acupuncture's basic concepts. These therapies use physical pressure or movement rather than needles to stimulate the same points targeted in acupuncture.

Ayurvedic and Chinese traditional medicine

Indigenous peoples everywhere have medical systems based on the use of herbal remedies. Two of these, India's Ayurveda and traditional Chinese medicine, have been systematized and studied to a great extent. The Ayurvedic medicine concept revolves around a life-force called prana; Chinese traditionalists talk about ch'i, as mentioned in the previous section on acupuncture.

Ayurvedic practitioners will give you a thorough exam and then tell you which type you are in their diagnostic system. Then they'll suggest an appropriate diet, lifestyle adjustments, and probably therapeutic meditation. They may also have various suggestions about cleaning out your digestive tract.

Chinese traditional practitioners take a very similar approach, although their dietary recommendations are usually less strict than a typical Ayurvedic plan.

There is a vast array of Ayurvedic and Chinese herbal remedies. Some of these concoctions are probably quite effective, others could be dangerous to your health. If possible, try to find out exactly which herbs are in a potion, and check out their effects. For example, the popular Chinese herb Ma Huang (ephedra) is a common ingredient in traditional nerve tonics. It is also a powerful central nervous system stimulant and should be taken with caution.

It is far safer to work closely with a practitioner who knows your state of health and can monitor you during treatment than it is to purchase Chinese or Ayurvedic remedies over the counter. See the sections "Other sleep supplements" and "Herbal remedies," later in this chapter, for more information on traditional remedies that are used for sleep disturbance, depression, anxiety, and agitation.

In the US, the primary certification agency for practitioners of Chinese medicine is the NCCAOM. There is no US certification commission for Ayurvedic practitioners or Western herbalists. The most active group promoting Ayurveda in the US is the National Institute of Ayurvedic Medicine, which can be reached at (914) 278-8700 or online at *http://niam.com/corp-web/index.htm.*

Holistic psychology

Holistic psychology is the practice of blending talk therapy with other non-pharmaceutical treatments. Besides seeing you in therapy sessions, a holistic psychologist might recommend a combination of dietary changes, nutritional supplements, exercise, biofeedback, and mood-control techniques, such as meditation or self-hypnosis. Helping you build a more effective support system is usually a part of the plan. These interventions would have the overall goal of helping to normalize your physical health, improve your mental stability, and have a more enjoyable and productive life.

Technically, a holistic psychologist should have the same credentials as a regular psychologist, plus training in holistic health-promotion practices. In practice, this may not be the case, so be sure to ask. Depending on the practitioner, holistic psychology may be helpful for people with bipolar disorders who are interested in a combination approach.

Homeopathy

Homeopathy practitioners use remedies containing infinitesimal amounts of substances that could cause a medical condition to prod your immune system into action against the condition. Homeopathy is considered to be fairly mainstream in the UK, although repeated studies have not verified that it works.[5]

In the US and Canada, homeopathic physicians are not licensed to practice medicine. However, some MDs and NDs do recommend homeopathic treatments, and a few homeopaths are fully licensed physicians. For information about homeopathic medicine and licensing for homeopaths in North America, contact the National Center for Homeopathy at (703) 548-7790 or on the Web at *http://www.homeopathic.org*.

Although homeopathic remedies can often be purchased at health-food stores, responsible practitioners recommend seeing a homeopathic doctor before choosing remedies. The remedies are generally used only as part of an overall treatment plan that may include diet changes and stress reduction. Even if the remedies themselves are of no value, as many skeptics believe, you might benefit from this part of the program.

Homeopathy does not seem to have a good track record as an intervention for bipolar disorders, although some patients report that certain homeopathic remedies can occasionally provide relief from anxiety and physical distress associated with mood swings.

Massage and bodywork

Bodywork is a general term that covers a wide variety of therapeutic practices. All of them involve massaging, manipulating, or moving the muscles and body parts in specific ways. These practices differ in style, intensity, and intent and include:

- **Acupressure** is similar to acupuncture, but employs firm or light pressure applied to specific sites on the body rather than needles. Acupressure helps with chronic pain and some physical disorders. Its efficacy for bipolar symptoms is unknown.

- **The Alexander Technique** is used to help people streamline and increase the gracefulness of their movements. Practitioners teach new, more balanced movement patterns. Its efficacy for bipolar symptoms is unknown. For more information, see the Alexander Technique web site (*http://www.alexandertechnique.com/*).

- **Craniosacral therapy** involves delicately manipulating the plates of the skull and energies that course through the body. Some question the scientific basis of craniosacral work, but it is gentle and noninvasive, and some people with neurological problems say it has been helpful. Most craniosacral therapists employ a certain amount of talk therapy along with the bodywork, which may or may not appeal to you. Its efficacy for bipolar symptoms is unknown. Although it was developed by osteopath John Upledger, craniosacral therapy is practiced by trained members of other professions, including some occupational therapists and physical therapists. Upledger includes some accounts of beneficial use of this therapy for people with mental illness in his book *Your Inner Physician and You: Craniosacral Therapy and Somatoemotional Release* (1997, North Atlantic Books). For more information, see the craniosacral therapy web site (*http://www.craniosacral.co.uk/*). Although anecdotal reports indicate that some people with bipolar disorders find craniosacral therapy useful, no peer-reviewed studies have been published on the topic. Some practitioners make claims of being able to cure manic depression, which has certainly not been proven.

- **The Feldenkrais Method**, developed by Moshe Feldenkrais, concentrates on rebuilding sensory and movement systems, particularly through unlearning poor movement patterns. A number of Feldenkrais practitioners work with people who have neurological problems. The therapy is gentle, but the efficiency of Feldenkrais for bipolar symptoms is unknown. For more information, see the movement educators web site (*http://www.movement-educators.com*).

- **Massage** comes in many forms, including Swedish, Shiatsu (which resembles acupressure), and more. It can promote relaxation, physical comfort, and body awareness. It may also help decrease sensory defensiveness. Its efficacy for other bipolar symptoms is unknown.

Some bodywork believers make extravagant claims. For any bodywork method, including those not mentioned here, check the practitioner's credentials, and make sure you feel comfortable with both the person and the methodology.

Norman says bodywork and relaxation techniques help to reduce his anxiety levels, especially when he's depressed:

> I do get energy work and massage from my wife, who is in that field. It's definitely useful. I go in probably once a month on average, although there was a time when I was getting it once a week, when I was working 40 hours a week after coming out of retirement.
>
> Also, about ten years ago I trained under a hypnotherapist, and I'm sure that's been an asset—I've always found it fairly easy to relax. I think what I'm doing is using a trigger, namely taking a deep breath, that sends me into a pretty relaxed state.
>
> I think any kind of relaxation is something that's helpful, and there are various ways of getting there—like soaking in a hot tub.

All of the modalities listed in this section have accrediting bodies in most Western countries. Generally speaking, accredited, well-trained practitioners are more likely to do beneficial work than self-trained or non-accredited practitioners.

Some massage schools and training centers for other bodywork methods operate free or low-cost clinics that allow students to practice under close supervision.

Naturopathy

Naturopaths are licensed to practice medicine in some US states, Canadian provinces, and other countries. They are trained and licensed as naturopathic doctors (ND). Naturopaths tend to see themselves as "wellness promoters," not just treaters of disease. Their practice stresses prevention of disease through diet, exercise, and vitamins. They may prescribe herbal remedies or Western pharmaceuticals (in states where they are licensed to do so) to those with illness, and may also suggest and/or administer complementary therapies like hydrotherapy (special baths or wet packs) or massage.

Naturopaths vary in their personal philosophy about Western medicine. Some will refer you elsewhere for ailments they feel are out of their league, others prefer to rely solely on nutritional and natural medicine.

People who want to try herbal remedies and nutritional interventions like the ones mentioned in this chapter can choose a naturopath as their primary care provider. Take care when making a choice, however: in the US, some people calling themselves naturopaths have not completed an accredited program. Properly licensed naturopaths receive medical training roughly comparable to traditional ("allopathic") medical school, though with a different emphasis.

For information about finding a licensed naturopath in the US or Canada, contact the American Association of Naturopathic Physicians (*http://www.naturopathic.org*) or the Canadian Naturopathic Association (*http://www.naturopathic.org/canada/Canada.Assoc. List.html*).

Rachel, mother of 19-year-old Lillian, says her daughter had mixed results from naturopathic treatment:

> *When Lillian was 13, she saw a naturopath a few times who tried to treat her with B-vitamin injections and a better diet. It seemed to clear up her constant bronchial symptoms a bit and brighten her mood, but the effects wore off quickly. On the other hand, the herbal remedy he gave her for a urinary tract infection worked as well as any pharmaceutical I've ever seen. I'm now convinced that naturopathy works for some kinds of medical*

conditions, but I felt the ND's approach to her bipolar symptoms was simplistic and not very useful.

Orthomolecular medicine

Orthomolecular medicine relies mostly on using vitamins and nutrition to prevent or cure illness. The most famous proponent of orthomolecular medicine was its late founder, Dr. Linus Pauling. Better known for receiving the 1954 Nobel Prize for Chemistry and the 1962 Nobel Prize for Peace, Pauling spent most of his later life studying and publicizing the effects of megadoses of vitamins, particularly Vitamin C. Many of Dr. Pauling's more extravagant claims have not been substantiated, but his reputation as a scientist forced the medical establishment to take his ideas seriously.

Some MDs are firm believers in orthomolecular medicine, and Pauling's principles underlie many of the megadose vitamin concoctions in health-food stores. Since large doses of vitamins can have side effects as well as potential benefits, discuss what you should expect with your doctor if he wants to try an orthomolecular approach. You shouldn't do megadose vitamin therapy without consulting a physician or a competent nutritionist. See the section "Vitamins," later in this chapter, for more information.

If a practitioner says she is an orthomolecular physician or doctor, that should mean she is a licensed MD or DO. You can check on the status of a physician's license with your state Medical Licensing Board. If a practitioner says he is board-certified, you can confirm it with the American Board of Medical Specialties at (847) 491-9091 or online at *http://www.certifieddoctors.com*. An appropriate board certification for an orthomolecular psychiatrist would be Psychiatry or Neurology. Unfortunately, some persons presenting themselves as orthomolecular physicians or psychiatrists are not licensed MDs or DOs.

Osteopathy

Osteopathic physicians are trained as primary care providers first, although they may then specialize as pediatricians, surgeons, allergists, and so on. They stress preventative care and look closely at the role of body structure in the disease process. They sometimes adjust the musculoskelatal system to effect improvement.

In the UK, licensed osteopaths participate in the National Health Service. They are licensed to practice medicine in all US states, and use the initials DO (Doctor of Osteopathy) instead of MD. You can find out if an osteopath is licensed to practice medicine in your state by calling your State Medical Board or State Osteopathic Board. You can find out more about DO certification and find a practitioner through the American Osteopathy Association at (800) 621-1773 or online at *http://www.aoa-net.org.*

Light therapy

Light therapy for seasonal mood swings is a rather mainstream intervention. If your episodes of depression and mania are clearly tied to the seasons (a fact that can best be determined by keeping a careful mood diary), your physician or psychiatrist may recommend light therapy.

The good news is that these devices are likely to help. Numerous scientific studies have shown that light therapy is effective for the reduction of seasonal affective depression (SAD). Light therapy also is sometimes effective for people with seasonal eating disorders.[6]

Recent medical research indicates that the retinas of people with seasonal affective depression and other forms of seasonal mood swings are less sensitive to light.[7] The presence of light suppresses the production of melatonin, the sleep hormone. It appears that bright light also has an effect on how the body produces and uses the neurotransmitter serotonin. Specific types and frequencies of light may have other, as yet unknown, effects.

Tony, age 31, says:

> I've got an Ott light [a brand-name full-spectrum light], which I try to use fairly regularly as a task light on my desk. It does seem to help. I get into certain work patterns with deadlines and will be inside a lot. Sometimes it's like I don't see the sun for days! That's when I think it has some benefit.
>
> But basically, I try to spend more time outside. Even with the depleted ozone layer, I think real sunlight is the best thing. If it's rainy and overcast you want to spend more time inside, and that doesn't help if I'm feeling depressed. I need to get out, get some sun, get some exercise.

The most frequently studied type of light therapy requires direct exposure to 2500-lux cool-white fluorescent light (filtered for UV rays) from a light box for two hours per day. The light box can be installed in any room where you are likely to be for two hours: the bedroom, the kitchen, or your office, for example.

Other studies have indicated that thirty minutes of direct daily exposure to a more intense 10,000-lux light source is just as effective, and it is considerably easier to build into your daily schedule.[8]

Although light boxes are the most common devices used in light therapy, inventors have also developed various head-mounted devices and light visors that are said to deliver the same effect while allowing people to move about freely.

Dawn simulation is a newer and more complex technique that involves exposure to increasingly bright light in the early morning hours, simulating a summer dawn. It has not been well studied, but could be as effective as the older forms of light therapy. Special devices with timers and lamps can provide dawn simulation therapy.

A new technology tested so far only on patients with the autoimmune disorder lupus uses the A-1 ultraviolet wavelength. This is not the same UV wavelength used in tanning-salon beds, which is quite dangerous for people with systemic lupus erythematosus (SLE). One of the most prominent features of SLE is severe mood swings, and patients in the NIH-sponsored study did find some relief in the areas of mood, energy levels, and skin rash.[9]

Light therapy can also improve the duration and quality of sleep in people who are in or about to be in a hypomanic or manic phase. It appears that exposure to bright light at mid-day increases the amount of melatonin naturally produced during night hours. This should encourage more restful and regular sleep. Using light therapy in the morning, as is usually done for depression, appears to increase cycling among manic or hypomanic patients.[10]

You can fit the time and amount of light therapy to address your cycling moods. That gives it a certain advantage over medications that usually must be taken daily to be effective and that should not be increased or decreased willy-nilly.

Further resources for starting a light therapy program are listed in Appendix A. The section "Vitamins," later in this chapter, contains related information.

Another light-related strategy is increasing your exposure to natural sunlight. If you tend to spend most of your day indoors, see if you can add thirty minutes to an hour of outdoor activity to your daily schedule. It is unlikely to be as effective as using direct exposure to a light box, but it costs nothing and could help with mood control.

Fixing sleep problems

If the heart of bipolar disorders is a built-in problem with the body's circadian clock, as many researchers believe, it naturally follows that re-adjusting that clock is a possible treatment. Light therapy is one approach that follows this reasoning, as described earlier in this chapter. There are other ways to regulate sleep, and both patients and researchers report that they can be highly effective. If you can control your sleep pattern, you can reduce the number of mood swings and also reduce their severity and length.

Leslie has found herbals and other alternatives helpful for sleep cycle problems:

> *I use kava kava, chamomile, and other herb teas to calm me, or ginseng tea if I need a lift. 5-HTP is a good substitute for tryptophan to help me sleep.*
>
> *I also drink coffee in the morning—psychiatrist's orders (really!)*
>
> *A lot of doctors get freaked out if you do herbals. Mine is a very enlightened fellow, and likes that I'm open to drinking herb tea at bedtime instead of taking a Klonopin.*

Sleep deprivation can definitely set off hypomanic and manic episodes, and one of the earliest visible signs of impending depression is a desire to sleep much more than usual (hypersomnia). Strict scheduling can be the key here. That means setting a bedtime and a wake-up time and sticking to them, no matter what. Social rhythm therapy, described in Chapter 5, *Talk Therapy*, includes these recommendations as part of a larger plan to regulate circadian rhythms.

Some clinical studies have used controlled, supervised sleep deprivation to break a depressive downswing.[11] Please don't try this without your doctor's help to set up a plan.

Other researchers have found that sleep schedules can be reset during manic episodes by inducing sleep, either through the use of medication or by high levels of activity that eventually wear the person out and bring on sleep.[12] Again, this isn't something to attempt without help—although you can probably safely add extra strenuous activity to your schedule when hypomania threatens. Most of the sleep-promotion strategies outlined in the rest of this section are also safe during hypomanic episodes.

Some advice for improving the quality, duration, and regularity of sleep applies to anyone who experiences occasional insomnia or oversleeping. The following are basic guidelines for maintaining a regular sleep schedule:

- Avoid unnecessary artificial stimulants and depressants, such as coffee, tea, and alcohol.

- Avoid over-the-counter medications that have a stimulating or depressive effect, such as allergy preparations, aspirin with caffeine, No-Doz and other non-prescription stimulants, and most commercial cough syrups.

- Avoid hyper-exciting television programs, music, or exercise right before bed.

- Use your bed for sleeping only, not for reading, watching television, or working. This helps associate the concepts of "bed" and "sleep" in your mind.

- If you can't get to sleep at the proper time, don't just lie there tossing and turning. Get out of bed and do something really, really boring—like housework or putting together an old jigsaw puzzle.

- Make a relaxing ritual, such as winding down with a book or quiet music, part of your end-of-day plans. A nice, long bath is another great way to prepare for sleep.

- Add aromatherapy to your relaxation plan, if you find that certain scents make you sleepy. These can be added to massage oil and rubbed into the skin for a doubly relaxing effect.

- Try relaxation audiotapes or background noise machines to sleep or return to sleep.

- Learn special breathing and muscle relaxation techniques for relaxation.

Melatonin

Melatonin (MLT) is a hormone produced by the pineal gland. It is responsible for helping the body maintain sleep and other biochemical rhythms. It is also involved in regulating immune function, particularly the inflammatory response, and affects reproductive hormones, growth hormones, thyroid hormones, and insulin as well.

Melatonin supplements given about half an hour before bed can address sleep problems. The effect may not last, however.

Melatonin's effects may also differ for people with bipolar disorders. Some studies have found that taking a melatonin supplement on a regular basis may help with depression, but could make mania worse.[13] Supplementing directly with any kind of hormone is problematic in the long run, because in some cases your body may respond by producing less of the natural substance.

George, age 61, was not bowled over by melatonin:

> I took a low dose of melatonin, just three or four milligrams, and it didn't
> do much. The sleep that I got was restless sleep. I wasn't all that impressed—
> it just didn't seem to promote a good night's sleep.

If you do decide to try melatonin, talk about it with your doctor or psychiatrist and set up a dosage plan and observation schedule first. Most people with bipolar disorders who have reported good results from melatonin use it only when their sleep cycle first begins to get out of kilter, and then only until it is back on track. Their stories of improvement are strictly anecdotal, though.

Other sleep supplements

You may be tempted to try "natural" sleep aids. Of the options mentioned here, chamomile and hops are probably the safest and mildest. Avoid using other central nervous system depressants, including alcohol, at the same time as these substances. Other depressants may make the active ingredients in some of these substances work even stronger, with possibly dangerous effects.

Indeed, although these herbal potions are not as dangerous as prescription sleeping pills, they are also not inconsequential. While most people agree that depending on a pill to sleep is a bad thing, the same is true of natural sleep aids—little is known about their long-term effects, or the effects of their over-the-counter counterparts, such as Ny-Tol or Sominex.

Eileen has tried herbals for sleep, but without benefits:

> On occasion, I have taken valerian to help me get to sleep, but that has not helped. When I'm not sleeping, it is because the mania has gotten out of control, and even valerian won't help. I know several people it works wonderfully for.... just not me.

Simply taking a good multivitamin may also help regulate sleep. The B vitamins (especially B2 and niacin), potassium, and magnesium all affect the sleep cycle.

Vitamin B2 may be of particular importance in regulating sleep. Scientists at the University of North Carolina discovered in 1998 that B2 binds to cryptochrome, a light-absorbing pigment found in the retina of the eye. UNC researcher Dr. Aziz Sancar believes that a B2 deficiency may be implicated in some cases of SAD and related disorders. Others with SAD may have a deficiency in one of the two varieties of cryptochrome itself.[14]

Supplements believed to affect sleep include:

- **Valerian (Valeriana officinalis).** Valerian is a strong herbal sedative (and one of the secret ingredients in the soporific liqueur Jagermeister). It can occasionally be used to fight episodic insomnia, but it's too strong for regular use.

- **Kava-kava (Piper methysticum).** This mild sedative herb has been used for centuries in the South Pacific. It does have addictive properties, however, and so should not be used regularly. Improper use may worsen Parkinson's disease, cause your skin to yellow, and cause muscle spasms, biochemical abnormalities, vision disturbances, or shortness of breath.

- **Chamomile (Anthemis nobilis).** Chamomile is a mild, but effective, sedative traditionally used to treat sleep disorders or stomach upsets. It is a member of the daisy family, so avoid this herb if you are allergic to its cousin, ragweed.

- **Passion flower (Passiflora incarnata).** This botanical has sedative, antispasmodic, and anti-inflammatory effects.

- **Skullcap (Scutellaria lateriflora).** Skullcap is an herbal sedative that has traditionally been used to treat tic disorders and muscle spasms, as well as seizure disorders, insomnia, and anxiety. Other traditional uses include menstrual irregularity and breast pain, indicating that it may have hormonal effects.

- **Hops (Humulus lupulus).** This herb is used to flavor beer, and it is the reason beer makes many people sleepy. It's available in capsules or as a dried herb for use in tea, and works as a gentle sleep aid.

- **Tryptophan.** This amino acid raises the levels of serotonin in the brain. It's not currently available in the US due to a badly contaminated batch several years ago, but it is sold over-the-counter in Europe and by prescription in Canada. It appears to help regulate sleep and to have an antidepressant effect not unlike that of an SSRI. For that reason, people with bipolar disorders should be wary of possible manic effects from taking tryptophan. In any case, do not take this substance with any pharmaceutical antidepressant. If you can purchase tryptophan, buy it from a trustworthy source. For maximum effect, take it at bedtime with sweetened milk or fruit juice or with vitamin B6. A 1997 study of adjuncts to light therapy found that SAD patients who were initially poor responders benefited more when they also took L-tryptophan, the type of tryptophan that is most easily absorbed.[15] Unusually low tryptophan levels have been found in people with bipolar disorders who take lithium[16], so L-tryptophan may also be a good adjunct for this medication.

- **5-HTP (5-hydroxytryptophan).** The substance 5-HTP is synthesized from tryptophan and is an even more direct precursor to serotonin than tryptophan. It is available in the US. It appears to help regulate sleep and to have an antidepressant effect not unlike that of an SSRI. For that reason, people with bipolar disorders should be wary of possible manic effects from taking 5-HTP. Do not take this substance with any antidepressant.

- **Taurine.** This amino acid can counteract insomnia by slowing down nerve impulses.

- **Black cohosh (Cimicifuga racemosa, squaw root).** Black cohosh is a nervous system depressant and sedative and is often used by people with autoimmune conditions for its anti-inflammatory effects. Its active ingredient appears to bind to estrogen receptor sites, so it may cause hormonal activity.

- GABA (gaba-amino butyric acid). GABA is an amino-acid-like compound that inhibits the activity of certain neurotransmitters. You shouldn't take antiepilepsy medications or mood stabilizers with GABA supplements, unless your physician recommends it and oversees the process. Supplementation with over-the-counter GABA is sometimes recommended for anxiety, nervous tension, and insomnia, especially insomnia associated with racing thoughts. If you experience shortness of breath, tingling, or numbness in your hands or feet when taking GABA, lower or discontinue this supplement.

Valerian, kava-kava, passion flower, black cohosh, and skullcap can help to ease extreme anxiety as well as insomnia, but their sedating qualities and side effects must be taken into account.

Essential fatty acids

Some of the most exciting complementary treatment news for people with bipolar disorders arrived in 1998, when Dr. Andrew L. Stoll and his colleagues at McLean Hospital in Belmont, MA, announced that Omega-3 fatty acids appear to act as a mood stabilizer for some people with bipolar disorders.[17] How they work is still unknown, but they are essential for building and maintaining the myelin sheath that surrounds nerve fibers and ensures the proper conduction of messages along the nerves.

Omega-3 fatty acids are a type of essential fatty acids (EFAs) that are found almost exclusively in fish oils. As the "essential" in their name implies, these fatty acids are needed to build cells and also to support the body's anti-inflammatory response. They are the good polyunsaturated fats that improve cardiovascular health when substituted for the bad saturated fats.

Two Omega-3 fatty acids are found in oily, cold-water fish: eicosapentaenoic acid (EPA) and docosahexanoic acid (DHA). Another Omega-3 fatty acid, alpha-linoleic acid, is found in flax-seed and perilla oils, among other sources.

Omega-6 fatty acids are also important for optimal health. The Omega-6 family includes linoleic acid and its derivatives, including gammalinolenic acid (GLA), dihomogamma-linolenic acid (DGLA), and arachidonic acid (AA). These substances also come from animal fats and some plants, such as evening primrose oil (EPO), which is a good source of GLA; flax-seed oil; black-currant seed oil; hemp-seed oil; and borage oil, which contains both GLA and very long chain fatty acids (VLCFAs).

Unfortunately, the high levels of arachidonic acid found in evening primrose oil have been reported to lower the threshold for frontal-lobe seizures, so people who have seizures should exercise caution. Also, the VLCFAs found in borage oil can be irritating to the liver and central nervous system and are therefore not recommended for use by people with nervous system disorders or those who take medications that place stress on the liver. Other oils with a high VLCFA content are canola oil, peanut oil (including the oil in peanut butter), and mustard-seed oil.

When oils are heated, most will convert at least part of their fatty acids into trans fatty acids, which are substances to be avoided. Hemp oil is one of the few that can resist this heat-driven conversion progress, and it has recently become available for cooking and medicinal use in the US.

Researchers believe that achieving a dietary balance between Omega-3 and Omega-6 fatty acids provides the most benefits. The ratios usually recommended are 3:1 or 4:1 Omega-6 to Omega-3.

EFA basics

Now that you know the good news about EFAs, here's the not-so-good news: to get the mood stabilizing benefits reported in the McLean Hospital study, patients took 9. 6 grams per day of concentrated fish oil. Think about that for a moment: 9.6 grams is a lot of oil to drink from a spoon, much less take in capsule form (almost 30 capsules per day). Many people who have tried to duplicate this experiment at home have found it difficult, both for the sheer amount they had to use and for the side effects that can ensue.

Since announcing his initial results, Dr. Stoll has produced an "Omega-3 Fatty Acid User Guide" that is highly recommended and has also written a book. Both are listed in Appendix A. He notes that 5 grams of Omega-3 fatty acids may be sufficient to stabilize mood. Although he recommends fish oil because it has been studied the most, Dr. Stoll says that the concentration of Omega-3 EFAs in flax-seed and perilla oils is actually higher, and the taste of these oils is far more palatable. Two to three teaspoons per day of these oils in their liquid form should be sufficient for an adult, he says, although you'll need to adjust the dose according to body size and individual chemistry. The maximum effective dose Dr. Stoll reports using is 15 grams of oil per day.

Dr. Stoll and others with experience at using EFAs as a mood stabilizer do not recommend using them as a sole remedy—the patients who were successful in the McLean study continued to take their regular mood stabilizer, and you should too.

Joe, age 33, found this out the hard way:

> A little more than a year ago I experimented with taking omega-3
> fatty acid supplements after a study at McLean Hospital suggested
> that these fatty acids, found often in brain tissue, could be as effective
> in treating bipolar disorder as lithium. I tried using only the fatty acid
> supplement instead of lithium, but relapsed into another episode.

EFAs can also affect more than your mood. They can impact blood clotting, a particular concern to anyone with a clotting disorder, heart problem, or particular susceptibility to stroke. As with all complementary therapies, discuss EFAs thoroughly with your doctor before use.

EFA tips

The following tips for using EFAs as mood stabilizers have been collected from a variety of sources, including researchers at NIH and US mood disorder clinics where patients are trying this approach, and patients themselves.

- You can take antioxidant supplements during treatment with EFAs to prevent your body from simply oxidizing the extra oil. One mood disorder clinic recommends 1200 IUs (International Units) of natural vitamin E and 2000 mg of vitamin C for adults weighing approximately 150 pounds, with doses reduced or increased according to body weight.

- If you choose fish oil, fishy burps are the most commonly reported side effect—and they are most unpleasant. Recommendations include swallowing a whole clove of garlic or a garlic tablet with the fish oil as a breath deodorant. You know these burps are not nice if garlic is recommended as a cover-up! Taking the fish oil at night or with orange juice also seems to help.

- In Iceland and Scandinavia, flavored fish oils have long been available as an old-fashioned health tonic (those flavored with mint are a favorite). If demand rises, these may be seen on North American shelves soon.

- Stomach troubles are reported from EFA use, as is excessive flatulence. Garlic or a garlic pill might also help with these problems. Some people report trying acidophilus capsules or other probiotics, yogurt with live cultures, or over-the-counter stomach or gas remedies. If you try over-the-counter medications, do be careful. Many of these can interact with or counteract psychiatric medications, and they just might affect the action of EFAs as well. Perilla oil seems less irritating to the stomach than fish oil or flax-seed oil.

- Diarrhea or oily stools are another unpleasant side effect, especially if the dose is more than 10 grams per day. In fact, flax seeds are rather well-known for promoting regularity, and when you ingest a lot, you may be a little too regular. Taking several small doses of oil rather than one large one should help.

It's great if you can get at least some of your EFAs in food. Low-fat diets are part of the reason some people, especially those who are trying to lose weight, may not get enough. Many cold-pressed salad oils, including olive, safflower, sunflower, corn, peanut, and canola oils, do contain EFAs, as do coconut oil and coconut butter. When these oils are processed with heat, however, the fatty acids may be changed or destroyed. Corn and soybean oils are both high in Omega-6 fatty acids. Olive oil is probably your best EFA choice for cold, oil-based dressings and marinades.

Oily, cold-water fish themselves are another great EFA source, although again, cooking may be a problem (and not everyone is a sushi fan).

It is possible to have lab tests done to discern EFA levels, although few doctors know much about them. You might have to send a blood sample to a specialty lab.

Diabetics may experience adverse effects from too high a dose of EFAs and should talk to their physician before supplementing with EFA products. If excess weight is already a problem, you should probably consult a nutritionist about how to substitute these good fats for bad ones, while cutting calories in other areas.

Commercial EFA preparations that you may hear about include the following:

- **Cod liver oil.** High in Omega-3 fatty acids, cod liver oil is also loaded with vitamins A and D. Look for a high-quality, toxicology-tested source of cod liver oil, because mercury and other toxins are deposited in the fish's liver if it is exposed to these substances.

- **Efalex.** This brand-name EFA supplement made by Efamol Neutriceuticals Inc. is widely touted as a supplement for people with ADD/ADHD. It contains a mix of Omega-3 fish oil, Omega-6 EPO and thyme oil, and Vitamin E.

- **Efamol.** Also from Efamol Neutriceuticals, Efamol is marketed as a treatment for PMS. It combines EPO; vitamins B6, C, and E; niacin, zinc, and magnesium. Both Efamol products are now available in the US, Canada, and the UK and can be purchased by mail order. Unlike many supplement manufacturers, Efamol adheres to strict standards, and it also sponsors reputable research.

- **EicoPro.** Made by Eicotec Inc., this supplement combines Omega-3 fish oils and Omega-6 linoleic acid. Eicotech is another supplier known for its high manufacturing standards.

- **Essential Balance.** This is a commercial EFA formula made from sesame, sunflower, flax-seed, pumpkin-seed, and borage oils.

- **Evening primrose oil (EPO).** Evening primrose oil is one of the best EFA sources around and has become a very popular supplement as a result. It contains high amounts of Omega-6 fatty acids, as do borage oil, flax-seed oil, and black currant seed oil. Evening primrose oil has been reported to lower the threshold for frontal-lobe seizures, however, so people who have these types of seizures should exercise caution. EPO and other plant-source oils are available in liquid form or as gelcaps from several different companies.

- **Fish body oil.** Like cod liver oil, fish body oil is made from oily, cold-water fish that are high in valuable Omega-3 fatty acids. However, there is less risk of mercury and other toxins in these oils, because they are not made from fish liver.

- **Monolaurin.** Your body makes this substance from lauric acid, another medium-chain fatty acid found in abundance in coconuts and some other foods, including human breast milk. It is known to have anti-bacterial and anti-viral properties. Monolaurin may be the active ingredient in colostrum, the "pre-milk" all mammals produce to jump-start a newborn's immune system. Cow colostrum is available in supplement form in some areas.

- **OmegaBrite.** This is a new EFA supplement designed by the researcher who headed NIMH's clinical trials on EFAs in bipolar disorder, Dr. Andrew Stoll. Based on fish body oil, it is toxicology tested and is available in gelcaps.

Contact information for suppliers listed above and other companies that sell EFA supplements is listed in Appendix A.

Diet

Some basic dietary advice applies to anyone who suffers from mood swings: eat a variety of healthy foods at regular intervals, do not skip meals, and avoid an excess of sugar and junk food. The problem with a poor diet is that it does not promote general health. Taken to the extreme, self-restricted diets can turn into full-blown eating disorders. Both anorexia nervosa and bulimia are more common in people with bipolar disorders and may have similar neurological triggers.

As the section on essential fatty acids earlier in this chapter indicated, one dietary change that may help with mood regulation is eliminating hydrogenated (trans) fats. Experts in fatty acid metabolization note that hydrogenated fats short-circuit the body's ability to metabolize the good fatty acids needed to, among other things, produce normal amounts of neurotransmitters and other hormones.

Simply raising the level of good fat in the diet could also help. In 1996 Dr. Keith Ablow published some intriguing thoughts on the relationship between fat intake and mental disturbances in the article "Fat Chance" (*http://www.mhsource.com/exclusive/psychandsoc0796.html*). His observations on fat intake and mood are echoed by anecdotal reports on the calming effects of high-fat foods.

Whether dietary changes are as effective as their proponents claim, one thing is certain: eating healthier never hurt anyone. Besides, changing your diet is relatively easy, inexpensive, and non-invasive.

Monique is still struggling to find the right eating habits to take off medication-linked pounds:

> *I have gained approximately 35 to 40 pounds since I started taking Depakote. That kind of weight gain is really devastating.*
>
> *I have tried dietary changes in order to combat my weight gain from Depakote. I tried the "Somercizing" diet from Suzanne Somers, where you cut down on the carbohydrates and you eat more protein. I lost some weight, but from what I read recently at the NAMI conference, you really need a more balanced diet rather than doing it the way I did. You need both carbohydrates and proteins mixed in. Now I'm trying to stay balanced, watching the amount I eat, watching fats, and cutting down on the sugar intake.*

If you need to make major changes in the way you eat, it's a good idea to work with a nutritionist. Nutritionists are experts in how food intake affects health. Some are employed by hospitals, clinics, and long-term care facilities to improve patient care through appropriate diet. Others work in private practice. Some nutritionists have very traditional views about diet, and others may recommend what seem like radical changes. Be sure to check the credentials and training of any nutritionist you consult, and pay attention to your intuition if her suggestions seem unreasonable or potentially unhealthy.

Checking the credentials of a nutritionist isn't always easy. Those who work with hospitals are usually registered dietitians (RDs). Others may hold credentials from the American Society for Nutritional Sciences (RSNS) or the American Society for Clinical Nutrition (ASCN). A good guide to nutritionist credentials—both reputable and dubious—is available on the Web at *http://www.quackwatch.com/04ConsumerEducation/ nutritionist.html.*

If you have an eating disorder in addition to manic depression, include a nutritionist with background in dietary interventions for eating disorders on your treatment team.

Battling medication-linked weight gain

Perhaps the most talked-about diet issue among people with bipolar disorders is weight gain caused by taking psychiatric medications. The neuroleptics are the most frequent offenders, but Depakote, Depakene, and lithium have also been implicated in packing on extra pounds.

When it's just a little extra weight, that's a small price to pay for effective mood control. But for many people who take these medications, the weight gain is substantial— up to 100 pounds, in some cases, and often gained very rapidly. This amount of extra weight can pose a danger to your health and is certainly no boost for your self-esteem.

Shannon, age 33, is looking for ways to cope with weight gain due to neuroleptic use:

> The newer neuroleptics (Clozaril and Risperdal) made me gain about 100 pounds altogether, although they virtually eliminated any psychotic symptoms. I'm trying via Weight Watchers to take the weight off, since I never had a weight problem before taking psychotropics.
>
> I also began taking L-Carnitine (brand name: Carnitor), a supplement, which acts as an appetite suppressant and is often deficient in people taking Depakote. However, I no longer take it, because my doctor wasn't sure about the drug interactions.
>
> I switched from Risperdal to Geodon recently, and have lost about ten pounds on this new med, which inhibits appetite and speeds up metabolism, at least for me. I had a little initial hypomania on Geodon, but that's under control now, and I'm happy with my new med.

Diet changes are the first thing to try when faced with weight gain. These medications may both increase your carbohydrate cravings and change your metabolism, and not every diet plan is a good way to deal with this type of weight problem. For example, a high-protein diet may add extra strain on your liver and kidneys—and so can some psychiatric medications. Generally speaking, a balanced, low-calorie diet is your best bet. If you need extra support or assistance, you may want to try a group like Weight Watchers or a commercial plan like Jenny Craig, which makes food choices even easier. Consult your doctor or a nutritionist prior to beginning any diet.

Medication changes for weight control

If you continue to gain weight despite changing your diet, talk to your doctor about changing your medication. Some mood stabilizers and neuroleptics are worse than others for causing weight gain. Older neuroleptics such as Haldol tend to cause more gain than the newer atypical neuroleptics, although individual experiences may vary. Ziprasidone (Geodon, also known as Zeldox), one of the newer atypical neuroleptics, was developed specifically to reduce the incidence of major weight gain and other side effects. It's not a good choice for people with heart trouble, but may work well for others.

For some people, adding another medication may be part of the answer. A recent study indicates that the antihistamine Axid (nizatidine) reduced weight gain by half among people taking the neuroleptic Zyprexa.[18] Other medications that affect metabolism may also help, including Topamax (topiramate)[19] and Glucophage (metformin).[20]

The supplement L-Carnitine is sometimes suggested for combating weight gain from Depakote and Depakene in particular. These mood stabilizers definitely deplete the body's natural supply of carnitine, which can cause stomach pain and may cause metabolic changes.[21,22] Naturally occurring carnitine is found throughout the body, including in the nervous system. It carries long-chain fatty acids through the inner mitochondrial membrane and is believed to affect metabolism. It may also help to protect brain tissue and prevent seizures.[23] However, the benefits of L-Carnitine supplementation have not been completely substantiated.[24]

Exercise is also a great way to prevent or reverse weight gain, and it can give you a psychological boost as well. Research indicates that exercise can also have a marked antidepressant effect of its own.[25]

For Sharon, age 47, a rigorous exercise program has been the key to weight loss:

> I was fat for ten years after my diagnosis—I gained 100 pounds in six
> months on lithium and Depakote. Yecchh! I finally finished losing 90
> pounds of it this fall, so that's a major burden lifted.
>
> For me, it's exercise, exercise, exercise. I believe utterly that running or
> walking five to ten miles per day is saving my life, from weight loss plus
> endorphins.

Allergy tests and treatments

No one knows why, but people with bipolar disorders tend to have a higher rate of allergies, including asthma, than people who have no neurological challenges. If you have allergies or asthma, that can affect your treatment choices. Many of the medications used for these conditions contain stimulants that could cause mania if you are not on an adequate mood stabilizer. Steroids used to treat asthma can also cause mood swings.

In addition, any medication can contain allergens, such as cornstarch, egg albumin, or wheat. If you have or suspect you have allergies and experience an unusual reaction to a new psychiatric medication, share this information with your doctor. Non-allergenic formulas are available.

You may also find that certain psychiatric medications ease your allergy symptoms, allowing you to reduce or discontinue allergy medications. All of the neuroleptics, for example, are based on antihistamines.

Allergies, and especially seasonal allergies, can also play a part in your pattern of mood swings. Chronic allergies sap your strength and energy, which can worsen depression. There may be other, more complex interactions between the immune system and the neurotransmitter system as well.

You can find out whether you have allergies by getting tested. The most common allergy tests done by doctors are the skin-prick test and the radioallergosorbent test (RAST). Although the skin test may actually be more sensitive, the RAST is more specific and reliable and is preferred for anyone with eczema. The RAST is a blood test that measures the level of immunoglobulin E (IgE) antibodies to specific foods or substances. If there are no IgE antibodies present in the blood, the person does not have an allergy to that item.

Tell the allergist what medications you take before the RAST is administered. Antihistamines (including neuroleptics), steroids, and some other medicines can skew results by inhibiting the inflammatory response.

Severe allergic reactions are rare, but those at risk must be extra careful about reading labels and should always carry an emergency kit. Your allergist can help you put this together. People who have both asthma and allergies have a higher risk of dangerous allergic reactions.

Elimination/reintroduction diet for food allergies

About 5 percent of all people have food allergies, but the rate of both food allergies and food sensitivities among people with bipolar disorders appears to be higher.[26]

The only sure treatment for food allergies is food avoidance. There are desensitization shots available for other types of allergens, such as pollens, but this therapy is only in its formative stages for food allergies. Some allergists are willing to try neutralization shots or sublingual drops that contain a tiny amount of the allergen, also called low-dose immunotherapy. The efficacy of these is not proven, although some clinical trials have been promising.[27]

Diets to detect and eliminate food allergies should be carried out under the aegis of an allergist or other knowledgeable physician. Most start patients out with an elimination diet, taking out all of the most common allergens: dairy products, eggs, all gluten-containing grains, corn, citrus fruits, bananas, nuts (especially peanuts), soy, and vegetables from the nightshade family (tomatoes, eggplant, potatoes, and peppers). Obviously, if you already know of or suspect an allergy to another food, this item should be eliminated as well. Most people stay on this very restricted diet for at least four weeks—some doctors recommend an elimination diet for as long as six months.

Next comes the reintroduction process: add back the foods that you eliminated, one at a time. Eat the reintroduced food at every meal. If you suffer no ill effects, you aren't allergic to that food, and it can be added back to your regular diet.

Food sensitivity reactions can sometimes be cut short with a simple dose of baking soda or commercial preparations containing bicarbonate of soda, such as Alka-Seltzer. These can counteract some psychiatric medications, however. According to Kristi, age 52, a gluten-free diet has been helpful in minimizing her mood swings, although it has not been a cure:

> I had to make a medication change two years ago and did not have as much control over my moods as I used to. I saw a naturopath and he said that because I also have some bowel problems I might try taking all gluten products out of my diet—that's wheat and some other grains. He said it is not an allergy, but that maybe my body can't handle these foods well, like some people are milk-intolerant.
>
> At first it didn't seem to be helping at all, but after about a month my physical problems got quite a bit better. Not long after that, I noticed that I was also less depressed.

I don't know if that's because these foods were making me depressed, or if I just felt better physically and that lifted my mood, but either way changing my diet has contributed to being more stable. I did not have a choice about changing my medication, so I'm glad this worked.

If you seem to have an allergic reaction to a food, eliminate it again for several weeks and then reintroduce it again. You may need to follow this last step several times to make sure you know which food is causing the possible allergic reaction.

Rotation diet for food allergies

If you find definite food allergies or food sensitivities, allergists usually recommend following a rotation diet. This plan requires that you eat different foods each day in a four-day period to decrease the likelihood of developing new allergies. People with mild food sensitivities may find that they can eventually tolerate foods that once caused them distress when they follow a rotation diet, but reintroducing these foods should be done very carefully.

Although proper treatment for allergies promotes better health, it may have little to no impact on bipolar symptoms, despite what you may read in some books or online.

When using allergy medication, always check for contraindications and watch out for side effects. Many allergy medications contain stimulants or steroids that can cause manic symptoms in people with bipolar disorders.

Hormonal treatments

Many women have noticed that hormones can have a profound effect on their mood swings. Birth control pills, the birth-control shot Depo-Provera (medroxyprogesterone, a synthetic cousin of the hormone progesterone), estrogen supplements and medications like Premarin (synthetic estrogen), and other hormone-based compounds can increase or decrease your stability, depending on individual circumstances. Lower levels of progesterone, which occur in the luteal phase of menstruation (right before your period), are already known to predispose some epileptic women to seizures and to cause an increase in migraine symptoms in others.

Medications used to treat bipolar disorders can also cause hormonal changes, as Monique discovered:

After I started taking Depakote, I found that this medication has affected my cycle. It's not as regular as it used to be. When I asked my first psychiatrist about this issue, he had no idea. He just said, "no, I don't think it could affect that." Then I showed him the side effects sheet from the pharmacist, which says that Depakote can affect your cycle.

I've been to doctors about it and they've run tests. Now they have me on birth-control pills to regulate it—great, another medication I have to take! I've just been really frustrated in this regard.

Considering the importance of the endocrine system in mood control, it's surprising that very little research has been done on how hormones influence bipolar symptoms. Few psychiatrists use hormonal treatments to target bipolar symptoms or to augment other treatments, and many are unaware that these treatments can have destabilizing effects as well.

That said, estrogen's ability to cause mania and rapid cycling is fairly well-known among doctors who specialize in hormone replacement therapy for older women. These doctors are also well aware that in the right dose, estrogen can also help with mild depression. It's a balancing act, and one that can be less than pleasant for women with bipolar disorder as they reach middle age and beyond.

Some clinicians have suggested that a combination of estrogen and progesterone could act as a mood stabilizer, but others suggest that hormones only be considered as an adjunct to regular mood stabilizers, much as thyroid hormone supplementation is sometimes used.[28]

Other studies have indicated an anti-manic role for drugs that block estrogen, specifically the breast cancer drug tamoxifen. Early research into tamoxifen, which is a protein kinase C inhibitor, indicates that it is effective and may turn out to be a well-tolerated drug for emergency treatment as well as, perhaps, for prevention of mania.[29]

New mood stabilizers may be developed soon that target catamenial (menstrual-cycle-linked) symptoms. One promising candidate is the antiseizure drug ganaxolone.[30] Although the FDA gave ganaxolone special "orphan drug" approval for treating infantile spasms several years ago, it's still being investigated as a treatment for other forms of epilepsy and migraine. No trials for treating bipolar disorder have been done.

It may be worthwhile for bipolar women to explore these possibilities with their physician. Women with manic depression frequently report menstrual irregularities and pre-menstrual mood problems, and evening out hormone levels may help with these problems as well as with mood.

Rachel says:

> *Because my daughter's bipolar symptoms first emerged at puberty, I have just always had the gut feeling that there is hormonal involvement in the illness itself, at least for her. She's an adult now, and still has severe problems with her cycle—very irregular, sometimes nonexistent, sometimes extremely heavy, sometimes painful. And it correlates very closely with her moods. She has talked to her doctors about this, but it's still a puzzle—birth control pills as a way to regulate her cycles have also caused mood swings. I really wish someone would do research on this topic!*

You might also consider looking at natural alternatives to hormone supplementation. Soy isoflavones, yams, Vitamin E, essential fatty acids, and other substances that affect estrogen or progesterone production could be beneficial—or could disrupt hormonal cycles that are functioning normally.

For those who may be sexually promiscuous when manic, birth control obviously has other attractions. Talk with your doctor about how birth control will interact with your psychiatric medications, and know the signs of impending trouble.

Because the hormonal cycles of men are less obvious than those of women, there has been almost no research into hormone-based treatments for physically healthy men. It's possible that at least some males with bipolar disorders also suffer from hormonal imbalances. Unfortunately, there isn't much information available at this time, anecdotal or otherwise.

If you're interested in pursuing the hormonal angle, be sure to work with a competent endocrinologist, even if you plan to use natural supplements only. Hormones are not something to experiment with on your own.

Anti-viral treatments and immunotherapy

Anti-viral treatments and immunotherapy may soon be moving into the mainstream of psychiatric care. There is ample reason to believe that for at least some people with bipolar disorders, viral infections of the central nervous system are part of the problem. Possible culprits include enteroviruses; various human herpes viruses, including varicella zoster (the virus that causes chicken pox) and the Epstein-Barr virus (EBV); paramyxoviruses (the family that includes measles, mumps, and some types of influenza-like viruses); retroviruses; cytomegaloviruses; or something completely new.

In the years before psychoanalytic theory, physical illness was often assumed to be the cause of mental illness, since it was well-known that syphilis, influenza, and other diseases could also cause dementia. It's only recently that medical researchers have taken up the quest for infectious agents again. Some practitioners, however, have long encouraged their mentally ill patients to pursue anti-viral therapies, sometimes with encouraging results.

Recent findings that give credence to viral infection theories include the following:

- Lymphocyte abnormalities: lymphocytes are white blood cells involved in immune system response

- Protein abnormalities

- Antibodies to the patient's own tissues (autoantibodies), including antibodies to brain tissue

- Increased levels of the immune system regulators called cytokines in some people with bipolar disorder or schizophrenia

The discovery that lithium and some other psychiatric medications have anti-viral properties has also intrigued researchers.

Viral infection could result in brain lesions or structural changes in the brain that cause bipolar symptoms, or it could have other effects on the nervous system. A virus may affect the use or production of certain neurotransmitters, for example, or it might impact the immune system in ways that cause psychiatric symptoms. The actual infection may occur before birth, which would help to explain the slightly higher number of minor birth defects seen in people with mental illnesses. Many viruses can lie dormant in the human brain or other tissue for years, only emerging when some other insult to the immune system (such as extreme stress or infection with another illness) sets them off.[31]

The re-emergence of viral theories of bipolar disorders doesn't mean that researchers are throwing out today's genetic theories, however—the two ideas are actually complementary. It's now known that particular types of unusual immune responses to infection and susceptibility to damage from viruses, are very much genetically linked.

Some of the most interesting work on viruses and bipolar disorders is being done at the Stanley Foundation Neurovirology Laboratory (*http://www.med.jhu.edu/stanleylab/*) at Johns Hopkins University's School of Medicine. Using cells from the brains of deceased people with either schizophrenia or bipolar disorders, researchers at this lab have identified the tell-tale signs of infection with a virus that seems to be from the paramyxovirus family. They've also found evidence of retroviral activity.[32]

So how can you find out if a virus is part of your problems, and what can be done to help? Doctors who specialize in this area of practice are known as neuroimmun-ologists—but this is a new specialty, and practitioners can be hard to locate. If you don't have a neuroimmunity specialist in your area, you might search for a practitio-ner who works with patients who have AIDS, multiple sclerosis, or other conditions that combine viral activity with neurological symptoms. He should be familiar with the major therapies and hopefully will be able to tailor a program for your specific case. There are medical tests available that can help to identify immune system impairments and/or viral activity. These include:

- **Blood count.** A low white blood cell count could indicate that there is a viral or other infection active somewhere in the body.

- **Sedimentation rate.** This test measures how quickly the red cells separate from the serum in a test tube. In most inflammatory or autoimmune diseases, they separate quickly, although unusually slow separation could also indicate trouble.

- **Immune panel.** This general screen may include a search for antibodies, mito-gens (substances that cause certain cells to proliferate), antigens (foreign proteins in the body), and lymphocyte surface markers and blood tests for various specific immune-dysfunction markers.

- **Anti-Neuronal Antibody screen.** An ANA screen looks for antibodies to brain tissue in the bloodstream. Their presence is a general indicator for a variety of auto-immune disorders, such as lupus. Note that the Anti-Nuclear Antibody test, also abbreviated as ANA, may also be ordered. This test is part of the screening procedure for several autoimmune inflammatory diseases.

- **Viral antibody tests.** Tests that look for unusual levels of specific viral anti-bodies, such as those associated with the Epstein-Barr virus, other human herpes viruses (HHV6, HHV7, HHV8, HSV-1, HSV-2), chronic mononucleosis syn-drome (CMS), cytomegalovirus (CMV), or rubella (German measles).

- **Immunoglobulin tests.** Tests to check for immunoglobulin G (IgG) subclass abnormalities (IgG1, IgG2, IgG3, IgG4), which are found in patients with increased susceptibility to viral or bacterial infections due to a compromised immune system, autoimmune diseases, or immune-mediated neurological dis-orders. It's possible to plot the distributions of IgG sub-types against patterns associated with specific viruses or conditions.

- **Amino acid profile.** Markers for an impaired immune system include low amounts of the amino acids lysine and arginine.
- **NeuroSPECT.** This brain scan shows the diffusion of blood through the brain, indicating areas of low and high activity.

A multi-faceted immune panel can turn up many small pieces of evidence that, taken together, indicate a compromised immune system.

Anti-viral treatments

If you find viral activity or immune system problems, there are many possible treatments, including prescription medications. AIDS research has resulted in new medications that are called "immune system stimulants" or "immune system modulators." The majority of these drugs have side effects that make them undesirable for use, except for patients faced with a life-threatening immune deficiency. Others may deserve a trial for treating bipolar disorders that are linked to the immune system. As the saying goes, "your mileage may vary" with these medications and supplements. Some vitamins and supplements are also believed to boost the immune system.

The following are some substances that may work as immune modulators:

- **Kutapressin.** A porcine liver extract comprised of very small proteins or polypeptides, kutapressin inhibits human herpes viruses (its best-known use is as a medication for herpes zoster, or shingles) and reduces inflammation. It is given in intramuscular injections, can be rather expensive because the supply is currently limited, and may not be a long-term solution for herpes infection.
- **Dimethylglycine (DMG, calcium pangamate, pangamic acid, vitamin B15).** This vitamin-like amino acid supplement appears to give a mild boost to the immune system, possibly by boosting the number of natural killer (NK) cells. DMG may help some people tolerate stress, reduce the frequency of seizures, and strengthen the immune system. DMG changes the way your body uses folic acid, so you may need to supplement with that vitamin. Increased hyperactivity may result from a lack of folic acid when taking DMG. A related product, trimethylglycine (TMG), is available in liquid form. Both DMG and TMG have roles in the chemical reactions that increase serotonin levels. Those who take medications that also affect serotonin should take care with these supplements.
- **Inosine pranobex (Isoprinosine).** This older anti-viral is also active against human herpes virus and other infections. It is a relatively weak immune modulator.

- Acyclovir (Zovirax). This potent anti-viral works against several human herpes viruses, Epstein-Barr virus, herpes zoster, varicella (chicken pox), cytomegalovirus, and other viruses.

- Foscarnet. This is another anti-herpes drug. Unfortunately, it's rather toxic and so is not used unless the infection is causing severe symptoms and other medications have been tried and failed.

- Ampligen. This nucleic acid compound apparently heightens production of the body's own immunological and anti-viral agents, such as interferon. It is expensive, is administered by intravenous infusion, and is not available to all patients or in all countries.

- SSRI antidepressants. These medications may affect neurotransmitters in ways that not only address depression and other neurological disorders, but directly or indirectly regulate the immune system. When used for this purpose, they are often given at very low doses.

- Lithium. As noted in Chapter 4, *Medical Care,* lithium also appears to have anti-viral action.

For some kinds of virulent infections, intravenous immunoglobulin G (IVIG) or plasmapheresis is sometimes prescribed. These invasive procedures involve cleansing and replacing blood components.

Herbal antibiotics and antivirals

Several herbs appear to have antiseptic, antiviral, antifungal, or antibiotic properties. Obviously, if these substances are active, you should use them carefully and sparingly, despite the claims of certain manufacturers who encourage daily use for disease prevention.

- Antioxidants. Natural antioxidants include vitamins A, C, and E; beta carotene; Coenzyme Q (CoQ10); gingko biloba; the minerals selenium and zinc; grapeseed oil and other proanthocyanidins; and the Mexican folk remedy Cat's claw (una de gato). Of these, the vitamins, minerals, and grapeseed oil have received the most attention from patients over the years. Anecdotal reports indicate that grapeseed oil may be especially effective for people who have episodes of extreme agitation or rage.

- Bitter melon (Momordica charantia). An antiviral from the Chinese herbal pharmacopoeia, bitter melon is the plant from which the active ingredient in some protease inhibitors (the powerful drugs used to combat AIDS) is derived.

- Echinacea (Echinacea purpurea). An herbal antiseptic, echinacea also dilates blood vessels. It is said to have anti-seizure qualities as well.

- Goldenseal (Hydrastis Canadensis L.). An alkaloid isoquinoline derivative related to the minor opium alkaloids. Its active ingredient, hydrastine, elevates blood pressure. This is a very strong herb that has antiseptic properties when taken internally or applied to the skin in powder or salve form. It acts on the mucous membranes of the GI tract when taken internally.

- SPV-30. Derived from the European boxwood tree, SPV-30 is a fairly new item in this category. It apparently includes some antiviral and steroidal (anti-inflammatory) compounds and has become very popular among people with AIDS as an alternative to pharmaceutical antivirals.

Herbal remedies

Many herbs have been used to treat neurological disorders through the ages. Herbalists call these substances nervines, and some may prove useful for treating specific symptoms of bipolar disorders.

Of all the herbal remedies, this group of plant extracts is among the strongest, and the most likely to cause serious side effects. Along with the herbal sleep aids, antibiotics, and antivirals mentioned earlier in this chapter, nervines that have been tried by people with bipolar disorders or related conditions include:

- Black cohosh (Cimicifuga racemosa, squaw root). Black cohosh is a nervous system depressant and sedative that is often used by people with auto-immune conditions for its anti-inflammatory effects. Its active ingredient appears to bind to estrogen receptor sites, so it may cause hormonal activity.

- Damiana (Turnera aphrodisiaca). This is a traditional remedy for depression. As its Latin name indicates, it is also believed to have aphrodisiac properties. Whatever the case may be there, it does seem to act on the hormonal system. Its energizing quality might be dangerous for bipolar patients.

- Gingko biloba. An extract of the gingko tree, this substance is advertised as an herb that can improve your memory. There is some clinical evidence for this claim. It is an antioxidant and is prescribed in Germany for treatment of dementia. It is believed to increase blood flow to the brain and body. By increasing blood flow to the genitals, it may help revive sexual response in people experiencing loss of libido due to medication.

- Ginger (**Zingiber officinalis**). Ginger can help to circumvent medication-induced nausea. Two or three slices of fresh ginger steeped in hot water makes a stomach-calming tea.

- Ginseng (**Panax quinquefolium**). Ginseng has an energizing effect that may be helpful to people whose depression is accompanied by extreme fatigue and lethargy.

- Gotu kola (**Centella asiatica, Hydrocotyl asiatica**). This Ayurvedic herbal stimulant is sometimes recommended for depression and anxiety.

- Licorice (**Glycyrrhiza glabra, Liquiritia officinalis**). Licorice boosts hormone production, including hormones active in the digestive tract and brain. Licorice can help with nausea.

- Sarsaparilla (**Hemidesmus indicus**). Like licorice, sarsaparilla seems to affect hormone production as well as settling the stomach and calming the nerves.

- St. John's Wort (**Hypericum perforatum**). This herb has gained popularity as an herbal antidepressant. It has the backing of a decent amount of research, but as noted in Chapter 4, those choosing to use this remedy should follow the same precautions as with pharmaceutical antidepressants in the SSRI and MAOI families. Like other antidepressants, St. John's Wort can cause mania in people with manic depression. It can also cause increased sensitivity to light. It is available by prescription in Germany, where it is the most widely used antidepressant. It is potentially dangerous to use St. John's Wort with prescription antidepressants, any other medication that could affect serotonin, or drugs used to treat HIV (particularly protease inhibitors like indivir).

Vitamins

A varied, healthy diet is your best source of vitamins. Some researchers believe that people with bipolar disorders may metabolize certain vitamins differently, and therefore require careful intake of food or supplements.

A small-scale study at the University of Calgary found that taking a broad-based multivitamin supplement plus antioxidants produced surprising benefits for people with bipolar disorders. According to early reports, symptoms were reduced by almost half, and some participants were able to reduce the number of medications or medication doses they needed to control mood swings.[33]

The supplement studied had 36 ingredients, including vitamins A, C, D, and E; multiple B vitamins; calcium; iron; magnesium; zinc; copper; potassium; and two antioxidants. A larger trial is now underway, with results expected in 2002.

Although this small study is certainly not conclusive, a general-purpose multi-vitamin is probably a good idea.

If you plan to pursue vitamin therapies, purchase a basic guide to vitamins and minerals that includes information about toxicity symptoms. Some people metabolize vitamins and minerals differently, making them more or less susceptible to potential toxic effects. Along with your doctor's guidance, a good reference book can help you avoid problems.

Also, take vitamin company sales pitches and dosage recommendations with a grain of salt. The testimonials these companies produce are intended to sell their products, not to help you develop a treatment plan. Consult a physician or a professional nutritionist who does not sell supplements for unbiased, individualized advice.

Vitamins often cited as important in mood regulation include the following:

- **The B vitamins.** If you are deficient in any of the Bs, depression, anxiety, and fatigue can result. The B vitamins work together, so it's best to take a "B Complex" supplement that mixes them in proper proportions along with folic acid. The Bs have a generally energizing effect and help build up the immune system. Some naturopaths recommend Vitamin B-12 shots for depressed patients. They don't always work, but sometimes they can have surprisingly quick mood-elevating effects. Because of that energizing effect, however, they are probably not a good idea for those who are hypomanic or manic. B vitamins are used up quicker when the body or mind is stressed, so supplementing during these times could help.

- **Vitamin B-1 (thiamin).** B-1 alone, or in addition to a regular B complex pill, might be a good idea for bipolar patients who suffer from circulation problems, tingling in the extremities, anxiety, irritability, night terrors, and similar symptoms.

- **Vitamin B-6 (pyridoxine).** B-6, in addition to a regular B-complex pill, might be indicated for bipolar patients who present with a great deal of irritability and for those with marked premenstrual symptoms and/or motion sickness. Vitamin B6 is taken in combination with magnesium for the best effect. If you start to experience tingling in your hands or feet, reduce or discontinue the B6.

- **Vitamin B-12.** This vitamin helps your body turn food into energy, and without enough of it you are likely to feel listless and fatigued. Vegetarians are often deficient in B-12, because it's found mostly in meat.

- **Vitamin E.** This vitamin is an anti-oxidant that can reduce the frequency of seizures in some people who have epilepsy.[34] It's especially important to take Vitamin E if you take Depakote, Depakene, or another anticonvulsant, because these drugs deplete vitamin E. If you have high blood pressure, monitor it carefully after starting vitamin E, and reduce the dose if your blood pressure rises.

Vitamins A and D are fat-soluble, so they are stored in the body's fat cells for later use. Having a little socked away for a rainy day is probably okay, but if you take too much, hypervitaminosis may develop. Symptoms of hypervitaminosis A include orangeish, itchy skin; loss of appetite; increased fatigue; and hard, painful swellings on the arms, legs, or back of the head. Symptoms of hypervitaminosis D include hypercalcemia, osteoporosis, and kidney problems.

Don't overdo it with any fat-soluble vitamin, and take care with fish-oil supplements, including cod liver oil, which is very high in both vitamins A and D.

Folic acid can counteract the iron-depleting effects of Depakote, Depakene, and some other anticonvulsants. However, it may also cause manic mood swings.

If you experience flushing when taking niacin, look for a "no-flush" brand that is buffered. Niacin can lower your blood pressure, so caution is necessary when taking it with blood pressure medication.

Troy takes a common-sense approach to vitamin supplements:

> *I agree that vitamins are very important for keeping mood swings in check. I take a multi-vitamin, Vitamin E and zinc every day just in case my diet slips a little bit in quality.*

Minerals

Minerals are basic building blocks for cells and chemical processes in the body. Most of them are needed in relatively small amounts that are provided through the combination of a reasonably decent diet and a regular multivitamin with minerals.

Supplementing with specific minerals can be helpful for alleviating bipolar symptoms, however. Minerals that are sometimes suggested include:

- **Calcium.** Calcium is important for the regulation of impulses in the nervous system and for neurotransmitter production. If you supplement with magnesium, you should also take twice that amount of calcium—these two minerals need each other to work. However, excessive levels of calcium in the blood (hypercalcemia) can result in stupor.

- **Chromium picolinate.** This substance may help control the sugar and carbohydrate cravings that many patients experience while taking Depakote or Depakene. Chromium picolinate can act like a stimulant, however, so keep an eye out for this side effect.

- **Magnesium.** Magnesium lowers blood pressure and is also important for the regulation of impulses in the nervous system and neurotransmitter production. Magnesium deficiency can cause anxiety and insomnia, and it can also lower your seizure threshold. This mineral is rapidly depleted during periods of stress, hard work, hot weather, or fever. If you are supplementing with vitamin B6, you will need to add magnesium as well.

- **Manganese.** A deficiency in this mineral is marked by fatigue, irritability, memory problems, and ringing or other noises in the ears. It is needed in trace amounts only, but some people's diets do not include enough.

- **Selenium.** This mineral works with vitamin E to produce the antioxidant peptide glutathione peroxidase. Selenium deficiency occurs in some people with celiac disease and other autoimmune disorders. If you want to use this mineral, try its easily absorbed chelated form, L-selenomethionane. When combined with zinc, selenium may promote improved thyroid function, which is important for people with thyroid involvement in their mood swings and rapid cyclers. This combo can sometimes also circumvent the hair loss that is associated with some mood stabilizers.

- **Zinc.** Zinc is another trace mineral that's often absent from the diet. Symptoms of deficiency can include mental disturbance. You may want to use a supplement of this mineral in its easiest-to-absorb chelated form, zinc aspartate or zinc picolinate. See the listing for selenium, above, for more information.

Nutritional supplements

If it's not an herb, vitamin, or mineral, you can simply call it a nutritional supplement. That means the manufacturer agrees not to market it as a drug, and the Food and Drug Administration agrees to consider it a food. Meanwhile, consumers are left unsure about whether these supplements provide nutrients (they usually don't), cure disease (rarely, if ever), or simply promote health.

The supplements category includes amino acids. There are 22 of these simple compounds, which combine to create all of the body's proteins. Most amino acids are produced by the body itself, but some people do report benefits from taking amino acid supplements. These may combine several amino acids or include just one.

Along with the amino acids listed in the section "Other sleep supplements," earlier in this chapter, supplements that are sometimes used for symptoms of bipolar disorders include the following:

- **Lecithin (phosphatidyl choline).** This phospholipid is found mostly in high-fat foods. You may hear that it improves memory and brain processes. Lecithin is necessary for normal brain development; however, double-blind studies of patients with Alzheimer's disease did not substantiate claims that it can help people recover lost brain function.[35] The ketogenic diet increases the amount of lecithin in the body, which may be one of the reasons for its success in some cases of hard-to-treat epilepsy. Some people with epilepsy have also reported reducing their number and severity of seizures from taking lecithin alone. Some studies of lecithin use by people with bipolar disorder indicate that it can stabilize mood, while others indicate that it tends to depress mood (and might therefore be more useful to a person who is manic or hypomanic).[36] Lecithin capsules are available, but many people prefer the soft lecithin granules. These are a nice addition to fruit-juice smoothies, adding a thicker texture. Lecithin is oil-based and should be refrigerated.

- **Choline.** Choline is one of the active ingredients in lecithin. It is needed by the brain for processes related to memory, learning, and mental alertness, as well as for the manufacture of cell membranes and the neurotransmitter acetylcholine. Acetylcholine is involved in emotional control and other regulatory functions. Its effectiveness for bipolar symptoms is unknown.

- **Inositol.** This is another active ingredient in lecithin. Inositol plays a part in the chemical process that carries messages for certain neurotransmitters, including serotonin and acetylcholine. It also seems to help boost the activity of serotonin receptors. It may help repair damaged areas of the myelin sheath that surrounds and protects nerves. Clinical studies indicate that inositol supplements may be helpful for some people with obsessive-compulsive disorder, depression, and panic disorder.[37,38,39] Its effectiveness for bipolar symptoms is uncertain.

- **Taurine.** This amino acid appears to have anti-seizure capabilities and has received good reviews from some adults with bipolar disorders. It inhibits abnormal electrical activity in the brain and is often found to be deficient in brain tissue where seizures have been occurring. Interestingly, rapid cyclers report the best results. Recommendations range from 500 to 1000 mg per day, divided into as many as three doses. Experts recommend buying only pharmaceutical-quality L-taurine from reputable manufacturers. Unusual EEG activity has been reported in patients using doses over 1000 mg per day.

- GABA (gaba-amino butyric acid). GABA is an amino acid-like compound that acts like a neurotransmitter by inhibiting other neurotransmitters. A number of medications are under development that would affect GABA production or usage; some existing drugs that affect GABA, such as Gabapentin and Depakote, are used to treat manic depression. You should not take these medications with GABA supplements unless your physician recommends it and oversees the process. Supplementation with over-the-counter GABA is sometimes recommended for anxiety, nervous tension, and insomnia, especially insomnia associated with racing thoughts. If you experience shortness of breath or tingling or numbness in your hands or feet when taking GABA, lower or discontinue this supplement.

- Tyrosine. This amino acid serves as a precursor to the neurotransmitters norepinephrine and dopamine. It may help the body form more of these neurotransmitters and is also believed to provide support for optimal thyroid gland function. Tyrosine can raise blood pressure, so talk to your doctor prior to using it.

- Phenylalanine. An essential amino acid, phenylalanine is also the precursor of tyrosine. It has an indirect effect of boosting production of norepinephrine and dopamine. Like tyrosine, phenylalanine can raise blood pressure.

- Methionine. This antioxidant amino acid is helpful for some individuals suffering from depression. It has an energizing effect—and as with SAMe, below, that could precipitate mania in bipolar patients.

- SAMe (S-adenosyl-methionine). SAMe, a metabolite of methionine, is used to treat depression and arthritis in Europe. It became available in the US in early 1999. It is believed to affect dopamine and serotonin and to have anti-inflammatory effects. However, it is not recommended for people with bipolar disorder, because it may cause mania.

Supplement cautions

It's very important to let your doctor know about any supplement you take, whether it is a vitamin, a mineral, or an herb. There are many possible interactions between these substances and prescription drugs. Here are just a few that are known at this time.[40]

- Echinacea adds to the toxic effects some medications have on the liver, including anabolic steroids, amiodarone, methotrexate, and ketoconazole, increasing the risk of liver failure.

- The anti-migraine effects of feverfew may be negated by non-steroidal anti-inflammatory drugs (NSAIDs), including aspirin.

- Feverfew, garlic, gingko biloba, ginger, and ginseng alter bleeding time, so should not be used with anti-coagulant drugs like warfarin (Coumadin). You should also report use of these supplements to your doctor if you are going to have surgery.

- When taken with the MAOI antidepresssant phenelzine (Nardil), ginseng can cause headache, tremor, and mania.

- Ginseng (and other herbs that may affect the hormonal system) may add to or work against the effects of estrogens, corticosteroids, or oral contraceptives.

- St. John's wort (and any other "natural" antidepressant, such as SAM-e) may add to the effects of prescription antidepressants, increasing the risk of serotonin syndrome. It also appears to impact the effectiveness of a wide variety of other prescription drugs.

- Valerian (and any other herbal sedative) should not be used with barbiturates or other prescription sedatives, because of an increased risk of over-sedation—and even coma or death.

- Kyushin, licorice, plantain, uzara root, hawthorn, and ginseng may interfere with the medical action of digoxin, as well as with digoxin monitoring.

- Evening primrose oil and borage oil may lower the seizure threshold, so should not be used by people with seizure disorders or with prescription anticonvulsants such as Depakote or Neurontin.

- The Ayurvedic remedy Shankapulshpi may decrease phenytoin levels as well as diminishing drug efficacy.

- Kava-kava can cause coma when combined with alprazolam. It can also damage the liver if used for more than thirty days in a row. It could worsen the effects of other drugs that can harm the liver, including many psychiatric medications.

- Immunostimulants like echinacea and antioxidants should not be given with drugs that suppress the immune system, such as corticosteroids or cyclosporine.

- St. John's wort, saw palmetto, and some other herbs have high levels of tannic acids, which may inhibit iron absorption.

- Karela, ginseng, and some other herbs may affect blood glucose levels and should not be used by people with diabetes.

- Folic acid blocks the action of the antiseizure medication Dilantin and the drug methotrexate.

There are surely many more unknown reactions that could occur between natural and pharmaceutical remedies. *The Herbal PDR*, listed in Appendix A, provides the results of medical research on herbal remedies.

One of the best online resources for information on medicinal herbs is MedHerb.com (*http://www.medherb.com*), which is sponsored by the professional journal *Medical Herbalism*. It includes information about herbs used in Western, Asian, Ayurvedic, and other traditional medicine systems, with links to scientific studies and information on adverse reactions.

Auditory integration training

Some people with unusual sensitivity to sounds or types of sounds have found relief with auditory integration training (AIT) or auditory processing stimulation, both relatively new approaches.

Although it's rarely addressed in the medical literature, extreme auditory sensitivity is actually fairly common in people with bipolar disorders. People with this problem describe many normal sounds as affecting them like fingernails scraping a blackboard. Naturally, this distortion can increase your level of anxiety and discomfort.

Monique has experienced this puzzling symptom:

> When I'm manic, everything—especially sound—seems 50 times worse than what it is. Everything affects me differently when I'm manic—you can irritate me so easily. I'm not a person who will usually yell or scream, but when I'm manic, my emotions are just so intense that it's ridiculous. I'm super-sensitive to everything.
>
> When I'm hypomanic or in a manic episode, bright lights also really affect me. It's like my mind just starts running wild because of bright lights.
>
> I think to some regard this is why therapists always tell me that when you're manic you should be in an environment where there's not sensory overload, without a lot of action going on, a lot of noise. It should be very quiet.

Many audiologists (hearing specialists) and other professionals can test for auditory sensitivity and offer therapeutic treatment. Based on principles first developed by French audiologist Guy Bérard, AIT involves listening to particular sounds through earphones. The process is believed to retrain the hearing mechanism, and there is some evidence that it is effective for many patients. A similar therapy is called the Tomatis Method.

The most dramatic results from AIT have been in people with autism or related disorders. You can learn more from the Society for Auditory Integration Training, online at *http://www.teleport.com/~sait*.

Occupational therapy

Occupational therapy (OT) is intended to help people with fine motor skill problems or other impediments improve their ability to perform daily activities, ranging from walking to writing. This can be useful for coping with tremor or balance problems caused by medication.

Another kind of OT focuses on self-care skills, vocational skills, esteem-building activities such as arts and crafts, and therapeutic exercise. You may encounter this type of OT when in a hospital or other residential facility.

Sensory integration

Sensory integration (SI) is a specific type of occupational therapy that can be invaluable for people whose sensory systems are unbalanced. Like the auditory processing problems described earlier in this chapter, sensory integration difficulties seem to be more common in people with bipolar disorders than the literature would indicate. These can include over- or under-sensitivity to smell, taste, texture, types of touch, and even the forces of gravity.

Sensory integration therapy can help reduce or enhance sensitivity levels as needed. It is used with increasing frequency for children with neurological problems, including cerebral palsy, autism, and ADHD, but has rarely been offered to bipolar adults. If you have symptoms of sensory dysfunction, ask your doctor or occupational therapist about SI.

In bipolar disorders, sensory disturbances can be cyclical. A person in a manic phase may find that they have a heightened response to certain types of sensation. This increased sensitivity may be perceived as pleasurable, but in some cases it can be painful. People with bipolar disorders seem to be especially sensitive to sensory input when they are in a depressed-irritable state, sometimes to the point of being unable to wear their usual clothes (jeans and socks are suddenly too scratchy), eat their regular diet (everything smells gross, tastes weird, and makes them feel like retching), or handle a normal level of sensory input (the sounds and smells of work or the shopping mall become rapidly overwhelming).

Occupational therapists trained in SI use simple techniques to retrain the body's sensory apparatus. These can include brushing and joint compression, exercises that improve and strengthen the sensory part of the nervous system, and targeted work on specific sensory difficulties. Much SI work does not require any special devices, or employs inexpensive items like stretchy strips of rubber for arm exercises or weighted vests for calming. Many SI specialists do use occupational therapy equipment, such as scooter boards, huge "therapy balls" for improving balance, and prone-position swings.

SI specialists recommend making a "sensory diet" part of your home environment. This means building experiences with different types of textures, tastes, smells, and physical sensations into daily activities. SI therapists can also teach you how to use self-calming activities and devices when you are reaching the point of sensory overload.

Dance, music, or art therapy

There is no proof that dance, music, or art therapy has curative value for people with bipolar disorders, but these activities often draw out hidden talents and bring a sense of joy and accomplishment. Sometimes dance, music, or art therapy is integrated into hospital or day-treatment programs.

Stress-busters

Being bipolar always brings with it the unwanted baggage of stress. When you're manic, your body and mind are being pushed to their very limits. When you're depressed, just going through the motions can be intensely stressful. And even when you're well, there's the stress of dealing with the mess you made during your last episode of illness and of worrying about what will happen next.

Everyone can benefit from knowing many ways to beat back stress. What works will depend on you, your state of mind, and the situation. It's not enough to say "just relax"—if you're totally stressed out, you need to have a plan to follow or it will seem like a hopeless task.

Perhaps the oldest stress-busters are meditation, prayer, and breathing exercises. These simple activities, either alone or in various combinations, relax the body and the mind simultaneously. There are many different schools of meditation, and types of prayer or contemplative thought have been developed over the centuries that can fit any individual, of any religion (or none), in any situation. For example, yoga offers many relaxation techniques that combine physical movements, special breathing patterns, and mental exercises. Working with a well-trained instructor can help you master various yoga positions.

Monique has found strategies that work for her:

> For stress relief, I try meditating and prayer. I find that praying and meditating helps me with my spirit, it helps me connect more with myself. When you're manic, you're not yourself—you think grandiose thoughts, you're running around and doing things non-stop for days, and you feel like you need hardly any sleep. But prayer and meditation just keep me grounded. Combined with taking my medications only at night, it also makes me drowsy and helps me sleep better.
>
> I also feel that just working on self-awareness and building your self-worth—not just as a woman but as a person—is important. Just treating yourself, like taking a bubble bath or getting your nails done. For me to stay feeling good and stay stable, I have to treat myself right and stay self-aware. That self-awareness lets me know when I'm not well, when I'm manic.

Breathing exercises can actually reduce the sensation of pain, gradually help agitation to subside, and even lower a racing heartbeat, as any woman who has tried Lamaze breathing during childbirth can tell you. One technique that works during anxiety or panic is sometimes called "candle breathing." You breathe in through your nose in short bursts, and breathe out forcefully, as if blowing out a stubborn candle a couple of feet away. Done repeatedly, this usually has a calming effect.

Hyperventilation is a common side effect of extreme mania, anxiety, and panic. It increases all the most unpleasant aspects of those states, can make a person pass out, and can even mimic the physical sensation of a mild heart attack if you are unaware that you are hyperventilating.

A hyperventilating person takes sharp, short, ragged breaths uncontrollably. Her whole body appears wracked by the effort of this forced breathing. To stop the process, breathe into a small paper bag. As less oxygen comes in, your breathing process will slow down and become more regular until the episode of hyperventilation ends.

Sensory integration techniques, described earlier in this chapter, are also effective stress-reducers. Some people may respond better to more traditional massage.

Exercise is another great stress-fighter. Running, which produces certain endorphins and depletes others, is a favorite strategy for many. Bicycling, aerobics, racquet sports, and jumping on a trampoline are other high-energy activities that may help take the edge off. If you're stuck indoors, calisthenics, stair climbing, or using a stationary bicycle or treadmill can also work well.

Troy, age 30, has found that exercise can short-circuit an impending manic episode and is one of several non-medication strategies that also helps with depression:

> It was the day before I had two final exams to take at the university I was attending, when I felt a manic episode coming on. I was very irritable and unable to concentrate on my studying. I took my basketball and went down to a local park that had some courts. I started shooting baskets, and then some people showed up and I ended up playing basketball until dusk. When I got home I was a little tired and able to study each subject for an hour or two. I took the exams the next day and ended up getting As on both of them.
>
> The best therapy for me when I'm really depressed is to take a long walk and then write in my journal.

The healing power of humor

Humor can be a powerful healing force. It lifts the spirits of people who are depressed and can gently show those whose thinking has become disordered how to get back on track.

Humor is the best way to defuse unthinking remarks from others and makes possible an offbeat perspective on things that could otherwise be overwhelming, like hospitalization and having to take psychiatric medication. With an intact sense of humor, you can better withstand what your health and the world throw at you without giving in to despair.

So when it all gets to be too much, take a page from Norman Vincent Peale and go to a funny movie, listen to a classic comedy record, rent some "Monty Python" or "Three Stooges" videos, or pick up the latest book by your favorite humorist. If you feel the need for something that speaks directly to your situation, Ernie Kovacs and Richard Pryor both seem to have a knack for everything about "craziness" that's funny, and tragic, and still funny after the tragic part has been touched on. So does Jonathan Winters—and as someone who's quite public about having bipolar disorder, he understands the topic first-hand.

Let go, let laughter wash over you, and remind yourself that the human condition is simply too absurd to be taken seriously.

CHAPTER 7

Healthcare and Insurance

MENTAL HEALTHCARE IS SOMETIMES DIFFICULT to get and manage, not to mention expensive. Many medical insurance plans don't cover anything more than prescription medication, while others give mental healthcare second-class status or make it hard to access.

This chapter explains how to access the best care through your existing health plan and offers suggestions on how to get medical care if you do not have insurance coverage. It covers private insurance, including health maintenance organizations (HMOs) and other forms of managed care, as well as public health insurance plans. It describes typical insurance roadblocks and shows you how to get around them. It also lays out strategies for handling service and insurance coverage denials. Both US options and the healthcare systems of other English-speaking nations are covered.

Public income assistance programs in the US and some other countries are closely tied to eligibility for public health benefits, so this chapter also explains Social Security disability income and other benefits that are sometimes available to people coping with bipolar disorders.

Health insurance and bipolar disorders

In the US and other countries where private medical insurance is the norm, the system can be hard to deal with under the best of circumstances. Each insurance company offers multiple plans with various rates and benefits, and there's no central oversight. As a result, a mental health diagnosis can come with an unpleasant surprise: the healthcare services you need aren't covered, even though you have paid your insurance premiums. Some insurance plans specifically refuse to cover any psychiatric or neurological disorder, and in many cases it's legal for insurers to make that choice.

Some insurance companies do a good job of covering plan members' mental health needs. The best plans do not put an arbitrary cap on visits to psychiatrists, neurologists, psychologists, or therapists. They provide informative materials on making the most of the mental health services they offer, and they reward practitioners for helping people recover—not just for helping them out the door. They promote best practices as defined by the latest medical research, encouraging practitioners to use effective medications and therapy techniques.

Other companies cover mental healthcare in a substandard way. For example, the company may cover only short-term therapy programs; it may have no qualified "in-plan" practitioners, but refuse to make outside referrals; or it may limit you to a certain number of outpatient visits or inpatient hospital days each year, regardless of what you actually need. The company may have a drug formulary that does not include safer, more effective medications, simply because they cost more than older, less effective medications that carry a higher risk of side effects.

Most insurers fall somewhere between these two extremes.

Shannon, age 33, is pleased with her insurance coverage:

> I have "high option" Blue Cross/Blue Shield insurance. That means that
> I pay a high premium, but that I have never had problems with coverage.
> Most of my symptoms are under excellent control with the right combination
> of medications and therapy.

Leslie, age 44, says managed care has been an up-and-down experience:

> I'm under my husband's insurance, an HMO. My psychiatrist isn't on their
> network and the ones who are that I've tried were of the "drool and let the
> client vent" philosophy. As a result, I pay out-of-pocket. My meds are covered.
>
> We are switching insurance soon, and my general practitioner isn't on the
> network. Nor are the orthopedist or the neurologist. It's very unsettling. I've
> used public services in the past when things got bad—free psychiatrist, free
> medical care, and a small stipend.

Making insurance choices

Whenever you are in the position of choosing a new insurance plan, try to find out in advance what its attitude is about treatment for mental illness in general and for bipolar disorders specifically. If there is a nearby medical center with expertise in treating bipolar disorders, does it accept one or more of the plans you're considering? How about the psychiatrist or therapist you would most like to see?

Most insurance plans do limit your choice of physicians and may also control the type and frequency of care you receive. Accordingly, you should interview the companies you are considering as if you were hiring one—because you are. Here are just some of the questions you may want to ask, as adapted from *Working with Your Doctor: Getting the Healthcare You Deserve* (Nancy Keene, O'Reilly & Associates, 1998).

- How many subscribers does the plan have in your area?

- How many primary care doctors are on its provider list? Are they all board certified? If you already have a doctor with whom you feel comfortable, make sure she is on the primary care provider list, or you will have to change doctors if you sign up. If your doctor is a specialist, most likely you will have to see a primary care doctor, known as a gatekeeper, who will decide when and if you need to see a specialist.

- What criteria does the insurer use when selecting providers? Is it still accepting additional providers?

- How are the doctors paid? Are they paid a flat monthly fee per patient, an arrangement called capitation? Do they get a bonus or penalty based on referrals to specialists, number of office visits, hospital admissions, prescriptions written, or any other action?

- Is there a maximum lifetime cap on medical payments? Is there a separate lifetime cap on mental health payments? Are there annual limits on the length of hospital stays?

- What hospitals, radiological services, home-health agencies, nursing homes, and other facilities does the managed care agency use? Are these facilities located close to your home?

- Is the plan accredited by the National Committee for Quality Assurance (NCQA)? This organization reviews more than 270 managed care organizations annually and gives them one of four ratings: full accreditation, which is good for three years; one-year accreditation, if the organization is equipped to make recommended changes within one year; provisional accreditation, for organizations with the potential for improvement; and denial of accreditation, for companies that do not meet NCQA standards. You can also get a report from NCQA that summarizes its findings for an individual HMO. Call the NCQA Accreditation Status Line at (888) 275-7585 or order a list of accredited HMOs by calling (800) 839-6487. The same information is available on the NCQA web site at *http://www.ncqa.org*.

- Does the plan pay for a second opinion if you request one?

- Can you change doctors anytime?

- Are the doctors bound by a "gag order" or other contractual provisions that prevent them from fully informing you of all treatment options? Are they barred from disclosing bonuses they receive from the plan if they limit care, referrals, or prescriptions? Ask for a copy of the HMO policy regarding gag clauses, and refuse to sign up until you get it. Some states now have laws that prohibit gag clauses for HMO doctors, and federal legislation has been proposed.

- Will you see a doctor at each appointment? How often and in what capacity are nurse practitioners and physician's assistants used? How long will you have to wait to get an appointment?

- Does the plan offer a point-of-service (POS) option to enable you to go outside the network if you think it is necessary to get the best care?

- What is the plan's coverage for pre-existing conditions? If you have a pre-existing condition, federal law (H.R. 3103—effective date: July 1, 1997) restricts group health plans, insurers, and HMOs from denying coverage because of pre-existing conditions if you already have coverage from another health plan. The law has several restrictions, so be sure to check it out if you have a pre-existing condition.

- Are mental health services accessed through a different company, an arrangement called a mental health "cut-out" or "carve-out"? If so, will your primary care physician have to approve each mental health service, or will the mental health provider be empowered to create a treatment plan, prescribe and manage medications, and make needed referrals?

- Does the plan have a formulary for prescription drugs? If so, are your drugs or those you are considering on it? Is there a way for physicians to make exceptions?

- Are providers required to use cheaper drugs first, before being allowed to use newer, more expensive drugs? This is a particular concern for people who take neuroleptics to control psychosis and other symptoms. Older neuroleptics like Haldol have a much higher potential for serious side effects than newer ones like Risperdal.

- Will you be limited to selected pharmacies? Is there a monthly drug budget, and are doctors penalized or rewarded for restricting prescription drugs?

- What are the plan's complaint and appeals policies? Who is on the appeals board? How quickly are complaints usually resolved?

If your coverage is provided by an employer through a group plan, the company is required to provide you with a Summary Plan Description (SPD) that outlines both the benefits and restrictions of the plan. The SPD must be written in easy-to-understand language, not legalese. However, the SPD often does not answer all of the questions listed above. To find out more, get a copy of the actual contract (not the glossy promotional material) and read it thoroughly. You may also want to ask your benefits manager at work and talk to your doctor. Do not rely on a salesperson's verbal answers. To see how 150,000 HMO members rate their HMOs, get the *Consumer's Guide to Health Plans,* which is published by the nonprofit Center for the Study of Service at (800) 475-7283.

Although doctors are rarely willing to speak ill of specific insurers, their office staff may not be as circumspect. Ask about whether the firm you're thinking of cooperates with them at billing time, buries them in unnecessary paperwork, or has a reputation for denying services the doctor requests. You can tell a lot about an insurance company or HMO by how it treats its business partners—and that's what doctors and their staff members are when it comes to healthcare plans.

In the absence of a plan that definitely covers the practitioners and facilities you want, your best bet is a plan that has an out-of-network clause. These plans allow you to choose your own providers if you can't find the right professional on the list of preferred providers or HMO members. You will generally pay more for out-of-plan visits, but you also won't have to run the referral gauntlet as often. The cost of using these providers regularly, such as for weekly therapy visits, may be more than your budget will bear.

Cindy, mother of 17-year-old Nathan, has insurance with a limited (and expensive) out-of-network option:

> We have Tricare (the federal insurance plan for US military personnel), formerly known as Champus. Anyone who thinks the military is great obviously is not in it. We can get no mental health benefits for my son at the Army hospital, which is supposed to be a major medical facility, and it costs us a $20 co-pay for every visit on the outside. If inpatient is allowed, we have to pay $20 a day. That may not sound like a lot to some people, but for someone on a very limited budget as we are, the money is just not there.

If your employer does not offer insurance that covers out-of-network providers or other needed services, take up the issue with the human resources or benefits department (or in small companies, the boss). When the cost is spread over a group, expanded benefits may not be very expensive. You can also make a very persuasive case that providing better coverage will keep employees on the job more days, because they will be less likely to need long periods off work due to health problems or caring for a sick family member.

The most difficult managed care plans to deal with are usually those that contract with a so-called carve-out for mental healthcare (and often for other services as well). These plans do not provide any mental healthcare themselves, but instead refer patients to outside providers. Sometimes these outside programs are very good. Unfortunately, you can end up feeling like a ping-pong ball as you are bounced between your major medical carrier and the mental health program, the substance abuse program, and other cut-outs. Your insurer or HMO, your medical care facility, and your outside provider may argue with each other about what kind of treatment is needed, who should deliver it, and who will pay for it. Meanwhile, you may go without appropriate care.

Carve-out problems are particularly acute in states that have very recently passed mental health parity laws, such as California. Some health plans were caught unprepared by the new requirement for equal service provision, and they chose outside providers that have been unable to meet the demand for services. Others have not yet surmounted the paperwork problems inherent in these arrangements.

One would think that integrated HMOs would do a better job. These are companies that provide both mental and physical care in the same plan and sometimes at the same site. Some integrated HMOs do live up to their promise of seamless mind/body care, but not all. Even within a single company there can be turf wars, payment disputes, and outright denial of services.

Be sure to check up on your prospective plan's solvency, too—in recent years many have gone under, sometimes leaving patients without coverage.

Shoshana, age 56, is still dealing with the aftermath of two health plan failures:

> We had one insurance company go into bankruptcy and one go into receivership, and we were left with about $70,000 in unpaid medical bills from my hospitalizations. I'm making payments on the last of it now, and still owe about $4,000.
>
> I had no medication coverage for several years, and that was difficult, as my psychiatric meds were running about $600 per month. Fortunately, I have no expensive tastes or hobbies. I have Medicare now, and for the last three years I have also been covered by my husband's small group plan.

COBRAs and individual plans

Insurance for people affected by any long-term disability is very hard to get in the private market (i.e., without going through an employer). It's available, but premium costs can be extraordinarily high. If you are leaving a job that provides health insurance for one that does not, pursue a COBRA plan. These plans allow you to continue your current, employer-sponsored coverage after leaving employment. You will pay the full rate, including the contribution previously made by your employer plus up to a 2 percent administrative fee, but it will still be less than what you'd pay as an individual customer.

If you do choose a COBRA, it's important to pay all of your premiums on time. COBRA plans generally have a higher claims ratio, so COBRA administrators are not lenient with late premiums.

A COBRA plan is not a permanent arrangement, but it can help you maintain your coverage for eighteen months—or longer, if you or another covered member of your family meets the Social Security Administration definition of disabled (see the section "SSI" later in this chapter). For this reason, it may be wise to apply for Social Security Income on the basis of that person's disability, even if you are quite sure that your family income would prevent actually receiving SSI or SSDI benefits. Once the Social Security Administration informs you in writing that the person has been found to be disabled, you must send a copy of that letter to your COBRA administrator within sixty days to arrange for an eleven-month extension of your COBRA coverage. This extension applies to the entire family, not just the person with a disability. Having a bipolar disorder does not always qualify a person as disabled under SSI regulations. If it prevents you or your family member from working or from carrying out some or all basic self-care tasks, qualification is possible.

If your COBRA is about to run out and cannot be extended, call your state insurance commission to see what your options are. Some states sponsor an insurance pool for people whose COBRA plan has expired. To qualify, you will have to show proof of state residency and COBRA status. It's best to apply at least a month before your plan is due to expire.

Maintaining continuous health insurance coverage is critical to prevent being locked out of healthcare by pre-existing conditions. If you don't qualify for either a group plan or a COBRA, you can sometimes obtain insurance directly from an insurance company. An insurance broker that works with many different individual plans can usually help you find the widest selection of options and assist you in making a choice that ensures the best possible quality of care.

If individual coverage is just too expensive, lower-cost possibilities include group plans offered by trade associations, unions, clubs, and other organizations. You may also want to look into public health insurance options, which are discussed later in this chapter, or see if you can get coverage through your spouse.

Jean, who is married to 61-year-old George, says a combination of public and private coverage has made access to care easier and less expensive:

> *I worked for the county for 20 years and took an early retirement.*
> *The insurance I get from the county covers both of us. We have to pay*
> *a premium, but it's not very high. When George became disabled and*
> *went on Social Security, after two years he got Medicare and that*
> *became his primary insurance. My employer's insurance became his*
> *secondary coverage—it covers almost anything that Medicare*
> *doesn't. We still end up paying at least 20 to 30 percent out of our*
> *pockets, but that's not bad, compared to what I've heard from other*
> *people.*

Several states also have income-based state plans for adults on public assistance or in low-wage occupations.

You can appeal the insurance coverage denial to the insurance company itself. Call the insurer's business office to find out what its procedures are for formally appealing denial of coverage. Ask to receive this information in writing. Your appeal should stress that if appropriate routine medical and preventative care is provided, it is highly unlikely that you will require expensive services, such as hospitalization.

Appendix A, *Resources,*' lists several books and publications that can help you in your quest to secure insurance coverage and appropriate healthcare services. For managed care issues, The National Coalition of Mental Health Professionals and Consumers maintains a useful (if opinionated) site at *http://www.NoManagedCare.org*.

Managing managed care

In most HMOs and other managed healthcare insurance companies, doctors earn more if their patients stay healthy. In many ways, this makes more sense than rewarding doctors for only taking care of people after they're sick, because many illnesses could be avoided with appropriate preventative care. It also removes the financial incentive for ordering unnecessary tests or padding the bill with extra office visits—at least, that's the theory.

For patients with long-term conditions, however, the reality of managed care is that sometimes you are perceived as an obstacle in the way of your physician's or HMO's profits.

Following the steps outlined in this section can help you obtain maximum benefits, whether you're dealing with an HMO, another type of managed care organization, an old-style fee for service arrangement, or a public health agency.

Learn how the system works

Informed insurance consumers are a rarity. Most people look at the fancy plan brochure and the provider list when their insurance first kicks in, but unless something goes wrong, that's about as much as they want to know. If you suspect that you may need to advocate for services, however, you'll need a copy of the firm's master policy.

You can obtain this document, which specifies everything that is and isn't covered, through your employer's human resources office (for employer-provided insurance or COBRA plans administered by a former employer) or from the insurance company's customer relations office (for health insurance that you buy directly from the insurer). Read it. It will be tough going, but the results will be worthwhile. If you need help interpreting this document, disability advocacy organizations and insurance-related sites on the Web can help. For a list of some helpful organizations, see Appendix A.

Find out in detail what the chain of command is for your healthcare provider and your insurer. You'll need to know exactly whom to call and what to do if you need hospitalization, emergency services, a referral to a specialist, or a medication that isn't in its formulary.

If your employer provides your insurance, find out if the plan is self-funded through your employer or if the employer is paying premiums to the insurer. If the plan is self-funded, always discuss any concerns with your company's benefits manager first, before contacting the insurer. Since the employer is, in effect, paying the benefits, it may be more generous than the insurer.

You will also need to find out about your plan's procedures for grievances and appeals, just in case (see the section "Fighting denial of care," later in this chapter).

Document everything

You should keep copies of all bills, reports, evaluations, test results, and other medical records. You should also keep records of when and how your insurance payments were made. This information is essential if you have a dispute with your healthcare provider or insurer.

It's also helpful to document personal conversations and phone calls. You needn't tape-record these, although if a dispute has already begun this can be wise (make sure to let the other party know that you are recording, if required by law.) Simply note the date and time of your call or conversation, whom you spoke with, and what was said or decided. If a service or treatment is promised in a phone conversation, it's a good idea to send a letter or fax documenting the conversation. For example:

> *Dear Dr. Smith:*
>
> *When we spoke on Tuesday, you promised to authorize a referral to Dr. Jones at the City Hospital Neurology Center for my neurological exam. Please fax a copy of the referral form to me at xxx-xxxx when it is finished, as well as to Dr. Jones at xxx-xxxx. Thanks again for your help.*
>
> *Sincerely,*
>
> *John Doe*

Referral forms are especially important. Most managed care firms send a copy to both the patient and the provider. This document usually has a referral number on it. Be sure to bring your referral form when you first see a new provider. If the provider has not received a copy of the form, your copy and the referral number can ensure that you'll still be seen and that payment can be processed. Without it, you may be turned away.

Form a partnership with your healthcare providers

Most doctors and other healthcare providers care about helping their patients, and they are the most powerful allies you have. Let them know how important their help is, and make sure they know your case well. Give them additional information about bipolar disorders if they need it. Your primary care provider may not be treating your mood disorder directly, but he does have the power to write referrals, to recommend and approve certain treatments suggested by specialists, and to advocate on your behalf within the managed care organization.

Don't rely on your providers completely, however. They have many patients, some of whose needs will likely take precedence over yours. A life-or-death emergency or a large caseload may cause paperwork or meetings on your behalf to be overlooked temporarily or even forgotten.

Another staff member, such as a nurse or office assistant, may help keep your provider on track, but you will have to be organized and persistent. Make sure that you return calls, provide accurate information, and keep the provider's needs in mind. For example, if you have information for your doctor about a new medication, summarize it on one page and attach the relevant studies or journal articles. The doctor can then quickly scan the basics in her office, and read the rest when time permits.

Semi-sneaky tips

Some people are better at managing managed care than others. The following suggestions may be a little shady, but they have worked for certain managed care customers:

- Subvert voicemail and phone queues. If you are continually routed into a voicemail system and your calls are never returned or if you are left on hold forever, don't passively accept it. Start punching buttons when you are stuck in voicemail or on hold, in hope of reaching a real person. If you get an operator, ask for Administration (Claims and Marketing never seem to have enough people to answer the phone). Nicely ask the operator to transfer you directly to an appropriate person who can help, not to the department in general. The old "Gosh, I just keep getting lost and cut off in your phone system" ploy may do the trick.

- Whenever you speak to someone at your HMO, especially if it's a claims representative, ask for his full name and direct phone number. It will make him feel more accountable for resolving your problem, because he knows you'll call him back directly if he doesn't.

- If you can't get help from a claims or customer service representative, ask for her supervisor. If you're told that she isn't available, get the supervisor's full name, direct phone line, and mailing address. Simply asking for this information sometimes makes missing supervisors magically appear.

- Use humor when you can. It defuses situations that are starting to get ugly and humanizes you to healthcare company employees. That can be an important factor in getting the job done: it's easy to dismiss the needs of a case or an ID number, but much harder to refuse help to a real person.

- Be ready to explain why your request is urgent and to do so in terms that non-doctors can understand. For example, if receiving a certain treatment now could mean avoiding expensive hospitalization later, that's an argument that even junior assistant accountants can comprehend.

- Whatever you do, stay calm. If you yell at managed care people, they'll dismiss what you have to say. That doesn't mean being unemotional. Sometimes you can successfully make a personal appeal. You can act confused instead of angry when you are denied assistance for no good reason. You may also want to make it clear that you're gathering information in a way that indicates legal action—for instance, asking how to spell names and asking where official documents should be sent.

One bright spot in insurance company practice is a move toward integrated case management for people with serious mental illness. One model, assertive case management, is intended to coordinate healthcare with social welfare agencies, family members, clergy, social workers, and others. This model should include weekly contact between patient and a permanent case manager. Your healthcare provider could initiate assertive treatment options, or you could access them through a third party, such as a social services agency or even your local NAMI chapter.

If this kind of case-management system is implemented more often, it should help people with bipolar disorders obtain more consistent care—including those whose symptoms are difficult to manage. That will prevent relapses and reduce the number of mental health crises and hospitalizations, saving both insurers and affected persons a great deal of money. With good case management, you will always have a person you can call when things aren't working well, even if you change insurers, lose your insurance, get a different job, or develop different health needs.

Fighting limits on psychiatric care

If your insurance company only provides treatment for persons with bipolar disorders as part of a limited mental health or nervous disorders benefit, you can challenge that limitation, even if your state does not have a mental health parity law on the books. It's easy to show that bipolar disorders are biologically based, so you may be able to avoid the mental health limit altogether.

Monique, age 30, worries about these arbitrary limits:

> I think those limits are standard, because on all the jobs I've had where I had health insurance, the plan says you get a certain number of visits a year. I had to call in to tell them I'm manic-depressive and need the mental health coverage, and they said after your visits are up, you can't go back until the next year.
>
> As a result, I have to keep track of when I went to see my doctor and how many times I've gone this year, so I'm under the limit. If you go over

and you need medicine, you have to call in to your doctor to get your script sent to the pharmacy instead of coming in.

I haven't been in a situation yet where I've had to appeal for more visits—right now they usually see me for medication review, so that's every three or four months—but it could happen.

One piece of information to get in advance is how the company treats acquired nervous system disorders, such as stroke, brain tumors, or traumatic brain injuries. If your insurance covers long-term care for these conditions, you can make a case that equal coverage for your own biologically based brain disorder is simply consistent.

Many people with bipolar disorders have concrete signs of neurological dysfunction, which can't be written off as purely psychological. A thorough neurological exam can help buttress your arguments.

Getting coverage for new treatments

All insurance plans bar coverage for experimental treatments. Some do have a compassionate care exception, which comes into play when regular treatments have been tried unsuccessfully and the plan's medical advisors agree that the experimental treatment might work. This exception is generally available only to people with life-threatening illnesses.

So what do you do to pay for promising new treatments for bipolar disorders, such as newly developed medications? You either pay out of pocket or work closely with your physician to get around the experimental treatment exclusion.

"Creative coding" is the term some doctors use to describe billing the insurer or managed care entity for something that's not quite what was actually delivered. For example, a therapist might bill participation in a social skills training group, which the insurance company probably would not pay for, as something else that the insurer will pay for, such as group therapy.

Creative coding is a form of fraud. Providers who do it take tremendous risks, and patients for whom it is done must remember that they can't discuss these services with the rest of their healthcare team for fear of exposing the deception.

You can appeal to your insurer or HMO for an exemption to policies that prevent you from accessing promising new treatments. Your physician may have to prepare a letter of medical necessity to support your request—or this task may fall to you. This letter must include the following information.

- The diagnosis for which the service, equipment, or medication is needed
- The specific symptom or function that the service, equipment, or medication will treat or help with
- A full description of the service, equipment, or medication and how it will help you
- If the service, equipment, or medication is new or experimental, evidence (such as medical studies or journal articles) to support your request
- If there are less expensive or traditionally used alternatives to the new or experimental service, equipment, or medication, well-supported reasons that these alternatives are not appropriate

Fighting denial of care

Refusal of appropriate mental healthcare is the top insurance complaint voiced by people with bipolar disorders. You can fight denial of care, but it isn't easy. Indeed, most healthcare consumers are so discouraged by the initial denial that they don't pursue it further. However, all insurance companies and managed-care entities have an internal appeal process, and it's worth your while to be persistent.

Rachel, mother of 20-year-old Lillian, says she was surprised that insurers can legally deny coverage in some cases:

> I'm self-employed, so we have to buy coverage directly from an insurer. When our last plan was canceled a couple of years ago, our whole family applied for coverage from Kaiser Permanente, which is very inexpensive. I couldn't believe it—they rejected all four applications, including my daughter's, on the basis of pre-existing conditions. For three of us it was a mental health diagnosis; for my husband it was sciatica. Apparently if you checked "yes" next to any of the sixty-plus conditions listed on the application form, you would be denied. You would have to be in absolutely perfect health to qualify!
>
> The insurance company's representative told me that we did have the right to appeal the decision, and mailed me the paperwork. But by then I had looked closer at what the plan would cover on these pre-existing conditions, and decided that I would instead take those denial letters and use them to get insurance through our state's insurance pool. This is a special plan for people who have been rejected by other insurers. It's not cheap, but the coverage is very broad and includes pre-existing conditions right away.

The appeals process should be explained in the master plan. If it's not, call the insurance company's customer service office or your employer's human resources department for information.

Grievances

A formal appeal is not the same thing as a grievance. Grievances are complaints about the quality of services you have received: for example, complaints about rude doctors, overly long waits, or lost paperwork.

These conflicts can usually be resolved person-to-person, by talking with your provider or the office staff. If this doesn't work, you may want to ask the insurance company or HMO to investigate your grievance and mediate a solution.

Appeals

Appeals are formal complaints about healthcare decisions made by insurers and providers. They have legal status, and healthcare consumers are entitled to have appeals addressed in a specific and timely manner.

The appeals process begins by addressing the issue directly with the provider or office in question. For example, if your provider refuses to give you a needed referral to a psychiatrist, set up a meeting with the provider to find out why and to let the provider know that you need to have a copy of this refusal in writing. Often this request will lead to a change of heart.

If it doesn't, make sure that you receive a written denial. If you do not, request it again in writing, asking for a list of the specific reasons for denial, as well as the names of all persons who took part in the decision. You should also ask for articles from the medical literature that support the plan's position. If the administration can't or won't provide any, your case is strengthened. In the meantime, do your own medical literature search—your local NDMDA or NAMI chapter may already have many of the basic documents you need on file or can order supporting material from the national office. You can also use web-based services like Medscape (*http://www.medscape.org*) to look up journal articles, best practices statements from medical boards, and other useful literature.

When you do receive a written denial of care, make sure that the reason you were given verbally is also the reason given in this document.

If your primary care provider disagrees with the decision involved in your appeal, it's very effective to have him appeal that decision directly. Ask if he will write a letter of appeal to the appropriate employee, office, or committee. If he will not, ask if you can get a second opinion from another doctor. If he cannot refer you for a second opinion, you may want to take the step of arranging to pay privately for a second opinion from another physician.

Rachel has successfully appealed an insurance company decision:

> *One of my children needs speech therapy, and our insurance would only cover treatment at one facility, not one of the city's better ones. We have a really good speech and hearing center at the medical school here, so when his doctor's request for a referral to that center was denied by the insurer, I wrote a letter explaining why he should go there instead, what was different about that center's approach, and also why he needed more speech therapy than was usually allowed on this plan.*
>
> *Although they didn't approve as many visits as were actually needed, they did finally approve using the medical school's center.*
>
> *I believe this same approach would work if, for example, your insurance company wouldn't pay for a cognitive behavioral therapist or newer medications. Just lay out your case, include some journal articles to buttress your position or a letter from your doctor, and be insistent.*

A psychiatrist or other healthcare provider you have seen previously may be able to help plead your case by providing evidence about your condition, such as test results and examination reports. These experts can also explain that consistent treatment for bipolar disorders is much more cost-effective than the alternative—particularly by showing the insurance company what the financial risk is of going without the treatment you need. Hospitalization, for example, is far more expensive than adequate medication and case management.

At this point you should also enlist the help of your company's benefits department or union benefits manager, if you have one. If the same problem has occurred before, she may know how it was resolved. She may also be able to support your position or, if such problems are happening often, to threaten the insurer with loss of its contract.

If your person-to-person efforts are unsuccessful, it's time to make a formal appeal to the insurance company or HMO management. This type of appeal should be made in writing and clearly marked "appeal" at the top of the document. Send it by certified mail and request a return receipt. This will document the date your letter was received and who signed for it.

Your appeals letter should contain a clear and concise definition of the problem, as well as your name, insurance policy number and/or patient ID number, any statements from your doctor or lab reports, and other pertinent materials. Make sure to state in the letter what action by the company would resolve the problem. Don't delay writing this letter: your right to start an appeal may expire in as few as 30 days after the original decision was made. Keep a copy of this letter and all other correspondence for your records

Every insurance company and every state have slightly different procedures for handling appeals. In most cases, the company must complete its reconsideration of the decision you have appealed within 60 days of receiving your letter. If you need an expedited appeal because waiting this long could endanger your health, say so in writing and enclose supporting documentation from a doctor.

When you file a formal appeal, the managed care entity should convene a committee made up of people who are not involved in your problem. This committee will meet to consider the matter, generally within 30 days of receiving your written appeal. Particularly in HMOs, where the committee is usually made up mostly of physicians, your medical arguments may fall upon receptive ears.

You usually can't attend an insurance company or HMO appeal. You can send written material to support your appeal, such as medical studies that support your position.

Some companies have more than one level of appeal resolution, so if you are denied at first, check your plan to see if you can appeal the committee's decision to a higher body. You may have the right to appear in person at this higher-level hearing, to bring an outside representative (such as a disability advocate, outside medical expert, or healthcare lawyer), and to question the medical practitioners involved. In other words, if a second-level procedure is available, it will be more like a trial or arbitration hearing than an informal discussion.

To prepare your appeal, look first at the insurance company's own documents. Somewhere in the fine print of the master policy that you should already have in your files, you will probably find a provision stating that if any of the company's policies are unenforceable based on state law, they are superceded by state law. Most insurance company claims adjusters know very little about state insurance law. Your job is to educate yourself and then educate them.

Now you need to find out what your state says about coverage in general and about bipolar disorders in particular. The answer may be found in actual legislation. Bipolar disorders are almost always included in the list of conditions covered under the mental health parity laws now found in some states: for example, California's state legislature has specifically declared that illnesses with organic causes, such as bipolar disorders and schizophrenia, are considered medical conditions under the law. Your state may have similar laws or public policies on the books. Laws protecting the disabled against discrimination may also have bearing. Both of these types of laws were written to ensure that people with disabilities or health problems get equitable treatment.

State chapters of advocacy groups like the NDMDA or NAMI will probably already have the information you need on hand, and the national NAMI office also collects information on state insurance laws. State insurance commission staff members should also be able to help you with general questions about what your state requires coverage for and can tell you about any protections written into state insurance, healthcare, or consumer protection laws. If you have Internet access, check to see if state laws, some public policies, and possibly state insurance commission decisions are available online. You could also call your state representative or senator's office and ask a staff member to research this issue for you.

Your state's protection and advocacy (P&A) office can also help you find out about what laws in your state apply to your insurance or healthcare problems. Sometimes P&A representatives, many of whom are lawyers, can resolve problems for you; in other cases, they can provide you with advice and referrals to other resources in your area (see the listing for the National Association of Protection and Advocacy Systems in Appendix A).

If you can show your insurance company that it is trying to assert a provision that violates a state or federal law, it should back down and provide treatment. The kinds of legal arguments needed to secure coverage are hard for non-lawyers to craft. Advocacy groups may help you write a persuasive letter of appeal on legal grounds.

Remember, actual state law trumps state policy statements every time, and that includes official policy statements issued by your state insurance commission. State laws may be more restrictive than federal regulations, in which case the state prevails. If state laws are less restrictive than federal mandates, the federal government prevails.

If you are still denied after all this time and trouble, you may be able to take the matter directly to your state's insurance commission. If your managed care plan is part of a public insurance program (for example, if you receive Medicaid or state medical benefits but you have been required to join an HMO), you can also appeal through a state agency, such as the county health department.

You can send a copy of your appeal to your state representative or senator or to your US representative or senator if any of the following situations occurs:

- Your insurance company or healthcare provider cites state or federal law as the basis for its decision
- You believe the company is acting in violation of a law, such as the Mental Health Parity Act or the ADA
- Your dispute is with a public healthcare program

These elected officials have staff members who try to help their constituents.

Sometimes going to the press (or at least threatening to) also gets results.

Arbitration

Formal arbitration is another possibility when appeals fail, although experienced advocates warn that since arbitrators are paid by the healthcare plans, it's a tough arena for consumers.

The average arbitration case costs less than $5,000, and that amount may be split with the HMO. In most cases, you can't recover your legal costs in arbitration. Sometimes arbitration can be quite expensive, however. According to Consumers for Quality Care, a division of the non-profit Foundation for Taxpayer and Consumer Rights (*http://consumerwatchdog.org*), your costs can reach $50,000 or more in complex cases, which may be more expensive than a court trial. Most consumer-law cases in the courts are taken by lawyers who work on contingency, meaning that you don't pay unless you win a financial settlement, which makes it hard to secure legal help for arbitration. If it is a binding arbitration, you may be unable to pursue help through the court system if the decision goes against you.[1]

Legal action

Taking your insurance company to court is something that you should consider only as a last resort. It's expensive, and it takes so long for a decision to come down and then be implemented that your current healthcare crisis may have passed long before the gavel bangs. If you have the means and the gumption, don't be dissuaded from making things better for others. Just don't pin all your hopes on a quick resolution by a judge.

In some cases your state disability protection and advocacy group (see the listing for the National Association of Protection and Advocacy Systems in Appendix A) can provide legal advice or even representation, and some lawyers are willing to take insurance cases on contingency.

Public healthcare in the US

The US does not have a national health plan that covers everyone, but instead supports a network of plans that cover some or all members of certain groups. Individual states and a few heavily populated counties and cities within them may also have health plans for certain citizens.

Groups that may have access to healthcare plans from the federal government include people over age 65, disabled people, and people in the military and veterans of military service. Not all people who fall into these categories are eligible for healthcare, and coverage is not total—most plans require co-pays at the time of service and other cost-sharing arrangements, as do the majority of private insurance plans.

Military healthcare coverage

Military personnel are one of the largest groups of people receiving publicly funded healthcare in the US. The federal government offers the Tricare Standard plan for active duty and retired members of the US military under the age of 65 and their families. A special service within Tricare, the Program for Persons with Disabilities, can help you with special medical needs, including mental illness. Tricare also includes dental benefits and access to Department of Defense pharmacies. A second program, called Tricare Extra, offers more benefits.

Retired service members over age 65 may move into a special Medicare program (Tricare Prime) operated by the Department of Defense, although this area of benefits is changing. Many former military personnel obtain much of their healthcare through Veterans Administration (VA) facilities.

If you rely on Tricare or the VA, you may encounter some special challenges with accessing expert services.

Raymond, age 36, is a former career serviceman. He says:

> I receive my services and medicines through the VA medical system. I am grateful for that, but I would prefer to have a job, and get outside care through my insurance carrier.
>
> For those in the VA system, if there is any way that you can obtain the funding to attend an outside facility, I would highly recommend it.
>
> I have been in several VA hospitals. At one, the corpsmen that worked there were good, the therapy sessions were present and somewhat helpful, but the doctors were residents and didn't have a clue. At another, there

*were good doctors, the staff cared, but no therapy occurred. A third was
set up for people with addictions to alcohol and drugs—not real helpful
for those patients with mental illness alone. They kept wanting to perform
ECT (electroconvulsive therapy) on me.*

Medicaid and Medicare

Medicaid is a federal health insurance program for eligible individuals who are not
senior citizens. It pays for doctor and hospital bills, including consultations with
neurologists and psychiatrists; six prescription medications per month; physical,
occupational, and speech therapy; and adaptive equipment.

You may be able to get Medicaid coverage by becoming eligible for SSI (see the
following section). In some states, such as Hawaii and Oregon, Medicaid may also be
delivered through a statewide healthcare system based on state funds plus a federal
Medicaid waiver. Medicaid is one of the few insurance plans that will pay for in-
home therapy services, partial hospitalization or day treatment, crisis services, and
long-term hospitalization or residential care for people with disabilities. Although it
is excessively bureaucratic, it is in many ways superior to private insurance coverage
for people who have disabilities.

Older adults sometimes qualify for Medicare, an insurance program for senior citizens who qualify for Social Security. To apply, call your local Social Security office or
call the Social Security hotline at (800) 772-1213 for an eligibility pre-screening.

SSI

Supplemental Security Income (SSI) is an income support program for people with
disabilities that limit their ability to work. In all states; Washington, DC; and the
Northern Marianas Islands, disabled people who qualify for SSI may be able to qualify for healthcare coverage through the federal Medicaid plan.

Being diagnosed with a bipolar disorder may or may not qualify you for SSI—it all
depends on how severely affected you are. If your symptoms are unresponsive to
medication, prevent you from working or limit your income from work, or make
self-care difficult, you may qualify. If your symptoms respond to medication but
medication side effects themselves prevent you from working or otherwise seriously
impact you, you may qualify.

SSI benefits range from around $300 to $500 per month for adults living in another
person's household to just over $500 per month for adults living independently. A

dependent adult's grant may be debited for such things as free room and board. Some states, such as New York and California, may supplement SSI to make up for higher living expenses.

This money is only provided for the direct needs of the disabled individual: it is not family income. You should keep receipts for all your expenditures.

Monique has not applied for SSI herself, but helping others with their SSI applications has been part of her job as an advocate:

> I have applied for SSI for other people through my job. The process is hell, to say the least. They want proof of everything—your doctor visits, your DSM-IV diagnosis, the works—and it is a difficult process, very tedious. When I was helping people fill out applications—they were for children, some of whom were in institutions—it was a 30-page application. They wanted incident reports, psych reports, and many other documents
>
> And for what—$500 a month? It's a tiny benefit. When you get to the point that you have it, you have to figure out what else you need to apply for and what other help you'll need. Just SSI alone will not get you food, rent, and incidentals.

To apply for SSI and/or Medicaid, go to your nearest Social Security office or call the Social Security hotline at (800) 772-1213 for an eligibility pre-screening. If you are given a green light by the eligibility screener, your next step is making an initial interview appointment and filling out a long form. This form asks dozens of difficult questions, including information about every physician or clinic that might have your medical records or test results, and information about your previous contacts with public health agencies. Provide copies of as many of your health records as you can—this may make the difference between winning and losing your claim.

If you need help in completing this form (and many people do), a social worker or someone from a disability advocacy group may be able to assist you. Some law firms specialize in helping people with new or pending SSI claims. Other firms only take cases that involve rejected claims.

Make sure your forms and records are complete when your initial interview takes place. Interviews may take place in person or over the phone. Most experienced applicants say in-person interviews are best, but they aren't always possible. During the interview, a Social Security representative will go over your application with you. It helps to have a file in front of you containing your health records; names, addresses, and phone numbers of doctors you see; and a list of social service personnel with whom you work.

Your Social Security caseworker will then send your documentation and application to a state agency for a decision about your claim. This agency may order a review of your medical documentation, sometimes including interviews and observation by doctors who contract with Social Security (a "consultative exam").

Social Security is supposed to arrange for your regular physician or psychiatrist to perform the consultative exam, if required. If you are instead told to see a different doctor, request that your own doctor be used instead or find out why the other doctor has been suggested.

Most applicants for SSI are rejected on their first try. You do have the right to appeal this denial, however—and you should, because a high percentage of appeals succeed. In addition, successful appellants get a lump sum equal to the payments they should have received, had their original application been properly approved. You must appeal the decision within 60 days, a process known as "reconsideration." You have a right to a hearing before an administrative law judge.

If your application is denied, contact a disability advocacy agency through the National Association of Protection and Advocacy Systems, which is listed in Appendix A. These publicly funded agencies can help you through the application process, and most can provide legal assistance if you need to appeal.

If you would prefer to work with a paid legal representative, you can find an SSI specialist through the National Organization of Social Security Claimants Representatives. You can reach NOSSCR at (800) 431-2804 or online at *http://www.nosscr.org*. If you win, a lawyer can charge a fee of 25 percent of your back due benefits, up to a maximum of $4,000. If you lose, you will be liable only for the cost of obtaining your medical records, copying fees, and possibly some other minor expenses.

Medicaid waivers

The reason one might need a Medicaid waiver is that SSI is an income-dependent program. If you or your spouse earns more than the regulations allow, you will not be eligible for SSI. In some cases, family income will reduce the amount of SSI received to as little as one dollar per month, but the beneficiary will get full medical coverage. Others must apply for a special income-limit waiver.

A waiver sets aside the income limits, allowing people who might not be eligible otherwise to get Medicaid coverage for themselves or a dependent. Medicaid waiver permissions come under the general title of Home and Community-Based Services, or 1915(c), waivers. These waiver programs are administered at a state level. Some states have severely limited the number of waivers they will allow; some have created their own disability-specific waiver pools for conditions like cerebral palsy and autism; and a few do not offer any waivers at all. Contact your county's Child and Family Services (CFS) department and ask for an appointment with a Medicaid worker, who can help you learn about and apply for waiver programs available in your state.

The appointment to apply for a waiver is usually long, and the questions are intrusive, so be prepared. You will need copious documentation, including the following:

- In most states, a rejection letter from SSI citing your income as the reason for rejection

- Copies of your birth certificate and Social Security card

- Proof of income (check stubs or a CFS form filled out and signed by your and/or your spouse's employer, and possibly income tax forms)

- Names, addresses, and phone numbers of all physicians who have examined you

- Bank account and safety deposit box numbers and amounts in these accounts

- A list of other assets and their value, including your house and car

- A medical report on a special form and a physician referral form signed by the doctor who knows you best (CFS will provide you with these forms)

If you have a caseworker with your county's mental health offices, this person may be able to help you navigate the SSI, Medicaid, and waiver process. Some state-by-state information about waiver programs is available online at *http://www.hcfa.gov/medicaid/ hpg4.htm.*

State and local public health plans

Some states, such as Hawaii, California, and Oregon, have public health insurance plans. These plans make innovative use of state funding combined with federal Medicaid payments. They may cover people on public assistance, low-income residents, residents with disabilities, and/or people who have been refused coverage due to preexisting conditions.

Some areas have public health plans that cover only mental healthcare. You may qualify for this coverage if you are uninsured, cannot obtain insurance, or have health insurance that either does not cover mental healthcare or imposes stringent limits on care.

To find out what's available and get the application process rolling, contact your state mental health department, listed in Appendix A.

In other areas, a pay-as-you-go system of public healthcare is available that relies on public health clinics. The cost of using these clinics is usually on a sliding scale, based on your income. Visits may be free for people with very low incomes.

Troy, age 30, used public care when he was younger:

> During the first few years after my diagnosis, I used county mental
> health services. Given my low level of income, I didn't have to pay much
> money for these services and they were very good. I was able to see the
> same therapist every month to talk about everything I was going through
> while coping with the illness, and then a psychiatrist would come into the
> session for about five minutes to prescribe lithium to me and discuss
> anything related strictly to the medication.

Unfortunately, millions of Americans who have government-provided health insurance find themselves limited to using county health clinics or public hospitals and to those private providers who are willing to work for cut-rate fees. Medicaid and state health programs pay healthcare providers less than private insurers do, and there's no law that says a given provider must take patients who have public insurance.

Some public facilities are run-down, understaffed, and hectic as a result of high demand and low budgets. In fact, the emergency rooms of some public hospitals are downright frightening on weekend nights! Familiarize yourself with all of the options covered by your public healthcare plan. You may have more choices than you are initially led to believe. In some cases you may have the option to join one or more HMO plans, receiving the same benefits as non-subsidized HMO members. Check with other recipients or local advocacy groups if you are offered this choice—some of these plans do a good job of caring for disabled clients, while others are not preferable to plain old Medicaid or state healthcare.

Sadly, there is also an anti-welfare attitude amongst some healthcare workers, who may not know or care what financial and medical troubles drove you to need public healthcare or income help. You shouldn't have to tolerate substandard or unbusinesslike treatment from providers. If it happens and you can't work things out with the provider directly, ask your caseworker about grievance and appeal options.

If you have problems accessing appropriate medical benefits under Medicaid, in state health plans, or through other public healthcare options, your mental health caseworker or a disability advocate may be able to help. If your problems are of a legal nature, such as outright refusal of services or discrimination, call your state Bar Association and ask for its pro bono (free) legal help referral service or contact the National Association of Protection and Advocacy Systems (see Appendix A). This national organization can put you in touch with your state's protection and advocacy agency, which provides free advice and legal help for issues related to disability. You can also consult the Health Law Project at (800) 274-3258.

Indirect financial help

In the US, tax deductions have replaced direct financial assistance to the poor in many cases. These benefits are provided just once a year, but people coping with the high cost of living with a disability should take advantage of them.

One of the most important tax benefits is the ability to itemize medical deductions on your federal income tax. You can write off not only the direct cost of doctor's visits not covered by health insurance, but also health insurance co-pays and deductibles, out-of-pocket expenses for medications, travel costs related to medical care, and at least some expenses related to attending medical or disability conferences and classes. Self-employed people can deduct most of their health-insurance premiums, even if they don't itemize.

Because itemized deductions limit your federal tax liability, they also reduce your state income taxes, if any. State taxes are usually based on taxable income figures taken from your federal form. Some states have additional tax benefits for the disabled.

Another important federal tax benefit is the Earned Income Credit (EIC) program. This benefit for the working poor can actually supplement your earnings with a tax rebate, not just a deduction. You can file for EIC on your federal 1040 tax form.

Participate in a Health Care Flex Spending Account (FSA), if your employer offers this opportunity. An FSA allows you to elect an amount that will be deducted from your paychecks on a pre-tax basis to pay for uncovered medical expenses. To participate in an FSA, you elect an amount at the beginning of the calendar year. As you accrue medical expenses, submit them for reimbursement, even if your paycheck deductions do not equal or exceed the amount of the reimbursement.

The one disadvantage of an FSA is that if your expenses do not total your election amount, you forfeit the difference. Accordingly, it's important to accurately estimate your anticipated uncovered expenses. Expenses recovered through a Health Care FSA cannot be deducted on your federal taxes, so this option works best if your combination of income and medical expenses does not allow you to itemize medical deductions.

Mortgage interest is also tax-deductible in the US, as most people are aware. Since your home is usually not considered as an asset when determining eligibility for direct financial assistance, such as SSI, this makes home ownership particularly attractive to people with a disability. Some banks and credit unions have special mortgage programs for low- and moderate-income families. Given the strong financial benefits of home ownership, including the opportunity to keep your housing costs from going up in the future, purchasing a house is very advisable.

Very low-income families may be able to get additional help in reaching the goal of home ownership from organizations like Habitat for Humanity. Disability advocacy and social service organizations have recently begun to push to increase the level of home ownership among disabled adults. In some cases, you can place your home in a special trust that provides professional management services.

Health Canada

In Canada, the Canada Health Act ensures healthcare coverage for all Canadian citizens and landed immigrants and for non-citizens who need emergency care. How healthcare is actually delivered is a provincial matter, however, and qualified providers can be hard to find in the less-populated northern provinces.

To initiate an evaluation for a bipolar disorder, you'll need to see your primary care physician. He can then make a referral to the appropriate specialist.

A wide variety of specialists are available through provincial health plans. Most of the best specialists are affiliated with university hospitals. Waiting lists are a reality, but reports indicate that calls and letters (especially if they come from your general practitioner) can often open doors.

If there is no qualified provider nearby, public assistance programs are available to help you get expert care elsewhere. This may include covering transportation costs and housing for out-of-town evaluation and treatment and facilitating regular consultations later on between the experts and a doctor closer to your home. Because each province has its own provincial insurance scheme, however, going out-of-province for care may mean paying up front and applying for reimbursement, which can be difficult.

Canadians also report that privatization and other changes are starting to limit their access to healthcare. Some families are now carrying private insurance to ensure timely access to care providers of their choice, although it is still rare.

Canadians in border areas may wish to consult with specialists in the US. Except for rare and pre-approved cases, public health insurance will not cover these visits.

Tony, age 31, says his public plan suffices for most needs, although he also carries supplemental insurance:

> I have medical insurance, both the Provincial Medical Services Plan and Extended Health coverage through my employer. I haven't really had to worry much about which plan covers what. I do pay a premium. I don't think it's expensive now, but if I was on a student budget, I probably would. They try to make the Provincial plan accessible to everyone, although you pay 100 percent at a certain income.
>
> As far as the blood work I get done for Epival (Depakote), that happens quarterly, and it's covered by the regular Provincial plan. I just give my Care card when I get my tests done. I also get 80 percent coverage of my prescriptions. I go see the psychiatrist every month lately, and I think that's also covered through Provincial—I don't need to fill out any claim forms or anything.
>
> I think the healthcare system's pretty good here, mostly because not much of it has been privatized. I think the whole approach of for-profit healthcare is that while it's supposed to increase access and give you more choice, in reality these ideas are capitalist propaganda.

Disability income in Canada

Welfare is available in Canada for people with disabilities, single parents, and unemployed adults with or without children. The amount of the monthly payment is set at the provincial level. The disability payment varies from a low of about $580 per month in New Brunswick to around $800 per month in more expensive Ontario and British Columbia.

To apply for welfare benefits, visit your nearest Ministry or Department of Social Services. Typically, you must be 18 years of age or older and have confirmation from a medical practitioner that the impairment exists and will likely continue for at least two years or longer or that it is likely to continue for at least one year and then reoccur. In addition you must require, as a direct result of a severe mental or physical impairment, one of the following:

- Extensive assistance or supervision in order to perform daily living tasks within a reasonable time
- Unusual and continuous monthly expenditures for transportation or for special diets or for other unusual but essential and continuous needs

There are limits on the amount and kinds of savings and other property that a person or family receiving benefits can have.

As in the US, welfare reform is a growing trend in Canada. Some provinces have introduced mandatory workfare programs for single adults and for some parents on welfare. These provisions generally do not apply to people receiving disability benefits, and parents with disabilities or caring for children with disabilities can usually have welfare-to-work requirements waived or deferred.

Canadians who are denied benefits or who have other problems with the benefits agency can appeal its decisions to an independent tribunal.

Some assistance for people with disabilities may also be available at the federal level or from First Nations (Native Canadian) agencies.

Indirect financial help in Canada

Sometimes indirect income assistance is available to Canadians, including income tax benefits. Some provinces provide a healthcare tax credit, which can cover medical costs not covered by public health insurance. College students with permanent disabilities can have their student loans forgiven and are also eligible for special grants to pay for hiring a note-taker, school transportation, and other education-related expenses.

Other direct and indirect income assistance is available to Canadians, such as subsidized travel and tax benefits. A disability tax credit is available that may reduce your income tax bill by $1,500 per year. It is also available to people caring for a disabled person at home. You will need to file form T2201 to receive this tax credit. You can get free help with this and other disability-related taxes at regional Revenue Canada offices.

You can get help with medical and disability issues from the support and advocacy organizations listed in Appendix A. These groups can also provide advice on working with Health Canada and public benefits agencies.

Benefits in the UK

The National Health system in England and Scotland has undergone tremendous upheaval over the past three decades. All services were once free to UK citizens, while private-pay physicians were strictly for the wealthy. Public services have since been sharply curtailed, and co-pays have been introduced. Nevertheless, services for people with mental illness are probably better now than they were in the past, when institutionalization was the norm.

Specialists are accessed through your general practitioner (GP). Referrals to specialists are notoriously difficult to obtain, even for private-pay patients.

You can get advice and help from the Manic Depression Fellowship (MDF) and other support and advocacy groups, several of which are listed in Appendix A.

Disability income in the UK

In the UK, people with disabilities have access to three major types of direct state benefits. You can apply for these programs at your local Benefits Agency Office.

The Disability Living Allowance (DLA) is for people with a disability. Payment ranges from fifteen to thirty-five pounds per week. The DLA forms are relatively complex, so find an experienced disability advocate to help you fill them out if possible. The MDF and other mental health advocacy groups may have DLA experts on staff, as may your local council.

Adults receiving DLA can also get a Mobility Allowance, a small sum of money to help them get to appointments and meet general transportation needs.

Your local council may also have its own benefits scheme. Benefits may include direct payments, such as a supplemental housing benefit, or tax offsets.

A number of supported work schemes are available for people with disabilities and adults receiving other forms of public assistance. In some cases, these programs are mandatory. Adults attending college or trade school may find themselves in a "Catch 22" situation: on some occasions benefits officers have decided that if they are well enough to pursue higher education, they're well enough to work, and canceled their benefits. You can appeal these and other unfavorable decisions to a Social Security Appeals Tribunal. Advice is available through your local Benefit Rights office.

Benefits in the Republic of Ireland

Disability Allowance and Disability Benefit are available in Ireland, but are far from generous. The Department of Social Welfare administers both programs. Disabled students can continue to receive these benefits while attending third level courses, although they may lose other types of public assistance, such as rent allowance. Maintenance Grant, a general benefit for poor families, is not affected by these benefits. Some direct mental healthcare is available from public or charitable hospitals and clinics in Ireland at low or no cost.

Supported work schemes are available, although your earnings may make you lose your disability benefits. The exception is work that the local welfare officer agrees is rehabilitative in nature.

A number of scholarship and grant programs are available to assist students with disabilities in Northern Ireland. An online report at *http://www.ahead.ie/grants/grants. html#toc* offers more information.

Benefits in Australia

Medicare, the Australian health plan, pays 85 percent of all doctor's fees. It also qualifies Australian citizens for free treatment in any public hospital. Many general practitioners and pediatricians bulk bill: they charge the government directly for all of their patient visits and let the 15 percent co-payment slide. Specialists usually won't bulk-bill. Once a certain cost level has been reached, Medicare pays 100 percent of the bill.

Patients can see the physician of their choice without getting a preliminary referral, but many specialists have long waiting lists. Access to qualified practitioners is especially difficult in rural areas, although the emergency healthcare system for rural Australia is enviable. In some situations, patients may be able to access professionals for advice or "virtual consultations" over the Internet, telephone, or even radio.

Medicaid does not cover some prescription medications, and there is a sliding-scale co-payment for those that are covered.

Jane, age 46, says it has been fairly easy to get her needs met:

> *My family and I moved from an outback town in Australia to the eastern coast. This move was my dream come true—everything was going well and I should have been happy, but I had a massive dive and would cry all the time over*

nothing. I went to a doctor, told him about how I was feeling, and he immediately diagnosed bipolar disorder and referred me to a psychiatrist.

When I had intense therapy and could not afford the gap, my psychiatrist bulk-billed so that I did not have to pay. I recently asked my psychiatrist if I could try a new drug, Topamax. He wouldn't give it to me, as it isn't used in Australia, but he has referred me to a mood disorder unit in Sydney that is doing research projects. I am happy with this at present, and am looking forward to the contact as they ask questions, do CAT scans, etc., and they might give me the drug.

Disability benefits in Australia

A variety of income support programs are available to Australian citizens, including direct financial assistance for adults with disabilities, parents caring for children with disabilities, single parents, unemployed single adults, youth, and students. Programs related specifically to disabled citizens and their families include Disability Support Pension, Related Wife Pension, Sickness Allowance, Mobility Allowance, Carer Payment, and Child Disability Allowance.

Employment programs for Australians with disabilities are many and varied, including the Supported Wage System (SWS), which brings the earnings of disabled workers in sheltered workshops or other types of supported or low-wage employment closer to the livability range.

You can find online information about all of Australia's benefit plans at the Centrelink Web site (*http://www.centrelink.gov.au/*). To apply for benefits or disability services, contact your local Department of Family and Community Services.

Indirect benefits in Australia

Indirect benefits may also be available under the Disability Services Act in the areas of education, work, and recreation. Examples include taxi vouchers from local agencies, elimination of sales taxes on aids and appliances related to a disability, and special home-buying programs.

The charity Carers' Taskforce Australia Inc. offers a "CarerCard" that can give people caring for a disabled person discounts on needed items and services at major stores. You can reach CTA at (02) 9543-6098 or on the Web at *http://www.carer.org.au*. This organization can also tell you about other benefits.

You can get help with disability income and health benefit issues from the support and advocacy organizations listed in Appendix A.

Benefits in New Zealand

About 75 percent of all healthcare in New Zealand is publicly funded. Care is delivered through private physicians who accept payment from the public health system. Treatment at public hospitals is fully covered for all New Zealand citizens, and also for Australian and UK citizens living and working in New Zealand. Privatization is a growing trend in New Zealand. Public hospitals and their allied clinics have been re-created as public-private corporations. However, the government still provides most of the funding, and it closely regulates healthcare.

Healthcare and disability services are both provided through a central Health Authority, which has for the past few years been making special efforts to improve the delivery of mental health services. To start an assessment for bipolar disorder, talk to your family physician about a specialist referral. Self-referral is also possible.

Urban patients may have access to group practices centered on Crown (public) hospitals, which often have excellent specialists. Māori patients may access healthcare and assessments through medical clinics centered around traditional iwi (tribal) structures if they prefer.

About 40 percent of New Zealanders carry private insurance, usually for hospitalization or long-term geriatric care only. This insurance is helpful when you need elective surgery and want to avoid waiting lists at public hospitals. It is not needed to access psychiatric care or other routine health or disability services.

New Zealanders complain that waiting lists for assessments and major medical treatments are sometimes excessive. For many years, patients on waiting lists were not given a firm date for their visits and were expected to be available immediately should an opening occur. A new booking system instituted in 1999 is said to be more reliable.

For patients in need of temporary or permanent residential care, volunteer organizations (particularly churches) are heavily involved in running long-term care facilities in New Zealand. These facilities are usually free of charge to the patient or family, although some are reimbursed by public health.

The social safety net in New Zealand is currently being revamped, and services for people with disabilities are expected to expand.

Direct benefits in New Zealand are similar to those provided in Australia, although the payments have historically been much lower. Domestic Purposes Benefit is for single parents, including those with disabled children. There are also a number of additional services available to the disabled and their carers, including training schemes, supported employment, and recreational assistance.

To apply for benefits or services, contact your local Ministry of Social Welfare office, which runs the Income Support program. If you need help with paperwork or appeals, Beneficiary Advisory Services at (03) 379-8787 or *http://canterbury.cyberplace. org.nz/community/bas.html* in Christchurch provides assistance and advocacy, as do a number of disability advocacy groups, particularly the information clearinghouse Disability Information Service at (03) 379-6189 or *http://canterbury.cyberplace.co.nz/ community/dis.html*.

Alternatives to insurance

No matter where you live, there are alternatives to expensive medical care. Those who don't have insurance or whose insurance is inadequate may want to investigate these resources.

For Heidi, simply having insurance has been no guarantee of getting optimum coverage:

> *It is almost impossible to do the company insurance thing and survive. My co-pays are $15 each for meds and doctor visits, and $25 if I want non-generic meds. Now I have four chronic conditions that must be monitored and several meds to take, so you can imagine how this adds up on a $9.50 an hour job. I have been sent to collections over doctor bills I cannot pay.*
>
> *It affects my choices: I wanted to try Lamictal but don't see it happening any time soon, especially the way it has to be titrated up slowly.*
>
> *If I had it all to do over, I would have remained on assistance where at least meds are $1 each on Medicaid. This is what I get for trying to better myself and be a good productive citizen.*

In some cases, creative private-pay arrangements may be possible with care providers. Parents have traded services or products for care, and others have arranged payment plans or reduced fees based on financial need. The larger the provider, the more likely it is to have a system in place for providing income-based fees. The smaller the provider, the more receptive an individual might be to informal arrangements, including barter.

Hospitals and major clinics usually have social workers on staff who can help you make financial arrangements.

Sources of free or low-cost healthcare or therapeutic services may include:

- Public health clinics and hospitals

- Medical schools that have teaching hospitals and clinics

- Hospitals and clinics run by religious or charitable orders, such as Lutheran Family Services clinics

- Charitable institutions associated with religious denominations, such as Catholic Charities, the Jewish Aid Society, and the Salvation Army

- United Way, an umbrella fund-raising organization for many programs that can often provide referrals

- Grant programs, both public and private

In the UK, special resources outside of National Health include:

- The Mental Health Foundation (*http://www.mentalhealth.org.uk/*)

- Community Trust associations, particularly The Zito Trust (0171 240 8422) and The New Masonic Samaritan Fund (for members and families of Masons)

- Samaritans (0345 909090)

The Mental Health Foundation Web site and *http://www.caritasdata.co.uk/ind_c181.htm* list many UK trusts related to mental illness, substance abuse, and related issues, including many that focus on particular ethnic or religious communities.

Medical savings accounts

Medical savings accounts (MSAs) are a new healthcare payment option that may benefit some people with bipolar disorders in the US. An MSA allows you to put away a certain amount of money specifically for healthcare costs. This income is then exempted from federal (and in some cases state) income taxes. Unused funds continue to gain tax-free interest. These accounts can be used to pay for insurance deductibles, co-payments, prescriptions, and medical services not covered by insurance.

People faced with paying out-of-pocket for expensive residential care or experimental medication are sometimes able to use an MSA to reduce their costs by an impressive percentage. You'll need to check the regulations of the specific MSA plan to see what expenses qualify.

MSAs are currently available through a wide variety of investment firms, as well as some banks. They are governed by rules similar to those for an Individual Retirement Account (IRA), except that you can make withdrawals as needed for qualified medical expenses. There are limits to how much you can place in an MSA, what expenses it can be withdrawn for, and who can have an MSA. Talk to a financial advisor at your bank or an investment firm for more information about this option.

Help with medications

Low-income people are sometimes able to get their medications for free by providing documentation to charitable programs run by pharmaceutical companies. In the US, the Pharmaceutical Research and Manufacturers of America Association (PhRMA) publishes a directory of medication assistance programs at *http://www.phrma.org/ patients*. Alternatively, you or your doctor can call the company that makes your medication to find out about its indigent patient program. Individual company programs are listed in Appendix A.

Most pharmaceutical companies require that you have no insurance coverage for outpatient prescription drugs, that purchasing the medication at its retail price is a hardship for you due to your income and/or expenses, and that you do not qualify for a government or third-party program that can pay for the prescription. An organization called The Medicine Program at (573) 996-7300 and *http://www.themedicineprogram. com* can help you apply to indigent patient programs.

Doctor's samples

Another source for free medications is your physician's sample cabinet. All you have to do is ask, and hope that the pharmaceutical rep has paid a recent visit. Samples can help you make it through a month when your budget is stretched too far, but you can't rely on getting them monthly.

Mail-order medications

In some cases, you can reduce the cost of your monthly medication bill by using a mail order or online pharmacy. These pharmacies can fill your prescription and mail it to you, sometimes at substantial savings. Medications may be available via mail order within your country or from overseas. The latter option can be surprisingly inexpensive and may provide you with access to medications that normally are not available where you live.

Your doctor may have to fill out some paperwork before you can use these mail-order services. As with any other transaction by mail or over the Internet, you should check out the company's reputation and quality of service before sending money or using your credit card.

These firms can usually send you a three-month supply in each order. If you are doing business with an overseas pharmacy, check Customs regulations that might prohibit you from importing medication before ordering, especially if the drug is not approved for use in your country.

Some mail order and online pharmacies were initially created to serve the market for AIDS medications, but have since expanded to provide a wide selection of drugs. Many will accept health insurance if you have a drug benefit—some will actually cover your medication co-payment as part of the deal.

If you have US military health benefits, contact your Tricare representative about mail-order arrangements. The main Tricare-approved mail-order service is Merck-Medco at (800) 903-4680 and *http://www.merck-medco.com/medco/index.jsp*.

Mail-order pharmacies that some people with bipolar disorders have worked with successfully are listed in Appendix A.

Clinical trials

Some people receive excellent medical care by taking part in clinical trials of new medications or treatments. Others have suffered unpleasant side effects or felt that they were treated like guinea pigs. Occasionally, serious harm or deaths have occurred.

Before enrolling in a clinical trial, make sure that you feel comfortable with the procedure or medication being tested, the professionals conducting the study, and the facility where it will take place. Clinical trials should be reviewed by an ethics committee. You should receive detailed information about potential benefits and risks, have all of your questions answered, and be given a consent form to sign.

An international listing service for current clinical trials is available at *http://www.centerwatch.com*. You can reach Center Watch by phone at (617) 247-2327. You can also find listings online at *http://www.clinicaltrials.gov*, a site maintained by the National Institutes of Health.

Miscellaneous discounts

A number of programs around the world help disabled people get access to computers and the Internet. One that offers free computers is the Center for Computer Redistribution at PO Box 70001, Richmond, VA 23255, or online at *http://www.freepcs.org*.

If you need medical care in a location far from home but you can't afford the cost of a flight or hotel, Appendix A lists resources in the US or Canada that may be able to help.

Similar corporate programs may be available in the UK, Europe, Australia, and New Zealand: contact the public relations office of your national airline to find out more. Social service agencies are sometimes able to give you an emergency travel grant to cover these needs.

Changing the rules

Advocating for changes in the insurance system or your national healthcare system is a big job, perhaps too big for any one person. But by working together, individuals can accomplish a lot.

Advocacy organizations are often the point of contact between healthcare consumers, insurers, HMOs, and public health. NAMI has been at the forefront of efforts to protect people with mental illnesses and their families by mandating insurance coverage and treatment, but it's an uphill battle.

The federal Mental Health Parity Act was passed with much fanfare in 1996 and went into effect at the beginning of 1998. Many people now believe that all insurance plans in the US must cover mental healthcare at the same level as they do physical healthcare. This is a misconception. This law affects only employer-sponsored group insurance plans that wish to offer mental health coverage. They are not required to do so. Additionally, if such coverage raises the company's premium cost by more than 1 percent, they need not comply with the law. Companies with fewer than 50 employees are also exempted.

The Mental Health Parity Act raises the annual or lifetime cap on mental healthcare in the plans that it covers, but it does not prevent insurance companies from limiting access or recovering costs in other ways. They may, for example, legally restrict the number of visits you can make to a mental health provider, raise the co-payment required for such visits, or raise your deductible for mental healthcare.

Currently, more than 30 states have passed their own mental health parity laws. As noted earlier in this chapter, these laws can supersede the federal regulations if they mandate higher levels of coverage. Twelve states have parity laws that surpass the federal act, while others have less-restrictive laws. Of the twelve with tighter restrictions, all of the laws are written in ways that should require coverage for bipolar disorders. Colorado, Connecticut, Maine, New Hampshire, Rhode Island, and Texas specifically require coverage for biologically based mental illnesses. For people living in these states, this is a step in the right direction, although it remains to be seen how these laws will be enforced and what steps some insurers may take to evade responsibility.

The University of South Florida maintains an informational web site on state and federal mental health parity research, laws, and proposed laws at *http://www.fmhi.usf.edu/parity/parityhome.html*.

In the US, most insurance regulation takes place at the state level, so that's probably where the most effective efforts for change will be made. There's still a need for education, for public advocacy, for legislative action, and in some cases for legal action. If you choose, you can make a big difference in these efforts. All of the mental health advocacy groups listed in Appendix A are involved in this effort in some way, as are many general healthcare consumer groups.

By working closely with allies in the public, private, and volunteer sectors, people can make change happen. People with mental illnesses can ally with healthcare providers, many of whom are angry at how their patients are being mistreated. For example, the Washington, DC-based American Psychological Association (APA) filed suit against Aetna U.S. Healthcare Inc. and related managed care entities in California, alleging that the company engaged in false advertising when it claimed to offer "prompt, accessible mental health treatment services." The APA has further alleged that Aetna put hidden caps on its already limited mental health benefits, disregarded what practitioners had to say about medical treatment of their patients, and deliberately delayed referrals.

In a 1998 press release, APA executive director for professional practice Russ Newman, PhD, JD, said:

> Despite the managed care industry's argument to the contrary, it's typically the managed care company that determines and controls the treatment of patients, not the doctor, and the financial bottom-line, not patient need, is usually the controlling factor.

Even insurance companies and managed care entities can be brought on board if they're shown the positive benefit of better-functioning patients, who require much less emergency care, fewer hospitalizations, and less expensive medications. Alternative models for delivery of care are evolving, and with hard work these new systems can be both more humane and more cost-efficient.

Other insurance issues

People with bipolar disorders in the US and other areas where litigation is common may want to consider carrying other types of insurance. For example, you might want to bolster your homeowners or renters insurance to cover damages to property that could occur if your behavior gets out of control and to ensure that your insurance includes liability coverage in case you injure someone.

If you fear that your symptoms could worsen in the future, long-term disability insurance could help you live more independently despite setbacks. If your employer offers a disability insurance policy, this is your best bet, because individual coverage is difficult to get and variable in quality.

Unfortunately, disability insurance vendors in the US and Canada are currently allowed to insist on mental illness exclusion clauses, which even apply to customers who have simply attended family therapy sessions. Other policies will not pay benefits unless the policyholder's mental illness confines him or her to a hospital, which is not the case when a policyholder has a physical disability. As of this writing, these provisions are being challenged in US state and federal courts, as well as by the Canadian Psychiatric Association. The Judge David L. Bazelon Center for Mental Health Law provides up-to-date information on insurance issues, including disability insurance, on its website at *http://www.bazelon.org,* but it directs individual inquiries to the appropriate state Protection & Advocacy office.

CHAPTER 8

Living with Bipolar Disorders

WHEN THE SYMPTOMS OF A BIPOLAR DISORDER STRIKE, they change your life. Everything from your personal priorities to your career can be affected.

This chapter takes a look at dealing with the behaviors, problems, and changes that often come with bipolar disorders. The emphasis is on being proactive: avoiding common dangers and thinking ahead about goals and how to reach them. It starts by discussing a basic shift in priorities that is helpful when setting personal goals. It then discusses keeping a mood diary and other steps that give you increased control over your symptoms and treatment. The following sections look at specific areas of life that the diagnosis often affects; they offer skills and strategies for coping with difficulties.

When you're caught in the maelstrom of mood swings, it seems to take all of your energy just to stay upright. The solution is setting small goals that you can reach, building on these successes to achieve those big, important goals that lie farther down the road.

If you've ever taken a college psychology course, you probably remember Maslow's hierarchy of needs, as shown in Fig. 8.1. Drawn up by behavioral scientist Abraham Maslow in 1943, it's a visual guide to the forces that motivate people, from the most basic survival instincts to the highest altruistic motives. It's also a good guide to handling the effects a bipolar disorder can have on your life. It will help you set goals, both small and large, to achieve recovery.

Maslow defined physiological needs as the basic things we need to survive: food, clothing, and shelter. Safety needs include freedom from physical danger and the feeling that your physiological needs will be met. At the next level is the need to relate to others socially and emotionally. Esteem needs refer to the desire to feel loved and accepted by others in return and to have adequate self-esteem.

Maslow identified additional needs that people strive for once these basic needs have been met. These include, at the very top, what he called "self-actualization": the need to reach one's fullest potential as a human being.

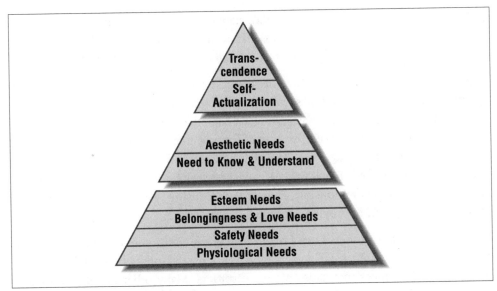

Figure 8-1. Maslow's hierarchy of needs

His hierarchy is a general guide, not an absolute. Many people reach their full human potential despite struggling daily to meet their most basic physical needs. But it's certainly true that when your survival needs are not being met, it's difficult to think about abstractions like the future, not to mention considering the impact of your behavior on the lives of others.

The following sections translate this hierarchy into a guideline for self-care.

Physiological needs

Eating properly and finding shelter from the elements is important—but for anyone with a serious mental illness, this isn't always as simple as it sounds. Meeting your physiological need for shelter and basic bodily safety can mean anything from taking special steps to keep your job to applying for public assistance if needed or considering hospitalization during a crisis.

Tony, age 31, has gained a new appreciation for the struggles of others coping with mental illness:

> *Because of my experience, I now look at street people differently. I believe that many homeless people and prison inmates suffer from mental disorders, so I think getting people effective help earlier will help with the problems of overcrowding prisons and too many street people.*

I can see the humanity in the confusion and incoherence of these people,
and I have more compassion and understanding for them now. I feel like
without the good fortune I experienced, I could very easily be in their shoes.

In the US, a large percentage of homeless people have a major mental illness. Many others coping with mental illness are just one paycheck away from losing their homes. The stress that comes with living on the edge financially can actually cause your symptoms to worsen. Seek the help of friends, family, support groups, and professional advocates as needed to lessen that anxiety, and plan ahead during periods when you're feeling well. For low-wage workers, seeking outside help is usually the only way to ensure secure housing. The section "Housing," later in this chapter, offers some specific ideas on improving your shelter situation.

People with bipolar disorders have a higher rate of eating disorders, including anorexia and bulimia. These are treatable medical conditions and possibly are related to the neurological differences that cause bipolar disorders. Many other people with manic depression are extremely picky eaters, willing to ingest so few foods that it can impact health. Medications that cause nausea can also impact your diet. Treatment for eating disorders and work on problems that may underlie self-limited food choices fall into the survival needs category. Hypersensitivity to textures and smells is a common but little-known cause for eating problems, and it can be treated (see Chapter 6, *Complementary Therapies*).

Another physiological need is continued treatment for any chronic physical illness you may have, such as diabetes or asthma. Even long-standing medical conditions are sometimes ignored during periods of mental health crisis, but if left untreated they can only contribute to further destabilization. Medications for these conditions can also interfere with the effects of psychiatric medications, so make sure your general practitioner and psychiatric practitioner are working together.

Safety needs

People with bipolar disorders are often their own worst enemies. They are at increased risk due to impulsive and self-destructive behaviors, including drug and alcohol abuse. Reducing, and hopefully eliminating, these behaviors should be the No. 1 priority of psychiatric treatment and therapy. Until these crises are dealt with, other symptoms may barely be noticeable, much less treatable.

People with bipolar disorders who avoid the trap of substance abuse have a far better prognosis than those who do not. If this issue is already impacting your health, seek treatment as soon as possible. It may literally save your life. Alcoholism, drug addiction, and even occasional binge drinking or drug use can substantially increase your risk of mood swings, health problems that contribute to destabilization, job and relationship loss, and death. See the section "Substance abuse" later in this chapter for more information.

If physical or emotional abuse is affecting your life, eliminating this major source of stress can have a profound impact. People with mental illness often end up in abusive relationships due to poor self-esteem or economic instability, factors that also make it hard to leave. Be sure to talk to your therapist about this issue—she may be able to help you work through your barriers to leaving and provide practical advice. Special services are available to people who need to escape abusive situations. Call your local health department, Mental Health Association, mental health advocacy group, or a crisis line to find out what is available in your community.

Your family and the larger community also have safety needs. If you are acting out in ways that put others in danger, these aggressive or abusive behaviors must be addressed. Stabilizing your moods via medication and therapy is a good start, but anger counseling and developing alternative ways to cope with stress, pressure, and anger are also essential. Chapter 6 offers some ideas, as does the section "Add joy to your life," later in this chapter.

If you frequently deal with overwhelming feelings of anger, you might add something to your home that helps you cope. A ceiling-mounted punching bag, some pillows to throw, or an exercise bike to pedal off the aggression can help. You can even store a box of thrift-shop crockery in the basement that you can break when the urge hits you, instead of smashing something valuable or, worse yet, taking it out on another person.

Monique, age 31, says irritability and anger have been challenging, and no one strategy is always successful:

> I try to exercise every week, so I just try to continue my routines when I'm manic and hope it will tire me out so I won't be aggressive or angry. Sometimes it works, sometimes it doesn't.
>
> I really haven't found a perfect remedy to the angry feelings I get when I'm manic. I am so thankful and blessed to have people who love me so much that my anger and harsh words have not made them go away. I have tried my best to stay away from people who might provoke me and to bite my lip, but if I'm manic I'm not always able to do that. I tell people it's a good idea not to say things that are likely to bug me, just stay out of my way if you can.

Finding a way to contain your rage and channel it into something productive may also protect you from entering the criminal justice system, an arena where you may not be able to protect yourself from harm. See the section "Criminal justice and mental illness" later in this chapter for additional information.

Eliminate as many suicide risks from your home as you can and build in safeguards. See the section "Suicide prevention" at the end of this chapter for more on this topic. Have a plan for preventing self-harm and stick to it. Talk to your therapist about writing up an "anti-suicide contract" that sets up this kind of plan, including whom to call when you need help right away.

Social needs

It's pretty hard to meet your own social needs. Others must be willing to be in relationship with you. The social world is fraught with problems for people with bipolar disorders, however. Impulsive or unusual behavior can make you a social pariah, or attract the kind of friends who encourage your worst tendencies. Finding good, supportive friends—or even any friends—is sometimes a real challenge.

Shoshana, age 56, says:

> Most of the former friends I had disappeared. My real friends stood out, and I suppose one is lucky to come through something like this with a couple of friends by her side.
>
> When one is fairly stable, the community can be a great place. It is not so friendly to obvious mental patients, and there are few places set up for us in local communities since mental health funding has been slashed.
>
> I have made some really good friends from support groups, both online and in real life. I've also found a good place to volunteer at the local Humane Society thrift shop, where I can help animals without taking them all home with me.

One way to find positive social relationships is to seek out an organization that needs your creativity, brains, and energy. Volunteer service groups, activist organizations, community theater, amateur sports leagues, and political campaigns are just some of the activities that have worked well for others.

As Shoshana notes, some communities do have drop-in community centers specially made for people with mental illness. See the section "Drop-in centers," later in this chapter.

Perhaps the two greatest social skills you can develop are a sense of humor and flexibility. These will help you weather life's setbacks.

Personality is based partly on inborn traits and partly on how relationships with others are experienced. A person who has experienced rejection may react by expecting rejection, avoiding social contact, or pushing others away deliberately. When these coping strategies combine to reinforce difficult inborn traits, the result can be a personality disorder, as discussed in Chapter 2, *Getting a Diagnosis*.

Like substance abuse, personality disorders make manic depressive illness harder to treat. If you have become uncomfortably withdrawn as a result of your illness or if you have developed personality problems that push others away, working on these issues in therapy can help your social life get back on track.

Esteem needs

You can think of self-esteem as the internal benefits of having your social needs met, an internal perception of self-value based in large part on the words, deeds, and reactions of others. One goal you could strive for is being an emotionally healthy person, despite mental illness. That's not a contradiction in terms at all. You need opportunities to see that you are socially acceptable, lovable, and cared for. You need to see that your attachments to others are valued and returned. You need chances to let your innate talents shine through, whatever they may be, and to give to others.

This may not be possible in the context of old relationships. Some members of your family may reject you in ways that are hurtful. Friends and coworkers can also be cruel, especially if they don't understand the nature of the illness. You may have to go the extra mile to educate the people whose opinions matter to you.

Jane, age 46, says she has had to seek outside support to keep her marriage going, but maintaining other relationships hasn't been as straightforward:

> *I have been married twice, and have hurt so many people that I have lost count.*
>
> *My husband and I saw a marriage counselor for a number of years before my diagnosis because I couldn't work out what was going on— we did not communicate with each other emotionally or physically for eighteen months. My husband listens, and is involved with any concerns I have with bipolar disorder. I must admit that we have only just started really talking about it recently, mainly after I found a mailing list on the Internet.*

My family—my siblings, mother, etc.—try to act interested, but are in denial.

Loving a person with a bipolar disorder is sometimes hard work. Do whatever you can to support your spouse, partner, family, and friends in their journey through life with you. In some cases, family or relationship counseling is useful. In other relationships, all that's needed is doing your best to understand the feelings and views of others and how your behavior might be perceived.

This isn't always easy for someone with a bipolar disorder, or any serious illness, for that matter. When things are not going well for you, there's a natural tendency to put your own needs first and perhaps to become a bit egocentric. Over time, you may lose the habit of considering how your actions or speech impact others. This is something you can recover, however—just as it's part of 12-step programs like Alcoholics Anonymous, seeking forgiveness for past misdeeds and repairing your relationships can also help you regain your self-esteem and get you one step closer to recovery.

Repair isn't always possible. People may disappear from your life because of their own discomfort or for an unrelated reason, not because of something you did. Not everyone is able to forgive the past misdeeds of others. Nevertheless, the act of trying to restore relationships is therapeutic in and of itself.

Taking charge of bipolar disorder

Medical care is an essential first step in tackling bipolar disorders, and medication is almost always the foundation of all subsequent interventions. Research the medications you take, make sure you take them regularly, watch out for side effects, and add therapy and complementary interventions as needed.

There are other tasks to undertake on the road to recovery, however, and these can be just as important. These include learning about the disorder and discerning personal patterns that are the key to proactive treatment. Books such as this one, films, online resources, and other materials can be helpful. Talking to others who have a personal experience with bipolar disorders is often invaluable.

The mood and behavior diary

Keeping a daily mood and behavior diary is an empowering activity. It can reduce the number of serious depressive and manic episodes by helping you see the early warning signs. It can also help you assess whether new medications or other treatments are working.

Marcia, age 26, is learning to recognize her mood variations:

> *The autumn season always seemed to be a down time for me, starting as early as age 5, while my springs and summers seem to have always been really "up." Obviously, the hypomania I experience can be quite enjoyable, but my depressions are very "down." I have not necessarily reached the point of suicide in my depressions, but have experienced constant sleeping, irritability, lack of interest, difficulty concentrating, obsessive thoughts, etc.*

What would this kind of diary look like? It depends on you and on how you want to use it. Some people love to write long diary entries, others might grudgingly check off a few boxes on a worksheet every day. No matter what the format is, it should hold a daily collection of information that illuminates early warning signs of incipient mania, hypomania, or depression. This data can help you recognize what emotions, activities, behaviors, and seasonal changes precede mood swings; what makes mood swings stronger and longer-lasting; and what makes mood swings milder and shorter.

Monique is also using mood charting to get ahead of her illness:

> *My doctor recently gave me this mood chart, which I really like. You just track how you're feeling by the day. Are you having ups and downs, are you getting less sleep?*
>
> *I do find it hard to recognize when my mood is changing, so I think it definitely does help. It asks things like "is your thinking irrational?" That's something you may not recognize til later unless you analyze your thought patterns every night and really think about it. Then you can say, "hmm, I have been thinking about some strange things today."*
>
> *I've been doing mood charting for about a month and a half now, and I'll definitely keep it up on a long-term basis.*

Some typical early warning signs are listed in the official criteria for depression, hypomania, or mania—pressured speech, for example, or decreased need for sleep. Others can be personal in nature, such as menstrual cycles, being stressed out over work, or overdoing it at the gym.

Figure 8-2 is an example of a daily mood and behavior worksheet that mostly uses a simple Yes/No style.

The Harvard Bipolar Research Group has also designed a detailed mood chart that can be downloaded from the Web and printed for use at home. See *http://www.manicdepressive.org/moodchart.html* for charts in HTML and PDF (Adobe Acrobat) format.

SLEEP

Did you sleep well last night?	☐ Yes ☐ No
Did you have a hard time getting to sleep last night?	☐ Yes ☐ No
Did you wake one or more times during the night and have a hard time getting back to sleep?	☐ Yes ☐ No
Did you have nightmares or very unusual dreams?	☐ Yes ☐ No
Was it hard to wake up on time this morning?	☐ Yes ☐ No

MEDICINE

Did you take all of your medicine on time today?	☐ Yes ☐ No
Did you start or stop taking any medication today, or change your dose? (If yes, which? _____)	☐ Yes ☐ No
Did you start or stop taking any vitamin or supplement today, or change your dose? (If yes, which? _____)	☐ Yes ☐ No
Did you see a doctor, therapist, or alternative healthcare practitioner today? (If yes, what happened? _____)	☐ Yes ☐ No

FOOD

Did you eat a complete breakfast today?	☐ Yes ☐ No
Did you eat a complete lunch today?	☐ Yes ☐ No
Did you eat a complete dinner today?	☐ Yes ☐ No
Did you have snacks after school or between meals?	☐ Yes ☐ No
Did you eat anything unusual, or anything that disagreed with your digestion? (If yes, what? _____)	☐ Yes ☐ No

WORK/HOME

Did you go to work or do your regular home routines today?	☐ Yes ☐ No
Did you have trouble paying attention today? (If yes, when? _____)	☐ Yes ☐ No
Did anything happen today that made you feel sad, angry, upset, or scared? (If yes, what? _____)	☐ Yes ☐ No
Did you find yourself talking "too much" today, or did other people say you were doing so?	☐ Yes ☐ No
Did you have a hard time staying still today, or did other people say you were fidgety?	☐ Yes ☐ No
Did you feel tired, sick, or "down" today?	☐ Yes ☐ No
Did you have any special activities today? (If yes, what? _____)	☐ Yes ☐ No
Did you get in an argument today? (If yes, why? _____)	☐ Yes ☐ No
Were you able to relax today, or did you feel like you had to keep on the move constantly?	☐ Yes ☐ No
Did you keep thinking strange, depressing, or scary thoughts today?	☐ Yes ☐ No
Is anything coming up soon that's making you nervous or excited? (If yes, what? _____)	☐ Yes ☐ No
Did you get some physical exercise today?	☐ Yes ☐ No
Did you get some exposure to natural sunlight or a light box today?	☐ Yes ☐ No
Did you do anything fun today?	☐ Yes ☐ No
What is the date and season today? _____	
If female, where are you in your menstrual cycle? _____	

Figure 8-2. Daily mood and behavior worksheet.

Jane, age 43, has found a mood diary useful, but warns that commitment is a must if it's to work properly:

> *When first diagnosed I kept a record daily of moods, rated with a graph of severity from 0 to 10. It was great, and I wish I could do it now, because you can pick up straight away what is happening. The only thing is, when I'm feeling good, I feel like I don't need to do it any more—and when I feel bad, I don't have the energy to fill it out.*

Preventing mood swings

Eventually, the information gained from keeping daily records can help head mood swings off at the pass. For example, many people with bipolar disorders enter a hypomanic or manic phase if their sleep schedule is severely disturbed for two nights in a row (some doctors call this familiar pattern the "Two Day Rule"). If you see a growing pattern of sleep disturbance, you can take steps to turn things around. For some people, the solution is as simple as a warm bath and a cup of herbal tea before bed. Others may need to try medication, either an over-the-counter preparation, a supplement like melatonin, or a prescription drug. When you know sleep deprivation is a trigger for mood swings, you can more easily prevent a problem.

Stress breeds anxiety, which can change eating and sleeping habits. Identifying and doing something about stressful situations can prevent problems.

For some people, certain dates or special events act as triggers. Holidays, for example, can be mood-swing minefields due to schedule and diet changes, and personal and family expectations. Anniversaries of past traumatic events may also drive increased symptoms.

Troy knows one of his trigger dates and makes sure he's ready to cope when it comes around:

> *It was the seventh anniversary of my stepfather's death that coincided with my first down swing. I was 17, and I remember crying for hours and not understanding why.*
>
> *Even though it's been thirteen years since I was diagnosed with a bipolar disorder, this date still consistently acts as a trigger for a down swing.*
>
> *Just knowing that a swing is possible during certain seasonal changes can help you cope—you're not taken by surprise. I try to schedule things around those times, although that doesn't always work. My advice is to just take it easy, and try to avoid whatever other stressors there are in your life so you don't make things worse.*

Your mood and behavior diary can also be a simple tool for thinking about moods, emotions, and behaviors. It identifies issues every day and can help you and your doctor identify patterns. Over time, you may note that you have a higher likelihood of a mood swing just before your menstrual cycle starts, at the beginning of spring, or following a physical illness. You can then use this information to be proactive. For example, if you note seasonal differences to mood, you can try some of the therapies that work for seasonal affective depression. Your doctor could also prescribe an "as needed" medication or change the dosing schedule for your regular medication to fit your cyclic pattern, or you can simply learn to cut back on stressful activities during times that tend to be problematic.

Thinking about thinking

Some of the most persistent problems that people with bipolar disorders have involve types of thinking that are irrational and difficult for others to understand. Once you can label and dissect an irrational thought, you take away some of its power.

Although these habits of thought contribute to development of the hard-to-treat personality disorders that often bedevil people with bipolar disorders, they can be overcome with knowledge and practice. Working with a therapist is often essential, especially if you have experienced irrational thoughts for years. Types of thinking that often get people into trouble include the following:

- **Catastrophizing.** This is defined as seeing only the worst possible outcome in everything. For example, you might think that just because the boss didn't like your work on a project you will be fired, everyone will think you're stupid, you'll never get another job, and on and on. No matter what soothing words or solutions well-meaning friends try to apply, the person who catastrophizes will insist that there's no remedy.

- **Minimization.** This involves minimizing your own good qualities or refusing to see the good (or bad) qualities of other people or situations. People who minimize are often accused of wearing rose-colored glasses or of wearing blinders that allow them to see only the worst. If a person fails to meet the minimizer's high expectations in one way—for example, by being dishonest on a single occasion—the minimizer will suddenly write the person off forever, refusing to see any good characteristics that may exist.

- **Grandiosity.** Having an exaggerated sense of self-importance or ability is grandiosity. For example, you may fancy yourself the all-time expert at stock-market investing and act as though everyone else should see and worship your fabulous skill as well—regardless of whether you are actually getting stellar results or not. You might believe that you know more than your broker or even (if you really let things get out of hand) think that you'll be tapped to head up a top investment firm any day now.

- **Personalization.** This is a particularly unfortunate type of grandiosity that presumes you are the center of the universe, causing events for good or ill that truly have little or nothing to do with you. You might believe your mean thoughts made your husband ill, for example, or that world peace depends on your writing a letter to the President.

- **Magical thinking.** Magical thinking is more common in people with obsessive-compulsive disorder, but it's sometimes seen in bipolar disorders as well. Magical thinkers come to believe that by doing some sort of ritual they can avoid harm to themselves or others. For example, you might believe that you can prevent harm from coming to your family by painting the doors and windows blue or by saying certain words several times a day. The ritual may or may not be directly connected with the perceived harm, and sufferers tend to keep their rituals secret. Others may come to feel that ritual behavior will bring about some positive event.

- **Leaps in logic.** Everyone's guilty of this one on occasion—making seemingly logic-based statements, even though the process that led to the idea was missing obvious steps. You may jump to conclusions, often negative ones. One special type of logical leap is assuming that you know what someone else is thinking. For instance, you might think that anyone who is whispering is talking about you. Another common error is assuming that other people will naturally know what you are thinking, leading to great misunderstandings when they don't seem to grasp what you're talking about or doing.

- **"All or nothing" thinking.** The "all or nothing" thinker is unable to see shades of gray in everyday life, leading to major misperceptions and even despair. A person who thinks only in black-and-white terms can't comprehend small successes. He's either an abject failure or a complete success, never simply on his way to doing better.

- **Paranoia.** In its extreme forms, paranoia slides into the realm of delusion. Many people with bipolar disorders experience less severe forms of paranoia because of personalizing events, catastrophizing, or making leaps in logic. A person with mildly paranoid thoughts might feel that everyone at work is watching and judging him, when in fact he's barely on their radar screen. A person with severe paranoia might feel that she is being tracked by the CIA through radio transponders in her teeth.

- **Delusional thinking.** Most of the other thought styles mentioned above are mildly delusional. Seriously delusional thinking has even less basis in reality and can include holding persistently strange beliefs. Believing that you were kidnapped by aliens during the night and then returned to your bed or that you need to cover your ceiling with tin foil to keep spies from reading your thoughts are examples of delusional thinking

Not only are these thought styles in error, they're intensely uncomfortable to the person who suffers from them, because no one would deliberately choose to experience the intense anxiety these thoughts produce. When such thoughts emerge in words and deeds, the damage can be even worse. Expressing these kinds of strange ideas can alienate friends and family, lead to ostracism and severe misunderstandings, and even cause you to be arrested or institutionalized.

Tony notes that watching out for delusional thinking is always a tough call:

> I can remember the mindsets of mania or depression, and my mind sometimes has shades of these states. Sometimes it seems like I can feel my brain pulling me one way or another. I think this experience has made me more careful about taking my emotions and feelings so seriously. I realize that I may feel something very strongly, but it is not how I really feel, it is a trick.

The same chemical imbalances that cause bipolar disorder are at the root of these thought errors, although they also have a basis in life experiences. If you were teased, bullied, and ridiculed as a child, for example, personalization and paranoia may not seem so far-fetched. If you've frequently been scapegoated on the job or within your family, it's easy to feel like you really are the cause of all problems.

The rigidity that these problematic thought patterns have in common may also come from life experiences, at least in part. Many clinicians suspect that because people with bipolar disorders often deal with illogical waves of emotion and activity, they try to impose strict structures on their thoughts and beliefs to compensate. These efforts to make sense of an inner world gone haywire sometimes work, but sometimes they become problems in and of themselves.

Unless you're in an acute depressed, hypomanic, mixed, or manic episode, which can sap you of your self-control, you probably try hard to keep these types of weird thoughts under wraps. That can be an exhausting use of mental energy and can leave you feeling terribly alienated. The good news is that there are ways to minimize these types of thoughts.

Because these thought styles have at least some chemical basis, medication helps in many cases. Having someone in your life who is willing to hear you out without being judgmental can be a real relief, whether it's a sympathetic spouse or a therapist. One therapeutic approach that works particularly well, especially when it's used in conjunction with medication, is cognitive therapy. This type of talk therapy is geared precisely toward helping people identify erroneous thinking and mistaken beliefs about themselves and the world. Chapter 5, *Talk Therapy*, explains more about this approach.

Bipolar disorders at college

If you are attending college or thinking of going back to school, don't let manic depression stop you. The Americans with Disabilities Act (ADA) prohibits discrimination against disabled persons in public facilities. This has been defined in multiple court decisions as encompassing both private and public colleges, including graduate schools and technical schools. That means it's against the law to deny admission to students based on disabilities. Of course, other admission criteria generally must be met.

Some national governments have instructed universities to make an effort to recruit students with disabilities. Recruitment programs tend to be geared toward people with physical barriers to access, but the directives are often written to cover those with mental illness as well.

Public universities and community colleges may waive some admission criteria for disabled students on a case-by-case basis if you can show that you are capable of college-level work. Standardized test requirements are sometimes set aside if your high school grades, previous college performance, or work portfolio look good. This option is very helpful if your education was disrupted by illness or in-patient treatment.

Joe, age 33, made it through a rigorous college program despite his illness:

> *The illness has interfered with work and school, but I have generally managed to do well in that part of my life. I missed months of school in my junior year of high school, as I was too depressed and agitated to function. A tutor helped me through some of the material, but when an Ivy League college I applied to noticed the irregularities in my school career, my guidance counselor told them about my episode.*
>
> *An episode in college caused me to cancel my plan to study in London for a semester, but that was about it.*

In graduate school, I was lucky to have a thesis advisor who was very understanding. He visited me while I was hospitalized, and lent me a tape and a book. He also introduced me to a successful professional in my field who was public about his manic depression.

Most people with bipolar disorder don't need anything special from the university to qualify for admission or to succeed. For those who do, such as people who also have a learning disability, almost all public universities and many private ones offer at least some special services, such as tutoring, counseling, mentoring programs, and study groups.

The freshman year of college is a very common time for symptoms to flare, and the rigors of high-stakes tests like the GRE, grad school, and heavy schedules can also fuel mood swings. Stress, all-night study sessions, and off-campus attractions such as drug and alcohol use can all play a role.

Before you leave for college in another city, make sure that you have secured safe and appropriate housing, and found competent local professionals to provide ongoing care. Plan ahead to keep your stress level as low as possible. A minimum course load in your first semester is a good idea, as is limiting additional stressors like work and relationship hassles. Give yourself time to figure out how to handle the basics before you throw yourself into the full swing of campus activities and outside commitments.

Work out a crisis plan, just in case things go wrong. Know whom to call and where to go. You can contact the NAMI or NDMDA chapter in the area you're moving to for more information about local care providers, crisis hotlines, and support resources. You may want to talk to the health services office on campus, if any. Some colleges have full-service clinics that can provide a convenient location for medication management and referrals for other services. Colleges with medical schools often offer quite excellent care on or near campus.

Bipolar disorders at work

There are two major on-the-job issues for people with bipolar disorders: getting work and keeping it. Most Western and Asian countries offer employees at least some protection from disability discrimination on the job. In the US, the ADA makes it illegal to refuse to hire a person simply because he has, or appears to have, a disability—as long as that disability will not prevent him from doing the job.

Careful preparation for job applications and interviews can help you avoid job discrimination. Make an honest assessment of your skills and job history when deciding what job to apply for. Working with a job counselor can help you prepare your resume and practice interviewing skills. Apply only for jobs that you are able to do, because employers have the right to reject you if you are not qualified for the job. If you have a choice, choose to work for a company with a large workforce; it is less likely to discriminate and more likely to offer group life and health insurance.

Interviewers are only allowed to discuss a job applicant's disabilities if they are visible or if the applicant brings up the topic. Accordingly, you don't need to volunteer information about your mental illness during a job interview.

Monique says:

> With my current employer (a mental health advocacy group) it has not been a big deal, and I've felt comfortable talking to people here about my mood disorder. But with other jobs that I've had, I have been hesitant and afraid of discussing it. I don't want to be treated differently than any other person,
>
> I think if it was a position where I felt I was going to stay there and I felt comfortable with my co-workers, I would reveal it—but not at the job interview.
>
> And even though I have told people here, I haven't told everyone. It's personal, and I want to feel comfortable with the person before we talk about it.

Unless you have specific mental or physical limitations that affect the type of work you are applying for, the fact that you have a bipolar disorder should have no bearing on your qualifications for the job. Knowing your rights and preparing strategies for your job interview can make the difference between being hired and being rejected. The following suggestions on how to conduct yourself during a job interview may help:[1]

- Do not volunteer information about your medical history. Employers have the right only to determine if you are capable of performing the job. They do not have the right to ask about personal or confidential information during an interview.

- Under the Americans with Disabilities Act, employers cannot ask about medical history, require you to take a medical exam, or ask for medical records unless they have made a job offer.

- Do not lie on a job application or during an interview. You can be fired later if your dishonesty is uncovered. Instead, answer only the specific questions asked. Try to steer the conversation toward your current ability to do the job, rather than explain your past.

- Do not ask about health insurance until you have been offered a job. Before accepting the job, get the benefits information and review it thoroughly.

- If your medical history becomes an issue after the job offer, get a letter from your physician that briefly outlines your treatment and stresses your current good health and ability to do the job. Ask the doctor to let you review the letter prior to giving it to your potential employer. If your doctor is willing, you might even prepare this kind of letter yourself and give it to your doctor for a signature.

- See the web site of the US Equal Employment Opportunity Commission (*http://www.eeoc.gov*) for the EEOC's technical assistance documents on Pre-Employment Disability-Related Questions and Medical Examinations. The EEOC also has a document on the definition of disability used in federal civil rights (anti-discrimination) laws.

- Both federal contractors and federal aid recipients (hospitals, universities, etc.) are required to actively recruit people with disabilities. If you are seeking a job with one of these employers, inquire about its affirmative action program.

People who need to take a pre-employment drug screen or whose jobs require regular screening for drugs will need to inform the tester about prescription medications they take. In most circumstances this information is not shared with the employer.

Americans with Disabilities Act

The Americans with Disabilities Act of 1990 prohibits many types of job discrimination based on actual disability, perceived disability, or history of a disability by employers, employment agencies, state and local governments, and labor unions. Any employer with 15 or more workers is covered by the ADA.

In addition, most states and some cities have laws that prohibit discrimination based on disabilities, although what these laws cover varies widely. If your state or city has laws that provide more protections than the ADA, those laws prevail. If the ADA provides more protection than local or state laws, it prevails.

The ADA requires that:

- Employer may not make medical inquiries of an applicant, unless:
  - Applicant has a visible disability, or
  - Applicant has voluntarily disclosed her medical history.

- Such questions must be limited to asking the applicant to describe or demonstrate how he would perform essential job functions. Medical inquiries are allowed after a job offer has been made or during a pre-employment medical exam. The employer must provide "reasonable accommodations" unless it causes undue hardship. An accommodation is a change in duties or work hours to help employees during or after treatment, when symptoms are worse, or when new health issues arise. An employer does not have to make these changes if they would be very costly, disruptive, or unsafe. If it seems likely that an increase in symptoms could jeopardize your job, work proactively with your employer to make needed accommodations.

- Employers may not discriminate because of family illness. For instance, if your spouse has a bipolar disorder, the employer cannot treat you differently because she thinks you will miss work to care for your spouse or file expensive health insurance claims.

- Employers are not required to provide health insurance, but if an employer does offer health insurance, the company must do so fairly to all employees.

The Equal Employment Opportunity Commission enforces Title 1 of the ADA, the section that covers employment. Call (800) 669-4000 for EEOC enforcement information and (800) 669-3362 for enforcement publications. Other sections of the ADA are enforced by, or have their enforcement coordinated by, the US Department of Justice (Civil Rights Division, Public Access Section). The Justice Department's ADA web site is *http://www.usdoj.gov/crt/ada/html*.

In Canada, the Canadian Human Rights Act provides essentially the same rights as the ADA. The Canadian Human Rights Commission administers the act. You can get further information by calling the national office at (613) 995-1151.

If you feel that you have been discriminated against due to your disability or a relative's disability, contact the EEOC, the Canadian Human Rights Commission, or the appropriate agency in your country promptly. In the US, a charge of discrimination generally must be filed within 180 days of when you learned of the discriminatory act. Although you do not need an attorney to file a complaint, an attorney experienced in job discrimination law can help you draft the complaint to make it more likely to be successful.

Leslie, age 41, experienced discrimination early in her career, but was not able to combat it because it occurred before the ADA extended protection to people with disabilities:

> *I had a summer hypomania in late 1987 and got transferred to a low-profile position in another department at work.*

When I was depressed again I started withdrawing at work and obsessing on what had happened at the other department. I couldn't concentrate on my work either, and spent a lot of time getting on support newsgroups and e-mail lists.

My project leader wrote up a humiliating questionnaire for me to fill out about why I didn't say hi to people in the hallways, why I spent so much time on the computer, and other behaviors. My first set of contrite, self-deprecating answers wasn't acceptable. It didn't occur to anyone present at the meeting that followed that my problem might be depression.

Eventually I got on the right medication. However, the damage at work was done, and when layoffs came around, I went with the first wave.

My career was going fairly well until I got on the psychiatric meds— many of them trash your short-term memory. Now I have trouble retaining verbal information especially, and keeping a job is very difficult.

The Federal Rehabilitation Act

The Federal Rehabilitation Act bans public employers and private employers that receive public funds from discriminating on the basis of disability. The following employees are not covered by the ADA, but by the Rehabilitation Act:

- Employees of the executive branch of the federal government (Section 501 of the Rehabilitation Act)

- Employees of employers that receive federal contracts and that have fewer than fifteen workers (Section 503 of the Rehabilitation Act)

- Employees of employers that receive federal financial assistance and that have fewer than fifteen workers (Section 504 of the Rehabilitation Act)

If you are a federal employee (section 501), you must file a claim within 30 days of the job action against you. If you are an employee whose employer has a federal contract (section 503), you must file a complaint within 180 days with your local Office of the US Department of Labor, Office of Federal Contract Compliance Programs. If your employer receives federal funds (Section 504), you have up to 180 days to file a complaint with the federal agency that provided funds to your employer, or you can file a lawsuit in a federal court. The Federal Rehabilitation Act is enforced by the Civil Rights Division of the Department of Justice, (202) 514-4609.

Section 504 of the Rehabilitation Act of 1973 includes protections for adults attending school or working for employers who get at least some public funds. That list includes colleges, government bodies, and many non-profits, and may sometimes cover private firms that accept government contracts.

If you live outside the US, talk to a disability advocacy group about the laws that affect you on the job. If you live in one of the nations within the European Community, you can cite European Union civil rights regulations as well as applicable local or national disability rights laws.

The ADA does have a hitch: it only applies if your bipolar disorder presents a significant disability or if your employer believes that it does—even if that belief is based on misconceptions about mental illness. This has led to a Catch-22 situation for many people with neurological conditions or mental illness: yes, there are drugs available that can treat the symptoms of these conditions, but those drugs don't work consistently for everyone and may not work at all for some. They also carry with them side effects and dangers.

However, recent Supreme Court cases uphold the idea that if a disability can be corrected with medication, eyeglasses, or other temporary measures, it does not qualify for ADA protection, despite many lower-court cases that say otherwise. Future challenges can be expected in this area of law; indeed, California recently passed a bill that removes the "significant impairment" criteria for persons in that state.

One way around this roadblock is showing that the medication itself creates a disability. Lithium, for example, effectively suppresses mood swings for many people who take it, but it can also cause hand tremors and brain fog. Slow thinking and shaky hands on the job can be disabling in and of themselves and may qualify you for ADA protection.

An attorney can explain where you stand legally and may be able to help you fix the problem without going to court. Mediation is an increasingly popular and less costly option.

Medical leave

If you need to be away from work temporarily due to worsening symptoms or treatment needs, you may have legal job protection available to you. Since August 1993, the Family and Medical Leave Act (FMLA) has protected US workers in public agencies or large companies who need a leave of absence. Only employees who have worked 25 hours per week or more for one year are covered, and only if they work for a company with 50 or more employees within a 75-mile radius.

The Family and Medical Leave Act:

- Provides twelve weeks of unpaid leave during any twelve-month period for one's own medical needs or to care for a seriously ill spouse, child, or parent—sometimes you can take intermittent leave, which means shortening your normal work schedule

- Provides twelve weeks of unpaid leave for the birth of a child or due to placement of a child in your home via adoption or foster care

- Requires employers to continue benefits, including health insurance, during the leave period

- Requires employees to attempt to schedule leaves so as not to disrupt the workplace and to give 30 days' notice if possible

- Requires employers to put returning employees in the same position or in an equivalent position

Employers should have procedures in place for medical leaves covered by the FMLA. Usually you will need to present your employer with documentation from your doctor stating why the leave is necessary and how long it is expected to be for.

The FMLA is enforced by the Employment Standards Administration, Wage and Hour Division, US Department of Labor and by the courts. You can find the nearest Wage and Hour Division office in the US Government pages of your telephone directory. You have up to two years to file an FMLA complaint or a lawsuit if your employer does not abide by the law.

Help with getting a job

For those having trouble getting a job, the public Vocational Rehabilitation (VR) system can be part of the solution. The VR system provides skills assessment, training opportunities, and job placement services for adults with disabilities. However, in many states the Vocational Rehabilitation system is severely overloaded, with wait times for placement ranging from three months to as much as three years. Typical opportunities range from sheltered workshop jobs (splitting kindling wood, sorting recyclables, light assembly work) under direct supervision to supported placement in the community as grocery clerks, office helpers, chip-fabrication plant workers, and the like. Often people in VR programs work with a job coach, a person who helps them handle workplace stresses and learn work skills. In some cases, the job coach actually comes to work with the person for a while.

Pam, mother of 20-year-old Jakob, says the Vocational Rehab department has helped him move into employment gradually:

> We had never even heard of Vocational Rehabilitation when Jakob left the hospital. His therapist at community mental health sent him there. They had a job counselor who worked with him on his first resume, how to dress, and what interviews were like. They placed him in a part-time file clerk job with a hospital near the community college, and they checked up on him regularly for quite awhile. That was perfect: he's been there two years, and now he's taking classes part-time also.

The Ticket to Work and Work Incentives Improvement Act of 1999, a federal law that is only now being implemented, will allow states to extend Medicaid health insurance coverage to people with disabilities who are working or who would like to work. This law is intended to prevent people whose health improves from staying on SSI because they can't afford to lose their health insurance. States will also be allowed to cover working adults with disabilities who have never been on SSI, but do need affordable health insurance. There may be an income-based charge for this insurance.

Some public and private agencies may also be able to help with job training and placement. These include your state employment department; the Opportunities Industrialization Commission (OIC); the Private Industry Council (PIC); and job placement services operated by Goodwill Industries, St. Vincent de Paul, and similar service organizations for people with disabilities.

Career choices

All people with disabilities should receive appropriate vocational counseling, including aptitude testing, discussion of their interests and abilities, and information about different employment possibilities. People with the ability to work should not be shunted into dead-end positions that leave them financially vulnerable. This can be a problem when in the VR system: some VR counselors assume that their job is to get you into a job, any job, regardless of your past accomplishments, educational level, or long-term aspirations.

Truthfully, very few career options are off-limits to people with bipolar disorders. If anything, people with bipolar disorders are over-represented in creative careers—art, acting, music, and writing. Many also gravitate toward high-excitement occupations, including brokerage work, the top levels of marketing and sales, medicine, and other jobs that feed their need for challenge and variety.

Of course, the more exciting the job is, the greater its potential for stress and mood swings. That shouldn't dissuade you from pursuing your dreams, but may require life-style adjustments to make things work out well.

Off-limits occupations

One door that is barred to most people with a bipolar disorder is the US military. Current regulations prohibit anyone who has ever taken a psychiatric drug from enlisting. If you have never taken medication, the diagnosis itself may not preclude enlistment if you can pass the preliminary mental health screening.

There is ample reason to believe that people who have taken psychiatric medications have entered the military, however, with varying degrees of success. Whether they did not divulge their medication use when enlisting, or whether the officers in charge simply chose to ignore this one "blemish" in an otherwise promising candidate, is an open question. With Ritalin and Prozac now topping the list of childhood prescriptions, it does seem likely that the military will have to take a second look at this policy to keep its ranks filled. Should the draft be reinstituted, the ban will almost certainly have to be lifted.

Other careers that involve firearms may also be off-limits, including work as a police officer or armed security guard. That's because under some gun control laws, a person who has been found mentally ill by a court or who has a "history of mental illness" as defined by the state involved is legally prohibited from purchasing or being licensed to carry a gun. Most police departments also put applicants through a mental health screening process. A person whose bipolar disorder is well-controlled by medication could probably pass one of these, however.

In some states and under some circumstances, a bipolar diagnosis could cause licensing problems for certain types of professionals. If you are in a profession that requires state licensing, such as law, medicine, nursing, or teaching, familiarize yourself in advance with the rules governing licensure. Under current US disability law, it would not be legal to fire someone simply because he has a certain diagnosis—there would have to be some kind of problem behavior or loss of ability involved. However, bar associations and medical boards are currently allowed to suspend or deny professional licenses on such grounds, and so far most challenges have been upheld by the courts.[2]

If a problem related to your illness does occur on the job and you are a licensed professional, there is usually an option to keep your license by entering a diversion program. Each state has its own regulations on diversion. In a diversion program, you practice under supervision and may need to satisfy treatment or performance-improvement guidelines. If you do well, your license is safeguarded.

Entering a diversion program is voluntary and confidential, although in some states that confidentiality can be breached if program officials feel you pose a danger to others. If you quit or do not comply with the program, you may not be able to enter it again. If you do complete a diversion program successfully, the records are usually destroyed after a specified period of time.

Low-stress work options

The world of high-stress employment is not for every person with a bipolar disorder, including many who initially choose it. You may find that life outside of the fast lane better suits your moods.

Shoshana did not expect to opt for a low-stress lifestyle:

> I lead a much quieter life now, but I'm not sure this would have been my choice. I loved intensity, and wanted to live life intensely—I went into law because it was a field where there was no mandatory retirement at age sixty-five.
>
> I've not returned to the practice of law, and it doesn't look too likely at this point, since stress triggers off nasty mood swings.
>
> How ironic it all is.

For some, part-time, temporary, or on-call work are the best options. Although these work styles may not offer the same level of financial security as full-time or permanent employment, they do provide more down time and flexibility. For others, a position that offers predictable hours, a steady workflow without too many crunch periods, and a relaxed atmosphere is sometimes worth taking a cut in pay.

You may be able to take the skills earned in your old high-stress job and apply them to something less hard to handle. For example, lawyers can become legal researchers or consultants, nurses can move from the ER into long-term care, and executives can drop down a rung on the corporate ladder to get out from under long hours and constant changes.

Sometimes an existing job can better meet your needs with a little restructuring. If you find that sleep deprivation caused by frequent travel is affecting your stability, see if you can pass the conference circuit responsibilities on to a co-worker and take on some in-office projects instead. It all depends on how flexible your employer, and you, are willing to be.

You don't have to talk about your diagnosis when making these kinds of changes. Simply tell curious co-workers and friends that you're simplifying your life, want more time for your family, or desire a more satisfying new career direction.

"Out" at work or not?

To tell or not to tell, that's the big work issue for most bipolar adults. Some feel that their employers might see them as unworthy of responsibility or promotion, or worry about how their mental health could affect company operations. Although it's illegal to discriminate on the basis of mental illness, most bipolar adults have personal experiences with job discrimination or know someone else who has. Your reticence is natural—and may be warranted. In a 1991 Harris poll about attitudes toward people with disabilities, 59 percent of people surveyed said they feel comfortable with someone who is in a wheelchair, but only 19 percent had the same level of comfort with someone who has a mental illness.[3]

If your symptoms are well-controlled, there's probably no reason to tell, unless it is required by company policy. If you occasionally have breakthrough symptoms, you may want to consider confiding in one key person at work. That person need not be your direct supervisor—the personnel department might be a better choice. You can ask the personnel department to place a letter in your personnel file outlining your diagnosis and any accommodations you might need if your symptoms worsen.

Lillian, age 19, says:

> Don't be embarrassed about it, but you don't have to tell everyone about it.
> A friend of mine told everyone when she got the diagnosis. It's not cool, it's not
> a status symbol, but it's not something to be ashamed of. It's who you are.

If you do have a sympathetic boss, approach the topic with caution. You might try making a joking reference to the illness (on a particularly frantic day, "I think I'm having one of those manic mood swings my doctor warned me about," for instance) to break the ice. Some people have simply left their medication in plain view one day—another conversation opener.

People who feel secure in their ability to manage on the job are often comfortable about addressing the issue forthrightly and openly. It would be wonderful if more people could do so.

You can get more information about the legal rights of disabled people on the job, including tips on approaching employers, from the Job Assistance Network at (800) ADA-WORK or the US Department of Justice Hotline, (800) 514-0301.

Marcia, age 26, says:

> When it comes to who you should and should not tell, honestly I am still unclear on what is best. All my immediate family and close friends know I am bipolar. Actually, I feel like my diagnosis has helped strengthen my relationship with my friends and family. Now that we have identified my symptoms, my family and friends know when it's me and not the illness talking.
>
> Even though I have been working now at the same company for almost three years, I have not told any of my coworkers about my bipolar disorder. Whether or not that is the right decision, I am still unsure.

Civil rights laws do protect you against workplace harassment based on your disability. As with other types of harassment cases, it's important to let harassers know exactly how you feel about their actions, to keep detailed records of incidents, and to go through any formal grievance procedure your company or labor union has before filing a lawsuit.

Most large firms have a staff member who handles internal complaints of sexual or racial harassment. This is probably the right person to see first if you find that your illness has become the topic of rude remarks, practical jokes, or other cruel actions by fellow employees or supervisors. You should inform this person about your disability and make it clear that you are bothered by the behavior. This will either bring down the weight of company policy on the offenders or form the legal basis for a future discrimination claim.

If you're not sure how to handle a workplace problem related to your bipolar symptoms, call your state's Protection & Advocacy system for free advice (see Appendix A, *Resources*). Some NAMI chapters can also refer you to legal counsel; occasionally, national advocacy groups get involved in prominent or groundbreaking cases.

Housing

Some disabled people in the US are eligible for financial assistance with housing and for housing preference programs through Housing and Urban Development programs. Some charitable organizations and churches also manage low-income housing projects or voucher programs and may have preferential treatment for people with disabilities.

The federal Section 8 program is one way to add to your housing choices. If you earn a low wage, ask your local social services department how to apply for a Section 8 voucher. The voucher acts as a supplement to what you can pay for rent, giving you a wider choice of housing options at a more affordable cost. The voucher is paid directly to your landlord. Most landlords are not required to take the vouchers, however, so you still find that your choices are limited.

Other forms of subsidized housing range from adult foster homes with full-time staff on up to private apartments that have no on-site support, but do have reduced rents. A number of innovative housing options are starting to spring up, including subsidized apartment buildings where each tenant has a maximum of personal autonomy despite having on-site medical management staff, therapy groups, AA and NA meetings, and the like.

Some subsidized housing is of poor quality, especially in areas where the supply of low-cost units is tight. You'll need to pay special attention to security concerns, such as locking doors and windows, having a personal telephone in case of emergencies, and the safety profile of the surrounding neighborhood. Some older housing projects and residential hotels are also unhygienic and may not even have fully functional plumbing, lighting, and heating. Landlords are responsible for bringing units up to code, but they may not respond until a social services agency or legal advocate gets involved.

Group homes that stress independent living, including self-managed group homes or co-ops, are also an option. These programs are covered out of personal monthly payments, long-term care insurance, health insurance, funds placed in trust, or public funds. Local advocacy groups should have information about special housing options for people with mental illness, or you can check with a public or private social services agency.

The wait for subsidized housing is often long (three years or more for Section 8 vouchers), so it's important to apply before there's a pressing need. This may mean applying now, even though you don't need housing assistance right away.

In Canada, the UK, Ireland, Australia, and New Zealand, your local housing authority or council housing office can help you get on the waiting list, and inform you of preference programs for the disabled and their caregivers that will move you up the queue faster.

People with severe symptoms may prefer relying on services for maintaining themselves in a regular apartment or home, rather than setting up a special housing arrangement. These services are usually less expensive than subsidized housing and are available through government or private social services. Options include housekeeping assistance, self-care help, medication and case management, and special transportation arrangements to help you with shopping, medical appointments, and recreation needs.

There is a growing trend toward helping adults with disabilities purchase their own homes. Sometimes grants are available for down payment assistance, along with special loan programs, trust arrangements, and home buying and home ownership training.

If you do own a home, you may want to consider purchasing insurance that will cover your mortgage payments in case of hospitalization or disability. Normally, financial advisors do not consider these policies a good deal, but they may be for people who would rest easier knowing that everything's covered should they need in-patient treatment. Maintaining your regular homeowners coverage and even enhancing it is also important—this insurance can cover any number of contingencies, from libel suits over poison-pen letters sent while manic to injuring someone in your home.

Legal and financial planning

While insurance is important just in case, the best defense against legal and financial problems is advance planning. People with bipolar disorders should take the same basic steps as other adults, of course. These include drawing up a will in case of your demise, keeping track of your day-to-day finances, and planning for later life. There are some additional steps, however, that can provide an extra measure of protection.

Psychiatric advance directive

You may have heard about medical advance directives—a type of legal document that sets out your wishes and guidelines for healthcare in the event that you are not able to make a personal decision. Medical advance directives are often used to discuss end-of-life care options, such as whether you wish heroic measures to be used in certain kinds of medical crises or to specify types of emergency medical care that you do not approve of for religious reasons, such as blood transfusions for people who are Jehovah's Witnesses.

A psychiatric advance directive is very similar, but it comes into effect if you are declared incompetent to direct your own mental healthcare. It can specify what kind of care you do and do not want. For example, your advance directive could name drugs that have resulted in adverse effects for you in the past and ask that they not be used. It can name treatments that you would not consent to, such as electroshock therapy, psychosurgery, or experimental drugs.

It can also appoint a trusted person to act as your representative for these decisions. Indeed, in most states, appointing an agent is required to make the advance directive valid. You can also appoint an agent using a general medical power of attorney form that explicitly includes psychiatric care.

Psychiatric advance directives are a fairly new area of law. No one is quite sure how courts will respond to them and if they will be respected—especially if a person who is judged to be suicidal or homicidal has a psychiatric advance directive that refuses care recommended by her doctors. You may wish to consult a lawyer before writing a psychiatric advance directive. Your state's Protection and Advocacy system (see Appendix A for more information) can also help.

The Judge David L. Bazelon Center for Mental Health Law offers information about psychiatric advance directives as well as downloadable templates on the web at *http://www.bazelon.org/advdir.html*.

Letter of intent

This isn't a legal document, but it's an important one when it comes to how your affairs are managed if you are temporarily or permanently unable to handle them yourself. It should be written as though intended for someone who knows nothing about you or your family and stored with your will and other legal documents.

The letter of intent should be comprised of at least four sections:

- **General information.** This section should include such things as your full name, date of birth, Social Security number, address, blood type, religion, and citizenship status. It should also include a list of all known family members, and any non-relatives (such as a friend, clergy member, or caseworker) whose advice and help a caretaker or court-appointed guardian or conservator could call on.

- **Medical history and care.** In this section, list all of your medical diagnoses, with a brief explanation of the symptoms of each that a caretaker, guardian, or conservator might need to be aware of. List any hospitalizations and surgeries you have had. Include complete contact information for all doctors involved in your care, as well as dentists and therapists, and provide insurance information.

- **Goals.** This section should state what your preferences are for living situation, daily activities, diet, social activities and hobbies, religious observance, etc. If you are unable to communicate your needs for any reason, this section will help guide your care.

- **Legal information.** List all assets, including bank accounts, annuities, property, life insurance policies, stocks, trusts, and safe-deposit boxes, in this section. Provide general information about the disposition of these assets—not for what would happen to them in the case of your demise (that is the purpose of a will), but what a helper should do if you are unavailable to carry out your usual duties. For example, this section could include a list of your regular monthly financial obligations; name a person to take charge of your pets; and identify when, how, and by whom your personal belongings could be put into storage. It can name a financial trustee, but this is something that should be done in a durable power of attorney as well. It should include contact information for any trustee or financial advisor who handles your finances or assets held in trust for you.

Power of attorney

A durable power of attorney appoints personal representatives for financial or medical decisions made on your behalf. In some circumstances, you will need to create a durable power of attorney for persons named in a psychiatric advance directive, letter of intent, and other documents created for self-protection.

Child custody arrangements

If you are a single parent with children under the age of 18, it's very important to set up a guardianship arrangement for your children, just in case. If you don't, a judge appoints a guardian if you are judged incompetent to care for your family. This person may or may not share your values or be the person you would have chosen. If no family member steps forward, your children could end up in foster care.

Mention guardianship arrangements in your psychiatric advance directive, if you have one.

Financial self-protection

If you have had problems with manic overspending or missing bill payments when ill, you may want to hire someone to handle your finances at all times. A Certified Public Accountant (CPA) is usually the best choice.

This individual can receive your income in a special account, carry out transactions approved by you, and provide you with a reliable weekly income for food, transportation, clothing, and other necessities, as well as an amount of pocket money that you can actually afford to spend. Remaining funds are put in savings or invested, as you wish. An accountant can also handle your income taxes.

Be sure to check the credentials of any accountant you are considering and call the Better Business Bureau or applicable state agency to see if there have been complaints by past clients. Ask for regular reports about your finances, and examine the books kept on your behalf regularly.

Case management

If you have a hard time managing your medical and personal needs due to your illness, case management is an option. Case management services can encompass arranging for healthcare, connecting you with community services as needed, certain kinds of financial management (such as being your payee for SSI), and more.

You can hire case managers privately, find them within government mental health or community services departments, or access them through advocacy agencies for the mentally ill. Some health insurance plans provide case management services as part of their behavioral health package, including coordination of outside services as well as managing your medical needs.

Especially for women

Changes in your hormonal balance due to birth control, pregnancy, and menopause can cause symptoms to flare. Some women with bipolar disorders find that using birth control pills, Depo-Provera injections, or Norplant has a beneficial effect on their moods, but others find that some or all of these make their symptoms worse. You absolutely must inform any physician providing you with birth control services about your diagnosis. You may need to consider alternative, non-hormonal methods of birth control, such as abstinence, an IUD, a diaphragm and spermicide, or condoms and spermicide. Except for abstinence, each of these methods of birth control has its own risks (including a higher risk of unwanted pregnancy with the latter two) that you will need to explore with your doctor and your partner.

Work closely with your psychiatrist, gynecologist, and/or obstetrician during your child-bearing years to ensure the greatest level of safety during pregnancy for yourself and your child. The most important step is making a decision about using medication before, during, and after pregnancy. All of the mood stabilizers carry some risk of causing serious birth defects, including neural tube defects. Your baby's risk can be lessened, but not eliminated, if you take a folic acid supplement before conception and during your pregnancy.

Explore your medication options with your doctor before you get pregnant, not after, because the risk to your fetus is greatest during the first trimester. That means it may be possible to take a temporary break from your medication, under careful medical supervision, while you get pregnant and make it through those crucial first months. The risk of birth defects is least during the third trimester, so you can then resume medication during the latter part of pregnancy or immediately after delivery.

The risk to your personal stability and safety if you stop taking your medication is also serious. Many women who take mood stabilizers do not stop before or during pregnancy, and the majority of their babies are born without birth defects.

Most pregnant women report some "weepy" and hypomanic moods, but some bipolar women seem especially susceptible to mood swings during pregnancy.

Post-partum psychosis is of special concern for women with bipolar disorders. This is the most severe version of the common post-partum depression or "baby blues" that many women experience after delivery. The normal risk of post-partum psychosis is one in 500—but for women with manic-depression, it is one in five.[4] This is a very serious risk, and every woman with a bipolar disorder should take steps well in advance of delivery to deal with it.

Making smart decisions about medication is paramount among these. Other wise decisions include researching the warning signs of psychosis, making sure your partner is also aware of them, and having a relative or mother's helper at home during the first weeks or months after delivery.

Kristi, age 52, says she wishes she had known more when she was a young mother:

> When I had my oldest boy I was 25 and had never even heard of post-partum depression. To tell you the truth, those first months after he was born were absolutely the worst. I didn't think anyone else had ever felt like this, and that I was a complete failure as a mother. I seriously considered suicide; knowing that there was no one else to take care of my baby was probably all that kept me going. Every day I had to struggle to get out of bed, much less feed the baby, do laundry, change diapers, and the rest.
>
> When my two other children were born, because things were so difficult the first time around, I asked my mother to come stay with me for the first month or so each time. This did help somewhat.

It's also especially important for women at greater risk of post-partum depression or psychosis to have a strong support system in place during and after pregnancy. If you are a single parent, calling on friends, family members, and professionals for extra help is not a sign of weakness—it may be essential for your good health and your baby's.

Some psychiatric medications can pass through breast milk to your baby. Breastfeeding is normally the best and safest form of feeding for infants, but your personal situation may make using a well-chosen formula a better solution. Talk over with your doctor before your baby is born the risks and benefits of breastfeeding when taking the medications you use.

Family relationships

Your family relationships have probably already suffered many blows due to your illness. Divorce is common when one spouse has a mental illness. There are also issues of guilt, blame, sorrow, and stress to work out.

Joe says his relationships have been stressed, but not broken:

> My parents and brother have been very supportive, but my episodes have cost them peace of mind, and time and energy they could have used productively in their own lives. Still, I fear having an episode without my parents around to steer me towards treatment.

Eileen, age 47, has not been so lucky—but feels that despite the stress her illness has placed on relationships, things have worked out fairly well:

> My marriage lasted 23 years, until I ran away. I was so crazy then that I blamed every wrong thing on the marriage, and I had to escape or die. Since then, my husband and I have re-established a dating/family sort of relationship where we spend time together doing family things, like holidays, but I cannot commit to anything beyond that. I cannot totally leave him, nor totally be with him. The history we have together draws us together, and also drives me away.
>
> My parenting as a young woman was like a yo-yo. My children called me "the marshmallow." I always saw the gray areas, black and white were impossible to define. This was terribly hard on them as children, but as young adults they have become the most compassionate people, and I am so proud of them.
>
> My kids have all stated that they would not like to be like "other" families— so what if we were different? They like us just the way we were!

It is possible to build (or rebuild) strong family relationships despite these additional challenges. Family therapy is a great place to work out problems that seem insoluble on your own. You may find that, as you and your family members discuss your difficulties and work to solve them together, your relationships will become deeper and stronger. If you can face your problems with a united front, the outlook for your health will also be much improved. Chapter 5 explains family therapy in more detail.

Behavior isn't the only issue that pits family members against each other. The financial burden of treating bipolar disorders can be heavy. In-patient hospitalization can cost over $1,000 per day if not covered by insurance, and therapy, medications, and regular healthcare add up to hundreds of dollars each month. Chapter 7, *Healthcare and Insurance,* discusses some options for reducing these costs, but there will surely be bills to pay.

For young adults, this can impact relationships with parents. Shannon, now age 33, says:

> As an adolescent and young adult just starting to manifest the illness, I caused my parents much worry and concern, and cost them a lot of money too, I'm sure. Now I have a more easy-going relationship with my parents, and they're not terribly hypervigilant for signs of illness to return in me. I think they trust that I'm always doing my best to stay well, which I am.

For older adults, the difficulties may be entirely personal or may impact a partner and/ or children. Sometimes the result is more than just a momentary budget problem. You may have to give up a demanding, stressful job, cut back on your hours, or turn down promotions that would require moving to an area with inadequate medical care. The chance to further your education or put away money for a comfortable retirement, material niceties, or even basic financial stability may be out of reach.

Your children or spouse may miss out on nice clothes, travel, or a free ride through college due to the cost of your medical care. This is something you'll need to discuss in advance, because financial issues can create huge amounts of resentment. Talk about and look for alternative ways to meet these needs. For example, a grandparent, aunt, or uncle might offer some special financial and personal support for your children if you cannot.

The ongoing chaos of life with someone whose moods swing wildly has a detrimental effect on family relationships and home life. In fact, people married to a person with a bipolar disorder often swear that the illness is contagious! It's essential to set and enforce consistent boundaries about the most important issues.

Jane says this has been a major issue in her life:

> Since my diagnosis, my husband is not as tolerant of my behavior as he was before—which is good. Before, he didn't say anything when I was a real bitch, now he doesn't take it any more.
>
> As for money… well, we both have had well-paid jobs for the 22 years we have been together, but because of my behavior, and my husband's lack of control over me, we have huge debts and no assets.

Suicide prevention

Suicide is the eighth leading cause of death in the US.[5] For people with a bipolar disorder, however, the suicide rate is five times higher than it is for those without a known mental disorder.[6] It is hard to cope with a long-term, chronic mental illness, especially when there's no easy cure. But it's worth hanging in there despite the difficulties and challenge.

Tips for friends and family members

Everyone should be aware of the warning signs of suicide, but for friends and spouses of people with bipolar disorders, this knowledge is especially urgent. Behaviors to watch out for include the following:

- Withdrawal from friends and family
- Inability to concentrate
- Talk of suicide
- Dramatic changes in personal appearance
- Loss of interest in favorite activities
- Expressions of hopelessness or excessive guilt
- Self-destructive behavior (such as reckless driving, drug abuse, and promiscuity)
- Preoccupation with death
- Giving away favorite possessions
- Suddenly "cheering up" after a deep depression (the new mood may mean a plan for suicide has been made, causing the person to feel relieved)

If you noticed that some of these warning signs are common characteristics of people with bipolar disorder, you're right. People with manic depression are predisposed to the despair and suffering that cause suicide because of the effect this illness has on their lives and relationships.

Never ignore the warning signs of suicide. Most people who try to kill themselves give advance notice. Be open to the verbal and non-verbal messages your spouse or friend may be sending you, and if your suspicions are aroused, act. Don't be afraid to come right out and ask if suicide is on his mind.

The crisis lines listed in the next section are there for you, too—you can call and get information about what to do if you are concerned.

Tips for people with bipolar disorders

Information and advance planning are your best allies in preventing suicide. If you are thinking about suicide, there are several resources that can get you in touch with immediate help.

National suicide prevention hotline (US)
Call this number to get information about the closest suicide prevention hotline.
(800) 999-9999

Suicide Awareness/Voices of Education (SA/VE)
http://www.save.org/

Suicide Information and Education Centre (SEIC)
http://www.siec.ca/crisis.html
SEIC maintains a list of suicide prevention hotlines and services in the US and Canada.

Befrienders International Online
http://www.befrienders.org/centre.html
The Befrienders maintain a list of crisis and suicide counseling centers throughout the world.

A suicide crisis is not something to keep quiet about or to handle discreetly at home. Successful suicide attempts mean death, and unsuccessful ones can cause permanent injury or brain damage. Because some people do make half-hearted "cry for help" suicide attempts in response to breaking up with a boyfriend or similar minor tragedies, emergency room personnel are not always as sympathetic as they should be when faced with the real thing. To protect yourself from callous treatment or too-early release, you need to have a hospital admission plan set up in advance.

The most helpful person for putting this plan in place is your psychiatrist. Set up a private session to talk about local mental health facilities. Most psychiatrists have had to commit a patient from time to time, so they're usually familiar with local facilities. They can tell you which hospitals have the best facilities and which staff person you should talk to in advance.

A county or provincial mental health professional or social worker may also have information about local resources, and of course people in local support groups can tell you about their experiences as well.

Make an appointment to visit the best facility or the top two in advance. Try to meet the program's director if possible. Find out what the admissions process is—where you would go in case of a crisis, whom you can call if you need help getting to the facility, and what the criteria for admission are.

Lack of information is one of the biggest problems people face when they need emergency mental health help. Transferring paper medical files and even computerized files seems to take forever, and sometimes the documents that do arrive are incomplete. You may want to provide the facility you would use in a crisis with an advance copy of your basic medical and mental health history, a list of medications used currently and in the past, your mental health advance directive, and your insurance data, just in case. Alternatively, make a copy of this information and store it where you or a friend can grab it en route to the facility.

In larger cities, there may be a crisis triage center for mental health admissions. This is usually a separate area of a hospital. If a suicide attempt causes injury, including attempted drug overdoses, you would almost certainly go to the emergency room first. If you have swung into a severe depression, mania, or mixed state, or if you have become psychotic, go to the crisis triage center instead. Professionals are available there to evaluate you, give emergency medications if needed, and direct you to an inpatient or day treatment facility.

In areas without a special intake center, you can call ahead to the emergency room and let them know if there are special security needs or medications that should be on hand when you arrive. In some areas you can go directly to a mental health facility, such as a county mental hospital, for immediate evaluation. Be sure to call first, as some facilities will turn you away unless they feel it is a matter of life or death. Others don't have good assessment facilities on site, and you'll only end up waiting or being redirected.

Of course, your insurance company, HMO, and public health policies can have a lot to do with how you go about accessing emergency mental healthcare. Chapter 7 includes more information about choosing a plan that meets your needs.

Removing hazards

Another important step you can take to prevent suicide is to remove implements of self-destruction from your home, particularly guns. Guns are a terribly final choice, and they are the weapons used in more than half of all suicides. If you currently keep a gun in the home for protection against criminals, get a burglar alarm, security bars, panic button, or watch dog instead.

If you are a hunter, consider that giving up your hobby may be essential to protect your life. You may want to take up hunting with a camera instead, or going on hunting trips with friends but not owning a firearm yourself. If your gun is needed for your job as a police officer, soldier, or security guard, store it securely at the station house, base, or company headquarters.

Family members and roommates also need to know that locking up a gun is not enough to stop a person who is determined to kill himself. Either get rid of it, or install a coded trigger lock.

Watch out for other suicide hazards as well. For example, choose disposable razors instead of razor blades, and toss out bottles of old medication.

Make sure you have a plan for what to do if suicide is on your mind. Know how to reach a crisis line right away. Program your phone to call a friend, family member, or 911 automatically at the push of a button, or keep these numbers right by the phone for when you need them most.

Raymond, age 36, uses his mood diary to watch out for deepening depression that could turn dangerous:

> I have been averaging one hospitalization every eight months since my diagnosis. The doctors have the manic phase under control for the most part, but the depressive end is far from under control.
>
> I can overcome most suicidal feelings, but I rate mine on a scale of 1 to 10, 10 being the worst. If I am at a 7 for half an hour or more, I know that it is beyond my coping skills, and I seek medical attention immediately.

Handling self-injurious behaviors

For a long time self-injurious behaviors, also known as SIB or self-mutilation, were a dirty little secret. With the publication of widely read books like *The Scarred Soul: Understanding & Ending Self-Inflicted Violence* by Tracy Alderman in 1997 and both Steven Levenkrom's *Cutting: Understanding and Overcoming Self-Mutilation* and Marilee Strong's *A Bright Red Scream: Self-Mutilation and the Language of Pain* in 1998, SIB is finally coming out into the open.

Common forms of SIB include cutting (usually this involves shallow cuts on the arms, legs, or torso), puncturing or piercing the skin (not to be confused with cosmetic piercing or tattooing), hitting (including banging the head on hard objects), burning the skin with lit cigarettes or matches, and picking at the skin or at scabs. People who have had SIB describe it as a way to relieve inner pain or stress, a form of self-punishment, or a way to create sensations that are almost enjoyable when compared to the out-of-control feelings they had before committing the act. It can also be entirely compulsive, with seemingly no rhyme or reason behind it.

You might compare SIB to the activities of ancient saints and mystics, many of whom used mortification of the flesh via hair shirts, whips, or beds of nails to achieve ecstatic states or to drive out what they considered impure thoughts. In some religions, these activities are still practiced and revered, but modern society usually views self-mutilation as repugnant and shameful. In truth, it's just another bad coping mechanism, not unlike drinking, using drugs, or becoming a workaholic.

People with bipolar disorders are at a high risk for SIB, especially if they do not learn other, safer ways to deal with emotional distress at an early age.

In "Self-Injury: A Quick Guide to the Basics" (available online at *http://www.palace. net/~llama/psych/guide.html*), Deb Martinson writes:

> *People who self-injure generally do so because of an internal dynamic, and not in order to annoy, anger or irritate others. Their self-injury is a behavioral response to an emotional state, and is usually not done in order to frustrate caretakers. In emergency rooms, people with self-inflicted wounds are often told, directly and indirectly, that they are not as deserving of care as someone who has an accidental injury. They are treated badly by the same doctors who would not hesitate to do everything possible to preserve the life of an overweight, sedentary heart-attack patient.*

Martinson's point is well-taken. People who self-injure deserve to be taken seriously when they come in for treatment. If not respected, they may not return. And although death from SIB is rare, it does occur, as can less severe forms of permanent harm.

Many medical people have very little experience in treating SIB, and some actually do more harm than good. Some doctors still assume that it always arises from some secret trauma. For a person with a chemical imbalance, this approach can be more harmful than getting no treatment at all. It essentially blames the patient, and it does nothing to assuage the actual feelings and impulses that cause repetitive self-injury.

If you need help, look for a psychiatrist who has expertise in this area and who understands the need to help you gradually develop safe substitute behaviors that can allay emotional pain and mood problems. Medication coupled with therapy designed to gradually reduce self-injurious actions does work and is worth going out of your way for. Support groups can also be helpful. The solitary nature of SIB can increase the sufferer's isolation, which only makes the behavior more frequent.

Criminal justice and mental illness

Jail can be the worst possible place for a person with a mental illness, but people with bipolar disorder are likely to tangle with the law one or more times. Impulsivity and sensation-seeking are a major part of the problem. Certain crimes, such as shop-lifting, drug- and alcohol-related offenses, and sexual escapades, are largely crimes of impulse and sensation.

Grandiose thinking is also an issue. It's not that people with bipolar disorders are too crazy to know right from wrong, or to know what the laws are—but when they're grandiose, they just think the laws don't apply to them. They may follow their impulses and desires without a second thought, even when they have been fully informed of the consequences.

Of course, when symptoms of psychosis are present, a person is usually not aware of rules, laws, or proper behavior. A person who is in a manic, depressed, or mixed state may also attract police attention due to bizarre behavior or appearance.

Tony narrowly avoided a legal crisis while manic:

> *I've had no legal problems, but I have come close.*
>
> *During my last manic episode, I sunk a lot of money into offshore tax shelters. I drove aggressively and for extended periods without sleep—*

one time I actually fell asleep at the wheel and left the highway travelling at 80 kilometers per hour. Luckily, I survived uninjured, with not much damage to the car either. The police were checking on me because my wife was worried I was building a bomb or something. I spent a lot of effort preparing for a possible cataclysm at the end of 2000, collecting supplies and thinking of ways of getting more, undetected. I remember planning to break into a local military base to steal weapons.

I ended up in the hospital. Of all the things that could have happened given my behaviors, the result could have been much worse.

Unless psychosis is present when the crime is committed, bipolar disorder rarely makes for a successful insanity defense. That means non-psychotic persons who have committed crimes, even if their bipolar symptoms had everything to do with the crime, are likely to go to a prison rather than being committed to a mental hospital for treatment. In the US, a person who commits a crime while psychotic can still be sentenced to prison, not a mental health facility. And that's not a good thing.

Since the closure of most large public mental hospitals in the US, increasing numbers of mentally ill persons are being sent to prison instead of getting appropriate health-care. In prison they rarely receive quality psychiatric care or medication, and they find themselves in the furthest thing imaginable from a therapeutic environment. This situation has reached crisis proportions, and advocacy groups for the mentally ill are crying out for a solution.

Until that solution is found, you must do your best to keep out of the criminal justice system. That means proactively finding appropriate treatment and medication that will prevent criminal behavior.

George, age 61, also urges people with bipolar disorder to get involved with changing the laws:

> *No bipolar individuals, except those who committed serious crimes, should be in jails or prisons. We need to have an excellent jail diversion system so the ones charged with misdemeanors and minor felonies are diverted to hospitals or other appropriate treatment settings.*

If you are incarcerated, you will face many obstacles to accessing proper mental healthcare. The worst abuses are often at the local level, in city lock-ups and county jails where prisoners awaiting trial and those convicted of minor offenses are usually held. These facilities were never intended for long-term prisoners, and they have few if any resources to provide even basic healthcare. Psychiatric care is minimal or non-existent—or just really, really bad. There have been hundreds of cases of suicide, abuse of mentally ill inmates by other prisoners, and serious self-harm in recent years.[7] You may not get your prescribed medications, and mental health evaluations are sometimes scheduled but never done. There's just no way around the fact that you will need a lawyer to have any influence at all. If you don't already have one who seems able to help ensure your safety, call your nearest chapter of NAMI or another mental health advocacy agency to get a referral.

There are facilities with caring professionals on staff, and others are willing to work with outside psychiatrists and social workers. They may have programs for counseling offenders, and hopefully they will have drug and alcohol treatment available (sadly, many do not, even though substance abuse is the No. 1 predictor for crime). Prisons are less used to recognizing, accommodating, and treating mental illness than hospitals, despite the fact that it is very common among offenders.

You or your family may need to use the legal system to ensure that you receive regular medical and psychiatric care and are properly medicated, that improper medications are not used as a chemical straightjacket, and that you are not physically restrained or isolated as a substitute for medical care. Usually a social worker is the best person to talk to about these issues at a corrections facility. The quality of prison social workers varies drastically, but a good one can be a true ally in helping you make it through this experience.

Maintaining your sanity

You've got to mobilize your inner and outer resources to protect your own peace of mind. That includes taking care of your physical health with regular checkups, eating right, and exercise. It also means caring for your own mental health.

Another thing you can do to maintain your sanity is keep careful health records. If you can keep your medical info neatly filed, you'll find that one major area of stress in your life will almost disappear.

Support and advocacy

No one can handle bipolar disorders well on his or her own. Besides the many professionals who can help, there are also others who have walked this road before. Their advice, support, and friendship can be a precious gift in your life. When you join a good support group for people coping with bipolar disorders, you'll gain shoulders to lean on, people you can call in a crisis, and a source of the latest information on services, healthcare, education, local doctors, and opportunities. You'll meet people who "get it," people you don't have to put up a brave front for.

Another kind of helpful group concentrates on advocacy for mentally ill people and their families. In the US, NAMI is the biggest of these, with chapters in almost every part of the country. These groups work to educate the public, reduce stigma, improve services and medical treatment, and change laws that adversely affect people with mental illness. Many also have a support group component, especially in more rural areas where support and advocacy go hand in hand. NDMDA is especially active in support.

Joe says these groups have already had an effect on the larger culture, but there is still much to be done:

> The reduction of stigma has a long way to go. There are some reactionaries out there who paint the mentally ill as dangerous, and want forced medication. There are still some negative and inaccurate media portrayals.
>
> On the other hand there are some good signs too: the deputy attorney general character in the movie "The Last Days of Disco" was manic-depressive and yet portrayed as in remission.

Support and advocacy groups also give people living with mental problems a way to give back to the community and to lift up those who are faced with a new diagnosis.

A new kind of support group has arrived with the advent of the Internet: online support communities. The great thing about these online groups is that they're available 24 hours a day. You can log in with your computer whenever it's convenient for you—late at night, when the kids are at school, or on your lunch break at work. All you need is a basic computer and an Internet account, either through a local Internet service provider or through a major commercial service like AOL or EarthLink.

Several online support options are listed in Appendix A. Each group is a little different in tone, rules, and activity level. In some cases, each subscriber receives each e-mail message sent to the group individually, or all of the messages sent each day may be combined into a single digest. You can answer messages via e-mail, or just read what other people have to say. Participants range from newly diagnosed people to old hands who can provide excellent advice based on their personal experiences. There are also some doctors, nurses, teachers, psychopharmacologists, and psychiatric researchers who lend their expertise in online forums.

You do have to be careful about online medical advice—it's no substitute for getting local medical care, and a treatment or medication that worked for one person may not be right for you. But these groups are a great place to ask about things like new treatments, medication side effects, and how other people cope with relationship and work issues.

Taking care of yourself

Many brain disorders bring with them built-in limits. Bipolar disorders do not. Some would even argue that these conditions may equip people with certain strengths: a high energy level, strong verbal skills, and sometimes an especially creative way of looking at the world and solving problems. Many people feel that these bonuses can help make up for the down side of their illness.

Joe agrees with this idea:

> In a millennium that will almost certainly see genetic engineering of human beings, we should be open to some relativism about what is "good" in human beings instead of trying to hold up a single ideal template. The extremes I've experienced have widened me and made me more sympathetic.

Make your home a safe haven

Sometimes something as simple as changing your home environment can reduce stress and improve your daily functioning. Just as parents look at their home in a new light when a new infant begins crawling and exploring, mood disorders can warrant some revisions. You might think of it as making your home a therapeutic environment or as a highly personal form of feng shui, the Chinese art of creating a harmonious environment.

Warm, soft colors tend to be soothing. Pastels and whites can also be calming, and they add brightness. Avoid colors that tend to make you agitated and aggressive. Lighting should be bright where it is needed for reading and studying, soft where the mood should be restful (lighting choices can literally help with mood control—see Chapter 6 for more information). Comfortable furniture can give you a cozy place to unwind.

A white noise generator or soothing music can drown out intrusive sounds from the street below or the neighbor's yard. The sound of running water, wind through the trees, or a cat purring can help you relax. Many people swear by keeping a pet as a way to reduce stress, although for others the time commitment involved is too much.

Drop-in centers

If your home isn't exactly a peaceful spot or if you feel the need to get out and social-ize in a low-stress situation, drop-in centers are available in some areas for people with mental illness. These can combine access to therapists, peer support groups, and socialization help. Well-run drop-in centers offer esteem-building activities, opportu-nities to learn new job skills, and an atmosphere of camaraderie. They may also be able to place visitors in supportive housing and work.

At a well-run drop-in center, like Liberty Place Clubhouse Downtown in Pennsylva-nia's Allegheny County, you can meet peers in a structured, supervised environment. Participants say the center works as a base for reintegration into society. The staff (most of whom are also people recovering from mental illness) provides transitional employment leads, housing help, and personal advice.[8]

Add joy to your life

Everyday life with a bipolar disorder can be a hassle. To keep stress from overwhelm-ing you, build affirmative, life-enhancing, joyful experiences into your life whenever you can. These activities nurture your spirit and can keep you going through the darkest days.

Shannon says:

> I firmly believe in the link that Kay Jamison, Nancy Andreasen, and others have found between bipolar illness and creativity. Personally, I've always been creative, even as a child writing poems and plays and endlessly drawing pictures. I still write poetry sometimes, have sung in choirs and bands, once in awhile even composing songs, acted in plays throughout high school, and turn to graphic art today as a catharsis. I don't have any delusions that I'm an artistic genius, but I genuinely enjoy creating artistically, and it fortifies my soul.

Here are just a few suggestions offered by people with bipolar disorders who were· interviewed for this book.

- Keep a personal journal or diary
- Pray or meditate
- Take time to play, dance, or listen to music
- Read books that uplift or that simply entertain
- Run, swim, or work out

- Turn off the television and computer in favor of relating to others
- Gain mastery of satisfying activities like cooking, mechanical work, or the arts
- Care for a pet or a garden
- Spend time with children or senior citizens who need a friend
- Help others in need, whether it's by participating in a charity marathon, volunteering in a homeless center, or donating money to a favorite cause

Many people with bipolar disorders are born adrenaline junkies. If you tend to feed this need, search out opportunities for safer risk-taking. Skiing, skydiving, rock-climbing, even activities like skateboarding or BMX bicycling that bring out the wild kid in you, can fill your need for high-energy excitement without putting your life at an unacceptable risk.

Despite the messages you may sometimes get from society, it's okay to be a sensation-seeker. The key is to find an outlet for this personality trait that keeps you out of legal and ethical trouble. Considering the popularity of extreme sports these days, you should find yourself with plenty of company out on the edge.

Just make sure to set some firm rules for yourself at the outset. Learn and employ all the safety precautions, so you can keep enjoying yourself for years to come. And know the signs of getting too hyped up, whether it's overspending on the activity or taking too many risks. Have a plan for what to do if you need to pull back and calm down.

Hold on to hope

People who have experienced years of worry, loss, and pain due to mental illness often fear that someday they will lose hope. You may know what kinds of resources are crucial to your recovery, but despair of ever finding them. It can make you feel powerless.

But your wishes are powerful, if you share them with others—if enough people coping with bipolar disorders wish out loud (and then add their shoulders to the wheel), these resources might become a reality.

Here are some ideas expressed by people interviewed for this book. If their visions resonate with you, advocate for change. You'll be glad you did.

> *I hope that I can accomplish something in my field that fulfills my*
> *promise, something that shows my unique way of thinking. I hope to find*
> *a fulfilling romantic relationship. I hope that a medication (or a natural*

supplement or diet, etc.) could be found with fewer side effects than lithium.

. . . . .

We need to have free meds for people with mental disorders, or some kind of help we could access without worrying if we can afford to pay for it for the rest of our lives. That has happened to me when I had no insurance and ended up in the hospital.

. . . . .

I would set up centers, run by recovered people with bipolar disorder, where other bipolars could go to partake in art therapy, music therapy, poetry therapy, etc., and where they could get peer counseling and support in crisis. They could also train for jobs, cook for themselves and other participants, and generally help in the running of the center. And at this kind of center, there would be no stigma about the "staff" people admitting they had a psychiatric illness—in fact this would be welcomed, because it would give these caretakers a unique and fitting perspective on how to help others.

. . . . .

I feel that mental illness advocacy is the civil rights movement of the new century. It is time for those concerned with the treatment of mental illness to stand up and be seen, heard, and counted! Actions speak louder than words!

. . . . .

I wouldn't change me for a million dollars. I have lived a lifetime in my half of a life already, and I can empathize with so many people, I can suffer with others, and I can rejoice with others.

I have been to hell—and returned.

Resources

THIS APPENDIX LISTS SUPPORT AND ADVOCACY organizations, as well as books, pamphlets, videos, and online resources on topics related to bipolar disorders, related conditions, family issues, insurance and healthcare, and medications. Contact information for some of the most prominent diagnostic and treatment centers is included, as is a list of national and state agencies in charge of mental healthcare.

Advocacy and support groups

United States

National Alliance for the Mentally Ill (NAMI)
Colonial Place Three
2107 Wilson Blvd., Suite 300
Arlington, VA 22201
(703) 524-7600
NAMI Helpline: (800) 950-6264
http://www.nami.org

NAMI is the largest organization for mentally ill people and their families in the US. It has state and local chapters around the country. It sponsors legislation, advocates for mentally ill people, and provides excellent information via its web site and publications.

National Depressive and Manic-Depressive Association
730 N. Franklin Street, Suite 501
Chicago, IL 60610-3526
(312) 642-0049 or (800) 826-3632
Fax (312) 642-7243
http://www.ndmda.org/

This support and advocacy group specifically for people with depression or bipolar disorders has chapters throughout the US and an informative web site.

Canada

Canadian Mental Health Association/L'Association Canadienne Pour La Santé Mentale
2160 Yonge Street, 3rd Floor
Toronto, ON M4S 2Z3
(416) 484-7750
Fax (416) 484-4617
cmhanat@interlog.com
http://www.cmha.ca/

The CMHA makes its support and advocacy materials available in French and English. It sponsors local groups throughout Canada.

Integrated Network of Disability Information and Education (INDIE)
info@indie.ca
http://www.indie.ca/

INDIE provides information about all aspects of living with a disability in Canada, in French and English.

Mood Disorders Association of British Columbia
2730 Commercial Drive, No. 201
Vancouver, BC V5N 5PN
(604) 873-0103
Fax (604) 873-3095
mdabc@telus.net
http://www.mdabc.ca/

MDABC sponsors support groups, conferences, and more for people in British Columbia.

United Kingdom

Glasgow Association for Mental Health
Melrose House, First Floor
15/23 Cadogan Street
Glasgow, G2 6QQ
(0141) 204-2270
Fax (0141) 204-2770
GAMH@colloquium.co.uk
http://users.colloquium.co.uk/~GAMH/

Manic Depression Fellowship
Castle Works
21 St. George's Road
London SE1 6ES
(020) 7793-2600
Fax (020) 7793-2639
mdf@mdf.org.uk
http://www.mdf.org.uk/

This organization has regional offices in Wales, Greater London, and Manchester, as well as 125 local groups throughout the UK. It provides support, advice, and information for people with manic depression, their families, friends, and carers.

The Mental Health Foundation (MHF)
20/21 Cornwall Terrace
London NW1 4QL
44 (0) 20 7535 7400
Fax 44 (0) 20 7535 7474
mhf@mhf.org.uk
http://www.mentalhealth.org.uk/

The MHF, which also has an office in Glasgow, Scotland, sponsors research, direct services, and informative resources for persons with mental illness and their families.

MIND
15-19 Broadway
London E15 4BQ
(020) 8215-2242
Fax (020) 8522-1744
Infoline: (020) 8522-1728 (London) or 08457-660-163
contact@mind.org.uk
http://www.mind.org.uk/

MIND campaigns against mental illness stigma, sponsors local offices and support groups, and provides printed and online information. Some information is also available in Welsh.

National Alliance of the Relatives of the Mentally Ill (NARMI)
Tydehams Oaks
Tydehams, Newbury
Berks RG14 6JT
(01635) 551923
Fax (01635) 550229

Northern Ireland Association for Mental Health
80 University Street
Belfast BT7 1HE
(01232) 328474

Scottish Association for Mental Health
Cumbrae House
15 Carlton Court
Glasgow G5 9JP
(0141) 568-7000
Fax (0141) 568-7001
enquire@samh.org.uk
http://www.samh.org.uk/

SANE
Cityside House, 1st Floor
40 Adler Street
London E1 1EE
(020) 7375 1002 (office)
Fax (020) 7375 2162
(0845) 767 8000 (National Helpline, daily from noon until 2 A.M.)
london@sane.org.uk
http://www.sane.org.uk/

SANE also has regional offices in Bristol and Macclesfield.

Ireland

AWARE
72 Lower Leeson Street
Dublin 2 Ireland
(01) 830-8449
(01) 679-1711 (Phone counseling service, daily 10 A.M. to 10 P.M.)

AWARE offers help by phone, sponsors support groups in 38 locations around Ireland, provides information and literature, does public advocacy, and supports research.

Mental Health Association of Ireland
Mensana House, 6 Adelaide Street
Dun Laoghaire, County Dublin, Ireland
(01) 284-1166
Fax (01) 284-1736
http://mhai.healthyirish.com/index.html

This site includes links to resources throughout Ireland, including Northern Ireland. Some information is available in Irish Gaelic.

Australia

Action Resource Network Inc.
266 Johnston Street
Abbotsford, Victoria 3067
(03) 9416-3488 or (800) 808-126
Fax (03) 9416-3484
TTY (03) 9416-3491

Association of Relatives and Friends of the Mentally Ill (ARAFMI)
195 Main Street, Suite 2
Osborne Park, WA
(61) 8 9228 0577 or (800) 811-747
http://www.arafmi.asn.au/

ARAFMI has chapters in most Australian states. Its Osborne Park office can help put you in touch.

Disability Action Inc.
62 Henley Beach Road
Mile End, SA 5031
(08) 8352 8599, (800) 805 495
Fax (08) 8354 0049
TTY (08) 8352 8022
brad@disabilityaction.in-sa.com.au

Mood Disorders Association (SA) Inc./Self-Help (MDP) Inc.
PO Box 310
Marleston, SA 5033
(08) 8221-5170
Fax (08) 8221-5159
http://homepages.picknowl.com.au/mda/

MDA sponsors support groups, a center with trained volunteers, and a library, and can link you with services.

SANE Australia
PO Box 226
South Melbourne, Victoria 3205
(61) 3 9682 5933
Fax (61) 3 9682 5944
info@sane.org
http://www.sane.org/

New Zealand

Richmond Fellowship New Zealand Inc.
249 Madras Street, Level 3
Christchurch, NZ
(64) 3 365-3211
Fax (64) 3 365-3905
national@richmond.org.nz
http://www.richmondnz.org/

Online support

The Internet is no substitute for local and family support, but for people who live in isolated areas or who are homebound, it's nothing short of wonderful. Many others find these web sites and discussion groups useful as well.

About Bipolar Disorder
http://bipolar.miningco.com/

This site presents a collection of articles, links, and a web-based chat group about bipolar disorders.

Bipolar Planet

http://groups.yahoo.com/group/BipolarPlanet/

The Bipolar Planet is a long-lived e-mail discussion list. To subscribe, visit the web site or send an email message to *BipolarPlanet-subscribe@yahoogroups.com*.

Bipolar Disorder Sanctuary

http://www.mhsanctuary.com/bipolar/

Bipolar Disorders Information Center

http://www.mhsource.com/bipolar/letter.html

This site includes clinical treatment information, information on conferences, and the "Bipolar Disorder and Impulsive Spectrum Newsletter" in PDF format. You'll need the free program Acrobat Reader to read the newsletter.

FyrenIyce

http://users.wantree.com.au/~fractal/

Information about bipolar disorders and links to support and advocacy groups in Australia and elsewhere can be found here. There's also a FyrenIyce e-mail list.

Massachusetts General Hospital Neurology Forums

http://neuro-www.mgh.harvard.edu/

This site features discussion groups (live and bulletin board-style) on almost every known neurological disorder, including bipolar disorders.

Pendulum Resources

http://www.pendulum.org/

You can find up-to-date information on bipolar disorders here, with a strong "mental health consumer" orientation.

WalkersWeb

http://www.walkers.org/

WalkersWeb (also known as Walkers in Darkness) is the home of several mailing lists geared toward people with bipolar disorders or depression. It also has excellent links to mental health sites, its own informational files, and online chat groups.

Online resources for family members

Beacon of Hope

http://www.lightship.org/

Managed by the spouse of a person with bipolar disorder, the Beacon of Hope site provides information about living with mental illness in the family, coping strategies, and more.

BPSO list
To subscribe, send a message to:
majordomo@lugdunum.net
With body text:
subscribe bpso
http://www.bpso.org/subscrib.htm

This list is for parents, spouses, siblings, and friends of people with bipolar disorder.

Suite 101: Children of Those with Mental Illness
http://www.i5ive.com/welcome.cfm/children_those_mental_illness

This site addresses the interests of this little-served population. It's geared primarily toward adults with mentally ill parents.

Books and publications

"Bipolar Network News"
http://www.bipolarnetwork.org/

The Stanley Foundation Bipolar Network produces this online newsletter, which includes reports on clinical trial results and new discoveries.

Berger, Diane, et al. *We Heard the Angels of Madness: A Family Guide to Coping With Manic Depression*. New York: Quill, 1992.

Fieve, Dr. Ronald R. *Moodswing: Dr. Fieve on Depression* (revised edition). New York: Bantam Books, 1997.

Guiness, David. "Inside Out: A Guide to Self-Management of Manic Depression." London: The Manic Depression Fellowship, 1998. This booklet is available from the MDF, listed earlier in this Appendix.

Halebsky, Mark. *Surviving the Crisis of Depression and Bipolar Illness: A Layperson's Guide to Coping with Mental Illness Beyond the Time of Crisis and Outside the Hospital*. Arvada, CO: Personal and Professional Growth Organization, 1997.

Jamison, Kay Redfield, MD. *An Unquiet Mind*. New York: Random House, 1997. Dr. Jamison is one of the most prominent experts on bipolar disorders—and is herself a manic-depressive. This is her fascinating memoir.

Jamison, Kay Redfield, MD. *Touched With Fire: Manic-Depressive Illness and the Artistic Temperament*. New York: The Free Press, 1996.

Videos

Mental Illness Education Project (MIEP)
PO Box 470813
Brookline Village, MA 02447
(617) 562-1111
info@miepvideos.org
http://www.miepvideos.org/

MIEP creates and sells affordable videos about many aspects of living with mental illness, including "I Love You Like Crazy: Being a Parent With Mental Illness" and materials on peer-to-peer support strategies.

General disability support and advocacy

The resources listed in this section provide legal information and, in some cases, practical help and advice on matters connected with disability.

United States

Disability Rights Education and Defense Fund Inc.
2212 6th Street
Berkeley, CA 94710
(510) 644-2555
Fax (510) 841-8645
dredf@dredf.org
http://www.dredf.org

FindLaw
http://www.findlaw.com/01topics/36civil/disabilities.html

FindLaw has a legal research search engine, as well as a wealth of specific information about disability law.

National Association of Protection and Advocacy Systems
900 2nd Street, NE, Suite 211
Washington, DC 20002
(202) 408-9514
http://www.protectionandadvocacy.com

Every US state has a federally funded Protection and Advocacy system. Call this group or check its web site to find a referral to your state's P&A organization. These organizations provide legal advice and, in some cases, legal representation to people with disabilities and their family members who have disability-related needs. This may include assistance with securing federal or state benefits, advocacy in the special education system, and helping with Americans with Disabilities Act compliance issues, among other areas.

National Organization of Social Security Claimants
6 Prospect Street
Midland Park, NJ 07432
(800) 432-2804
http://www.nosscr.org

United Kingdom

Disability Rights Commission
DRC Helpline
Freepost MID 02164
Stratford-upon-Avon CV37 9BR
(08457) 622633
Fax (08457) 778878
http://www.drc-gb.org/drc/default.aspddahelp@stra.sitel.co.uk

UK Advocacy Network
Volserve House
14-18 West Bar Green
Sheffield SI 2DA
(0114) 272 8171
Fax 0114 272 8172
ukan@can-online.org.uk

Australia

Disability Action Inc.
62 Henley Beach Road
Mile End, SA 5031
(08) 8352 8599 or (800) 805-495
Fax (08) 8354 0049
TTY (08) 8352 8022
brad@disabilityaction.in-sa.com.au

Related conditions and symptoms

If you have other diagnoses that contribute to your mood swings or affect treatment decisions, these books, organizations, and online resources may help.

Attention Deficit Disorder

Hallowell, Edward, MD. *Driven to Distraction: Recognizing and Coping With Attention Deficit Disorder from Childhood Through Adulthood.* Reading, MA: Addison-Wesley, 1994. This is the classic book on ADD/ADHD.

Children and Adults with Attention Deficit Disorder (CHADD)
8181 Professional Place, Suite 201
Landover, MD 20785
(301) 306-7070 or (800) 233-4050
Fax (301) 306-7090
national@chadd.org
http://www.chadd.org/

Attention Deficit Disorder Ontario Foundation
Station R, Box 223
Toronto, ON M4G 3Z9 Canada
(416) 813-6858
ADDO@addofundation.org
http://www.addofoundation.org

ADDnet UK
http://www.btinternet.com/~black.ice/addnet/addnetmain.html
44 (0) 181 269-1400 or 44 (0) 181 516-1413

Eating disorders

Eating Disorders Shared Awareness (EDSA)
http://www.mirror-mirror.org/

This site includes links to US and Canadian support and informational sites on anorexia and bulimia.

Eating Disorders Association (EDA)
Wensum House, 1st Floor
103 Prince of Wales Rd.
Norwich NR1 1DW UK
(0870) 770-3256
Fax (01603) 664-915
(01603) 621-414 (Helpline, available 9 A.M. to 5:30 P.M. weekdays)
(01603) 765-050 (Youth Helpline, available 9 A.M. to 5:30 P.M. weekdays)
info@edauk.com
http://www.edauk.com/

Immune-system disorders

Cournos, Francine, MD, and Nicholas Bakalar, eds. *AIDS and People With Severe Mental Illness: A Handbook for Mental Health Professionals.* New Haven, CT: Yale University Press, 1996. This is currently the only book available for clinicians on this topic—it may prove helpful to patients as well.

Goldstein, Jay A., MD. *Betrayal by the Brain: The Neurologic Basic of Chronic Fatigue Syndrome, Fibromyalgia Syndrome, and Related Neural Network Disorders.* New York: Haworth Press, 1996. This book presents something of a grand unified field theory and is rather controversial. A companion volume for self-help is also available.

Leonard, Brian E., and Klara Miller, eds. *Stress, the Immune System, and Psychiatry.* New York: John Wiley & Sons, 1995. This book provides a medical overview of how these factors interact.

Williamson, Miryam Erlich. *Fibromyalgia: A Comprehensive Approach: What You Can Do About Chronic Pain and Fatigue.* New York: Walker & Co., 1996. Written by a woman with FMS, this is a well-written, practical self-help book.

HRSA Action CARES
http://hab.hrsa.gov/publications.html

You can download a special issue of this newsletter on mental illness and AIDS at no charge. It's in PDF format, which requires the free program Adobe Acrobat.

Seasonal affective disorder (SAD)

Rosenthal, Norman E., MD. *Winter Blues.* New York: The Guilford Press, 1993.

National Organization for Seasonal Affective Disorder (NOSAD)
PO Box 40190
Washington, DC 20016
(301) 762-0768
http://www.nosad.org

NOSAD provides information about seasonal affective disorders and how to treat them.

Circadian Lighting Association
http://www.claorg.org

This is a trade organization for manufacturers of special light boxes for treating SAD. You can find out about products and vendors in the US, Canada, and UK here.

Self-injurious behavior (SIB)

Almost all easily available materials on SIB take a strongly psychoanalytic approach, which may not be appropriate for those whose self-injurious behaviors have primarily neurobiological underpinnings.

Alderman, Tracy. *The Scarred Soul: Understanding and Ending Self-Inflicted Violence.* Oakland, CA: New Harbinger Publications, 1997.
Levenkron, Steven. *Cutting: Understanding and Overcoming Self-Mutilation.* New York: W. W. Norton & Company, 1998.
Strong, Marilee. *A Bright Red Scream: Self-Mutilation and the Language of Pain.* New York: Viking Press, 1998.

Bodies-Under-Siege mailing list
To subscribe, send mail to:
majordomo@majordomo.pobox.com
with the message body:
subscribe bus
http://www.palace.net/~llama/psych/busfaq.html

Bodies-Under-Siege is an online support group for people with self-injurious behavior.

Secret Shame
http://www.palace.net/~llama/psych/injury.html

Secret Shame is a web site about self-injury, offering information and support to people with SIB and their families.

Sleep disorders

Idkidowski, Chris, MD. *The Insomnia Kit: Everything You Need for a Good Night's Sleep.* New York: Viking Penguin, 1998. This self-help package includes everything from information on insomnia and its causes to self-hypnosis tapes aimed at helping you get to sleep without medication.

SleepNet.com
http://www.sleepnet.com

On SleepNet you can learn about the various types of insomnia and sleep disorders and find information about techniques for coping and medical treatments.

Substance abuse

Dual Diagnosis
http://users.erols.com/ksciacca/

This web site provides information about treating both mental illness and substance abuse at the same time.

Sobriety and Recovery Resources
http://www.recoveryresources.org

This site is built around information from Alcoholics Anonymous, Narcotics Anonymous, and other resources that can help you stop using drugs and alcohol.

Centre for Addiction and Mental Health (CAMH)
33 Russel Street
Toronto, ON M5S 2S1
(416) 535-8501, (416) 595-6111 or (800)-463-6273
http://www.camh.net/

CAMH provides public information about drug and alcohol use and abuse, with much information specific to those with a dual diagnosis.

Drugline Ltd.
9A Brockley Cross
Brockley, London SE4 2AB UK
(0181) 692-4975

Drugline provides public information about drug use and abuse.

Healthcare and insurance

Beckett, Julie. *Health Care Financing: A Guide for Families.* Iowa City: National Maternal and Child Health Resource Center. This overview of the healthcare financing system includes advocacy strategies and information about public health insurance in the US. The author is the mother of Katie Beckett, the child whose case inspired the creation of Medicaid waiver programs. Order from: NMCHRC, Law Building, University of Iowa, Iowa City, IA 52242, (319) 335-9073.

Keene, Nancy. *Working With Your Doctor: Getting the Healthcare You Deserve*. Sebastopol, CA: O'Reilly & Associates, 1998. This is a general-purpose guide to navigating the healthcare and insurance system, including skills for communicating with medical professionals, appealing denial of care or coverage, and managing your own healthcare.

National Association of Insurance Commissioners (NAIC)
444 National Capitol Street, NW, Suite 309
Washington, DC 20001
(202) 624-7790
http://www.naic.org/

Contact NAIC to locate your state insurance commissioner, who can tell you about health insurance regulations in your state.

General medical information

Glanze, Walter, and others, eds. *The Signet Mosby Medical Encyclopedia* (revised edition). New York: Signet, 1998. This book is a condensed paperback version of *Mosby's Medical, Nursing, and Allied Health Dictionary* for health consumers.

Andreasen, Dr. Nancy C. *The Broken Brain: The Biological Revolution in Psychiatry*. New York: HarperCollins, 1985. Although it concentrates on the biology of psychiatric illness, *The Broken Brain* also does an excellent job of explaining neurochemistry concepts in accessible language.

Beers, Mark H., MD, Robert Berkow, MD, and Andrew J. Fletcher, eds. *The Merck Manual of Medical Information: Home Edition*. Whitehouse Station, NJ: Merck Research Laboratories, 1999. This is a consumer version of the standard medical reference book.

Diamond, M. C., A. B. Scheibel, and L. M. Elson. *The Human Brain Coloring Book*. New York: HarperPerennial, 1985. This book, a favorite of medical students, makes brain anatomy visual from the cellular level on up.

Medscape
http://www.medscape.com

Medline is a searchable online index to hundreds of medical journals. Many articles are available in full, others as abstracts only.

PubMed
http://www.pubmedcentral.nih.gov/

Free interface for searching the MEDLINE medical database, which can help you find out about studies, medications, and more.

Genetic counseling resources

Genetic counselors have special training in helping families understand the implications of having a member diagnosed with a genetic disorder. They can explain whether these disorders can be passed on to a diagnosed person's children and help you assess associated risks. They can also provide information about genetic testing for other family members.

American Board of Genetic Counseling Inc. (ABGC)
9650 Rockville Pike
Bethesda, MD 20814-3998
(301) 571-1825
Fax (301) 571-1895
http://www.faseb.org/genetics/abgc/abgcmenu.htm

The ABGC credentials professionals in the field of genetic counseling and can help you find a reputable member via phone, mail, or its web site.

GeneTests
Children's Hospital and Regional Medical Center
PO Box 5371
Seattle, WA 98105-0371
(206) 527-5742
Fax (206) 527-5743
genetests@genetests.org
http://www.genetests.org

GeneTests is a genetic testing resource funded by the National Library of Medicine of the NIH and Maternal & Child Health Bureau of the HRSA. It provides a list of genetic research and clinical laboratories, description of genetic testing and counseling, and information for genetic professionals.

European Society of Human Genetics
Clinical Genetics Unit
Birmingham Women's Hospital
Birmingham B15 2TG UK
(44) 0-121-623-6820
esgh@esgh.org
http://www.eshg.org/

Human Genetics Society of Australasia
Royal Australian College of Physicians
145 Macquarie Street
Sydney, NSW 2000 Australia
(02) 9256-5471
Fax (02) 9251-8174
hgsa@racp.edu.au
http://www.hgsa.com.au/

Information about medications

There are a number of books available that list side effects, cautions, and more regarding medications. The biggest and best is the *Physicians Desk Reference* (PDR), but its price is well out of the average person's league. You may be able to find a used but recent copy at a good price. The PDR is in the reference section of most public libraries.

If you are allergic to food dyes or to corn, wheat, and other materials used as fillers in pills, consult directly with the manufacturer of any medication you take.

British Medical Association and the Royal Pharmaceutical Society of Great Britain. *The British National Formulary*. London: British Medical Association and the Royal Pharmaceutical Society of Great Britain, 2001. This is the standard reference for prescribing and dispensing drugs in the UK, updated twice yearly.

Preston, John D., John H. O'Neal, and Mary C. Talaga. *Consumer's Guide to Psychiatric Drugs*. Oakland, CA: New Harbinger Publications, 1998.

Silverman, Harold M., ed. *The Pill Book* (eighth edition). New York: Bantam Books, 1998. This is a basic paperback guide to the most commonly used medications in the US.

Sullivan, Donald. *The American Pharmaceutical Association's Guide to Prescription Drugs*. New York: Signet, 1998.

Canadian Drug Product Database
http://www.hc-sc.gc.ca/hpb-dgps/therapeut/htmleng/dpd.html

Dr. Bob's Psychopharmacology Tips
http://www.dr-bob.org/

This site offers excellent information on psychiatric drugs, including things like the MAOI dietary restrictions and common SSRI interactions.

Federal Drug Administration (FDA)
http://www.fda.gov/cder/drug/default.htm

Official US information on new drugs and generic versions of old drugs can be found here, along with FDA warnings and recalls.

The Internet Drug List
http://www.rxlist.com/

The RxList includes information on prescription drugs as well as many herbal, Chinese, and homeopathic remedies. Many listings are available in Spanish as well as English.

PharmWeb
http://www.pharmweb.net/

Public Citizen's eLetter on Drugs for Severe Psychiatric Conditions
http://www.citizen.org/eletter/articleindex.htm

This consumer watchdog group's newsletter often breaks stories on dangerous side effects and interactions before the mainstream media. It also includes background info on the drug approval process.

The Royal Pharmaceutical Society's Technical Information Center
http://www.rpsgb.org.uk

There is a nominal fee for use of the RPS database, but one might be able to have it waived.

RXmed
http://www.rxmed.com/

Drug company patient assistance programs

If you do not have health insurance or if your health insurance does not cover prescriptions, you may be eligible to receive some or all of your medications at no charge. Most major pharmaceutical companies will accommodate requests for free or reduced price drugs; others may have reimbursement programs.

Check the package inserts for your medications to find out who makes them, and then call the patient assistance program directly. If the manufacturer's name is not listed below or if you live outside the US, talk to your pharmacist or check one of the pharmaceutical information web sites listed earlier in this appendix for more information.

Pharmaceutical Company	Phone Number
3M Pharmaceuticals	(800) 328-0255
Abbott Labs Patient Assistance Program (includes Survanta)	(800) 922-3255
American Home Products (includes Lederle)	(800) 395-9938
Amgen	(800) 272-9376
Astra-Zeneca (includes Ici-Stuart)	(800) 488-3247
Aventis Pharmaceuticals (includes Rhone-Poulenc Rorer, Hoecht Roussel)	(800) 207-8049
Bayer Indigent Patient Program	(800) 998-9180
Berlex	(800) 423-7539
Boehringer Ingleheim	(203) 798-4131
Bristol Myers Squibb	(800) 736-0003
Genetech	(800) 879-4747
Glaxo Wellcome Inc. (includes Burroughs)	(800) 722-9294
Immunex Corp.	(800) 321-4669
Janssen Pharmaceutica (includes Johnson & Johnson)	(800) 526-7736
Knoll	(800) 526-0710

Pharmaceutical Company	Phone Number
Lilly Cares Program (Eli Lilly)	(800) 545-6962
Merck National Service Center	(800) 672-6372
Novartis Patient Support Program (includes Sandoz, Ciba-Geigy)	(800) 257-3273
Ortho-McNeil Pharmaceuticals	(800) 682-6532
Pfizer Prescription Assistance Program (includes Parke-Davis, Warner-Lambert)	(800) 646-4455
Pharmacia Inc. (includes Upjohn)	(800) 242-7014
Proctor & Gamble	(800) 448-4878
Roche Labs (includes Syntex)	(800) 285-4484
Roxane Labs	(800) 274-8651
Sanofi Winthrop	(800) 446-6267
Schering Labs	(800) 521-7157
Searle	(800) 542-2526
SmithKline Access To Care Program	(800) 546-0420 (patient requests)
Solvay Patient Assistance Program	(800) 256-8918

Medical facilities

Sometimes bipolar symptoms become so challenging that your local psychiatrist may need to seek the help of experts. These facilities are among the world's best-known centers for treating bipolar disorders.

United States

Bipolar Disorders Research Center
Payne Whitney Clinic
New York Presbyterian Hospital
525 East 68th Street
Box 140
New York, NY 10021
(212) 746-5937
http://www.paynewhitney.yourmd.com/ypol/user/userMain.asp?siteid=17674

Harvard Bipolar Research Program
Massachusetts General Hospital
50 Staniford Street, 5th Floor
Boston, MA 02114
(617) 726-6188
http://www.manicdepressive.org/
Contact: Gary Sachs, MD

Along with providing care for patients, Massachusetts General Hospital coordinates the Systematic Treatment Enhancement Program for Bipolar Disorder (STEP-BD), a large, multi-site, NIMH-funded program seeking more effective treatments. STEP-BD includes studies specific to treatment-resistant bipolar disorders, including rapid cycling and ultra-rapid cycling variants. For more information specifically about STEP-BD, call (866) 398-7425.

Montefiore Medical Center
Department of Psychiatry and Behavioral Sciences
111 East 210th Street
Bronx, NY 10467
(718) 920-6215
http://www.montefiore.org/prof/clinical/psych/index.html

National Institutes of Mental Health (NIMH)
Biological Psychiatry Branch
Building 10, Room 3N212
9000 Rockville Pike
Bethesda, MD 20892
(301) 496-6827
(301) 402-0052
http://www.nimh.nih.gov/publicat/bipolar.cfm
NIMH Patient Recruitment and Referral Service
(800) 411-1222
prcc@cc.nih.gov

Stanford Bipolar Disorders Clinic
401 Quarry Road
Stanford, CA 94305-5723
(650) 498-4689
bipolar.clinic@stanford.edu
http://www.stanford.edu/group/bipolar.clinic/

The Stanley Clinical Research Center
Case Western Reserve University/University Hospitals of Cleveland
Department of Psychiatry
11100 Euclid Ave.
Cleveland, OH 44106
(216) 844-3880
Fax (216) 844-1703

The Stanley Center for the Innovative Treatment of Bipolar Disorders
3811 O'Hara Street, Suite 279
Pittsburgh, PA 15213
(412) 624-2476 or (800) 424-7657
Fax (412) 624-0493.
http://www.wpic.pitt.edu/stanley/

Currently the Stanley Center in Pittsburgh takes inquiries only from persons within 150 miles of Pittsburgh.

Stanley Foundation Bipolar Network
5430 Grosvenor Lane, Suite 200
Bethesda, MD 20814
(800) 518-7326
Fax (301) 571-0768
info@bipolarnetwork.org
http://www.bipolarnetwork.org/

This is a multi-center research effort, including the Stanley Foundation Center at Johns Hopkins University, NIMH, and several other institutions.

University of California, Los Angeles
Mood Disorders Research
300 Medical Plaza, 1544
Los Angles, CA 90095
(310) 794-9913
Fax (310) 794-9915
Contact: Joni Zuckerbrow-Miller, *JZuckerbrow@MEDNET.ucla.edu*

University of Texas Southwestern Medical Center
Department of Psychiatry
5353 Harry Hines Blvd.
Dallas, TX 75390
(214) 648-7492
Fax (214) 689-7499
Contact: Eileen Grace Fischer, *efisch@mednet.swmed.edu*

Canada

Canadian Network for Mood and Anxiety Treatments (CANMAT)
http://www.canmat.org/

This is a consortium of university medical schools and other research organizations concentrating on depression, bipolar disorders, and anxiety disorders. The CANMAT web site can link you with a center near you; it also provides information about diagnosis and treatment options.

University of British Columbia Mood Disorders Clinic
Department of Psychiatry
Vancouver Hospital & Health Sciences Centre, UBC Site
2211 Wesbrook Mall
Vancouver, BC V6T 2A1
(604) 822-9745
Fax (604) 822-7922
http://www.psychiatry.ubc.ca/mood/

Alternative medicine resources

The following books present information for those interested in approaching depression and mood swings with dietary changes, vitamins, supplements, and other alternative or complementary therapies, such as relaxation techniques. Always be sure to discuss any changes with your doctor. Be especially careful about trying "natural" antidepressants, because they can cause hypomania or mania in persons with bipolar disorders.

Balch, James F., MD, and Phyllis A. Balch, CNC. *Prescription for Nutritional Healing* (third edition). Garden City Park, NY: Avery Penguin Putnam, 2000.

Baumel, Syd. *Dealing with Depression Naturally: Complementary and Alternative Therapies for Restoring Emotional Health* (second edition). New York: McGraw-Hill, 2000.

Eades, Mary Dan, MD. *The Doctor's Complete Guide to Vitamins and Minerals* (revised edition). New York: Dell, 2000.

Elkins, Rita. *Depression and Natural Medicine* (second edition). Pleasant Grove, UT: Woodland Publishing, 1999.

Gruenwald, Joerg. *Physicians Desk Reference for Herbal Medicines* (second edition). Montvale, NJ: Medical Economics Co., 2000.

Murray, Michael T., ND. *Natural Alternatives to Prozac*. New York: Quill, 1999.

Norden, Michael J., MD. *Beyond Prozac: Brain-Toxic Lifestyles, Natural Antidotes, and New-Generation Antidepressants*. New York: HarperCollins, 1996.

Stoll, Andrew L., MD. *The Omega-3 Connection: The Groundbreaking Anti-Depressant Diet and Brain Program*. New York: The Free Press, 2001.

Tyler, Varro E., and Stephen Foster. *Tyler's Honest Herbal: A Sensible Guide to the Use of Herbs and Related Remedies* (fourth edition). Binghamton, NY: The Haworth Press, 1999.

National Center for Complementary and Alternative Medicine
NCCAM Clearinghouse
PO Box 8218
Silver Spring, MD 20907-8218
(888) 644-6226
Fax (301) 495-4957
http://nccam.nih.gov/

NCCAM examines claims made about herbal medications, bodywork, acupuncture, and other complementary treatments.

EFA supplement suppliers

Before trying essential fatty acids as a mood stabilizer, consult with your doctor and get as much information as you can about the source of the product, whether it has been toxicology tested, and the recommended dose. Researchers currently suggest trying EFAs to augment, not replace, pharmaceutical mood stabilizers.

Kirkman Laboratories Inc.
PO Box 1009
Wilsonville, OR 97070
(503) 694-1600 or (800) 245-8282
Fax (503) 682-0838
http://www.kirkmanlabs.com/

Kirkman Labs offers toxicology-tested cod liver oil, which contains high levels of EFAs.

Nordic Naturals
3040 Valencia Ave., Suite 2
Aptos, CA 95003
(831) 662-2852 or (800) 662-2544
Fax (831) 662-0382
http://www.nordicnaturals.com

Nordic Naturals is the original source of most fish-oil-based Omega-3 fatty acid supplements sold in the US.

OmegaBrite
Omega NaturalHealth
1050 Winter Street, Suite 1000
Waltham, MA 12451
(800) 383-2030
Fax (413) 556-0015
CustomerService@omegabrite.com
http://www.omegabrite.com

OmegaBrite is an EFA supplement formulated according to Dr. Andrew Stoll's specifications.

Martek Biosciences Corp.
6480 Dobbin Road
Columbia, MD 21045
(410) 740-0081 or (800) 662-6339
Fax (410) 740-2985
http://www.martekbio.com/Nutritional_Products/Introduction.asp

Martek's "Neuromins" product contains vegetable-based EFAs.

The Vitamin Connection
72 Main Street
Burlington, VT 05401
(802) 846-2026 or (800) 760-3020
Fax (802) 846-2027
http://www.vitaminconnection.com/

The Vitamin Connection carries EFAs and other supplements.

Public mental health agencies

The agencies listed here provide advice and direct services to persons with mental health needs. Even if you have private health insurance, these agencies may offer referrals to community services, specific treatment programs, support programs, and other resources.

United States

Alabama

Department of Mental Health and Mental Retardation
RSA Union
100 N. Union Street
PO Box 30140
Montgomery, AL 36130-1410
(334) 242-3417
Fax (334) 242-0684
http://www.mh.state.al.us/

Alaska

Alaska Division of Mental Health and Developmental Disabilities
50 Main Street, Room 214
PO Box 110620
Juneau, AK 99811-0620
(907) 465-3370
Fax (907) 465-2668
TDD/TTY (907) 465-2225
http://www.hss.state.ak.us/dmhdd/

Arizona

Arizona Department of Health Services
Behavioral Health Services
2122 E. Highland
Phoenix, AZ 85016
(602) 381-8999
Fax (602) 553-9140
http://www.hs.state.az.us/bhs/home.htm

Arkansas

Department of Human Services
Donaghey Plaza West
Slot 3440
PO Box 1437
Little Rock, AR 72203-1437
(501) 682-8650
http://www.state.ar.us/dhs/

Colorado

Mental Health Services
3824 W. Princeton Circle
Denver, CO 80236
(303) 866-7400
Fax (303) 866-7428
http://www.cdhs.state.co.us/ohr/mhs/index.html

District of Columbia

Department of Human Services
801 East Building
2700 MLK Jr. Avenue, SE
Washington, DC 20032
(202) 463-6211

Florida

Department of Health and Human Services
1311 Winewood Blvd.
Building 5, Room 215
Tallahassee, FL 32301
(904) 488-4257
http://www.doh.state.fl.us

Georgia

Department of Human Resources
878 Peachtree Street NE, Room 706
Atlanta, GA 30309
(404) 894-6670
http://www2.state.ga.us/Departments/DHR/

Hawaii

Department of Human Services
1000 Bishop Street, No. 615
Honolulu, HI 96813
(808) 548-4769
http://www.hawaii.gov/dhs/

Idaho

Department of Health and Welfare
450 W. State Street
Boise, ID 83720-0036
(208) 334-5500
http://www.state.id.us/dhw/hwgd_www/home.html

Illinois

Department of Mental Health and Developmental Disabilities
402 Stratten Office Building
Springfield, IL 62706
(217) 782-7395
http://www.state.il.us/agency/dhs/mhddfsnp.html

Indiana

Division of Mental Health
Social Services Administration
117 E. Washington Street
Indianapolis, IN 46204-3647
http://www.state.in.us/fssa/servicemental/dmh/

Iowa

Department of Human Services
Hoover State Office Building
Des Moines, IA 50319
(515) 278-2502 or (800) 972-2017
http://www.dhs.state.ia.us/

Kansas

Department of Social and Rehabilitative Services
915 SW Harrison, Room 603
N. Topeka, KS 66612
(785) 296-3959
Fax (785) 296-2173
http://www.srskansas.org

Kentucky

Department of Mental Health and Mental Retardation Services
100 Fair Oaks Lane, 4th Floor
Frankfort, KY 40621
(502) 564-4527
http://dmhmrs.chr.state.ky.us/

Louisiana

Department of Health and Hospitals
1201 Capitol Access Road
PO Box 629
Baton Rouge, LA 70821-0629
(225) 342-9500
Fax (225) 342-5568
http://www.dhh.state.la.us/

Maine

Department of Behavioral and Developmental Services
40 State House Station
Augusta, ME 04333-0040
(207) 287-4200
(888) 568-1112 (Crisis Hotline)
Fax (207) 287-4268
http://www.state.me.us/dmhmrsa/

Maryland

Department of Health and Mental Hygiene
201 W. Preston Street
O'Connor Building, 4th Floor
Baltimore, MD 21201
(410) 767-6500 or (877) 463-3464
http://www.dhmh.state.md.us/

Massachusetts

Department of Mental Health
25 Staniford Street
Boston, MA 02210
(617) 727-5600
Fax (617) 727-4350
http://www.state.ma.us/eohhs/agencies/dmh.htm

Minnesota

Minnesota Department of Human Services
444 Lafayette Road
St. Paul, MN 55155
(651) 297-3933
http://www.dhs.state.mn.us/

Mississippi

Department of Mental Health
1101 Robert E. Lee Building
239 N. Lamar Street
Jackson, MS 39201
(601) 359-1288 or (877) 210-8513
Fax (601) 359-6295
http://www.dmh.state.ms.us

Missouri

Department of Mental Health
1706 East Elm Street
PO Box 687
Jefferson City, MO 65102
(573) 751-3070 or (800) 364-9687
dmhmail@mail.state.mo.us
http://www.modmh.state.mo.us

Montana

Department of Public Health and Human Services
PO Box 4210
111 Sanders, Room 202
Helena, MT 59604
(406) 444-2995
http://www.dphhs.state.mt.us/

Nebraska

Department of Health and Human Services
Office of Community Mental Health
PO Box 94728
Lincoln, NE 68509-4728
(402) 471-2306 or (402) 479-5126
http://www.hhs.state.ne.us/beh/behindex.htm

Nevada

Department of Human Resources
State Capitol Complex
505 E. King Street, Room 600
Carson City, NV 98701-3708
(702) 684-4000
http://www.hr.state.nv.us/

New Hampshire

Division of Mental Health
Department of Health and Welfare
State Office Park South
105 Pleasant Street
Concord, NH 03301
(603) 271-5000
http://www.dhhs.state.nh.us/

New Jersey

Division of Mental Health Services
New Jersey Department of Human Services
50 E. State Street
PO Box 727
Trenton, NJ 08625-0727
(609) 984-0755 or (800) 382-6717
dmhsmail@dhs.state.nj.us
http://www.state.nj.us/health/index.html

New Mexico

Department of Health
1190 S. St. Francis Drive
PO Box 26110
Santa Fe, NM 87502-6110
(505) 827-2613
http://www.health.state.nm.us

New York

New York State Office of Mental Health
44 Holland Street
Albany, NY 12229
(518) 473-3456
http://www.omh.state.ny.us/

North Carolina

Department of Health and Human Services
620 N. West Street
PO Box 26053
Raleigh, NC 27611
(919) 733-6566
http://www.dhhs.state.nc.us/

North Dakota

Department of Human Services
State Capitol Building
Bismarck, ND 58505
(701) 224-2970
http://lnotes.state.nd.us/dhs/dhsweb.nsf

Ohio

Ohio Department of Mental Health
State Office Tower
30 E. Broad Street, 8th Floor
Columbus, OH 43266-0315
(614) 466-1483
http://www.mh.state.oh.us/

Oklahoma

Oklahoma Department of Mental Health and Substance Abuse Services
1200 NE 13th Street
PO Box 53277
Oklahoma City, OK 73152-3277
(405) 522-3908
http://www.odmhsas.org/

Oregon

Office of Mental Health Services
Department of Human Resources
2575 Bittern Street NE
PO Box 14250
Salem, OR 97309-0740
(503) 945-9700
Fax (503) 373-7327
http://omhs.mhd.hr.state.or.us/

Pennsylvania

Pennsylvania Department of Health
PO Box 90
Harrisburg, PA 17108
(800) 986-4550
http://www.health.state.pa.us

Rhode Island

Department of Mental Health, Retardation, and Hospitals
14 Harrington Road
Cranston, RI 02920-3080
(401) 464-3201
Fax (401) 462-3204
http://www.mhrh.state.ri.us/

South Carolina

Department of Mental Health
2414 Bull Street, Room 304
Columbia, SC 29202
(803) 898-8581
scdmh@yahoo.com
http://www.state.sc.us/dmh/

South Dakota

Department of Human Services
East Highway 34, Hillsview Plaza
c/o 500 East Capitol Avenue
Pierre, SD 57501-5070
(605) 733-5990
Fax (605) 733-5483
http://www.state.sd.us/dhs/

Tennessee

Department of Mental Health and Developmental Disabilities
Cordell Hull Building, 3rd Floor
425 Fifth Avenue North
Nashville, TN 37243
(615) 532-6500
Fax (615) 532-6514
http://www.state.tn.us/mental/

Texas

Department of Mental Health and Mental Retardation
909 W. 45th Street
PO Box 12668
Austin, TX 78711-2668
(512) 454-3761 or (800) 252-8154
http://www.mhmr.state.tx.us/

Utah

State Division of Mental Health
Department of Human Services
120 N. 200 W., Room 415
Salt Lake City, UT 84145
(801) 538-4270
http://www.hsmh.state.ut.us/

Vermont

Department of Developmental and Mental Health Services
103 S. Main Street
Weeks Building
Waterbury, VT 05671-1601
(802) 241-2610
Fax (802) 241-1129
http://www.state.vt.us/dmh/

Virginia

Department of Mental Health, Mental Retardation, and Substance Abuse Services
PO Box 1797
Richmond, VA 23218-1797
(804) 786-0992
http://www.dmhmrsas.state.va.us/

Washington

Mental Health Division
Health and Rehabilitative Services Administration
PO Box 1788, OB-42C
Olympia, WA 98504
(800) 737-0617 or (800) 446-0259 (emergency)
http://www.wa.gov/dshs/hrsa/hrsa2hp.html

West Virginia

Bureau of Behavioral Health & Health Facilities
Department of Health and Human Resources
350 Capitol Street, Room 350
Charleston, WV 25301-3702
(304) 558-0298
http://www.wvdhhr.org/bhhf/

Wisconsin

Bureau of Community Mental Health
Department of Health and Family Services
1 W. Wilson Street, Room 433
PO Box 7851
Madison, WI 53707
(608) 261-6746
Fax (608) 261-6748
http://www.dhfs.state.wi.us/mentalhealth/index.htm

Canada

British Columbia

Ministry of Health Services
Parliament Buildings
Victoria, BC V8V 1X4
(250) 952-1742 or (800) 465-4911
http://www.gov.bc.ca/healthservices/Manitoba

Manitoba

Manitoba Health
Legislative Building
Winnipeg, MB R3C 0V8
(204) 786-7101 or (877) 218-0102
http://www.gov.mb.ca/health/

New Brunswick

New Brunswick Department of Health and Wellness
PO Box 5100
Fredericton, NB E3B 5G8
(506) 453-2536
Fax (506) 444-4697
http://www.gnb.ca/HW-SM/hw/index.htm

Newfoundland and Labrador

Newfoundland and Labrador Department of Health and Community Services
Division of Family and Rehabilitative Services
Confederation Building, West Block
PO Box 8700
St. John's, NF A1B 4J6
(709) 729-5153
Fax (709) 729-0583
http://www.gov.nf.ca/health/

Nova Scotia

Nova Scotia Department of Health
PO Box 488
Halifax, NS B3J 2R8
(902) 424-5886 or (800) 565-3611
http://www.gov.ns.ca/health/

Prince Edward Island

Prince Edward Island Health and Social Services
Jones Building, Second Floor
11 Kent Street
PO Box 2000
Charlottetown, PEI C1A 7N8
(902) 368-4900
Fax (902) 368-4969
http://www.gov.pe.ca/hss/index.php3

Quebec

Quebec Ministére de la Santé et Services Sociaux
1075 Chemin Sainte-Foy, R.-C.
Québec, QC G1S 2M1
(418) 643-3380 or (800) 707-3380
Fax (418) 644-4574
http://www.msss.gouv.qc.ca/

Saskatchewan

Saskatchewan Health
T. C. Douglas Building
3475 Albert Street
Regina, SK S4S 6X6
(306) 787-3475
Fax (306) 787-3761
http://www.health.gov.sk.ca/

United Kingdom

People in England, Scotland, Wales, and Northern Ireland will generally need to be referred to a specialist at a clinic or hospital by their general practitioner.

The National Health Service Confederation
http://www.nhsconfed.net/

This site lists all local NHS authorities and boards, as well as specific sites for healthcare (including mental health services).

Ireland

Eastern Health Board
Mill Lane, Palmerstown
Dublin 20
(01) 620 1600
Fax (01) 620 1601
http://www.erha.ie

Midland Health Board

Central Offices, Arden Road
Tullamore, County Offaly
(353) 506 21501
http://www.mhb.ie

Mid-Western Health Board

31-33 Catherine Street
County Limerick
(061) 316655
http://www.mwhb.ie

North-Eastern Health Board

Navane Road
Kells, County Meath
(046) 40341
http://www.nehb.ie

North-Western Health Board

Manorhamilton, County Leitrim
(072) 20400
Fax (072) 20431
http://www.nwhb.ie

South-Eastern Health Board

Lacken, Dublin Road
County Kilkenny
(056) 51702
http://www.sehb.ie

Southern Health Board

Aras Slainte, Dennehy's Cross
Wilton Road
Cork, County Cork
(021) 4545011
Fax (021) 545748
http://www.shb.ie

Western Health Board

Merlin Park Regional Hospital
County Galway
(091) 751131
http://www.mayo-cs.ie/

Australia

Australian Capitol Territory

ACT Mental Health Services
Regional Community Mental Health
Belconnen Health Centre
Corner Benjamin Way and Swanson Court
Belconnen, ACT
(02) 6205-1110
Crisis line: (800) 629-354
http://www.health.act.gov.au/mentalhealth/index.htm

New South Wales

NSW Health
73 Miller Street
Sydney, NSW 2060
(02) 9391-9000
Fax (02) 9391-9101
nswhealth@doh.health.nsw.gov.au
http://www.health.nsw.gov.au/

Northern Territory

Northern Territory Health Services
PO Box 40596
Casuarina, NT 0811
(08) 8999-2400
Fax (08) 8999-2700
http://www.nt.gov.au/nths/

Queensland

Queensland Health
GPO Box 48
Brisbane, Queensland 4001
(07) 323-40111
http://www.health.qld.gov.au/

South Australia

Commonwealth Department of Human Services
Disability Services Office
55 Currie Street
Adelaide, SA 5000
(08) 8226-6721
Fax (08) 8237-8000
http://www.dhs.sa.gov.au/default.asp

Tasmania

Commonwealth Department of Human Services
34 Davey Street
Hobart, Tasmania
(03) 6233-3185 or (800) 067-415
http://www.dhhs.tas.gov.au/Victoria

Department of Human Services
Disability Programs
Casselden Place
2 Lonsdale Street
GPO Box 9848
Melbourne, Victoria 3001
(03) 9285-8888
http://www.dhs.vic.gov.au/

Western Australia

Department of Health and Family Services
Central Park, 12th Floor
152 St. George Terrace
Perth, WA 6000
(08) 9346-5111 or (800) 198-008
Fax (08) 9346-5222
http://www.public.health.wa.gov.au/

New Zealand

New Zealand Ministry of Health
133 Molesworth Street
PO Box 5013
Wellington, NZ
(04) 496-2000
Fax (04) 496-2340
http://www.moh.govt.nz/

The Genetics of Bipolar Disorders

SEVERAL POPULATION STUDIES have been done on families affected by bipolar disorders. Children of bipolar parents are definitely at increased risk for these conditions: between 10 and 27 percent have bipolar disorder, which is 10 or more times the rate in the rest of the population.[1,2] Among identical twins, if one twin has bipolar disorder, there's a 60 percent likelihood that the other twin will, too.[3] If both parents are bipolar, the risk of their offspring having a bipolar disorder rises exponentially.[4] These facts make bipolar disorders one of the most strongly familial of all mental illnesses.

However, the genetics involved are definitely not simple. Researchers believe that multiple genetic differences are involved, with varied combinations of genes producing different combinations of symptoms. For example, one combination might be more likely to produce the ultra-rapid-cycling type of bipolar disorder, and another combination might only result in symptoms when transmitted to female offspring.

Currently, a great deal of attention is being paid to sites on chromosome 18, because some of the strongest evidence to emerge from genetic studies implicates differences in a particular area of its genetic material.[5] Chromosome 22 is also considered a likely culprit.

Other genes have been linked to bipolar disorders in small studies, many of which have not been successfully repeated by other researchers to check for accuracy (replicated). These genes may have no involvement at all, or they may only be involved in a small number of persons with a bipolar disorder. In the second column of the table below, these sites are listed in parenthesis.

Genes linked to conditions that may occur more often in persons with bipolar disorders may also play a role in specific cases; they are listed in four separate columns.

It's important to understand that inheriting bipolar genes may only confer susceptibility to the disorder—it may be necessary for something else to happen for those genes to be expressed. That might be a viral infection, extreme stress, an injury, or some other environmental factor. As the identical twin studies mentioned earlier show, not everyone who carries the genes will have a bipolar disorder.

Chromosomes that may be linked to bipolar disorders	Specific genes on those chromosomes that may be linked	Velo-cardio-facial syndrome (VCFS)	Schizophrenia	ADD/ADHD	Other disorders that may be genetically linked
1			1q21-1q22		
4	(4q35)				Autistic-spectrum disorders (5q22.1; duplications)
5	(D5S392: Gene near dopamine transporter gene [DAT])				Autistic-spectrum disorders (6p21.3-6p21.3: complement C4 protein gene; duplications)
6			6p22-6p24		
8			8p21		Autistic-spectrum disorders (9q34)
9					
10			10p11-10p15		
11	(Gene for tyrosine hydroxylase)		Dopamine receptor 2 gene (11q22, 11q23)	Dopamine receptor 2 gene (11q22, 11q23)	Alcoholism (11q22, 11q23)
12	(12q23, 12q24)				
13			13q32		Autistic-spectrum disorders
15					Autistic-spectrum disorders (GABA receptor genes, 15q11-13, duplications)

Chromosomes that may be linked to bipolar disorders	Specific genes on those chromosomes that may be linked	Velo-cardio-facial syndrome (VCFS)	Schizophrenia	ADD/ADHD	Other disorders that may be genetically linked
17	Serotonin transporter gene: 5-HTT (D17S798)				Depression, autistic-spectrum disorders, post-partum psychosis (5-HTT)
18	D18S453, D18S37, D18S40, D18S45		D18S53		
21	(21q22)				
22	D22S278 22q11 deletion or variation, including catechol O-methyltransferase (COMT) gene	22q11 deletion, COMT gene	22q11, COMT gene, gene for WKL1 protein		Alcoholism, OCD (COMT gene)
X and Y	(X-linked MAO type B gene)				Substance abuse (X-linked gene affecting MAO receptors) Autistic-spectrum disorders (Fragile X, MECP2, HRAS)

Persons with bipolar disorders who find through genetic testing that a chromosome 22 deletion or difference is involved may want to visit the Chromosome 22 Central web site at *http://www.nt.net/~a815/chr22.htm*. The site includes a library of research on chromosome 22-linked disorders, such as velo-cardio-facial syndrome and trisomy 22, links to support groups for patients and families, and a discussion group.

If you're interested in participating in genetic studies, there are many current programs that would welcome your help. Usually filling out a questionnaire and giving a blood sample are all that's required. In some cases, you may be compensated for your time.

Contact NIMH (listed in Appendix A, *Resources*) or one of the following for more information:

The National Alliance for Research on Schizophrenia and Depression (NARSAD)
60 Cutter Mill Road, Suite 404
Great Neck, NY 10021
(516) 829-0091
Fax: (516) 487-6930
info@narsad.org
http://www.mhsource.com/narsad/bd/bipres.html

NARSAD funds researchers at several different sites in the US and Canada and around the world. Some projects are purely genetic; others cover medication responsiveness, brain function studies, and other aspects of bipolar disorders.

Collaborative Genomic Study
Washington University School of Medicine
(888) 292-1210
http://www.psychiatry.wustl.edu/bipolar/

Bipolar Disorder Genetics Research Project
University of Chicago
Department of Psychiatry
5841 S. Maryland Avenue, MC 3077
Chicago, IL 60637
(773) 834-3493 (collect calls are accepted)
Contact: Gail King
http://psychiatry.uchicago.edu/research/family-bipolar.html

Indiana University
Institute of Psychiatric Research
(312) 274-0173
http://www.iuinfo.indiana.edu/HomePages/111398/text/genetics.htm

Diagnostic Tests

THE DIAGNOSIS of bipolar disorders is mostly a matter of observation, collecting data, and matching symptoms with established criteria. This process is covered in Chapter 2, *Getting a Diagnosis,* along with the criteria most frequently used.

Standardized questionnaires, tests, and instruments designed to measure everything from symptom severity to intelligence may also have a place in the diagnostic process, however. This Appendix presents several types of tests that your doctor or diagnostic team may request. Many of these are also used by disability benefits programs and vocational assessment professionals.

If you are curious about your symptoms and would like to try a self-test, the National Depression and Manic Depression Association (NDMDA) offers a Mood Disorder Questionnaire online at *http://www.ndmda.org/screening_intro.asp.* This screening instrument is not appropriate for diagnosis, but it can help you understand the severity of symptoms you may be experiencing and indicate if you should seek medical treatment.

Psychiatric and neurological assessments

Some of these tests are highly clinical instruments used to tell disorders with similar symptoms apart or to diagnose disorders like ADHD or developmental delay that may coexist with bipolar disorders. Others are more subjective and are used by therapists and other non-physicians to rank behavior problems or uncover emotional difficulties.

Like the Rorschach Blot interpretation test, which is rarely used anymore, tests for emotional disturbance that ask people to make a picture and interpret what they've drawn are highly subjective. These projective tests have little use in diagnosing bipolar disorders, but are sometimes administered as part of a routine work-up.

No test should ever be used as the sole means of diagnosing or measuring emotional disturbance. The following is a list of tests sometimes used to help the diagnostic team get more information.

- Aberrant Behavior Checklist (ABC). One of the most popular behavioral checklists, the ABC also has a good reputation for accuracy. Versions are available for children and adults. Scores are expressed as scales in the areas of irritability and agitation, lethargy and social withdrawal, stereotypic behavior, hyperactivity and noncompliance, and inappropriate speech.

- Attention Deficit Disorders Evaluation Scale. Versions of this questionnaire about behaviors linked with ADD/ADHD are available for use by adults as well as for diagnosing children. Scores are expressed as a scale.

- DuPaul AD/HD Rating Scale. This instrument rates the severity of ADHD symptoms. Scores are expressed as a scale.

- **House-Tree-Person Projective Drawing Technique.** In this projective test, the patient is asked to draw a house, a tree, and a person, and then is asked a series of questions about these drawings. Sometimes these drawings are separate; sometimes they are done on a single page. Ratings are subjective interpretations, not objective measures.

- **Kiddie-Sads-Present and Lifetime Version (K-SADS-PL).** This test is designed to obtain severity ratings of symptoms and to assess current and lifetime history of psychiatric disorders in children and adolescents; it may be appropriate for use with older teens and some adults. It includes a questionnaire and a structured interview. There are supplemental tests for various types of disorders, including ADHD and affective disorders. Results are scaled.

- **Luria-Nebraska Neuropsychological Battery (LNNB).** The LNNB contains eleven scales with a total of 149 test items, which measure motor skills, rhythm, tactile performance, visual acuity, receptive speech, expressive language, writing, reading, arithmetic, memory, intelligence, and the maturation level of the brain areas that help people control their behavior. Each test item is scored on a scale, and a total scale for all items is also derived.

- **Mood Disorder Questionnaire (MDQ).** Based on the longer Primary Care Evaluation of Mental Disorders (PRIME-MD), the MDQ is a short screening instrument for use by primary care physicians.

- **Psychiatric Assessment Schedule for Adults with Developmental Disability (PAS-ADD).** Used primarily in the UK, this is a self-reporting questionnaire used to assess psychiatric state in people with developmental delay, learning disability, neurobiological disorders, or senility, among other conditions. Score is expressed as a scale.

- **Reitan-Indiana Neuropsychological Test Battery (RINTB).** These may be the most widely used neuropsychological tests and are intended to look for signs of brain damage. The RINTB contains the following tests: category, tactile performance, finger oscillation, sensory-perceptual measures, aphasia screening, grip strength, lateral dominance examination, color form, progressive figures, matching pictures, target, individual performance, and marching. Results are usually expressed as a scale (the Neuropsychological Deficit Scale). Additional information about right-left dominance or performance patterns may also be derived.

- **Structured Clinical Interview for DSM-IV (SCID).** The SCID is a set of interview questions for in-person or telephone interviews. As its name indicates, it's based on the DSM-IV; it is used to help identify and categorize persons who present with psychiatric symptoms.

- **Vineland Adaptive Behavior Scales.** These tests measure personal and social skills from birth to adulthood, using a semi-structured interview with the patient and/or a caregiver. Social and behavioral maturity in four major areas—communication, daily living skills, socialization, and motor skills—is assessed. Responses are rated on a 100-point scale for each area, and a composite score is also provided. Scores can be translated into developmental or mental ages.

- **Zeigler Rating Scale for Mania.** The Zeigler scale helps doctors or psychiatrists rate the presence and severity of manic symptoms. Scores are expressed on a scale from 0 to 4, with a higher score correlating to more severe mania. This test is also available online at *http://www.mhsource.com/disorders/zieglerrating.html*.

IQ, development, and academic tests

Some school and medical programs require IQ testing for all newcomers. Don't let these tests or scores give you too much worry: repeated studies have shown that IQs can and do change when they are measured differently or when a person is taught differently and then re-tested. Some people may find these tests especially difficult. For example, a person with hand tremor due to medication may perform poorly at tests of skill and dexterity, such as fitting pegs into a board.

IQ testing has been supplanted in some programs by tests that measure adaptive behavior, which can be loosely described as how well and how quickly a person can come up with a solution to a problem and carry it out. These provide a more realistic measure of intelligence as most people think of it, as opposed to measuring cultural knowledge.

Developmental tests rank the individual's development against the norm, often resulting in a mental age or developmental age score. Some of the tests listed in the "Psychiatric and neurological assessments" section in this appendix also chart a patient's developmental stage.

Academic testing is used with adults to identify undiscovered learning disabilities, design transition programs for teenagers and adults re-entering the workplace after becoming disabled, and design adult learning programs. Some clinicians like to compare the results of various types of tests, a practice that provides a picture of actual achievement against the background of supposed innate capability.

Following is a list of some intelligence, developmental, and academic tests in common use.

- **Leiter International Performance Scale, Revised (Leiter-R).** This non-verbal IQ test has puzzle-type problems for the areas of visual, spatial, and language-based reasoning. It produces scaled results.

- **Peabody Individual Achievement Test (PIAT).** These short tests measure performance in reading, writing, spelling, and math. Scores are expressed as a grade level.

- **Stanford-Binet Intelligence Test, Fourth Edition (S-B IV).** This intelligence test relies less on verbal answers than some. The score is expressed as an IQ number or as a scale.

- **Vineland Adaptive Behavior Scales.** A standardized measure of adaptive behavior, the Vineland scale tests problem-solving and cognitive skills. Scores are presented as a scale, IQ-style number, or age equivalent.

- **Weschler Adult Intelligence Scale (WAIS-R).** The Weschler Scale is an intelligence test that uses age-appropriate word-based activities and mechanical, puzzle-like activities to test problem-solving skills. It returns scores for verbal IQ and performance IQ, which may be broken down into several categories.

- **Wide Range of Assessment Test, Revision 3 (WRAT 3).** This standardized test determines academic level in reading, writing, spelling, and math. Scores are expressed as raw numbers or grade level equivalents.

- **Kaufman Adolescent-Adult Intelligence Test (KAIT).** This is a general test of intelligence for persons aged 11 through 85. It tests reasoning and planning skills, auditory comprehension, and mental status. A short version of this test, the Kaufman Brief Intelligence Test (K-BIT), is also available. Scores for each of the KAIT's ten sections are returned as age-based scales.

- Woodcock-Johnson Psycho Educational Battery, Revised (WJPEB-R, WJ-R). An individual test of educational achievement in reading, writing, spelling, and math, the WJ-R has many sub-tests that can be given as a group or separately. Standard scores are derived that compare the test-taker against US norms; they can also be expressed as an age or grade-level equivalency. One popular sub-test, the Scales of Independent Behavior-Revised (SIB-R/Woodcock-Johnson Battery, Part IV) is a standardized measure of adaptive behavior. SIB-R scores are raw numbers similar to IQ scores, but may be shown as a grade or age equivalency.

Notes

Chapter 1: What Are Bipolar Disorders?

1. J. D. Lish, et al. "The National Depressive and Manic-Depressive Association (DMDA) Survey of Bipolar Members," *Journal of Affective Disorders* 31 (1994): 281–294.

2. Hagop S. Akiskal, MD, A. H. Djenderedjian, R. H. Rosenthal, and M. K. Khani. "Cyclothymic Disorder: Validating Criteria for Inclusion in the Bipolar Affective Group." *American Journal of Psychiatry* 134 (1977): 1227–1233.

3. Margaret L. Moline, et al., editors. "Premenstrual Dysphoric Disorder: A Guide for Patients and Families," *A Postgraduate Medicine Special Report* (*Expert Consensus Guideline Series*), McGraw Hill (March 2001): 108–109: *http://www.psychguides.com/DinW%20PMDD.pdf*.

4. Hagop S. Akiskal, MD, et al. "Re-evaluating the Prevalence of and Diagnostic Composition Within the Broad Clinical Spectrum of Bipolar Disorders." *Journal of Affective Disorders* 59 (Supplement 1, 2000): 5s–30s; and written comments to the author.

5. G. Perugi, Hagop S. Akiskal, MD, et al. "Clinical Subtypes of Bipolar Mixed States: Validating a Broader European Definition in 143 Cases." *Journal of Affective Disorders* 43 (1997): 169–180.

6. Hagop S. Akiskal, MD (editor). *Bipolarity: Beyond Classic Mania.* Philadelphia: Psychiatric Clinics of North America/W. B. Saunders, September 1999.

7. T. A. Wehr and N. E. Rosenthal. "Seasonality and Affective Illness," *American Journal of Psychiatry* 146 (1989): 829–839.

8. National Depressive and Manic Depressive Association. "In Bipolar Illness: Rapid Cycling and Its Treatment," Revised (1996.) Chicago, IL: National NDMA: *http://www.ndmda.org/rapidcyc.htm*.

9. Ellen Leibenluft, MD. "Circadian Rhythms Factor in Rapid-Cycling Bipolar Disorder," *Psychiatric Times* 8 (5) (May 1996): *http://www.mhsource.com/edu/psytimes/p960533.html*.

10. Charles Nemeroff. "The Neurobiology of Depression," *Scientific American* (June 1998): *http://www.sciam.com/1998/0698issue/0698nemeroff.html*.

11. J. Rice, et al. "The Familial Transmission of Bipolar Illness," *Archives of General Psychiatry* 44 (1987): 441–447.

12. M. Strober. "Relevance of Early Age-of-Onset in Genetic Studies of Bipolar Affective Disorder," *Journal of the American Academy of Child and Adolescent Psychiatry* 31 (1992): 606–610.

13. Demitri F. Papolos, MD, et al. "Bipolar Spectrum Disorders in Patients Diagnosed with Velo-Cardio-Facial Syndrome: Does a Hemizygous Deletion of Chromosome 22q11 Result in Bipolar Affective Disorder?," *American Journal of Psychiatry* 153 (1996): 1541–1547.

14. Aziz Sancar, MD. "Cryptochrome: The Second Photoactive Pigment in the Eye and its Role in Circadian Photoreception," *Annual Reviews of Biochemistry* 69 (2000): 31–67.

15. Arline Kaplan. "Imaging Studies Provide Insights into Neurobiology of Bipolar Disorders," *Bipolar Disorders Letter* (February 1998): *http://www.mhsource.com/bipolar/bp9802image.html*.

16. J. Kerbeshian, L. Burd, and M. G. Klug. "Comorbid Tourette's Disorder and Bipolar Disorder: An Etiologic Perspective," *American Journal of Psychiatry* 152 (11) (November 1995): 1646–51.

17. E. H. Aylward, et al. "Basal Ganglia Volumes and White Matter Hyperintensities in Bipolar Disorder," *American Journal of Psychiatry* 151 (1994): 687–693.

18. L. R. Baxter, et al. "Caudate Glucose Metabolic Rate Changes with Both Drug and Behavior Therapy for OCD," *Archives of General Psychiatry* 49 (1992): 681–689.

19. F. A. Elliot. "The Episodic Dyscontrol Syndrome and Aggression," *Neurologic Clinics* 2 (1984): 113–125.

20. Robert M. Post, D. R. Rubinow, and J. C. Ballenger. "Conditioning and Sensitization in the Longitudinal Course of Affective Illness," *British Journal of Psychiatry* 149 (1986): 191–201.

21. R. W. Kupka, M. H. J. Hillegers, W. A. Nolen, N. Breunis, and H. A. Drexhage. "Immunological Aspects of Bipolar Disorder," *Acta Neuropsychiatrica* 12 (2000): 86–90.

22. Gay Men's Health Crisis. "Treatment Issues Fact Sheet: Toxoplasmosis," New York: GMHC (1995): *http://www.gmhc.org/living/treatment/toxo.html.*

23. Robert H. Yolken and E. Fuller Torrey. "Viruses, Schizophrenia, and Bipolar Disorder," *Clinical Microbiology Reviews* (January 1995): 131–145.

24. *Ibid.*

25. Jay D. Amsterdam, MD, et al. "A Possible Anti-Viral Action of Lithium Carbonate in Herpes Simplex Virus Infections," *Biological Psychiatry* 27 (1990): 447–453.

26. S. C. Sonne and K. T. Brady. "Substance Abuse and Bipolar Comorbidity," *Psychiatric Clinics of North America* 22, No. 3 (1999): 609–627.

27. Kathleen Brady, MD. "Substance Abuse and Bipolar Disorder," Presentation to the 9th Annual US Psychiatric & Mental Health Congress, *Medscape Online Coverage* (November 14–17, 1996): *http://www.medscape.com/Medscape/CNO/1996/ PsychCongress/11.15.96/1115.2b.html.*

28. *Ibid.*

29. Katherine Brady, MD, and R. B. Lydiard. "Bipolar Affective Disorder and Substance Abuse," *Journal of Clinical Psychopharmacology* 12 (1) (1992): 17–22.

30. Elizabeth Costello, MD. "Child Psychiatric Disorders and Their Correlates: A Primary Care Pediatric Sample," *Journal of the American Academy of Child and Adolescent Psychiatry* 28 (1989b): 851–855.

31. Anne Brown, "Mood Disorders in Children and Adolescents," *NARSAD Research Newsletter* (Winter 1996): *http://www.mhsource.com/advocacy/ narsad/childmood.html.*

32. Jennifer Ianthe Downey, MD. "Recognizing the Range of Mood Disorders in Women," *Medscape Women's Health* 1 (8) (1996): *http://www.medscape. com/Medscape/WomensHealth/journal/1996/v01. n08/w159.downey/w159.downey.html.*

33. National Alliance for the Mentally Ill. "The Criminalization of Mental Illness: Where We Stand," Arlington, VA: NAMI (2001): *http://www.nami.org/ update/unitedcriminal.html.*

34. Kelley Suttenfield, editor. "Current Topic Review: National Strategy for Suicide Prevention: Goals and Objectives for Action: A Summary of Goals and Objectives Set Forth by the US Surgeon General," *Medscape Mental Health* 6 (3) (2001): *http:// www.medscape.com/medscape/psychiatry/journal/ 2001/v06.n03/mh0511.sutt/mh0511.sutt.html.*

Chapter 3: Differential Diagnosis

1. Jane Wozniak, J. Biederman, and K. Kiely, et al. "Mania-like Symptoms Suggestive of Childhood-Onset Bipolar Disorder in Clinically Referred Children," *Journal of the American Academy of Child and Adolescent Psychiatry* 34 (1995): 867–876.

2. Demitri F. Papolos, MD, and Janet Papolos. "Night Terrors in Children With Bipolar Disorder," *The Bipolar Child Newsletter* 4 (July 2000): *http://www. bipolarchild.com/newsletters/0007.html.*

3. D. E. Nease, R. J. Volk, and A. R. Cass. "Investigation of a Severity-Based Classification of Mood and Anxiety Symptoms in Primary Care Patients," *Journal of the American Board of Family Practice* 12 (1999): 21–31.

4. M. Kovacs and M. Pollack. "Bipolar Disorder and Comorbid Conduct Disorder in Childhood and Adolescence," *Journal of the American Academy of Child and Adolescent Psychiatry* 34 (6) (1995): 715–723.

5. Stephanie Kasen, et al. "Childhood Depression and Adult Personality Disorder: 'Alternative Pathways of Continuity'," *Archives of General Psychiatry* 58 (2001): 231–236.

6. Annie M. Paul. "Painting Insanity Black: Why Are There More Black Schizophrenics?," *Salon* (Dec. 1, 1999): *http://www.salon.com/books/it/1999/12/01/ schizo/.*

7. The Thyroid Society for Education and Research. "Can Depression Be Caused by Thyroid Disease?," Houston, TX: The Thyroid Society (1996): *http:// www.the-thyroid-society.org/faq/.*

Chapter 4: Medical Care

1. Paul Perry. "Clinical Psychopharmacology Seminar: Lithium Intoxication," University of Iowa (1996): *http://www.vh.org/Providers/Conferences/CPS/32.html.*

2. Maura Lerner. "The Secret Behind Drug Side Effects May be in Your Genes," *Minneapolis-St. Paul Star Tribune,* November 15, 2000.

3. *Ibid.*

4. Alan Brier, MD. Data presented at The International Congress on Schizophrenia Research (May 3, 2001): *http://www.pslgroup.com/dg/1f9e2e.htm.*

5. G. D. Tollefson, et al. "Blind, Controlled, Long-Term Study of the Comparative Incidence of Treatment-Emergent Tardive Dyskinesia with Olanzapine or Haloperidol," *American Journal of Psychiatry* 154 (9) (1997): 1248–1254.

6. Michael W. Miller. "A Little Lithium May Be Just What the Doctor Ordered," *Wall Street Journal* (September 23, 1994): *http://www.pendulum.org/meds/lithium_wsj.htm.*

7. Jay D. Amsterdam, MD, et al. "A Possible Anti-Viral Action of Lithium Carbonate in Herpes Simplex Virus Infections," *Biological Psychiatry* 27 (1990): 447–453.

8. B. Lubrich and D. von Calker. "Inhibition of the High-Affinity Myo-Inositol Transport System: A Common Mechanism of Action of Antibipolar Drugs?," *Neuropsychopharmacology* 21 (4) (October 1999): 519–529: *http://biopsychiatry.com/inosbi.htm.*

9. B. Tudorache and S. Diacicov. "The Effect of Clonidine in the Treatment of Acute Mania," *The Romanian Journal of Neurology and Psychiatry* 29 (3–4) (July 1991): 209–213.

10. P. J. Pizzaglia, R. M. Post, and T. A. Ketter, et al. "Nimodipine Monotherapy and Carbamazepine Augmentation in Patients with Refractory Recurrent Affective Illness," *Journal of Clinical Psychopharmacology* 18 (5) (October 1998): 404–413.

11. Peter M. Brigham. "Psychopharmacology of Bipolar Disorder," (2001): *http://people.ne.mediaone.net/pmbrig/BP_pharm.html.*

12. L. Bobo, et al. "Correlation of Schizophrenia and Bipolar Disorder with Cytokine and Cytokine Receptors in the Ventricular Fluids and Post-morten Brain Tissue," (abstract), Baltimore, MD: Stanley Neurovirology Laboratory (1996): *http://www.stanleylab.org/Document/bobo%20abstract%201996%20mtg.htm.*

13. Kupka, op cit.

14. Howard S. Shapiro, MD. "Depression in Lupus," Rockville, MD: Lupus Foundation of America Inc. (1995): *http://www.lupus.org/topics/depression.html.*

15. National Institutes of Mental Health. "NIMH Fact Sheet: Depression and HIV," Bethesda, MD: NIMH (2000): *http://www.nimh.nih.gov/publicat/hivdepression.cfm.*

16. "More Uses for 'Miracle Drug,' Lithium, Sought in its 50th Year," *Psychopharmacology Update* 10 (1) (1999): 1–2.

17. M. G. Gordon, et al. "Understanding HIV-Related Risk Among Persons with a Severe and Persistent Mental Illness," *The Journal of Nervous and Mental Disease* 187 (4) (1999): 208–216.

18. Mirella Salvatore, S. Morzunov, M. Schwemmle, W. Ian Lipkin, and the Bornavirus Study Group. "Borna Disease Virus in Brains of North American and European People with Schizophrenia and Bipolar Disorder," *Lancet* 349: 1813–1814.

19. Yolken, op cit.

20. *Ibid.*

21. F. K. Goodwin and Kay Redfield Jamison. *Manic-Depressive Illness.* New York: Oxford University Press (1990.)

22. Russell Joffe, MD, and A. J. Levitt, MD. *The Thyroid Axis and Psychiatric Illness.* Washington, DC: American Psychiatric Press (1993).

Chapter 5: Talk Therapy

1. Edward Dolnick. *Madness on the Couch: Blaming the Victim in the Heyday of Psychoanalysis.* New York: Simon & Schuster (1998): 39.

2. Baxter, op cit.

3. N. A. Huxley, S. V. Parikh, and R. J. Baldessarini. "Effectiveness of Psychosocial Treatments in Bipolar Disorder: State of the Evidence," *Harvard Review of Psychiatry* 8 (3) (2000): 126–140.

4. Arline Kaplan. "Adjunctive Psychotherapy for Bipolar Depression," *Psychiatric Times* 17 (7) (July 2001): *http://www.mhsource.com/pt/p010746.html.*

5. Gary Sachs, MD. "Bipolar Mood Disorder: Practical Strategies for Acute and Maintenance Phase Treatment," *Journal of Clinical Psychopharmacology* 16 (supplement 1) (April 1996): S32–S47.

Chapter 6:
Complementary Therapies

1. National Institutes of Health. "Acupuncture," *NIH Consensus Statement* 15 (5) (November 1997): 1–34: *http://odp.od.nih.gov/consensus/cons/107/107_statement.htm*.

2. Y. Li, G. Tougas, S. G. Chiverton, and R. H. Hunt. "The Effect of Acupuncture on Gastrointestinal Function and Disorders," *American Journal of Gastroenterology* 87 (10) (1992): 1372–1381.

3. National Institutes of Health, op cit.

4. Karen Dale Dustman. "Margot Kidder's Search for Sanity," *Natural Health* (March 2000): *http://www.karendustman.com/Magazine_Clips/Search_for_Sanity/search_for_sanity.html*.

5. National Council Against Health Fraud. "Homeopathy: A Position Statement by the National Council Against Health Fraud," Loma Linda, CA: National Council Against Health Fraud (1994): *http://www.skeptic.com/03.1.jarvis-homeo.html*.

6. R. W. Lam, E. M. Tam, and A. J. Levitt. "Treatment of Seasonal Affective Disorder: A Review," *Canadian Journal of Psychiatry* 40 (1995): 457–466.

7. R. W. Lam, et al. "Low Electrooculographic Ratios in Patients with Seasonal Affective Disorder," *American Journal of Psychiatry* 148 (1991): 1526–1529.

8. M. Terman, J. S. Terman, F. M. Quitkin, et al. "Light Therapy for Seasonal Affective Disorder: A Review of Efficacy," *Neuropsychopharmacology* 2 (1) (1989): 1–22.

9. H. McGrath, P. Martinez-Osuna, and F. A. Lee. "Ultraviolet-A1 (340-400 nm) Irradiation Therapy in Systemic Lupus Erythematosus," *Lupus* 5 (4) (August 1996): 269–274.

10. Ellen Leibenluft, MD. "Circadian Rhythms Factor in Rapid-Cycling Bipolar Disorder," *Psychiatric Times* 8 (5) (May 1996): *http://www.mhsource.com/edu/psytimes/p960533.html*.

11. C. Colombo, F. Benedetti, B. Barbini, E. Campori, and E. Smeraldi. "Rate of Switch from Depression into Mania after Therapeutic Sleep Deprivation in Bipolar Depression," *Psychiatry Research* 86 (3) (June 30, 1999): 267–270.

12. Leibenluft, op cit.

13. S. H. Kennedy. "Melatonin and Cortisol 'Switches' During Mania, Depression, and Euthymia in a Drug Free Bipolar Patient," *Journal of Nervous and Mental Disease* 177 (5) (May l989): 300–303.

14. Aziz Sancar and Yasuhide Miyamoto. "Vitamin B2-based Blue-light Photoreceptors in the Retinohypothalamic Tract as the Photoactive Pigments for Setting the Circadian Clock in Mammals," *Proceedings of the National Academy of Sciences* 95 (11) (May 26, 1998): 6097–6102.

15. R. W. Lam, R. D. Levitan, E. M. Tam, L. N. Yatham, S. Lamoureua, and A. P. Zis. "L-tryptophan Augmentation of Light Therapy in Patients with Seasonal Affective Disorder," *Canadian Journal of Psychiatry* 42 (3) (April 1997): 303–306.

16. C. Benkelfat, et al. "Tryptophan Depletion in Stable Lithium-Treated Patients with Bipolar Disorder in Remission," *Archives of General Psychiatry* 52 (February 1995): 154–155.

17. Andrew L. Stoll, MD, et al. "Omega 3 Fatty Acids in Bipolar Disorder: a Preliminary Double-Blind, Placebo-controlled Trial," *Archives of General Psychiatry* 56 (5) (May 1999): 407–412.

18. E. Sacchetti, L. Guarneri, and D. Bravi. "H2 Antagonist Nizatidine May Control Olanzapine-Associated Weight Gain in Schizophrenic Patients," *Biological Psychiatry* 48 (2000): 167–168.

19. S. M. Dursun and S. Devarajan. "Clozapine Weight Gain, Plus Topiramate Weight Loss," [letter] *Canadian Journal of Psychiatry* 45 (2000): 198.

20. E. M. Cottingham, J. A. Morrison, and B. A. Barton. "Metformin Leads to Weight-Loss in Pediatric Patients on Psychotropic Drugs," [abstract] presented at the 47th Annual Meeting of the American Academy of Child and Adolescent Psychiatry in New York, NY (October 24–29, 2000).

21. J. P. Van Wouwe. "Carnitine Deficiency during Valproic Acid Treatment," *International Journal for Vitamin and Nutrition Research* 65 (1995): 211–214.

22. M. E. Nurge, C. R. Anderson, and E. Bates. "Metabolic and Nutritional Implications of Valproic Acid," *Nutrition Research* 11 (1991): 949–960.

23. H. Igisu, M. Matsuoka and Y. Iryo. "Protection of the Brain by Carnitine," *Sangyo Eiseigaku Zasshi* 37 (2) (March 1995): 75–82.

24. D. C. De Vivo, T. P. Bohan, and D. L. Coulter, et al. "L-carnitine Supplementation in Childhood Epilepsy: Current Perspectives," *Epilepsia* 39 (1998): 1216–1225.

25. J. A. Blumenthal, et al. "Effects of Exercise Training on Older Patients with Major Depression," *Archives of Internal Medicine* 159 (19) (October 1999): 2349–2356.

26. K. J. Rix, et al. "Food Antibodies in Acute Psychoses," *Psychological Medicine* 15 (2) (1985): 347–354.

27. W. P. King, R. G. Fadal, W. A. Ward, R. J. Trevino, W. B. Pierce, J. A. Stewart, et al. "Provocation-Neutralization: a Two-Part Study. Part II. Subcutaneous Neutralization Therapy: a Multi-Center Study," *Otolaryngology and Head and Neck Surgery* 99 (1988): 272–277.

28. Chouinard, G., et al. "Estrogen-Progesterone Combination: Another Mood Stabilizer?" *American Journal of Psychiatry*, 144 (June 1987): 826.

29. J. M. Bebchuk, C. L. Arfken, S. Dolan-Manji, J. M. Murphy, and H. K. Manji. "A Preliminary Investigation of a Protein Kinase C Inhibitor (Tamoxifen) in the Treatment of Acute Mania," presented at the American College of Neuropsychopharmacology (1997).

30. D. S. Reddy and M. A. Rogawski. "Enhanced Anticonvulsant Activity of Ganaxolone after Neurosteroid Withdrawal in a Rat Model of Catamenial Epilepsy," *Journal of Pharmacology and Experimental Therapeutics* 294 (3) (September 2000): 909–915.

31. Yolken, op cit.

32. I Dé, et al., and The Stanley Neuropathology Consortium. "Detection of Viral Particles in Glial Cells Inoculated with Brain Tissue From Individuals with Schizophrenia and Bipolar Disease," [abstract] (1997): *http://www.med.jhu.edu/stanleylab/*.

33. Daily University Science News. "Nutritional Supplement Of Benefit In Bipolar Disorder," Cape Coral, FL: UniSci (October 9, 2000): *http://unisci.com/stories/20004/1009006.htm*.

34. A. O. Ogunmekan. "Vitamin E Deficiency and Seizures in Animals and Man," *Canadian Journal of Neurological Science* 6 (1979): 43–45.

35. P. Etienne, D. Dastoor, and S. Gauthier, et al. "Alzheimer's Disease: Lack of Effect of Lecithin Treatment for Three Months," *Neurology* 31 (1981): 1552–1554.

36. B. M. Cohen, et al. "Lecithin in the Treatment of Mania: Double-blind, Placebo-controlled Trials," *American Journal of Psychiatry* 139 (1982): 1162–1164.

37. M. Fux, J. Benjamin, and R. H. Belmaker. "Inositol Versus Placebo Augmentation of Serotonin Reuptake Inhibitors in the Treatment of Obsessive-Compulsive Disorder: a Double-Blind Cross-Over Study," *International Journal of Neuropsychopharmacology* 2 (3) (September 1999): 193–195.

38. J. Levine. "Controlled Trials of Inositol in Psychiatry," *European Neuropsychopharmacology* 7 (2) (May 1997): 147–155.

39. A. Palatnik, K. Frolov, M. Fux, and J. Benjamin. "Double-Blind, Controlled, Crossover Trial of Inositol Versus Fluvoxamine for the Treatment of Panic Disorder," *Journal of Clinical Psychopharmacology* 21 (3) (June 2001): 335–339.

40. Lucinda G. Miller. "Herbal Medicinals: Selected Clinical Considerations Focusing on Known or Potential Drug-Herb Interactions," *Archives of Internal Medicine* 9 (November 1998) and other sources.

Chapter 7: Healthcare and Insurance

1. Consumers for Quality Care. "HMO Arbitration Abuse Reports," Santa Monica, CA: The Foundation for Taxpayer and Consumer Rights (2000): *http://consumerwatchdog.org/healthcare/st/index_abuse.php3*.

Chapter 8: Living with Bipolar Disorders

1. Oregon Disabilities Commission. "Pre-Employment Disability-Related Questions and Medical Examinations Under the ADA," Salem, OR: ODC Technical Assistance Center (2001): *http://www.odc.state.or.us/tadoc/ada29.htm*.

2. Phyllis Coleman and Ronald A. Shellow. "Restricting Medical Licenses Based on Illness is Wrong—Reporting Makes It Worse," *Journal of Law and Health* 9 (2) (1994-1995): 273–302: *http://www.asam.org/phc/coleman.htm*.

3. Andrew J. Imparato (general counsel and director of policy, National Council on Disability). Testimony before the US Commission on Civil Rights, Americans with Disabilities Act Hearing in Washington, DC (November 13, 1998): *http://www.ncd.gov/newsroom/testimony/usccr_11-13-98.html*.

4. Z. N. Stowe and C. B. Nemeroff. "Women at Risk for Postpartum-Onset Major Depression," *American Journal of Obstetrics and Gynecology* 173 (2) (1995): 639–645.

5. National Center for Health Statistics. "FASTATS: Suicide," Hyattsville, MD: US Department of Health and Human Services, Centers for Disease Control (1998): *http://www.cdc.gov/nchs/fastats/suicide.htm*.

6. S. G. Simpson and Kay Redfield Jamison. "The Risk of Suicide in Patients with Bipolar Disorders," *Journal of Clinical Psychiatry* 60 (supplement 2) (1999): 53–56.

7. The Center on Crime, Communities and Culture. "Research Brief: Mental Illness in US Jails: Diverting the Non-Violent, Low-Level Offender," Occasional Paper Series 1, Open Society Institute (November 1996): *http://www.soros.org/crime/research_brief__1.html.*

8. Sally Kalson. "Clubhouse Helps the Mentally Ill Work Toward Independence," *Pittsburgh Post-Gazette* (January 28, 1999): *http://www.post-gazette.com:80/magazine/19990128clubhouse1.asp.*

Appendix B

1. J. Kelsoe. "The Genetics of Bipolar Disorder," *Psychiatric Annals* 27 (1997): 285–292.

2. National Alliance for the Mentally Ill—Vermont. "Family to Family Education Program," Arlington, VA: NAMI (1990).

3. NIMH Genetics Workgroup. "NIH Publication No. 98-4268: Genetics and Mental Disorders," Rockville, MD: National Institutes of Mental Health (1998).

4. National Alliance for the Mentally Ill, op cit.

5. Wade Berrettini, MD. "Latest Findings on Human Chromosome 18 in Bipolar Illness," Presentation to the Second Annual Conference on Bipolar Disorder in Pittsburgh, PA: (June 1997).

Index

American Board of Medical Specialties, 28
  orthomolecular physicians, 173
American Board of Professional Psychology, 146
American Board of Psychiatry and Neurology, 28
American College of Rheumatology, 50
American Group Psychotherapy Association, 148
American Home products, 312
American Osteopathy Association, 174
American Psychiatric Association Axis system, 6–7
American Psychological Association (APA), 248
American Society for Clinical Nutrition (ASCN), 185
American Society for Nutritional Sciences
  (RSNS), 185
Americans with Disabilities Act (ADA), 263, 266–268
Amgen, 312
Amino acids
  profile, 195
  supplements, 201–203
Amitriptyline. See Elavil
Amitriptyline/chlordiazepoxide, 109
Amitriptylyne/perphenazine, 114
Amoxapine, 107
Amphetamines, 58
Ampligen, 196
Amygdala, 18
Anafranil
  general information on, 106–107
  grapefruit juice and, 76
  for unipolar depression, 49
Androgen, 52
Anesthesia, medication interactions, 75
Anger. See also Rages
  in conduct disorder (CD), 49
  destructiveness and, 45
Anorexia nervosa, 184, 252
Antabuse, 121
Anthemis nobilis, 179
Anticholinesterase inhibitors, 128
Antidepressants, 102–105. See also Selective
    Serotonin Reuptake Inhibitors (SSRIs);
    Tricyclic antidepressants
  Caucasians and, 82
  for fibromyalgia, 51, 131
  low dosages, 75
  MAOIs (monoamineoxidase inhibitors), 112–113
  sensitivity to, 71
  for unipolar depression, 49
Antigens, 194
Antihistamines, 53
  allergy testing and, 188
Anti-Neuronal Antibody screen, 194
Antioxidants
  as antivirals, 196
  with essential fatty acids (EFAs), 182
Antipsychotics. See Neuroleptics
Anti-suicide contracts, 254

Antivirals, 192–197. See also AIDS
  for fibromyalgia, 131
  herbal antivirals/antibiotics, 196–197
Anxiety disorders, 24, 47–48
  medications for, 122–127
A-1 ultraviolet wavelength treatment, 175
Appeals
  health insurance denials, 224–228
  Supplement Security Income (SSI), denial of, 232
Arachidonic acid (AA), 180–181
Arachnophobia, 47
Arbitration of denial of insurance coverage, 228
Aricept, 128
Arizona, public mental health agencies in, 318
Arkansas, public mental health agencies in, 318
Armour, 132
Aromatherapy, 177
Arthritis, rheumatoid, 57
Art therapy, 207
Asendin/Asendis, 107
Asia, medications approved in, 89
Aspartate transaminase, 80
Aspirin, 74
  thyroid hormones and, 132
Assertive case management, 221
Association of Relatives and Friends of the Mentally
  Ill (ARAFMI), 300
Association of State and Provincial Psychology Boards
  (ASPPB), 146
AST (aspartate amino transferase), 80
Asthma, 188–190
  inhalers, 74
  treatment of, 252
Astra-Zeneca, 312
Ativan, 68, 122–123
Attention Deficit Disorder Ontario Foundation, 306
Attention Deficit Disorders Evaluation Scale, 37, 336
Attention deficit hyperactivity disorder (ADHD), 24
  appendix listings on, 305–306
  Attention Deficit Disorders Evaluation Scale, 37
  beta-adrenergic blockers for, 127
  categories of, 45
  diagnosis of, 43–46
  Diagnostic and Statistical Manual of Mental
    Disorders (DSM-IV) criteria, 44–45
  essential fatty acids (EFAs) and, 183
  morning behaviors, 46
  stimulants for, 118
Attorneys
  Americans with Disability Act (ADA)
    protections, 269
  arbitration issues, 228
  criminal justice system and, 291
  Health Law Project, 235
  insurance companies, actions against, 228
  Supplemental Security Income (SSI) appeals, 232

Brain. *See also* Neurotransmitters
    electrical miswiring in, 22
    imaging research, 18
    parts of, 17
    structural differences in, 17–23
    substance abuse and, 57–59
    viruses and, 193
Breastfeeding, 282
Breathing exercises, 207–208
Brewer's yeast, 166
A Bright Red Scream: Self-Mutilation and the Language of Pain (Strong), 288
Bristol Myers Squibb, 312
British Columbia, public mental health agencies in, 327
British Medical Association, 311
British National Formulary, 90
Bromo Seltzer, 92
Brushing and joint compression, 207
Bulimia nervosa, 184, 252
Burproprion. *See* Wellbutrin
BuSpar, 68
    alcohol abuse, use in, 121
    for attention deficit hyperactivity disorder (ADHD), 120
    general information, 123
    grapefruit juice and, 76
    sexual side effects and, 84
Buspirone. *See* BuSpar
B vitamins, 53, 199
    sleep cycle and, 178

C

Caffeine, 119
    lithium level and, 92
Calan, 121
Calcitron, 61
Calcium acetylhomotaurinate, 121
Calcium channel blockers, 127
    lithium level and, 92
Calcium pangamate, 195
Calcium supplements, 76, 200
Calendar, use of, 30
California, public health insurance, 233–235
Calisthenics, 209
Canada
    disability income in, 237–238
    employment rights, 267
    health care in, 236–238
    homeopathy in, 170
    housing authority in, 276
    indirect financial help in, 238
    medical facilities in, 315
    naturopathic physicians in, 172
    new medications, approving, 77

public mental health agencies in, 327–328
    referral system in, 34
    support and advocacy groups, 298
    therapists, locating, 144
Canada Health Act, 236
Canadian Drug Product Database, 311
Canadian Human Rights Act, 267
Canadian Mental Health Association, 144
    appendix listing, 298
Canadian Naturopathic Association, 172
Canadian Network for Mood and Anxiety Treatments (CANMAT), 315
Canadian Psychiatric Association, 249
Cancer, complementary therapies and, 163
Candida albicans, 62
Candle breathing, 208
Canola oil, 181, 183
Capitation arrangements, 33
Carbamazepine. *See* Tegretol
Carbolith. *See* Lithium
Carbonic anhydrase inhibitors, 92
Career choices, 271–272
Careless destructiveness, 45
Carers' Taskforce Australia, Inc., 241
Carnitor, 186
Carve-out for mental health care, 215
Case management systems, 221, 280
Catalepsy, 12
Catamenial symptoms, 191
Catapres, 127
Catastrophizing, 260
    cognitive therapy for, 152
Catatonic, 12
Cat's claw as antiviral, 196
Caudate nucleus, 18
Celexa, 103
Celiac disease, 161
Centella asiatica, 198
Center for Computers Redistribution, 246
Center for Mental Health Research on AIDS Web site, 131
Center for the Study of Service, 214
Center Watch, 246
Central nervous system (CNS), 17
Centrax, 123–124
Centre for Addiction and Mental Health (CAMH), 308
Centrelink Web site, 241
Certificate of Professional Qualification in Psychology (CPG), 146
Certified Clinical Mental Health Counselor (CCMHC) certificates, 148
Certified professional counselors (CPCs), 147
Certified Public Accountants (CPAs), hiring, 279–280
Certified Rehabilitation Counselor (CRC) credentials, 148

Chamomile, 179
Chanting, prolonged, 56–57
Charitable institutions, 244
Chemotherapy, 129
Ch'i, 167, 168
Chicken pox, 23, 192
    Acyclovir and, 196
Child custody arrangements, 279
Children and Adults with Attention Deficit Disorder
        (CHADD), 305
Chinese medicine
        acupuncture, 167–168
        traditional medicine, 168–169
Chiropractic for fibromyalgia, 51
Chloral hydrate, 69
Chlordiazepoxide, 124
Choline, 202
Christian counselors, 148
Chromium picolinate, 201
Chromosomes, 16–17, 332
Chronic fatigue immune deficiency syndrome
        (CFIDS), 63
        treatments for, 131
Chronic fatigue syndrome, 63
Chronic mononucleosis syndrome (CMS), 194
Cigarette smoking
        with Ativan, 123
        Clorazil and, 116
        Luvox and, 104
        Zyban and, 113
Cimicifuga racemosa. See Black cohosh
Cipramil, 103
Circadian Lighting Association, 307
Circadian rhythms, 14–16
        nightmares and, 46
        stimulants and, 119
Citalopram, 103
Civil Rights Division, Justice Department, 268
Civil rights law, 275
Claustrophobia, 47
Cleft palate and velo-cardio-facial syndrome
        (VCFS), 17
Clinical trials, 246
Clomipramine. See Anafranil
Clonidine, 127
        for attention deficit hyperactivity disorder
            (ADHD), 120
Clozapine, 115–116
Clozaril, 115–116
        weight gain from, 186
COBRA plans, 216–217
Cocaine
        antagonists, 121
        mania and, 58
Coconut oil/butter, 183

Cod liver oil, 183
    supplements, 200
Coenzyme Q (CoQ10), 196
Cogentin, 85, 87
Cognitive therapy, 143, 152–153
Cold turkey detox, 120–121
Collaborative Genomic Study, 335
College, bipolar disorders and, 263–264
Colorado, public mental health agencies in, 319
Colors in home environment, 293
Colostrum, 184
Commission on Rehabilitation Counselor
        Certification (CRCC), 148
Community drop-in centers, 254, 294
Community Trust associations, 244
Compassionate use laws, 89
Complementary therapies, 161–209. See also Herbal
        remedies
        acupuncture, 167–168
        allergies, treatment of, 188–190
        antiviral treatments, 192–197
        appendix resources, 316–317
        art therapy, 207
        auditory integration training, 205–206
        Ayurvedic medicine, 168–169
        cautions about supplements, 203–205
        Chinese traditional medicine, 168–169
        dance therapy, 207
        diet, 184–190
        evaluating, 164
        evaluating supplements, 164–165
        herbal remedies, 197–198
        holistic psychology, 169
        homeopathy, 169–170
        hormonal treatments, 190–192
        immunotherapy, 192–197
        light therapy, 174–175
        massage, 170–172
        minerals, 200–201
        music therapy, 207
        naturopathy, 172–173
        nutritional supplements, 201–203
        occupational therapy (OT), 206
        orthomolecular medicine, 173
        osteopathy, 173–174
        in pregnancy, 163
        record keeping of, 167
        role of, 162–163
        sensory integration (SI), 206–207
        stress-busters, 207–209
        vitamins, 198–200
Complete blood count (CBC), 81
        agranulocytosis, avoiding, 84
Compounding pharmacies, 76
Compulsive disorder. See Obsessive-compulsive
        disorder (OCD)

Computers, access to, 246
Computer tomography (CAT), 18
Condoms, 280
Conduct disorder (CD), 48–49
Consumers for Quality Care, 228
Consumer's Guide to Health Plans, 214
Corn oil, 183
Corticosteroids, 53
    echinacea and, 204
Cortisol level test, 37
Cough syrups, 74
Coumadin, 204
Counselors, 34–35. *See also* Therapists
County health departments, 34, 234
Craniosacral therapy, 170–171
Cranitine, 187
Creative coding, 222
Creativity, 25–26
    hypomania and, 10
Criminal justice system, 25, 289–291
Crises, prevention of, 134–136
Crushing pills, 75
Cryptochrome, 178
Cryptosporidium, 62
Culture, effect of, 25
Cushing's disease/disorder, 49
Cutting: Understanding and Overcoming Self-Mutilation
        (Levenkrom), 288
Cyclic dosing, 103
Cyclosporine, 204
Cyclothymia, 63, 162
Cyclothymic disorder, 4–5
    premenstrual dysphoric disorder (PMDD) as, 5
Cylert, 119
Cyproheptadine, 119
Cytokines, 128
    increased levels of, 193
Cytomegalovirus (CMV), 192
    Acyclovir and, 196
    viral antibody tests, 194
Cytomel, 83, 132

D

DA. *See* Dopamine
Damiana, 197
Dance therapy, 207
Das, 119
Dawn simulation, 175
Day treatment facilities
    after hospitalization, 141
    increasing medications in, 73
Decongestants, 74
Definition of bipolar disorders, 1–2
Dehydration, lithium and, 93
Delirium tremens (DTs), 58

Delusions, 262
    depression with, 9
    paranoia, 261
    psychosis and, 14
    schizophrenia and, 60
Dendrites, 19
Depakene, 95–96
    chromium picolinate and, 201
    folic acid and, 200
    L-Carnitine and, 187
    vitamin E and, 200
    weight gain from, 186
Depakote, 69
    chromium picolinate and, 201
    folic acid and, 200
    GABA (gaba-amino butyric acid) and, 203
    general information on, 96–97
    hormonal changes and, 190–191
    L-Carnitine and, 187
    for mood swings, 50
    Prozac after, 75
    vitamin E and, 200
    weight gain from, 185, 186
Depo-Provera, 52, 190–192, 280
    for hormonal disorders, 51
Depression, unipolar, 2, 8–9, 49–50
    mixed state, 11–12
Depression and Related Affective Disorders
        Association (DRADA), 28
Depressive personality disorder, 56
Dervish dancing, 56–57
Desensitization shots, 189
Desipramine, 110
Desoxyn, 119
Destructiveness, 45
Desyrel, 113
Developmental delays, 24
Development tests, 338
Dexamethasone suppression test, 37
Dexampex, 119
Dexedrine, 119
    sexual side effects and, 84
Dexedrine Spansule formulation, 119
Dextroamphetamine/amphetamine, 119
Dextroamphetamine sulfate, 119
Dextromethorphan, 119
Dextrostat, 119
Diabetes mellitus, 50
    essential fatty acids (EFAs) and, 183
    herbal supplement cautions, 204
    treatment of, 252
Diagnoses. *See also* Differential diagnosis; Dual
        diagnosis
    of attention deficit hyperactivity disorder
        (ADHD), 43–46
    common problems, consideration of, 42–43

Family and Medical Leave Act (FMLA), 269–270
Family physicians, 27–28
Family therapy, 143, 153–155
    behavioral family management (BFM), 155
    labels in, 155
Farmer, Frances, 138
"Fat Chance" (Ablow), 185
Fat intake and mood, 185
Faverin. *See* Luvox
Federal Rehabilitation Act, 268–269
Feldenkrais, Moshe, 171
Feldenkrais method, 171
Fellow in the Academy of Clinical Psychology
        (FAClinP), 146
Feng shui, 293
Ferndex, 119
Feverfew, 203, 204
Fibromyalgia, 50–51
    occurrence of, 24
    treatments for, 131
Fibromyalgia and Bipolar Disorder Web site, 131
Fibrositis disease. *See* Fibromyalgia
Financial self-protection, 279–280
FindLaw, 304
Firearms
    careers involving, 272
    suicidal behaviors and, 287
First Nations (Native Canadian) agencies, 238
Fish, essential fatty acids (EFAs) from, 183
Fish oils, 180–184
    fish body oil, 184
    flavored fish oils, 182
    supplements, 200
5-HTP (5-hydroxytryptophan), 179
5-hydroxytryptamine or 5-HT. *See* Serotonin
Flashbacks, 58
Flatulence, 182
Flax seed oil, 180
Florida, public mental health agencies in, 319
Fluoride mouthwashes, 83
Fluoxetine. *See* Prozac
Fluvoxamine. *See* Luvox
Folic acid, 200
    cautions on, 204
    dimethylglycine (DMG) and, 195
Food allergies
    elimination/reintroduction diet for, 189–190
    rotation diet for, 190
Food and Drug Administration (FDA)
    lithium, approval of, 91
    new medications, approving, 77
    Web site, 311
Foscarnet, 196
Foundation for Taxpayer and Consumer Rights, 228
Frances, 138

Freud, Sigmund, 142–143, 144
FyrenIyce Web site, 302

G

GABA (gaba-amino butyric acid), 180, 203
Gabapentin, 98–99
    GABA (gaba-amino butyric acid) and, 203
Gabitril, 128
    general information on, 97
Gag orders, physicians bound by, 213
Gammalinolenic acid (GLA), 180
Ganaxolone, 191
Gardening, 295
Garlic, 182
    cautions on, 204
Gastrointestinal problems, 24
Gender, 24–25. *See also* Women's issues
Generalized seizures, 64
General practitioners, 29
Generic names of medications, 73
Genetech, 312
GeneTests, 310
Genetics
    appendix information on, 310, 332–335
    counseling resources, 310
    diabetes mellitus, 50
    factors involving, 16–17
Genital herpes, 23
Geodon, 83
    general information on, 117–118
    weight control and, 186
    weight gain and, 187
Georgia, public mental health agencies in, 319
Gestalt therapists, 144
GGT (gamma glutamyl transpeptidase), 80–81
Ginger, 198
    cautions on, 204
Gingko biloba
    as antiviral, 196
    for bipolar disorder, 197
    cautions on, 204
Ginseng, 198
    cautions on, 204
    diabetes and, 204
    digoxin and, 204
Glasgow Association for Mental Health, 298
Glaxo Wellcom Inc., 312
Glial cells, 18, 20
Glucophage, 187
Glucose tolerance test, 37
Glutathione, 165
Gluten-free diet, 189
Glycyrrhiza glabra. *See* Licorice
Gold, Mark, 47

Goldenseal, 197
The Good News About Depression (Gold), 47
Gotu kola, 198
Grandiose thinking, 9, 46, 61, 260–261
    criminal justice system and, 289–291
Grants for housing, 277
Grapefruit juice, medications with, 76
Grapeseed oil as antiviral, 196
Grave's disease, 163
Grievances with insurance plans, 224
Group homes, 276
Group therapy, 143, 157
    credentials for therapists, 148
Guanfacine. *See* Tenex
Guardianship arrangements, 279
Guns. *See* Firearms

H

Habitat for Humanity, 236
Habitrol, 87
Hair loss, Depakote and, 97
Halcion, 76
Haldol, 213
    liquid form, 75
    tardive dyskinesia (TD), 86
    weight gain and, 187
Hallucinations, 56
    alcohol abuse and, 58
    with mania, 9
    MAOIs (monoamineoxidase inhibitors) and, 113
    in psychosis, 12–13
    schizophrenia and, 56
Happy Camper, abuse of, 119
Harassment legislation, 275
Harvard Bipolar Research Program, 313–314
    mood chart, 257
Hawaii
    insurance in, 233–235
    mental health agencies in, 319
Hawthorn, 204
Headaches. *See also* Migraine headaches
    auras and, 66
Health Canada, 238
Health care. *See also* health insurance; HMOs (health
        maintenance organizations); Medicaid;
        Medicare; Public health care
    alternatives to insurance, 243–247
    appendix resources on, 308–309
    in Australia, 240–241
    in Canada, 236–238
    indirect financial help, 235–236
    in Ireland, 240
    medical savings accounts (MSAs), 244–245
    military health care coverage, 229–230
    in New Zealand, 242–243

public health care, 229–235
    Supplemental Security Income (SSI), 230–232
Health Care Flex Spending Accounts (FSAs),
        236–237
Health insurance, 29. *See also* HMOs (health
        maintenance organizations)
    advocacy organizations, 247–248
    alternatives to, 243–247
    appeals process, 224–228
    appendix resources on, 308–309
    arbitration of denial of coverage, 228
    assertive case management, 221
    bankrupt plans, 215
    in Canada, 236–238
    carve-out for mental health care, 215
    choices in, 211–215
    COBRA plans, 216–217
    coverage of bipolar disorders, 210–217
    creative coding, 222
    denial of coverage, fighting, 217, 223–228
    grievances, 224
    group plans, 217
    legal actions against, 228
    limits on psychiatric care, 221–222
    managing, 217–221
    new treatments, coverage of, 222–223
    in New Zealand, 242
    out-of-network provider coverage, 214
    partnering with physicians, 219–220
    phone calls, documenting, 219
    point-of-service (POS) options, 213
    questions on choosing, 212–213
    record keeping for, 218–219
    referral forms, 219
    state and local health plans, 233–235
    substandard coverage, 211
    Summary Plan Description (SPD), 213–214
    tips for dealing with, 220–221
    United Kingdom, benefits in, 239
    urgent care, obtaining, 136
    written letters of denial, 224–225
Health Law Project, 235
Heart conditions
    electrocardiogram (EKG) testing, 81
    medications and blood tests, 78–79
    velo-cardio-facial syndrome (VCFS), 17
Hemidesmus indicus, 198
Hemp-seed oil, 180, 181
Hepatitis, 63–64
    tests for, 42
The Herbal PDR, 166, 205
Herbal remedies
    antivirals/antibiotics, 196–197
    cautions about, 203–205
    medications and, 74
    for neurological disorders, 197–198

Labrador, public mental health agencies in, 327
Lamaze breathing, 208
Lamictal, 69, 98
Lamotrigine, 98
Latitude sensitivity, 6
Lauric acid, 184
Law enforcement careers, 272
L-Carnitine, 186, 187
LDS, 13
Leaps in logic, 261
Learning disabilities, 17
Lecithin, 202
Legal issues. *See also* Attorneys
    American Psychological Association (APA), action
        by, 248
    insurers, actions against, 228
    letters of intent, 278–279
    planning and, 277–280
    power of attorney, 279
    psychiatric advance directive, 277–278
Leiter International Performance Scale, Revised
    (Leiter-R), 338
Lentizol. *See* Elavil
Lethargy
    hormonal disorders and, 51
    as medication side effect, 73
Letters of intent, 278–279
Levenkrom, Steven, 288
Levothyroxine (T4), 132
Liberty Place Clubhouse Downtown, Allegheny
    County, Pennsylvania, 294
Librium, 124
Licensed professional counselors (LPCs), 147
Licorice, 198
    digoxin and, 204
Life experiences, 22
Lifestyle changes, 68
    for fibromyalgia, 131
    immune system, boosting, 129
    intensity, recapturing, 72
Light sensitivity, 6
Light therapy, 174–175
    sleep problems and, 175–177
Lilly Cares Program, 313
Limbic system of brain, 18
Limbitrol, 109
Linoleic acid, 180
Liothyronine (T3), 132
Liquiritia officinalis. *See* Licorice
Lithane. *See* Lithium
Lithium, 47, 69, 70, 88
    AIDS-bipolar disorder, 130
    Americans with Disability Act (ADA)
        protections, 269
    antiviral effects of, 23
    as antiviral treatment, 196

    blood tests for, 79–80
    calcium channel blockers and, 127
    discontinuing, 91
    facts about, 91–93
    general information on, 90–95
    hormonal disorders and, 52
    liquid form, 75
    for mood swings, 50
    Prozac after, 75
    schizophrenia and, 60
    side effects of, 70
    weight gain from, 186
Lithizine. *See* Lithium
Lithobid. *See* Lithium
Lithonate. *See* Lithium
Lithotabs. *See* Lithium
Liver. *See also* Hepatitis
    medications and testing, 78
    understanding liver function tests, 80–81
Liver function test, 37
Logic, leaps in, 261
Lorazepam, 122–123
Louisiana, public mental health agencies in, 320
L-selenomethionane, 201
L-taurine, 202
L-tryptophan, 179
Lupus, 23, 52
    A-1 ultraviolet wavelength treatment, 175
    bipolar mood swings and, 129
    mood swings and, 128–129
Lupus and Bipolar Disorder Web site, 131
Luria Nebraska Neuropsychological Battery
    (LNNB), 337
Lustral. *See* Zoloft
Lutheran Family Services clinics, 244
Luvox
    general information on, 103–104
    grapefruit juice and, 76
Lymphocyte abnormalities, 193
Lymphocyte surface markers, 194

M

McLean Hospital, Belmont, MA, 180
Magical thinking, 261
Magnesium, 201
    sleep cycle and, 178
Magnetic resonance imagery (MRI), 18
Ma Huang, 169
    abuse of, 119
Mail-order medications, 245–246
Maine, public mental health agencies in, 321
Managed care. *See* Health insurance; HMOs (health
    maintenance organizations)
Manganese, 201

Methotrexate, 129
    folic acid and, 204
Mexiletine, 128
Mexitil, 128
Midol-IB. *See* Ibuprofen
Migraine headaches
    aura, 56
    kindling process and, 22
    occurrence of, 24
Military. *See also* Tricare
    as career choice, 272–273
    health care coverage, 229–230
Milk thistle, 163
MIND (UK), 299
Minerals, 200–201
Minimization, 260
Minnesota, public mental health agencies in, 321
Mirtazapine, 113
Mississippi, public mental health agencies in, 321
Missouri, public mental health agencies in, 322
Mitogens, 194
Mixed states, 2, 11–12
    hospitalization for, 133
Mobility Allowance (UK), 239
Moclobemide, 113
Molipaxin, 113
Momordica charantia, 196
Monoamineoxidase inhibitors. *See* MAOIs
    (monoamineoxidase inhibitors)
Monolaurin, 184
Mononucleosis, 64
Montana, public mental health agencies in, 322
Montefiore Medical Center, 314
Mood and behavior diary, 37–38, 256–259, 294
    at consultation appointment, 30
    medication responses and, 77
    suicidal behaviors, watching for, 287
Mood disorder NOS, 5
Mood Disorder Questionnaire (MDQ), 337
Mood Disorders Association of British Columbia, 298
Mood Disorders Association (SA) Inc./Self-Help
    (MDP) Inc., 301
Mood stabilizers, 88–101
Mood swings, 1
    AIDS and, 62
    with diabetes, 50
    epilepsy and, 65
    hepatitis and, 64
    hormonal disorders and, 51–52
    immune disorders and, 23
    preventing, 259–260
    steroids and, 58
    toxoplasmosis and, 23
Morning behaviors, 46
Mortgage interest deductions, 237
Motipress, 107–108

Motival, 107–108
Motrin. *See* Ibuprofen
Mouth and velo-cardio-facial syndrome (VCFS),
    16–17
Mouth guards, 83
Movements, circadian rhythm and, 15
Multi-level marketing schemes, 165
Multiple diagnoses, 23–24
Multiple sclerosis (MS), 54
    neuroimmunology and, 194
Multivitamin supplements, 198–199
Mumps, 192
Music, 293, 294
    therapy, 207
Mustard-seed oil, 181
Myalgic encephalopathy (ME), 63
Myelin sheath, 202
Myofascial pain syndrome. *See* Fibromyalgia

N

Naloxone hydrochloride, 121
Narcan, 121
Narcotics Anonymous (NA), 72, 158
Nardil. *See* Phenelzine
National Alliance for Research on Schizophrenia and
    Depression (NARSAD), 335
National Alliance for the Mentally Ill (NAMI), 28, 247
    appealing denial of coverage, assistance on, 227
    appendix listing, 297
    electroconvulsive therapy (ECT) study of, 139
    medication information, 90
    psychiatric facilities, opinions on, 137
    support from, 292
    support group model, 158
    therapist qualifications, 149
National Alliance of the Relatives of the Mentally Ill
    (NARMI), 299
National Association of Insurance Commissioners
    (NAIC), 309
National Association of Protection and Advocacy
    Systems, 227, 228, 304
    legal help from, 235
    Supplement Security Income (SSI), denial of, 232
National Association of Social Workers (NASW), 147
National Board for Certified Counselors (NBCC), 148
National Center for Complementary and Alternative
    Medicine, 164, 316
National Center for Homeopathy, 170
National Certification Commission for Acupuncture
    and Oriental Medicine (NACCOM),
    168, 169
National Certified Counselor (NCC) credentials, 148
National Coalition of Mental Health Professionals and
    Consumers, 217

New Zealand, mental health agencies in, 331
  United Kingdom, agencies in, 328
  United States, agencies in, 318–326
PubMed Web site, 309
Pulse dosing, 103
Punching bags, 253
Pycogenol, 165
Pyridoxine, 199

Q

QMHA (Qualified Mental Health Associate), 149
QMHP (Qualified Mental Health Professional), 149
Qualified clinical social workers (QCSWs), 147
Quebec, public mental health agencies in, 328
Queensland, public mental health agencies in, 330
Questionnaires, 36
Quetiapine, 116–117

R

Race
  diagnosis and, 25
  harassment and, 275
Racquet sports, 208
Radioallergosorbent test (RAST), 188
Rages
  attention deficit hyperactivity disorder (ADHD) and, 45
  controlling, 253–254
  grapeseed oil and, 196
  mania and, 10
  seizures and, 22
  steroids and, 58
Rapid cycling, 11, 12
  estrogen and, 191
  gender and, 25
  taurine and, 202
  thyroid dysfunction and, 131–132
Razors, disposable, 287
Rebelliousness, 46
Reboxetine, 113
Recklessness, 9, 46
  hypomania and, 11
Record keeping
  for complementary therapies, 167
  for health insurance, 218–219
  medical records, 31
Recovery, availability of, 39–40
Referrals, 28
  roadblocks to obtaining, 33–34
  self-referrals, 33
Reflexology, 168
Registered dietitians (RDs), 185
Regulin. See Tetrabenazine

Reitan-Indiana Neuropsychological Test Battery (RINTB), 337
Religion
  and altered states of consciousness, 56–57
  charitable institutions, 244
  and diagnosis, 25
  self-injurious behaviors and, 288
  therapists associated with, 148
Remeron, 113
Renter's insurance, 248–249
Reproductive side effects, 74
Residential care facilities, 137
Restraints, 138, 140
Retroviruses, 192
ReVex, 121
ReVia, 120–121
Rheumatoid arthritis, 57
Rheumatrex, 129
Rhode Island, public mental health agencies in, 324
Richmond Fellowship New Zealand Inc., 301
Risk-taking behaviors, 295
Risperdal, 69, 213
  general information, 116
  liquid form, 75
  weight gain from, 186
Risperidone. See Risperdal
Ritalin, 44, 118, 119
  military and, 272
  sexual side effects and, 84
Ritalin SR, 119
Roche Labs, 313
Rock-climbing, 295
"Roid" rage, 58
Rorschach Blot interpretation test, 37
Rotation diet for food allergies, 190
Roxane Labs, 313
Royal Pharmaceutical Society of Great Britain, 311
  Technical Information Center Web site, 312
Rubella, viral antibody tests, 194
Running, 208
RXmed, 312

S

Safety needs, 252–254
Safflower oil, 183
St. John's Wort, 86, 198
  cautions on, 204
Salt, lithium and, 92
Samaritans, 244
SAMe (S-adenosyl-methionine), 203
  cautions on, 204
Sancar, Aziz, 178
SANE Australia, 301
SANE (UK), 300
Sanofi Winthrop, 313

Sarsaparilla, 198
Saskatchewan, public mental health agencies in, 328
Saw palmetto, 161
    tannic acids and, 204
The Scarred Soul: Understanding & Ending Self-Inflicted Violence (Alderman), 288
Schering Labs, 313
Schizoaffective disorder, 61
Schizophrenia, 59–61
    hallucinations in, 56
    as medical condition, 227
    psychosis and, 59
School social work specialists (SSWS), 147
Scotland. *See* United Kingdom
Scottish Association for Mental Health, 299
Scutellaria lateriflora, 179
Searle, 313
Seasonal affective disorder (SAD), 6, 63, 162
    appendix resources for, 307
    light therapy for, 174–175
    L-tryptophan and, 179
    vitamin B2 deficiency and, 178
Secret Shame Web site, 307
Sedimentation rate, 194
Seizures, 22, 64–66. *See also* Epilepsy
    arachidonic acid (AA) and, 181
    aura, 56
    diagnosis of, 41–42
    dimethylglycine (DMG) and, 195
    evening primrose oil (EPO) and, 184
    ganaxolone for, 191
    hospitalization for, 133
    Lamictal and, 98
    as medication side effect, 84–86
    occurrence of, 24
    taurine and, 202
Selective Serotonin Reuptake Inhibitors (SSRIs)
    alcohol abuse, use in, 121
    as antiviral treatment, 196
    for bipolar disorders, 50
    discontinuing, 78
    general information on, 102–105
    orthostatic hypotension, 85
    for unipolar depression, 49
    weight gain/loss and, 83
Selenium, 201
    as antiviral, 196
Self-actualization, 250–251
Self-esteem, 250
    needs, 255–256
Self-hypnosis, 169
Self-injurious behaviors, 252. *See also* Suicidal behaviors
    appendix resources on, 307
    dealing with, 288–289

emergency care for, 133–134
types of, 288
"Self-Injury: A Quick Guide to the Basics" (Martinson), 288–289
Self-medication, substance abuse as, 57–58
Self-referrals, 33
Sensation-seeking, 295
Sensitivity
    to medications, 71
    rapid cycling and, 12
    special drug formulas for, 75–77
Sensitivity training, 144
Sensitization techniques, 84
Sensory integration (SI), 206–207
    stress reduction and, 208
Serax, 125
Seroquel, 116–117
Serotonin
    effects of, 21
    5-HTP (5-hydroxytryptophan), 179
    hormones and, 52
    light and, 15
    tryptophan affecting, 179
    weight gain/loss and, 83
Serotonin syndrome, 86
Seroxat. *See* Paxil
Sertraline. *See* Zoloft
Serzone, 113
Sexual harassment, 275
Sexual issues
    precociousness, 46
    side effects, 83–84
SGOT (serum glutamic-oxaloacetic transaminase), 80
SGPT (serum glutamate pyruvate transaminase), 80
Shankapulshpi, 204
Shelter, need for, 251–252
Shiatsu massage, 171
Shift work, 119
Shingles, 195
Shoplifting, 289
Side effects, 82
    counteracting medications, 87–88
    of essential fatty acids (EFAs), 182
    hepatitis as, 63
    hospitalization for, 133
    of lithium, 70
    major side effects, 84–86
    minor side effects, 82–84
    of neuroleptics, 115
    vitamins, large doses of, 173
Sinequan, 110–111
Single-payer system, 34
Single photon emission computed tomography (SPECT) scans, 18
Skateboarding, 295
Skiing, 295

Toxoplasmosis, 23
    AIDS infection and, 130
Trace minerals, 201
Trace states, 56
Trade names of medications, 73
Tramadol, 129
Trampoline jumping, 209
Tranquilizers, 122
Trans fatty acids, 181, 184–185
Tranxene, 125–126
Tranylcypromine sulfate, 113
Trazodone, 113
Treadmills, 209
Trexan, 121
Triage facilities, 135
Triavil, 108–109, 114
Tricare, 214, 229
    mail-order medications, 246
Tricyclic antidepressants
    alcohol abuse, use in, 121
    for bipolar disorders, 50
    general information on, 106–112
    orthostatic hypotension, 85
    tardive dyskinesia (TD), 86
    for unipolar depression, 49
Triggers, 30, 259–260
Triiodothyronine (T3), 61
Trilafon, 108–109, 114
Trileptal, 101
Trimethylglycine (TMG), 195
Trimipramine, 111
Trough levels, 79
Tryptizol. See Elavil
Tryptophan, 179
Tumors, Cushing's disease, 49
Turnera aphrodisiaca, 197
Tyrosine, 203

U

UK Advocacy Network, 305
Ultram, 129
Una de gato, 196
Unipolar depression, 49–50
United Kingdom
    alternatives to insurance, 244
    benefits in, 239
    disability support and advocacy resources, 305
    housing authority in, 276
    osteopaths in, 173
    public mental health agencies in, 328
    support and advocacy groups, 298–300
United States
    disability support and advocacy resources,
        304–305

medical facilities in, 313–315
public mental health agencies in, 318–326
support and advocacy groups, 297
University of British Columbia Mood Disorders
        Clinic, 315
University of Calgary, 198
University of California, Los Angeles, 315
University of North Carolina, 178
University of South Florida, 248
University of Texas Southwestern Medical Center, 315
Upledger, John, 170–171
Urea, lithium and, 92
Urecholine, 83
Urine, blood in, 84
Utah, public mental health agencies in, 325
Uzara root, cautions on, 204

V

Valerian, 178
    cautions on, 204
Valium, 126
    grapefruit juice and, 76
Valpro. See Depakote
Valproic acid, 95–96
Varicella zoster, 192
Velo-cardio-facial syndrome (VCFS), 16–17
Venlafacine, 113
Verapamil, 121
Vermont, public mental health agencies in, 326
Very long chain fatty acids (VLCFAs), 180–181
Viagra, 84
Video resources, 303
Vineland Adaptive Behavior Scales, 337, 338
Viral antibody tests, 194
Viral infections. See also AIDS; Antivirals
    fibromyalgia and, 50
Virginia, public mental health agencies in, 326
Visual hallucinations, 56
Vitamin A, 200
    as antiviral, 196
Vitamin B1, 199
Vitamin B2, 178
Vitamin B6, 199
Vitamin B12, 199
Vitamin B15, 195
Vitamin C, 173
    as antiviral, 196
    with essential fatty acids (EFAs), 182
    methamphetamine addiction and, 121
The Vitamin Connection, 317
Vitamin D, 200
Vitamin E, 166, 200
    as antiviral, 196
    with essential fatty acids (EFAs), 182
    hormonal problems and, 192

About the Author

Mitzi Waltz has been a professional author, journalist, and editor for over a decade, covering topics ranging from computers to health care. She has been heavily involved in parent support work, and has also advocated for special-needs children within the medical, insurance, and education systems. She is currently completing her PhD in England with the University of Sunderland's Autism Research Unit.

Ms. Waltz has also authored *Pervasive Developmental Disorders: Finding a Diagnosis and Getting Help, Bipolar Disorders: A Guide to Helping Children and Adolescents, Obsessive-Compulsive Disorder: Help for Children and Adolescents, Partial Seizure Disorders: Help for Patients and Families* and *Tourette's Syndrome: Finding Answers & Getting Help* for the Patient-Centered Guides series.

Colophon

Patient-Centered Guides are about the experience of illness. They contain personal stories as well as a combination of practical and medical information.

The cover of *Adult Bipolar Disorders* was designed by Kristen Throop of Combustion Creative. The warm colors and quilt-like patterns are intended to convey a sense of comfort. The use of repetitive patterning was inspired by tile work seen by the designer on a trip to Turkey. The layout was created on a Macintosh using Quark 4.0. Fonts in the design are: Berkeley, Coronet, GillSans, Minion Ornaments, Throhand, and Univers Ultra Condensed. The design was built with tints of three PMS colors.

Rad Proctor designed the interior layout for the book based on a series design by Nancy Priest and Edie Freedman. The interior fonts are Berkeley and Franklin Gothic. The text was prepared using FrameMaker.

The book was copyedited by Paulette Miley and proofread by Marianne Rogoff. Tom Dorsaneo, Marianne Rogoff, and Katherine Stimson conducted quality assurance checks. Katherine Stimson wrote the index. The illustrations that appear in this book were produced by Rob Romano. Interior composition was done by Rad Proctor and Tom Dorsaneo.